Augsburger Rechtsstudien

Herausgegeben im Auftrag der
Juristischen Fakultät der Universität Augsburg von

Professor Dr. Arnd Koch
Professor Dr. Thomas M.J. Möllers
Professor Dr. Matthias Rossi

Band 87

Thomas M.J. Möllers/Hao Li (eds.)

The General Rules of Chinese Civil Law

History, Reform and Perspective

Nomos

Die Deutsche Nationalbibliothek verzeichnet diese Publikation in der Deutschen Nationalbibliografie; detaillierte bibliografische Daten sind im Internet über http://dnb.d-nb.de abrufbar.

The Deutsche Nationalbibliothek lists this publication in the Deutsche Nationalbibliografie; detailed bibliographic data are available on the Internet at http://dnb.d-nb.de

ISBN 978-3-8487-4745-0 (Print)
978-3-8452-9110-9 (ePDF)

British Library Cataloguing-in-Publication Data
A catalogue record for this book is available from the British Library.

ISBN 978-3-8487-4745-0 (Print)
978-3-8452-9110-9 (ePDF)

Library of Congress Cataloging-in-Publication Data
Möllers, Thomas M.J. / Li, Hao
The General Rules of Chinese Civil Law
History, Reform and Perspective
Thomas M.J. Möllers / Hao Li (eds.)
372 p.
Includes bibliographic references.

ISBN 978-3-8487-4745-0 (Print)
978-3-8452-9110-9 (ePDF)

1. Auflage 2018

Foreword: The Current Reform of Chinese Civil Law

University of Augsburg's law faculty looks back on a long history of scientific contact to China. Already in May 2006, several colleagues of the law faculty, namely the Professors *Marion Albers*, *Ivo Appel*, *Volker Behr*, *Michael Kort*, and *Thomas M.J. Möllers*, undertook a research trip to China and established first contacts there. In 2015, these close contacts led to the foundation of a research center for Chinese law (Research Center of Innovation and Legal Studies between China and Europe – *RICE*) at the University of Augsburg.

When the German Civil Code (*BGB*) was introduced in Germany on January 1, 1900, it was considered "a new code for a new century". The People's Republic of China now plans the same. It will certainly be a feat of strength before the civil code will be completed in 2020. China pursues a vision as well: introducing a modern, progressive, overall codification which is competent to overcome the challenges of the 21st century.

This was reason enough for us to hold a conference on the already completed general part of this civil code, the General Rules of Civil Law (*GRCL*), on July 20, 2017. In this context, we wanted to learn how the GRCL and the BGB, which was created more than a 100 years earlier, differ. It is even more surprising how similar they are. This conference transcript depicts these very similarities and differences.

We would like to sincerely thank the Bavarian Academic Center for China (*Bay-China*) whose financial support was indispensable for the conference. Special thanks go to the persons primarily responsible, *Dr. Liuhua Shen* of the research center for Chinese law and *Pirmin Herz* for the preparation of the conference and this transcript. We thank *Professor Dr. Knut Benjamin Pißler, Dr. Peter Leibküchler* und *Nils Klages* for providing a German translation of the Chinese legal text. The research assistant *Sandra Paulson* kindly translated the legal text into English. Lastly, we owe great thanks to the staff of the Augsburg Center for Global Economic Law and Regulation (*ACELR*), in particular *Michael Biesinger* and *Tristan Eickholt*, for their support in performing the conference as well as supervising the conference transcript.

Professor Dr. Thomas M.J. Möllers (Augsburg)
Professor Dr. Hao Li (Beijing)

March 2018

Contents

Introduction

Today, China is the second largest economy worldwide. No other nation exports an amount comparable to that which is exported by China. Being aware of its global influence, the 12th Chinese National People's Congress passed a new general part of Chinese civil law on March 15, 2017 which replaced the until then valid General Principles of Civil Law (GPCL) and came into force on October 1, 2017. This general part, now known as the General Rules of Civil Law (GRCL), is the first step for the new Chinese Civil Code that is to be finalised by 2020.[1]

The general part of the German Civil Code (BGB) has its foundation in the three-part structure, which was first introduced by the famous Roman legal practitioner Gaius in 162 AD and also builds the basis of todays French and Austrian Civil Codes: personae, res, actiones. The GRCL, on the other hand, consists of 11 parts. At the same time however, similar to the general part of the German Civil Code, the GRCL contains a general set of approximately 100 rules on natural and legal persons (sections 13–108 GRCL). The legal transactions which are laid out by sec. 104 et seq. in the German Civil Code, find a similar placement in the GRCL under the chapter civil legal transactions in sections 133 et seq. GRCL. The conference follows the classical four-step method of law comparison[2]: What is the current legal situation in one's own country? Which legal solutions does the foreign legal system present? What are the similarities that exist between both legal systems? Which solutions could appropriately be assimilated into the own legal system and which solutions cannot, and why?

In hindsight of the importance of such a codification in Chinese Law, the Research Center of Innovation between China and Europe (RICE) at the Law Faculty of the University of Augsburg under the leadership of Professor Dr. *Thomas M.J. Möllers* held a conference entitled "The Current Reform of Chinese Civil Law" on July 20, 2017. Aim of the conference was to recognise the fundamental changes made to the General Principles and to analyse these in a comparative way. For this occasion, seven renowned legal academics from throughout China were invited to Augsburg and engaged in a constructive dialogue with German scholars. Representative of

---

1 A German and English version of the General Principles of Law is attached as an Annex at the end of this publication, p. 295. For an overview oft he GRCL see *Yuanshi Bu*, ZChinR 183 et seq. (2017).

2 *Zweigert/Kötz*, Einführung in die Rechtsvergleichung, 3. Aufl. 1996, p. 45 et. seq.

the Consulate General at the Chinese Embassy in Munich, Professor Dr. *Chongling Huang*, emphasised in her opening speech the great significance of this first legal dialogue between Germany and China on the topic of the Chinese Civil Law reform. She stated that this reform would herald a "new era of Chinese jurisprudence".

This symposium is just the fruit of this first dialogue and shows mutual understanding between Germany and China. This publication includes 14 contributions selected from the contributions made during the conference and afterwards on other conferences in Germany and China by Chinese and German scholars on the topic of the reform. These articles show the historic development of Chinese civil legislation, the main controversies in the civil code drafting process and the main contents of the new General Part of the Chinese Civil Code. The topics include basic principles, natural persons, legal persons, civil juristic acts (particularly gross misunderstanding) and agency, unjust enrichment, and civil liability. They also discuss theoretical controversies and the future improvement of the new General Part as well as make a comparison between the German Civil Code and the new General Part of Chinese Civil Law. In addition, two articles examine the contentious topics in the field of Chinese property law and contract law.

Since the beginning of the 20th century, China has made numerous attempts to introduce a general codification of civil law. Professor Dr. *Hao Li* (Beihang University, Beijing) further explains this development in his article "The Codification of Chinese Civil Law – Innovations and Controversies". First Chinese civil codifications dated from the late Qing Dynasty, but all attempts since then were frustrated. The Kuomintang Party introduced the first Chinese civil code, the Republican Civil Code, in 1930. This civil code showed a strong orientation towards the German Civil Code. After the founding of the People's Republic of China in 1949, this civil code was abolished as it was considered reactionary and western. The new People's Republic tried to draft new civil codes three times from 1950s to 1980s, which were inspired by the foundations of the Soviet Civil Code. The General Principles of Civil Law (GPLC) introduced in 1986 was the result of the third drafting attempt, which still showed the heavy influence of the Soviet Union's legal system. The new GRCL is the result of the fourth attempt towards a complete civil code, one of whose most significant aims is to introduce a progressive, market-economy orientated code, which is able to withstand the challenges of the 21st century. Nonetheless, *Li* raises the question whether China is ready for such a modern codification of civil law. Because of the unique nature of the political system and cultural history of China, he warned that it was essential to find a way to unify reform and tradition. The new GRCL should have paved the foundation for such unification. Further progress must however be made when it comes to law enforcement.

As opposed to the German Civil Code, the GRCL include a number of general principles of law such as the freedom of contract (section 5 GRCL) and the principle of equal treatment (section 4 GRCL). Professor Dr. *Thomas M.J. Möllers* (University of Augsburg) further examines this in his article on the "Principles in the Chinese Civil Code" by defining the nature and work process with these general principles. When considered in an abstract manner, general principles of law are not yet subsumable and thus not tangible for law practitioners. Further substantiation through legal principles and the consideration of relevant circumstances is needed.

In this regard, *Möllers* introduces three possible techniques: First, the legal principles of *lex specialis* and *lex superior* can be used to concretise; in the case of a collision between legal principles these must be weighed up. He is however critical of section 3 GRCL, which protects absolute rights against all forms of legal violation. The absolute rights are concretised by special rules such as section 107 et seq. GRCL. Second, *Möllers* illustrates the way in which a principle is derived from applicable law and in a second step further refined as a legal institution with the example of private autonomy. Third, the principle of *lex superior derogat legi inferiori* allows for further concretisation. Superior rules of law for example are found when examining the legal relationship between federal law and state law. Furthermore, the "Green Principle" in section 16 GRCL is touched upon, although *Möllers* considers this more of a legal idea, than a legal principle as such.

Under the GRCL, the Chinese Civil Law on natural persons is no longer only applicable to citizens of the People's Republic of China but to everyone. This shows a clear abdication from the earlier influence of Soviet Union law. With this realisation, the article by Professor Dr. *Hongjie Man* (Shandong University, Qingdao) "The Law of Natural Persons in the GRCL: Innovations, Debates and Prospects" introduces the main progress of the GRCL in the field of natural persons. Section 16 GRCL for the first time bestows legal capacity even on the foetus under certain circumstances. As a precautionary measure to deal with China's ageing population and the threat of the increasing number of persons suffering fading consciousness due to health problems such as Alzheimer's disease, sections 21 and 22 GRCL lay out rules for cases of the limited legal capability of fully aged persons and guardianship. As a result of Alzheimer's disease, experts assume that approximately 24 million persons in China will be limited in their legal capacity by 2040. Whilst the interests of these persons became the focus of the legislative procedure, *Man* notes that the regulations on guardianship are not yet precise or comprehensive enough to cope with this threatening challenge.

In German law, the general part of the Civil Code and the part on family law include rules on natural persons. Section 1 of the German Civil Code declares all people as natural persons. As illustrated by Professor Dr. *Raphael Koch* and *Finn Mrugalla* (University of Augsburg) in their article "The Natural Person in German Civil Law", legal capacity in German Civil Law is bestowed on an individual with the completion of birth. German law however, also protects unborn life. By analogy to section 16 GRCL, section 1923 para. 2 of the German Civil Code renders unborn life as capable to inherit and is protected by tort law. *Koch* mentions however, that the case law of the German Federal Court of Justice on the matter of "wrongful life" (see BGHZ 86, 240, 251 *et seq.*) must be taken into account when considering protection through tort law. Similar to Germany, China also has cases in which unborn life is protected, especially in tort liability cases such as traffic accidents, medical malpractice and liability for environmental pollution. But it is still unclear exactly how China will continue dealing with this issue in the coming years. Each country's regulations on legal capability only differ slightly. Like the German Civil Code (section 828), Chinese civil law also contains specific rules on the liability of minors for civil wrongs (Chinese Tort Liability Law section 32). In German Law, persons with limited legal capacity can only obligate themselves to legal transactions that provide them solely with a legal advantage. In contrast, Chinese Law allows in section 19 GRCL persons with limited legal capacity to obligate themselves if the legal transaction provides them solely with an economic advantage or if the transaction is appropriate when considering the age and understanding of the individual.

Under the influence of the reform of the state-owned enterprises of 1986, the GPCL divided legal entities into four categories: enterprises, state institutions, institutions and social organisations. Professor Dr. *Tong Zhang* (China University of Political Science and Law, Beijing) describes the renunciation from the socialist character in the new GRCL in her article "Classification of Legal Entities in General Section of the Civil Code: Reforms and Problems". The GRCL distinguishes between for-profit and non-profit legal persons. There are specific regulations for Special Legal Persons such as state bodies, village committees and neighbourhood committees. *Zhang* mentioned however, that there still ceases to be a clear differentiation between legal persons of public law and those of private law. She also criticised the lack of harmonisation between civil and commercial law in relation to legal persons.

Professor Dr. *Michael Kort* (University of Augsburg) notes in his supplementary article "Recent Developments of the Legal Capacity of Economic Entities and Legal Persons" that case law is developing in a direction slowly closing the gap between economic entities with legal capacity and legal persons. In this context, he referred to a decision passed by the German Federal Court of Justice in 2017 (BGH, NZG 2017, 696) on the consumer status of private companies which involve a legal person. In addition, *Kort* stated that the fundamental right protected by section 19 para. 3 of the German Constitution also includes economic entities. When it comes to liability issues however, economic entities and legal persons still find their differences.

Sections 113 et seq. GRCL, which contain rules on property law questions, have been almost entirely taken over from the Chinese Statute on Property Law. At the beginning of his article "Introduction to New Property Rules in the GRCL", Professor Dr. *Jiayuan Zhuang* (Shanghai Jiaotong University, Shanghai) notes that the fundamental principles of Chinese property law are comparable with those contained in the German Civil Code. The Numerus Clausus concept is in this sense also known to Chinese law (section 117 GRCL). The existing legal structures for the ownership of real estate still reflect the early socialist influence. Private property ownership is only possible for buildings, not however, for land ownership. In the case that one wishes to actually use or build on a plot of land, a right of use must first be applied for. *Zhuang* compares this structure to that of the German Heritable Building Law. In addition, the right of the state to expropriate property in China is closely tied to the public interests (section 117 GRCL).

Similarly to earlier codes, the GRCL only contain a general rule for the issue of unjustified enrichment (section 122 GRCL). This general clause is then substantiated through further rules contained in contract law and other more special laws. In his article "The Chinese Civil Code and Unjustified Enrichment: Evaluation and Future Prospects", Professor Dr. *Guangyu Fu* (University of International Business and Economics, Beijing) mentions that unlike in Germany, the dogmatic foundations of enrichment law were never thoroughly examined in China. Because of the prevailing view that there is no such thing as the German "Abstraktionsprinzip" (Abstraction principle) in Chinese law, it is disputed which role enrichment law plays. Also unclear remains the relationship between enrichment law and other restitution claims. As the future Civil Code could probably refuse a general part of the law of obligations, unjustified enrichment would be located in the book of contract law as part of 'quasi contracts'. It is desirable, that the future Civil Code could, to a certain extent, reduce disputes and uncertainty concerning unjustified enrichment with further supplementary regulations.

Under the title "Civil Juristic Acts: History, Comparison and Problems" Professor Dr. *Yongqiang Chen* (China Jiliang University, Hangzhou) illustrates the prerequisites of the civil juristic acts in section 143 GRCL. These include legal capability and an honest intent. In addition, the acts may not violate mandatory rules, general discipline or social morals. *Chen* continues by examining the similarities to sections 134 and 138 BGB. The Chinese rules on interpreting declarations of intent (section 142 GRCL) are of specific interest. In cases of a unilateral agreement, the literal sense of the declaration as a whole must be considered. In addition, individual concepts, habits and the principle of good faith are to be borne in mind. In cases of one-sided declarations, it is necessary to identify the declaring party's real will.

"Significant misunderstandings in Chinese Civil Law" are the topic of the article by Dr. *Tianfan Wang* (Beihang University, Beijing). Section 147 GRCL rules that a legal transaction that was entered into as a result of a significant misunderstanding can be revoked. Part of *Wang's* article therefore revolves around the question how a "significant misunderstanding" is to be differentiated from the German legal idea of a "misconception" consequently. To further ascertain this issue, *Wang* points out that the Civil Code of the Republic of China, which finds strong parallels to the German Civil Code and was abolished in China in 1949, is still valid in Taiwan. She adheres to the idea, that when considering the literal meaning, a "misconception" always occurs on the side of the declaring party, whereas a significant misunderstanding arises on the part of the recipient. It is therefore all the more complicated that section 147 GRCL does not contain any concrete legal conditions, which allow drawing a clear line between the two.

On the symposium in July 2017, Professor Dr. *Martin Maties* (University of Augsburg) explained how the concept of a "misunderstanding" is treated in German law (His talk, however, has not been put in writing). A misunderstanding occurs, when a declaration is not understood by the recipient in the way that was initially intended. Here the law differentiates between three cases: whilst invalidity ipso iure is the result of the cases in sections 116 and 118 of the German Civil Code, cases in which a misconception has occurred require an appeal (sec. 119 German Civil Code). In both cases, a one-sided misconception exists on the side of one of the involved parties. The essential issue here is the question of causality: would the declaring party have decided differently, if he were to have had subjective knowledge of the situation and an objective understanding of the case? Section 313 para. 2 sentence 1 BGB allows for a collaborative adaptation of the contract in case of a misconception on both parts. The corrective measure here is the concept of reasonability.

Dr. *Jieqiong Li* (Sun Yat-sen University, Guangzhou) contributes with her article on "Civil Liability Provisions in the GRCL". According to *Li*, the chapter on civil liability of the GRCL is still characterised particularly heavily by socialist morals (see for example the protection of heroes and martyrs in section 185 GRCL). *Li* also draws particular attention to section 184 GRCL, which contains a "Good Samaritan" clause. The clause contains an comprehensive exemption from liability with the aim of encouraging the willingness to help in accident situations. This exemption goes beyond the regulation of section 680 BGB. During the conference, the continuing discussion quickly found its focus on section 179 GRCL, which contains a clause for punitive damages. Because of its systematic position in the GRCL, section 179 GRCL is applicable to all legal rights protected by section 109 et seq. GRCL that have a general preventive effect. This could, in individual cases, lead to very high compensation claims.

Besides the above-mentioned articles, this conference transcript also includes two articles from Ms. *Qiangzhi Hu* (University of Bochum) and Assistant Professor Dr. *Jing Jin* (China University of Political Science and Law, Beijing).

In her article "The Prohibition of Self-contracting in section 168 para. 1 GRCL: From the Perspective of Comparative Law", *Hu* analyses the legal effect of the issue of self-contracting by an agent. Generally, there exists a conflict between the representative's personal interests and those of his principal. It is assumed especially in the case of so-called self-contracting that the agent may act to maximize his own economic interests rather than those of his principal. Section 168 para. 1 GRCL, section 181 para. 1 BGB, Art. 2. 7. 7 PICC and Art. 3: 205 PECL regulate this situation. Section 168 para. 1 GRCL stipulates that an agent can't contract between the principal and himself, unless he has been expressly authorised or approved to do so. However, the legal consequence of violating this rule is missing. In German Civil Code, sec. 177 et seq. could apply to this situation. According to Art. 2. 7. 7 PICC and Art. 3: 205 PECL, the principal could also avoid the contract. These provisions could be commendable for the section 168 para. 1 GRCL by considering its main aim to provide protection to the principal.

Under the title "The Conflicting Standard Terms in Chinese Contract Law: The Way of Interpretation and the Possibility of Codification during the Drafting of Chinese Civil Code" Assistant Professor Dr. *Jing Jin* (China University of Political Science and Law, Beijing) illustrates the theoretical development of the battle of forms in commercial transactions. This evolved from the "first blow doctrine" in the beginning, to the prevailing "last shot doctrine" in the 20th century, and ultimately to the current "knock out doctrine". *Jin* states that China should carefully examine the relationship between Article 19 of the CISG and Article 30 of the Contract Law. With respect to the background of the compilation of Chinese Civil Code, China should try to construct or update relevant systems through legislation, introduce special rules on the conclusion of contract or on standardised terms and supplement them with clear rules on interpretation. In doing so, China could get itself out of the dilemma of normative application and the interpretation of the battle of forms.

This conference transcript gives an extensive insight into the current reform of Chinese Civil Law and its background. It becomes apparent, that the German Civil Code has an ongoing worldwide influence and is often used as an exemplary code for proposed legislation. Throughout the conference, it was however often mentioned, that "learning" is certainly not a one-way street. It is imperative that Germany also takes interest in the developments made by such modern civil law codes as the GRCL and how these could give inspiration for future reforms.

Professor Dr. Thomas M.J. Möllers (Augsburg)
Professor Dr. Hao Li (Beijing)

March 2018

The Codification of Chinese Civil Law: Innovations and Controversies

*Hao Li**

Abstract: *In 2015, the codification of Chinese civil law has set off its new journey. The agenda of the Chinese civil codification is divided into two steps: firstly the promulgation of the General Part in 2017, secondly the announcement of the Special Parts and the whole code in 2020. On March 15, 2017, the General Part of the Chinese Civil Code was finally reviewed and passed by the National People's Congress of China. The innovations of the new General Part appear in the field of basic principles, legal resources and the basic systems of civil law, such as civil subjects, the protection of civil rights, civil legal acts and agency, and limitations of periods. Along with these innovations, quite a few problems in the General Part still exist, such as apparent flaws in certain provisions, politics overriding academy, deficiency of legislative skills and academic foundations for an advanced civil code. Strong controversies still remain within the frame and structure of the Chinese Civil Code, especially the problem of the fusion or separation of civil law and commercial law, the preferential place of property law and personal law, the independence of the law of personality rights, the general part of the law of obligations, the law of intellectual property and the application of law on foreign-related civil relationships.*

Keywords: Development of Chinese Civil Law, Civil Rights, Controversies

* *Dr., LL.B., LL.M. (Peking)*; Associate Professor, Beihang University, School of Law. Chair for Civil Law, Commercial Law and Comparative Private Law.

I. Introduction

In the past decades, China has influenced the world with its rocketing economy. With the rapid development of China's market economy, the need for an autonomous civil code has arisen.

In 2015, the codification of Chinese civil law has set off its new journey. According to the official explanation of the Draft of the General Part of the Chinese Civil Code, the goal of this codification task is to establish an advanced civil code in the 21st century, which could solve the problems and satisfy the new demands of the modern society. To fulfill this objective, the codification not only includes systematical and comprehensive integration of the existing civil legislations, but also needs to amend the existing civil provisions that do not meet the actual situations.[1]

The National People's Congress of China (NPC) has also published an agenda according to which the task of civil codification is divided into two

1 See National People's Congress (NPC) Standing Committee, Statement on the Draft of the General Rules of Chinese Civil Law (Mar. 8, 2017) ("关于«中华人民共和国民法总则（草案）»的说明——2017年3月8日在第十二届全国人民代表大会第五次会议上"), http://www.npc.gov.cn/npc/xinwen/2017-03/09/content_2013899.htm (last visited Jul. 7, 2017).

steps : Firstly, the General Part should be read by the Standing Committee of the NPC in 2016 for three times and finally should be approved by the NPC in March 2017. Subsequently, from 2017 to 2020, the Special Parts, including property law, contract law, tort law, family law, succession law, etc., will be drafted and are expected to be passed by the NPC to finally form an autonomous Civil Code with the General Part.[2]

In June 2016, the twelfth session of the Standing Committee of the twelfth NPC read the General Part for the first time. The first reviewed draft consisted of 11 chapters and 186 articles. Compared with the old General Principles of Civil Law (GPCL), the first reviewed draft has made many changes, laying the foundation for the following draft versions.

The second reviewed draft published in October 2016 was made of 11 chapters and 202 articles. Compared to the first reviewed draft, the second draft has made quite a few changes, especially in the field of guardianship and legal persons.[3]

In December 2016, the third reviewed draft of the General Part was published, including 11 chapters and 210 articles. It has made only some small changes in comparison with the second draft, which had been the most important one as special legal persons were codified for the first time.[4]

Based on the third reviewed draft on March 15, 2017, the General Part of the Chinese Civil Code (i.e. General Rules of Civil Law, GRCL) was

---

2 See NPC Standing Committee, Statement on the Proposal of the General Rules of Chinese Civil Law (Jul. 6, 2016) ("关于«中华人民共和国民法总则（草案）»的 说 明"), http://www.npc.gov.cn/npc/lfzt/rlyw/2016-07/05/content_1993422.htm (last visited Jun. 19, 2017); the statement also asserts that compiling the Civil Code is an arduous and complicated project. In accordance with the requirements of the Central Committee of the Communist Party of China, it is necessary to promote actively and steadily the quality of legislations under the premise of strengthening the political foundation. The Civil Code will be composed of the General Part and the Special Parts (currently including contract law, property law, tort law, marriage and family law, and succession law). The General Part stipulates the basic principles and general rules that must be followed in civil activities and directs the special parts.

3 Li Hao, *The History and Recent Development of the Codification of Chinese Civil Law – Is China Ready for an Advanced Civil Code in the 21st Century?*, in Die Kodifikation des Zivilgesetzbuches der VR China, 1, 9–11 (Yuanshi Bu ed., 2017).

4 Li Hao, *The History and Recent Development of the Codification of Chinese Civil Law – Is China Ready for an Advanced Civil Code in the 21st Century?*, in Die Kodifikation des Zivilgesetzbuches der VR China, 1, 11–14 (Yuanshi Bu ed., 2017).

finally reviewed and passed by the NPC. It is the milestone of civil legislation in China and its promulgation has taken a solid step towards the whole task of a civil codification.

II. The history and current situation of Chinese civil legislations

1. A short but intricate history of the Chinese Civil Code

Before considering the current legislations of Chinese civil law, we need to take a short review of its history. The traditional China lacked the concept of separation of civil and criminal law. Most of the codes were the result of the fusion of administrative and criminal matters, and provisions about civil matters just appeared as ancillary. However, reforms of the Chinese legal system took place in the late Qing Dynasty. The legal reformers of the late Qing drafted a civil code modeled on the German Civil Code enacted in 1900. With the help of Japanese scholars, the first three books of the Great Qing's Draft of the Civil Code – General Part, Law of Obligations and Law of Rights over Things – were finished by 1911, shortly before the fall of the Dynasty. Thus, they were never promulgated within the Qing Dynasty. Moving to the pre-modern period, the successor of the Qing Dynasty, the Northern Warlords Government of China, followed the Draft of the Civil Code of the Great Qing and drafted its own civil code in 1925 (Draft of the Civil Code of the Republic of China), which still didn't go into force and could only be cited by courts as jurisprudence. As a consequence, the Republic of China continued to use the civil parts of the Criminal Code of the Great Qing until 1930. The first Chinese civil code, the Republican Civil Code, was finally adopted in 1930, after the Kuomintang came into power in 1927. Nevertheless, the Republican Civil Code was hardly implemented in the vastness of China, due to the chaotic political situation and long-term wars in the 1930s and 1940s. After 1949, the Republican Civil Code was repealed by the new people's government in the mainland of China, but is still used in our Taiwan District nowadays.[5]

5 For a brief history of Chinese civil codification before 1949, see Liang Huixing, *The Reception of Foreign Civil Law in China* ("中国对外国民法的继受"), 1 Shandong University Law Review 1, 1–4 (2003). For a detailed description, see Zhang Xinbao & Zhang Hong, *The Last Hundred Years of China's Civil Law* ("中国民法百年变迁"), 6 Social Sciences in China 67, 68–70 (2011).

After the Chinese Communist Party (CPC) swept into power in 1949, the new government abandoned the Republican legal system and adopted certain elements of the Soviet legal system in the 1950s. The primary way to settle civil matters was through politicized mediation then.

From the 1950s to the beginning of the 21st century, political authorities and academic pioneers have made three attempts to draft an autonomous civil code. In the second half of 1954, the Standing Committee of the first NPC set up a special team and began drafting a Civil Code. The drafting team finally finished several drafts, including four parts, i.e. the general part, ownership, obligations and succession. At that time, the structure of the drafts of the Civil Code was of course strongly affected by the Soviet Civil Code.[6] However, the first drafting process was interrupted because of political movements. Again, in December 1962, the civil law teaching and research section of the Renmin University of China proposed an Outline of the Draft of Civil Law. In 1963, other institutions submitted different versions of drafts. In July 1964, the tentative draft of Chinese civil law was finished, which included only three books, i.e. the general part, ownership of property and transfer of property. However, the process was cut off by the movement of the "four clean-ups" erupted in 1964. In 1979, the political situation restored to stability, and three years later, four drafts of a Chinese civil code were finished. Unfortunately, none of them had turned into formal legislations.[7] At the same period, certain special statutes like the Marriage Law (1980), the Succession Law (1985) and the GPCL (1985) were adopted and promulgated.

In December 2002, a brand-new draft of the Chinese Civil Code, including 9 books and 1209 articles, was completed. It mainly followed the German pandect system, and consisted of General Part, Property Law, Contract Law, Personal Rights Law, Marriage Law, Succession Law, Adoption Law, Tort Law, and Choice of Law for Foreign-Related Civil Relationships. This civil code was a fusion of civil law and commercial law with separate books

6 Wang Liming, *The Retrospective of and Expectations towards the Chinese Civil Code* ("中国民法典制定的回顾与展望"), 5 Legal Forum 5, 7–14 (2008).

7 For a brief history of Chinese civil codification after 1949, see Liang Huixing, *The Reception of Foreign Civil Law in China* ("中国对外国民法的继受"), 1 Shandong University Law Review 1, 5–7 (2003); Liang Huixing, *About the Compilation of the Chinese Civil Code* ("关于中国民法典编纂问题"), http://www.iolaw.org.cn/showArticle.aspx?id=4200 (last visited Sep. 25, 2017). For collections of drafts of Chinese civil codes from the 1950s see The General List of Drafts of Civil Codes of New China («新中国民法典草案总览»(上中下卷)) (He Qinhua, Li Xiuqing & Chen Yi eds., enlarged ed. (增订本), 2017).

for personal rights and tort law, compared with the traditional pandect system.

Because of the complicated political situations and immature economic foundations, all these attempts mentioned above have failed and never came into force. On the one hand, it has proved that civil codification needs suitable political chances and society situations; on the other hand, it has also revealed that the process of civil codification can be very challenging and China's legislative capacity to accomplish a civil code has always been insufficient. An integrated civil code thus became a dream of Chinese civil law scholars of several generations.

2. A brief list of current Chinese civil legislations and legal resources

Since 1979, the NPC and its Standing Committee have enacted and amended a huge number of laws and decisions. In the realm of civil law, the GPCL, promulgated and enacted in 1986, has provided the foundation for all laws concerning civil matters. As a continuation of the late Qing and the Republican Civil Codes, the GPCL is still modeled after continental civil codes, especially the German Civil Code (BGB).

Since the GPCL, a series of "special laws" regulating specific civil relationships have been promulgated. The Contract Law (1999, CL) is the combination and replacement of the Law of Economic Contracts (1981), the Law of Foreign-Related Economic Contracts (1985) and the Law of Technology Contracts (1987). Statutes concerning property are composed of the Property Law (2007, PL), the Guaranty Law (1995), and the Law of Rural Land Contracts (2002). As for intellectual property, statutes include the Patent Law (1984, latest amendment in 2008), the Trademark Law (1982, latest amendment in 2013) and the Copyright Law (1990, latest amendment in 2010). Moreover, in 2010, the Tort Law of the People's Republic of China came into effect. Besides property relationships, the People's Republic of China has also enforced three statutes to adjust personal relationships including the Marriage Law (1950, which was the first civil legislation of the People's Republic of China and later replaced by the Marriage Law of 1980, which was amended in 2001), the Succession Law (1985) and the Adoption Law (1991).

Chinese civil legislation also appears in six kinds of legal resources.[8] Statutes adopted by the NPC and its Standing Committee are the first references in the realm of Chinese civil law. Successively, State Council regulations, local legislations, judicial interpretation documents, customs, international conventions and treaties (such as the CISG) are all important legal resources to regulate civil matters. Yet in the judicial practice, judicial interpretation documents have been rendered more important than other statutes.

III. Innovations of the new General Part of the Chinese Civil Code

In March 2017, the final version of the General Part was publicly reviewed and passed by the NPC, which has gone into force since October 1st, 2017. The final version includes 11 chapters and 207 articles. Compared with the third reviewed draft, there are 126 amendments made in the final version, which will apparently have tremendous effects on the society.

1. Enrichment of basic principles

The core contents of the General Part are basic principles, which guide civil activities and judicial practice and fill in loopholes of statutes. Compared with the old GPCL, the new General Part has enriched the principle of good faith and added a new principle, the green principle.

a) The "most cited" principles of the GPCL and relevant cases

The GPCL has provided several basic principles in Arts. 3 to 7. The most important ones are the principles of voluntariness, fairness and good faith (Art. 4), and the principle of public order and good morals (Art. 7).

---

8 See Li Yu, Essentials of the General Part of Chinese Civil Law, Interpretation of Rules and Variorum of Judgments («民法总则要义：规范释论与判解集注»), 54–59 (2017).

(i) Art. 4. The Principles of Voluntariness, Fairness and Good Faith

Art. 4 of the GPCL provides that in civil activities, the principles of voluntariness, fairness and good faith shall be followed. A statistic shows that Art. 4 of the GPCL is cited in more than 50591 cases.[9]

Initially, the principle of good faith is characterized as an essential element to constitute a lawful juristic act. In other words, the insufficiency of authenticity might directly lead to the result of an invalid juristic act and damages bearing. However, the meaning of this principle has become intricate as different judges are using the principle differently. The cases concerning the principle of good faith have mounted up to 33583 insofar.[10] In a judgment ruled by the Supreme People's Court (SPC), the judge stated that, since the defendant had admitted a fact in the first instance, therefore, a contradictory assertion was rejected because the principle of good faith does not allow it.[11] From this judgment, we can see that the principle of good faith can reach outside its apparent meaning.

As for the principle of voluntariness, it is not only an important principle for the establishment of civil relationship, but also has some procedural efficacy. The Civil Procedure Law (hereafter "CPL") provides that, with respect to a legally effective conciliation statement, if evidence furnished by a party proves that the conciliation violates the principle of voluntariness, or that the content of the conciliation agreement violates the law, the party may apply for a retrial. If the foregoing proves true after the examination of the People's Court, the case shall be retried (Art. 201 CPL).

The principle of fairness also has an important derivation in Art. 114 CL. The article states that, based on the principle of fairness, where the amount

9 Result of a search on the website of China Judgments Online (裁判文书网), http://wenshu.court.gov.cn/list/list/?sorttype=1&conditions=searchWord+QWJS+++全文检索:民法通则第四条 (last visited Jul. 7, 2017). On Jan. 1, 2014, the SPC published a statement to formally implement the requirement about letting all the judgments be published on the internet. The statement clarified that the website, China Judgments Online, would be officially established to unify the publication of all documents and judgments made by the courts.

10 Result of a search on the website of China Judgments Online (裁判文书网), http://wenshu.court.gov.cn/list/list/?sorttype=1&conditions=searchWord+QWJS+++全文检索:诚信原则 (last visited Jul. 8, 2017).

11 See (2014) Min Yi Zhong Zi No. 108 ((2014)民一终字第108号), available at http://wenshu.court.gov.cn/content/content?DocID=024d6ead-5f35-41ca-bf8c-22f7d5305ac0&KeyWord=民一终字第108号 (last visited Jul. 8, 2017).

of liquidated damages prescribed is below the loss resulting from the breach, a party may petition the People's Court or an arbitration institution to increase the amount; where the amount of liquidated damages prescribed exceeds the loss resulting from the breach, a party may petition the People's Court or an arbitration institution to decrease the amount as appropriate. In 2005, in Zhejiang, a southern China province, Company X and Plant Y signed a mold production contract, with the contract price being 150 thousand Yuan. As agreed in the contract, if Plant Y delays in delivery, it shall pay 120 thousand Yuan as contract damages. The delivery of Plant Y then delayed for 36 days and Company X sued Plant Y to claim the aforementioned damages. However, the judge held that the damages provided in the contract were relatively too high according to Art. 114 CL and as a result, instead of spending 120 thousand Yuan, the defendant paid only 3900 Yuan to cover the damages.[12]

(ii) Art. 7. The Principle of Public Order and Good Morals

Art. 7 GPCL provides that civil subjects engaging in civil activities should have respect for social ethics and shall not harm public interests or disrupt social economic order. A statistic shows that this article appears in more than 1655 cases.[13]

There was an impactful case related to this principle in Sichuan, a southwest province of China, in 2001. The parties of this case were Mr. Huang's legitimate wife and his unlawful lover, Mrs. Zhang. Before his death, Mr. Huang had lived with his unlawful lover for five years and they even had a daughter. When the late stage of liver cancer was diagnosed to Mr. Huang, he made a will, and decided to donate his entire legacy to Mrs. Zhang. When Mr. Huang died, Ms. Zhang sued Mr. Huang's wife for her refusing to execute the will of Mr. Huang. The court of first instance dismissed Mrs. Zhang's complaint on account that the will violated the principle of good

12 (2005) Shan Min Chu Zi No. 473 ((2005)善民二初字第473号), available at http://wenshu.court.gov.cn/content/content?DocID=7b01e547-913d-465e-a649-274620ee2688&KeyWord=合同法第一百一十四条%7C违约金 (last visited Jul. 8, 2017).

13 Result of a search on the website of China Judgments Online (裁判文书网), http://wenshu.court.gov.cn/list/list/?sorttype=1&conditions=searchWord+QWJS+++全文检索:民法通则第七条 (last visited Jul. 8, 2017).

morals and therefore was invalid.[14] The appellate court upheld the judgment.[15]

In reality, China has the tradition of holding a very restricted tolerance towards adultery. When the story was spread all over the country, the public and social media overwhelmingly stood in the favor of the legitimate wife.

Nevertheless, Art. 16 of the Succession Law of the People's Republic of China has clearly stated that a citizen may, by making a will, donate his personal property to the state or a collective, or bequeath it to persons other than the statutory successors. However, this rule was ignored. Both courts of the first instance and the second instance had judged that the will was invalid solely based on the principle of good morals (Art. 7 GPCL), ignoring the fact that Ms. Zhang had lived a long time with Mr. Huang and they also had a daughter. From my perspective, issues concerning family relationships and inheritance relationships must be analyzed separately. Even if the adultery with a third party is not tolerated in the social ethics and should be regarded as violating good morals, the will to bequeath the third party should not be wholly invalid just because living with the third party is immoral. The application of the principle of good morals should consider the motive and aim of the donation and the concrete circumstances of each case. At the same time, the autonomy of the testator should also be respected. If the adultery is not the condition for the donation and the motive and purpose of the donation might aim at safeguarding the livelihood of the lover and

---

14 Zhang Xueying v. Jiang Aifang (张学英与蒋伦芳遗赠纠纷案), (2001) Naxi Min Chu Zi No. 561 (2001) 纳溪民初字第561号), available at http://www.pkulaw.cn/case/pfnl_1970324837012371.html?keywords= 纳 溪 民 初 字 第 561 号 &match=Exact (last visited Sep. 27, 2017).

15 Zhang Xueying v. Jiang Aifang (张学英与蒋伦芳遗赠纠纷案), (2001) Lu Min Yi Zhong Zi No. 621 (2001) 泸民一终字第621号), available at http://www.pkulaw.cn/case/pfnl_1970324837023525.html?keywords= 泸民一终字第621号&match=Exact (last visited Sep. 27, 2017).

their child, the will should be valid in the realm of the testator's own property.[16] The aforementioned judgments were apparently distorted by the public opinion and media.[17]

b) Introducing new principles into the new General Part

Compared to the GPCL, basic principles are enriched and supplemented in the new General Part of the Chinese Civil Code. The three principles stipulated in Art. 4 of the GPCL are divided into three separate articles (Secs. 5–7 GRCL). Especially the principle of good faith (Sec. 7 GRCL) is concretized in the General Part, which specifically clarifies that the principle of good faith means civil subjects engaging in civil activities shall adhere to honesty and keep their commitments.

Another outstanding change in this section is that it involves the environmental-friendly principle, known as the green principle (Art. 9 GRCL), to become a basic principle. This principle serves as the cornerstone to regulate natural persons and legal persons to conduct civil activities without doing harm to the environment and save public resources as much as possible.

In order to cooperate with the green principle, on June 27, 2017 the Standing Committee of the twelfth NPC amended the CPL, and authorized the Supreme People's Procuratorate (SPP) to bring public interest litigations in the field of environment and resources protection (Art. 55 Para. 2 CPL).[18]

---

16 As to the similar opinions, see Yu Fei, Studies on the Principle of Public Order and Good Morals («公序良俗原则研究»), 202–213 (2006); Xiao Han, *The Suspended Succession Law* ("被架空的继承法"), Vol. 2 No.1 Private Law Review 300, 300–313 (2002); Jin Jinping, *When Donation Meets Extramarital Cohabitation: Public Order, Good Morals and the Coordination of System* ("当赠与（遗赠）遭遇婚外同居的时候：公序良俗与制度协调"), 6 Peking University Law Review 287, 289–303 (2005).

17 See Xu Mingyue & Cao Mingrui, *Another Analysis of the Luzhou Bequest Case* ("泸州遗赠案的另一种解读"), 2 Research on Judicial Judgments 72 et seq. (2002).

18 Public interest litigation was established in China in 2015, when the Supreme People's Procuratorate (SPP) published a pilot program. For more information see the website of the SPP spp.gov.cn: http://www.spp.gov.cn/zdgz/201507/t20150703_100706.shtml (last visited Jul. 7, 2017). Recently, the SPC published a report about the examples of filing public interest litigations. In 2016, many air pollution cases were accepted, the reports of these litigation have been published on the website ChinaCourt.org, http://www.chinacourt.org/article/detail/2017/04/id/2738851.shtml (last visited 7 Jul. 2017).

The green principle, which closely relates to the system of public interest litigation, would clearly stimulate new progress on environmental protection and resource conservation. Yet it remains in doubt how the special parts of the Chinese Civil Code could reflect this principle and how judges should use this principle in judicial practice. Otherwise, this principle would be just a slogan without any practical value.

c) Dilemma about the derivation and substantiation of basic principles

When analyzing the development of Chinese civil law, it is prevailed that basic principles entrust judges with more freedom to make decisions, and enable them to carry out their discretion creatively to adapt to the change of political, economic and cultural situations in the society. Considering the reality, basic principles of Chinese civil law are playing too many roles. They are miscellaneous provisions of civil legislations to close loopholes in the statutes, they are the legal resources for civil jurisdiction, and they could integrate social norms and morality that guide civil subjects' civil activities. However, the meanings of basic principles are ambiguous, easily leading to the phenomenon of abuse, thus suppressing and restricting private autonomy. Lots of contradicting judgments within similar cases exist.

In 2016, Ms. Zhang and Ms. Wei signed a house-selling contract in Tianjin, with a concerted price of 1.3 million Yuan. However, after the contract was signed, the value of the house increased to 1.960 million Yuan. In view of the difference, Ms. Wei, the seller, refused to sell the house and claimed the termination of the contract according to the principle of changed circumstances.[19] When Ms. Zhang, the buyer, sued Ms. Wei, the court ruled that the principle could not be applied to this case. However, it decided the

19 According to Art. 26 of the Interpretation II of the Supreme People's Court of Several Issues concerning the Application of the Contract Law of the People's Republic of China (2009), when any unforeseeable major change is not a business risk and is not caused by a force majeure occurs after the formation of a contract, if the continuous performance of the contract is obviously unfair to the other party or cannot realize the purposes of the contract and a party files a request for the modification or rescission of the contract with the people's court, the people's court shall decide whether to modify or rescind the contract under the principle of fairness and in light of the actualities of the case. This provision reflects the principle of changed circumstances ("Störung der objektiven Geschäftsgrundlage" in German civil law).

termination of the contract and ruled as a punishment that the defendant should pay 330 thousand Yuan for her breaching of the contract in the first place.[20] In fact, this ruling partially recognized the legal effect of the principle of changed circumstances, i.e., that both parties should share the risk of the significant rising of the value.

In another very similar case, the concerted price was 830 thousand Yuan, and later, according to the claim of the defendant, the market price rose up by 60 or 70 percent. The court also excluded the application of the principle of changed circumstances to this case, but ruled that the initial contract remained effective and the seller should continue to perform the contract, i.e., to sell the house at the previously concerted price, without any other condition attached.[21]

Due to the indetermination of the principle of changed circumstances, the rulings from the courts in the abovementioned both cases were inconsistent. In both cases, the difference was beyond 30%. By analogy with Art. 29 Para. 2 of the Interpretation II of the Supreme People's Court of Several Issues Concerning the Application of the Contract Law of the People's Republic of China (2009), which regulates the adjustment of too high liquidated damages, 30% might be regarded as a boundary to judges whether the difference between prices shall constitute changed circumstances. In a famous case in the 1990s, which might be the first case citing the principle of changed circumstances in China, the significant rising of the price of raw materials was regarded as a kind of changed circumstances.[22]

To avoid the discretionary application of the basic principles, we still need the necessary technique of typification to concretize them and delimit their application.

---

20 Zhang Tong v. Wei Xia (张彤等诉魏霞房屋买卖合同纠纷案), (2016) Jin 0106 Min Chu No. 7587 (2016) 津 0106 民 初 7587 号), available at http://www.pkulaw.cn/case/pfnl_1970324877008705.html?keywords= 情 势 变 更%20房屋买卖合同&match=Exact (last visited Sep. 27, 2017).

21 Yan Fuxin v. Zhang Yuan (阎富信诉张媛等房屋买卖合同纠纷案), (2017) Jin 0102 Min Chu No. 2143 ((2017) 津 0102 民 初 2143 号), available at http://www.pkulaw.cn/case/pfnl_1970324877590512.html?keywords= 房 屋 买 卖合同%20上涨&match=Exact&tiao=3 (last visited Sep. 27, 2017).

22 Wuhan Municipal Coal Gas Corp. v. Chongqing Measuring Instrument Factory (武汉市煤气公司诉重庆检测仪表厂煤气表装配线技术转让合同、煤气表散件购销合同纠纷案), 1996 No. 2 Sup. People's Ct. Gaz. 63 («中华人民共和国最高人民法院公报»1996年第2期， 第63页), available at http://www.pkulaw.cn/case/pfnl_1970324837041389.html?keywords=煤气表散件购销合同&match=Exact (last visited Sep. 27, 2017).

2. Enrichment of legal sources

The sources of law are a special concept in civil law systems. The methodology of using a specific rule to address legal resources originates from Art. 1 of the Swiss Civil Code (ZGB). Similar provisions can also be found in the Korean and Taiwanese Civil Code, whereas they do not exist in the German, French and Japanese Civil Codes. According to the examples from civil law countries or districts, legal sources can be summarized into three levels: the first is statutes, including administrative regulations, the second is customs, and the third is jurisprudence (doctrines).

Similar to other civil law countries, statutes are the most important kind of legal sources in China. Beside statutes, sec. 10 GRCL adds customs, which are not contrary to public order and good morals, as another kind of legal sources to settle civil disputes, provided that there is an absence of statutes. This is a brave attempt of the new General Part, since it is the first time for the Chinese civil law to formally admit customs as one of the legal sources. This admission might break the limit of *numerus clausus* in the Chinese Property Law (Art. 5 PL).

3. Amendments concerning the basic systems

a) Natural persons and guardianship[23]

A considerable change in this chapter is that the legislator lowers the standard age of natural persons with limited civil capacity from 10 years old to 8 years old (Sec. 19 GRCL). The new law also provides that adults who could not recognize or fully recognize their behaviors have no or limited civil capacity for juristic acts (Secs. 21–22 GRCL). This could be regarded as a great improvement, since in the GPCL, this scope is strictly restricted to mentally disabled persons (Sec. 13 GPCL).

Another advancement is that the new law formally provides protection to fetuses. In the GPCL, a fetus could not possess civil capacity. Only Art. 28 of the Succession Law provides legally reserved portion in heritage for a fetus. In the new General Part, for the first time, fetuses are given the legit-

---

23 For a more detailed introduction about natural persons and guardianship in the new General Part, see Man Hongjie, The Law of Natural Person in the New General Rules of Civil Law (in this Symposium, p. 87).

imate status of possessing partial civil capacity to inherit legacy, accept bestowal or any other benevolent donation, except in the case that the fetus is dead when it comes out of the womb (Sec. 16 GRCL).

In respect of guardianship, changes are also obvious. Firstly, the statutory order of guardians is established. Secondly, the new law stipulates that the guardian could be assigned through a testament or an agreement. More importantly, the new law also involves civil affairs departments as competent guardians.

In addition, the new law provides the revocation system of guardianship. Since the guardian might infringe upon the lawful rights and interests of the ward, the new law provides three situations for the ward to appeal to the People's Court to revoke the guardianship and replace the guardian (Sec. 36 GRCL).

In a word, the aim of this section is to regulate the guardianship system in details to respect the ward's own will and best protect his or her interests.

b) Legal persons and unincorporated organizations[24]

The new law chooses a brand-new methodology to classify legal persons and to regulate their civil rights and civil liabilities.

In the GPCL, legal persons are classified in respect of their ownership, like "state owned company" or "collectively owned company". The new law divides legal persons, according to their purposes, into "profit-oriented legal persons", "non-profit legal persons" and "special legal persons" (Chapter 3).

"Profit-oriented legal persons", inherited from the term "enterprises as legal persons", refers to limited liability companies, companies limited by shares and other corporate legal persons (Sec. 76 GRCL). "Non-profit legal persons" refers to institutional units, social organizations, foundations, social service agencies and any other legal person aiming for charity (Sec. 87 GRCL). For non-profit legal persons, the new law expresses the rules for prohibiting the distribution of surplus property, i.e., the remaining property shall be used for public purposes (Sec. 95 GRCL).

---

24 For a more detailed introduction about legal persons in the new General Part, see Tong Zhang, Klassifizierung der Juristischen Personen im Allgemeinen Teil des chinesischen Zivilgesetzbuchs: Reformen und Probleme (in this Symposium, p. 129).

Furthermore, some delegates of the Standing Committee of the NPC have suggested that there are certain organizations and units that could not be classified either as profit-oriented legal persons or as non-profit legal persons. Therefore, it is necessary to add a special section. The third draft invented a new type of legal person, known as the "special legal persons", which refers to official organs, rural collective economic organizations[25], cooperative economic organizations and residents' and villagers' committees (Chapter 3 Section 4 GRCL).

Also, "unincorporated organizations" are the last kind of civil subjects, defined as organizations which could engage in civil activities with their own names, but do not possess independent legal personality as legal persons, including individual proprietorship enterprises, partnership enterprises, professional services, etc. (Sec. 102 GRCL). The new law also stipulates that investors or founders of the unincorporated organizations should bear unlimited liability for the debts of the organizations (Sec. 104 GRCL).

c) Agency

The aim of this section is to abstract different forms of agency existing in reality and govern them respectively.

The new law also emphasizes the prohibition of self-agency and bilateral-agency (Sec. 168 GRCL). More importantly, the new law reaffirms the validity of apparent agency first appearing in the CL of 1999 (Sec. 49 GRCL). Where the agent acts without authority, beyond authority or after the termination of agency but the third party has reason to trust it, then the contract between the third party and the agent shall be admitted and protected by law (Sec. 172 GRCL). Comparing the three drafts, the final version does not list the cases of exception any more. The new law also stipulates an independent agency based on the position and regulation, that the inner limitation on agency could not be raised against the counterparty in good faith (Sec. 170 GRCL). The relation of these regulations to the apparent agency is still unclear.

25 Rural collective economic organizations refer to a kind of organizations that specifically exist in rural areas, which possess the collection of a cluster of people and their investment and conduct business activities for the aim of economic development.

4. Improvement of the protection of civil rights

a) The protection of personal information and virtual property

To meet the development of the internet, the new General Part emphasizes that natural persons' personal information shall be protected by law. No organization or individual may illegally collect, use, or transmit personal information, and shall not illegally provide, disclose or sell personal information (Sec. 111 GRCL). Although the provision of personal data follows special personality rights, its legal attribute is still controversial because the relationship between personal information and data in Sec. 127 GRCL is still unclear.

Besides, the new law emphasizes the protection of virtual property and data (Sec. 127 GRCL), but detailed stipulations are still left to special statutes.

b) The protection of intellectual property

In order to strengthen the protection of intellectual property and to promote scientific and technological innovation, the new General Part stipulates that intellectual property covers drafts, patents, trademarks, geographical indications, trade secrets, integrated circuit layout designs, as well as new varieties of plants and other objects prescribed by law (Sec. 123 GRCL). The protected scope reflects over thirty years of rapid development in the field of intellectual property in China and greatly exceeds the GPCL.

c) The protection of personality rights

The protection of personality rights is one of the biggest amendments in the new General Part.

In the realm of special personality rights, besides the traditional ones – for example the rights to life, health, reputation, name, and portrait – the new law lists the right to physical integrity and the right to privacy as two independent special rights (Sec. 110 GRCL). In the times of the GPCL, privacy was regarded as a part of the reputation.[26] The right to physical integrity was classified in the same way. However, with the development and changes in the complex social life, there will always be some new uncovered rights. Therefore, in accordance with Arts. 37 and 38 of the Constitution, the new law clearly stipulates that the personal freedom and dignity of natural persons shall be protected by law (Sec. 109 GRCL). The intention of this provision is not only to protect personal freedom and personal dignity, but also to protect all the personal interests of natural persons. The provision uses these two concepts (personal freedom and dignity) to express the sum of the natural persons' personality interests. Therefore, Sec. 109 is regarded as the provision of "general personality rights".

More importantly, the new General Part adds that an infringement of heroic martyrs' names, portraits, fame or honor, which causes damage to public interests, shall be subject to civil liability (Sec. 185 GRCL).

d) The protection of Good Samaritans[27]

On the one hand, the new General Part has confirmed the right for Good Samaritans to request compensation. If one's rights and interests are prejudiced during the process of protecting others' civil rights, the infringer shall bear the liability of compensation, while the beneficiary could give proper compensation at the same time. Where there is no infringer, the infringer escapes or is unable to bear the liability, and meanwhile the Good Samaritans requests compensation, then the beneficiary should give appropriate compensation instead (Sec. 183 GRCL).

On the other hand, it has remained disputable whether Good Samaritans shall bear liabilities in the case that the rescue process has caused further damage to the sufferer. In the third reviewed draft of the General Part, Good Samaritans were supposed to be responsible for their gross mistake, while

---

26 Typical example: Art. 140 para. 1 of the Opinions of the Supreme People's Court on Several Issues concerning the Implementation of the General Principles of the Civil Law of the People's Republic of China (For Trial Implementation) of 1988 (最高人民法院关于贯彻执行«中华人民共和国民法通则»若干问题的意见（试行)).

27 For a another analysis of the Good Samaritan provision in the new General Part, see Jieqiong Li, Civil Liability Provisions in the New General Principles of Civil Law (in this Symposium, p. 269).

the final version of the General Part confirms that Good Samaritans are excused from all liabilities (Sec. 184 GRCL). It is believed that the goal of this article is to free citizens from worries about liability while giving help.

4. Amendments concerning limitation periods

The first and foremost change in this chapter is the extension of the ordinary limitation period from two years to three years (Sec. 188 Para. 1 GRCL).

Furthermore, for maximizing the protection of minors' interests, Sec. 184 establishes that the limitation period of claiming sexual assault by a minor shall be calculated from the day the victim reaches the age of 18 years.

The new law also separately stipulates the scheduled period ("Ausschlussfrist" in German) but therefore uses the expression of the "duration of rights" instead of its academic name for the public to understand (Sec. 199 GRCL).

It is also clarified in Sec. 197 that limitations of actions and scheduled periods are compulsory, which could not be excluded by agreements.

IV. Problematic issues of the new General Part of the Chinese Civil Code

1. Flaws of certain provisions

a) Legal sources

As I have mentioned above, the new General Part has confirmed that customs not contrary to public order and good morals could be a legal basis for civil cases. Therefore, the remaining issue is how parties and judges can identify and determine customs, especially trade practices.

Another important issue is the status of judicial cases. Unlike the precedents of common law countries, judicial judgments have not been recognized as a formal kind of sources of law in Chinese legal theory and judicial practice. Sec. 10 GRCL has also not mentioned them as a source of law. Yet, since 2010, our SPC has been actively promoting the case guidance system (案例指导制度). Until now, it has published 17 batches of guiding cases, i.e. 92 cases in total. According to Art. 7 of the Provisions of the

Supreme People's Court on Case Guidance[28] («关于案例指导工作的规定») and Arts. 9 and 10 of the Detailed Rules for the Implementation of the Provisions of the Supreme People's Court on Case Guidance[29] («〈关于案例指导工作的规定〉实施细则»), People's Courts at all levels should refer to key points of guiding cases when the pending cases are similar in facts and legal application. Apart from that, the guiding cases cannot be cited as a basis of ruling but as judicial reasons. However, when People's Courts do not refer to guiding cases or make wrong reference, the issue whether they belong to the situation of the wrong application of law and thus constitute the cause of trial on appeal or retrial remains to be observed in judicial practice.[30]

The last issue is whether jurisprudence (doctrines) could be involved as one kind of legal sources. Different from the abovementioned Swiss, Korean and Taiwanese Civil Codes, jurisprudence is still not included in Sec. 10 GRCL as a source of law, which might also reflect the current situation of Chinese civil law theories, i.e. there still exists no prevailing legal opinion ("herrschende Meinung" in German). When considering relevant cases, it is apparent that in practice, certain cases have quoted jurisprudence as reference.[31] Some scholars claim that judges could still cite jurisprudence as a legal source in case no statutes, customs or guiding cases exist.[32] If so, because the level of our judges is uneven and they cannot accurately understand and apply the jurisprudence, the concern would arise that as a result the power of jurisdiction may be abused.

b) Civil juristic acts

Most scholars, starting from the promulgation of the GPCL, have been insisting on directly applying the concept of "juristic acts", because this is the concept used universally in civil law systems. They believe it is wrong that

---

28 No. 51 [2010] of the Supreme People's Court (法发 [2010] 51号).

29 No. 130 [2015] of the Supreme People's Court (法 [2010] 130号).

30 Li Yu, Essentials of the General Part of Chinese Civil Law, Interpretation of Rules and Variorum of Judgments («民法总则要义：规范释论与判解集注»), 61–62 (2017).

31 There are quite a few examples citing jurisprudence, see Li Yu, Essentials of the General Part of Chinese Civil Law, Interpretation of Rules and Variorum of Judgments («民法总则要义：规范释论与判解集注»), 65–69 (2017).

32 Liang Huixing, *The Understanding and Application of Some Important Articles of the General Provisions of Civil Law* ("«民法总则»重要条文的理解与适用»"), 4 Journal of Sichuan University (Philosophy and Social Science Edition) 51, 52 (2017).

the GPCL created the concept of "civil juristic acts" to represent lawful and valid juristic acts. This opinion was once adopted in the internal draft of the GRCL by the Legislative Affairs Committee of the NPC in 2015, which initially accepted the concept "juristic acts". However, when it came to the first official draft in 2016, the concept "civil juristic acts" returned to the paper. The reason for this was that other legal scholars outside the civil law community resisted the concept of "juristic acts". They believed that if the civil code used the concept of "juristic acts", it would leave no space for jurisprudence, administrative law, economic law and other legal disciplines to use "administrative juristic acts", "commercial juristic acts", etc. Accordingly, the concept of "civil juristic acts" was adopted until the final version of the General Part of Chinese Civil Code.

My understanding is that this result is the consequence of clearing off the entanglement for the completion of the legislation of the General Part. Although the term "civil juristic acts" used in the Chinese Civil Code is relatively different from the concept of "juristic acts" used in civil codes of the German legal system, their essence is identical. According to Sec. 133 GRCL, a civil juristic act is the act conducted by a civil subject through the expression of intention with the purpose of establishing, altering or terminating civil legal relationships.

c) Agency

In comparison with the third reviewed draft, 11 amendments were made in the section concerning agency. However, many problems are still unclear.

Firstly, Sec. 168 states that an agent shall not perform any juristic act in the name of the principal with himself/herself or other principals he/she represents, unless it is consented to or ratified by the principal. The problem is that the article fails to indicate the legal consequence of these acts.[33]

Secondly, Sec. 171 describes three situations that invoke the abuse of the power of agency, i.e., agency without authority, beyond authority, or after the termination of authority. However, this article does not consider a situation where the agent does act "within" his/her authority, but his/her act is

33 For a more detailed analysis of Art. 168 Para. 1 GRCL see Hu Qiangzhi, Das Verbot des Selbstkontrahierens nach Art. 168 Abs. 1 GRCL – aus rechtsvergleichender Perspektive (in this Symposium, p. 187).

still detrimental to the principal and is usually maliciously harmful to the principal's interests. Should this situation be considered as an abuse of agency power? If the answer is negative, how should the interests of the principal be protected?[34]

In the new law, the rule of the anonymous agency system originating from Art. 402 CL, which has appeared in the previous three reviewed drafts, was finally not integrated. It is still uncertain if the anonymous agency system will finally be applied universally or only in the field of foreign trade.

d) Structural issues of the chapter of civil liability

According to the legislator, the aim of the chapter of civil liability is to integrate the liabilities of torts and breach of contracts. However, most contents of this chapter have already been reflected in the Tort Law of 2009. Especially Sec. 179 does not follow the traditional distinctions between obligations and liability ("Schuld und Haftung" in German) and between means of relief for absolute rights and for relative rights. These issues might cause structural problems for the future consolidation of the Chinese Civil Code.

2. Procedural problems during the drafting process

a) Drafting a civil code is just a "political task": politics override academy

On October 20, 2014, the fourth plenary session of the 18th Central Committee of the CPC was held. The resolution of the conference affirmed that China is now in great need to strengthen its legislation in key areas to ensure that citizens' economic, cultural, and social rights are respected. More importantly, the conference placed a political order to codify Chinese civil legislations.[35]

---

34 Xie Gen, A Brief Commentary on the General Rules of Civil Law of China ("«民法总则»简评"), Speech delivered at the University of Nanjing (Mar. 25, 2017), http://www.sohu.com/a/134714997_748103 (last visited 5 Oct. 2017).

35 The Communist Party of China, Resolution on Several Important Issues in Promoting the Rule of Law («中共中央关于全面推进依法治国若干重大问题的决定») http://www.china.org.cn/china/fourth_plenary_session/2014-12/02/content_34208801.htm (last visited Apr. 19, 2017).

It indeed provoked the concern at this time, that the civil codification process is politically oriented. Pressure from the political realm would accelerate the process of civil codification but definitely undermine its quality.

b) Deficiency of legislative skills

Fact is that even though quite a few departments and institutions have engaged in the codification task, the newly passed General Part did not turn out to be a satisfying start of the Chinese Civil Code.

Under the leadership of the Legislative Affairs Commission of the NPC Standing Committee, five units have participated in the legislative process, including the SPC, the SPP, the Legislative Affairs Office of the State Council, the Chinese Academy of Social Sciences, and the China Law Society (hereafter "CLS"). As for the coming special parts, five scholarly teams have also been founded by the CLS to discuss legislative issues and expand channels to ensure that the Civil Code is created in a strict, standardized, impartial form.

However, the legislatures are void of professionalism. Instead of becoming a comprehensive legal resource for legal professionals, the new General Part has been degenerated to a "guide book" for all civil activities to some extent, thus dramatically diminishing the use of legal terms for the public to understand easily.

On top of that, the legislative process is not transparent enough. Discussions in the legislative process are not fully publicized and many scholars' opinions are not adequately considered. What is the purpose of each article? How are they created? What controversies have arose during the process of legislation? These issues could never be answered clearly and publicly. There are no detailed legislative explanations, and some of the provisions are shuffled up right before the public review.

Moreover, scholars who are active in the codification do not possess firm stances. This is mainly because many of them are hurrying to finish the task and proactively compromise to the pressure from politicians.

All these phenomena have implied that the procedure of drafting the Civil Code is certainly politically oriented and non-professional, making it difficult to be fully justified.

3. Lack of solid foundations for an advanced civil code: Immature dogma and practices

a) Lack of necessary academic foundations

The most needed academic foundation for a civil codification is the dogma ("Dogmatik" in German). Unfortunately, the dogma of civil law is still under-developed in China. Without the help from relatively mature dogma, it would be extremely hard to standardize legal terms, establish effective expression patterns, and even more difficult to accomplish a universally accepted civil law system and fully refresh the current legislations.

In addition, even though the new draft proposal of the European civil code (Draft Common Frame of Reference – DCFR) and other new civil codes have been translated into Chinese by scholars, the legislative process has failed to pay enough attention to comparative legal materials to back up the work. Also, the participation of foreign scholars should be increased, like the German Corporation for International Cooperation (Deutsche Gesellschaft für Internationale Zusammenarbeit – GIZ), to give us more helpful instructions and different experiences.

b) Immature judicial practices

In the past three decades, judges have been faced with more and more cases. This heavy burden makes the argumentation in judgments to be very luxurious. Different judgments for same issues have been common in China, which makes it difficult to strike definite conclusions in hard cases.

More importantly, a huge gap between theories and judicial practices exist because of the lack of effective interaction. As a result, it is difficult to form a consensus to solve the problems appearing in suits. For example, the legal effect of unauthorized disposition of property has remained unclear and debated for a very long time, which, unfortunately, remains unsolved in the new GRCL.

V. Remaining controversies and perspective of the Chinese Civil Code

1. The fusion of civil law and commercial law

In the past centuries, many civil law countries like France, Germany, Spain, Portugal and Japan, were having their own separate commercial codes. The foundation of the separation of the civil code and the commercial code is based on historical facts. In the early days of capitalism, European countries formed a special class of merchants, established commercial practices and separate commercial courts, and thus formed commercial law, which was independent from the civil law. The commercial code is regarded as a special law of the civil code, and its application is superior to the latter.

In the history of China, the Qing Dynasty had tried to draft a civil code and a separate commercial code at the very beginning of the 20th century. Yet the Civil Code of the Republic of China finally did not provide a separate commercial code. The mode of a fusion of civil and commercial law was adopted. In 1949, the People's Republic of China was established. The mainland China followed the Soviet Union's legal system, which incorporated the commercial law into the civil law. Unfortunately, before the 1980s, the mainland China was devoted to abolish capitalism and establish a planned economy. During that special period, there was no space for commercial law to develop. After the 1980s, not only the legislature, but also the judiciary branch and academia have all been consciously following the mode of the fusion of civil and commercial law. However, there still are a few separate commercial statutes, such as the Company Law of 1993 (latest amendment in 2013), the Securities Law of 1998 (latest amendment in 2014), the Insurance Law of 1995 (latest amendment in 2015), the Law of Negotiable Instruments of 1995 (latest amendment in 2004) and the Maritime Law of 1992, etc.

After entering into the modern society, the free-market economy has highly developed. Any person can be engaged in business, so the distinction between businessmen and ordinary persons becomes blurred. Consequently, the necessity and possibility to set up a separate commercial code or general rules for commercial activities, independent from the civil code or an independent chapter for commercial activities in the civil code, had vanished.[36]

In my understanding, the fusion of civil and commercial law does not mean a disdain of commercial law. Its essence is that the general rules of the civil code could be applicable for people's commercial activities and the entire market economy. For specific types of legal persons and special market rules, special statutes are sufficient, such as company law, securities law, insurance law, maritime law and so on. This means the fusion or separation of civil and commercial law is just a quarrel about the form of a civil code, and it is hardly possible to integrate the whole system of commercial law into an individual civil code. The frequent amendments of special commercial laws would also influence the stability of the civil code.

2. Which comes first: Property law or personal law?

In the history of the civil law system, there are two main methodologies for the compilation of civil codes: the German style and the French style. The German style, also known as the pandectic type, has its origin in the Roman Pandects ("Digesten" in German). Its characteristics are as follows: firstly a "general part" is positioned in the beginning of the civil code; secondly a distinction between property rights and creditor's rights is made; thirdly the property law is placed before the personal law. The French style, which originates from the Institutes of Justinian, is a style that does not adopt many general rules and is usually divided into three parts (personal law, property law and methods of acquisition of property). However, the French Civil Code has changed from the original three volumes to five volumes, and the guarantee law has been separated as the fourth volume. In the recent years, the two major styles show the trend of amalgamation, such as the Hungarian New Civil Code (2013) and the Brazilian New Civil Code (2002).

In the Chinese Civil Code, there are two legislative plans for the upcoming parts. The first plan decides to inherit the German style, with the property law placed prior to the personal law (family law and succession law).

---

36 See Liang Huixing, Several Issues about the Style and Structure of the Chinese Civil Code ("民法典编纂体例若干问题"), Academic Report on the 40th Anniversary of the Chinese Academy of Social Sciences (May 17, 2017), http://www.iolaw.org.cn/showArticle.aspx?id=5168 (last visited on 27 Sept. 2017).

The second plan is characterized by the French style, with the personal law placed before the property law.[37]

Sec. 2 GRCL stipulates that the civil law regulates personal relationships and property relationships among natural persons, legal persons and unincorporated organizations as equal parties. This article, at the beginning of the Chinese Civil Code, has placed the "personal relationship" before the "property relationship". Therefore, some scholars suggested that the future structure of the Chinese Civil Code should be coherent with Sec. 2 GRCL, thus adopting a German style but the personal law should be arranged before property law.[38] Because the same rules regulate patrimonial relationships in family law, property law and the law of obligations, I think the traditional pandectic structure should be still obeyed in the Chinese Civil Code to avoid redundancy.

3. An independent book for personality rights?

As abovementioned, the new General Part confirms the protection of two kinds of personality rights, i.e., the general personality right and specific personality rights. Sec. 110 GRCL also confirms that besides natural persons, legal persons and unincorporated organizations also enjoy personality rights.

Since there are only three articles in the new General Part about personality rights, it is heavily debated whether we should have a separate book for them.[39]

---

37 See Liang Huixing, Several Issues about the Style and Structure of the Chinese Civil Code ("民法典编纂体例若干问题"), Academic Report on the 40th Anniversary of the Chinese Academy of Social Sciences (May 17, 2017), http://www.iolaw.org.cn/showArticle.aspx?id=5168 (last visited on 27 Sept. 2017).

38 See Liang Huixing, Several Issues about the Style and Structure of the Chinese Civil Code ("民法典编纂体例若干问题"), Academic Report on the 40th Anniversary of the Chinese Academy of Social Sciences (May 17, 2017), http://www.iolaw.org.cn/showArticle.aspx?id=5168 (last visited on 27 Sept. 2017).

39 Prof. Wang Liming from Renmin University of China is the main proponent of the independence of personality rights as a separate book, whose recent important articles are as follows: *On the Reasons of the Independence of the Section of Personality Rights* ("论人格权独立成编的理由"), 6 Law Review 1 (2017); *On*

An argument put forward was that an independent book for personality rights could best carry forward the protection of personality rights and show how it is valued in China. The supporters point out that although the new General Part has enumerated several personality rights, they still require further explanations, such as the definition of "privacy", the boundary of the right of name etc. It is inappropriate for tort law to meet these demands, so it is necessary to create an independent book to solve the problems.[40]

Codification is not like political propaganda. Personality rights are developing rights and their demarcation is indefinite. It is difficult to enumerate all personality rights and define their contents. In fact, the People's Courts are responsible for defining existing personality rights and for developing new ones.[41] It is reasonably predicted that even after the accomplishment of the Civil Code, People's Courts, especially the SPC would still maintain that function. Besides, in China's tort law, there existed many provisions that regulated the remedies of violating personality rights, which could satisfy most needs of protecting personality rights, it is not worth sacrificing the coherence among legislations just for the purpose of "emphasizing" personality rights.

---

the Promulgation of the General Principles of the Civil Code and the Establishment of the Section of Personality Rights ("论我国«民法总则»的颁行与民法典人格权编的设立"), 8 Political Science and Law 2 (2017); *On the Positive Confirmation of Personality Rights: The Relationship between the Law of Personality Rights and the Tort Law* ("人格权的积极确权模式探讨——兼论人格权法与侵权法之关系"), 2 The Jurist 2 (2016); *The Exclusion of Personality Rights from the General Provisions of China's Civil Law: The Independent Compilation of Personality Rights* ("论民法总则不宜全面规定人格权制度——兼论人格权独立成编"), 3 Modern Law Science 82 (2015). The main opponent of the independence of personality rights is Prof. Liang Huixing from the Institute of Law of the Chinese Academy of Social Sciences. His main ideas have been reflected in his recent article: *The Personality Rights can't be as a Separated Part in the Chinese Civil Code* ("中国民法典中不能设置人格权编"), 2 Academic Journal of Zhongzhou 48 (2016).

40 Wang Liming, Speech delivered at the Annual Meeting of the Civil Law Society of China at Fudan University School of Law (Jun. 10, 2017), http://www.fxcxw.org/index.php/Home/So/artIndex/id/14968.html (last visited Oct. 5, 2017).

41 The SPC has promulgated plenty of judiciary interpretations concerning personality rights, e.g. Interpretation of the Supreme People's Court on Several Issues Concerning the Application of Law in the Trial of Civil Disputes in the Use of Information Network against Personal Rights and Interests.

Therefore, it is not necessary to create a separate book outside tort law solely for some rhetoric work like the explanation of the meaning of some personality rights.[42]

4. An independent book for the general part of the law of obligations?

Chinese scholars have been heavily arguing about whether to set up an independent book for the general part of the law of obligations, which could provide general rules especially for contract law and tort law.[43] As it can be seen in the content of the newly passed GRCL, part of the general rules of the law of obligations have been moved into the new GRCL, such as obligations in portions and solidary obligations (Arts. 177–178 GRCL).

In my belief, eliminating an independent book for the general part of the law of obligations would weaken the strength of extracting common factors among the provisions about the obligations. In addition, some important legal institutions would have difficulties to find their place in the Civil Code, such as different types of obligations, unjust enrichment, benevolent intervention into another's affairs, rules of damages, etc. Some similar rules in contract law would have to appear again in tort law, which would lead to duplications, redundancy or too many cross references.

42 See Sun Xianzhong, Several Issues about the Chinese Civil Code ("民法典编纂的若干问题"), Speech delivered at Zhongnan University of Economics and Law (May 24, 2015), http://law.cssn.cn/fx/fx_cgzs/201511/t20151117_2617565.shtml (last visited Oct. 5, 2017).

43 E.g., Cui Jianyuan, *The General Principles of the Law of Obligations and the Making of the Chinese Civil Code* ("债法总则与中国民法典的制定"), 4 Journal of Tsinghua University (Philosophy and Social Sciences) 67 (2003); Qin Youtu & Ma Changhua, *The Abolition or not of the General Principles of the Law of Obligations in the Chinese Civil Code* ("我国民法典中债法总则的存废"), 5 Legal Science 101 (2003); Liu Jingwei, *Several Issues about the Establishment of the General Rules of the Law of Obligations in the Chinese Civil Code*("我国民法典应设立债法总则的几个问题"), 4 China Legal Science 3 (2007); Yang Lixin, *Whither the Section for the General Principles of the Law of Obligations?* ("论民法典中债法总则之存废"), 6 Tsinghua University Law Journal 81 (2014); Wang Liming, *The Relation between the General Principles of the Law of Obligations and Contract Law* ("论债法总则与合同法总则的关系"), 5 Social Sciences in Guangdong 224 (2014); Zhang Suhua, *Some Basic Theoretical Issues on the Abolition of the General Principles of the Law of Obligations* ("有关债法总则存废的几个基本理论问题"), 2 Law Review 129 (2015).

5. An independent book for intellectual property?

On the issue of the legislation of intellectual property, there was a boom of discussions among Chinese scholars from 2002 to 2003. At that time, most scholars believed that intellectual property law has formed a relatively independent normative system, which should not be incorporated into the Civil Code, but should be, as a single law, placed outside the Civil Code. There are two main reasons for this. Firstly, there is no successful example of the fusion of intellectual property and civil law in the world. Secondly, intellectual property is a kind of right that needs to be granted by administrative agencies, and if these provisions are incorporated into the Civil Code, many administrative procedures would be required to be integrated into the Civil Code, too. As a result, the Civil Code would become too complicated.

Later, in 2016, some scholars suggested that the legislation on intellectual property rights should be integrated into the Civil Code as a separate book, and when there is the right time, intellectual property could be compiled separately from the Civil Code, therefore forming a separate "intellectual property code".[44] Recently, the Intellectual Property Law Association has published its experts' proposal of the book of intellectual property.[45]

In my understanding, whether intellectual property law can be included in the Civil Code is not determined by stance of any scholar, but by the particularity of intellectual property and the logical relationship required by the compilation of the Civil Code. There is a wide range of intellectual property rights that could not provide common factors for a civil code to adopt, like the acquisition or grant of rights, the restrictions of rights, the alteration of rights, to name a few. Intellectual property law is also inclined to be

---

44 Wu Handong, *Intellectual Property Law in the Civil Law Codification* ("民法法典化运动中的知识产权法"), 4 China Legal Science 24 (2016). In this article, Prof. Wu states that the separated legislation of intellectual property has become an important trend universally. The codification of China's intellectual property law should take the "two step strategy": The first step is to achieve convergence between the Civil Code and the intellectual property law, i.e., to establish a separate book for intellectual property in the Civil Code for the purpose of demonstrating intellectual property also as a private right. The second step is to develop a special code for intellectual property, to unify rules and regulations about intellectual property.

45 Intellectual Property Law Association, *The Experts' Proposal of the Specific Part of Chinese Civil Code: The Book of Intellectual Property* ("民法分则・知识产权编"专家建议稿), http://www.fxcxw.org/index.php/Home/So/artIndex/id/15238.html (last visited Sept. 28, 2017).

amended more frequently. It is not necessary to include various provisions of intellectual property into the Civil Code, which might make the Civil Code extremely enlarged and unstable. On the reverse, even if intellectual property law as a special law is placed outside the Civil Code, the general rules of the Civil Code could still be applicable to the intellectual property.

From foreign experiences, France has an independent intellectual property code, but the relationship between the French Code of Intellectual Property and the Civil Code still reflects a classic relationship between special law and general law. The rules in the intellectual property code should be applied superiorly. Although intellectual property law has been codified, its basic position as a special law has not changed. Moreover, the French Code of Intellectual Property clearly omits essential elements of codification that are, lack of general principles and rules. In essence, it is just a collection of various laws and regulations. On the contrary, the Russian Federation Civil Code includes a separate book for intellectual property rights. Some other countries have also incorporated the copyright into their civil codes, such as the Turkmenian Civil Code of 1999. However, these legislations are not good examples for successful experiences.[46]

In short, I believe that it is not the right time for China to make the attempt of integrating intellectual property law into the Civil Code. It is enough that Art. 123 GRCL has showed that intellectual property is a kind of private right.

6. An independent book for the application of law on foreign-related civil relationships?

There exists a separate part for the rules concerning the application of law in foreign-related civil relations in the GPCL (chapter 8). Besides this, rules concerning the application of law on foreign-related civil relations are also scattered across numerous special laws. For a very long time, scholars in the field of international private law have been longing for an independent code for it. In the draft of the Civil Code of 2002, the rules concerning the

46 See Liang Huixing, Several Issues about the Style and Structure of Chinese Civil Code ("民法典编纂体例若干问题"), an academic report on the 40th anniversary for Chinese Academy of Social Sciences on May 17, 2017, http://www.iolaw.org.cn/showArticle.aspx?id=5168 (Last visited on Sept. 27, 2017).

application of law in foreign-related civil relations were included as a separate book, i.e., Book 9. Based on the draft of 2002, China promulgated the Law on the Application of Law in Foreign-Related Civil Relations in 2010.

Yet, the statement of March 15, 2017 on the Draft of the General Part of the Chinese Civil Code did not mention the arrangement of the law on the application of law in foreign-related civil relations,[47] which shows that the issue is not yet solved.

From my perspective, even though the conceptual system of international private law originates not independently from itself, but is rooted deeply in the civil law, it is still inappropriate for the Chinese Civil Code to seize the realm of private international law. This is because the international private law, including the rules on the application of law in foreign-related civil relations, whether substantively or procedurally, is unique, and it is overwhelming for the Civil Code to include it.[48] Furthermore, given the complexity and particularity of China's jurisdictional background, it is expected that the international private law of China should be self-consistent in the first step, before it is the right time to consider the relationship between the private international law and the civil law.[49]

VI. Conclusion

The birth of the Chinese Civil Code has been full of twists and turns, and thus it has become the dream of Chinese civil law scholars for generations. The promulgation of a civil code can systematically sort out existing legal theories, resolve conflicts and even promote the unification of judicial judgments. Therefore, it is still of great necessity to have a civil code in China. Now we have a suitable political environment and must seize the opportunity tightly.

---

47 See National People's Congress (hereafter “NPC”) Standing Committee, Statement on the Draft of the General Rules of Chinese Civil Law (Mar. 8, 2017) (“关于«中华人民共和国民法总则（草案）»的说明——2017年3月8日在第十二届全国人民代表大会第五次会议上”), http://www.npc.gov.cn/npc/xinwen/2017-03/09/content_2013899.htm (last visited Jul. 7, 2017).

48 Song Xiao, *The Combination of Private International Law and the Civil Code* (“国际私法与民法典的分与合”), 1 Chinese Journal of Law 175 (2017).

49 The international private law of China has its own problematic issues to be solved. For an analysis of them, see Tu Guangjian, *Forum Non Conveniens in the People's Republic of China*, 2 Chinese Journal of International Law 341 (2012).

However, China's legal system is facing much more complex social situations and difficulties. To fulfill the task of civil codification, China still lacks the necessary organizational system, theoretical preparations and the integration of judicial practices and legal theories (dogma). Hence, an ideal civil code is still out of reach.

We need to not only carefully draw lessons from western legal systems and legal theories, but also to discover and creatively deal with China's special problems, which poses a greater challenge for dogmatic researchers and judges in the future, even after the codification.

In conclusion, I believe that one of the most critical tasks faced by Chinese lawyers is still to learn, to transplant and to create a suitable way for China.

An Emperor's New or Old Clothes? – Understanding Some Basic Principles of China's General Rules of Civil Law (Summary)

*Wei Shen**

Civil law in China not only contains time-honored principles ready to be applied to existing situations, but also embodies fundamental principles from which new principles can be deduced. Despite a long history of codification, imperial China never developed a codified system of civil law or an independent court system for its administration. In 1986, the General Principles of Civil Law (GPCL) represented a victory over the economic interventionism of the post-Mao pragmatic thinking. This change ushered in a market economy reform and embodied a rights discourse, which was previously condemned as revisionist, thus bourgeois and anti-socialist. The general nature of the GPCL has been made sufficiently elastic to accommodate most of the changes in China's economy since 1986.

The General Rules of Civil Law of 2017 (GRCL) make quite a few adjustments and innovations. Firstly, the GRCL represent a great shift gearing toward the rights-based legal ideology. As to the protection of private (or personal) rights, the GRCL protect the rights of persons and the rights of assets. In addition, the GRCL protect the citizens' personal information, safety and rights to privacy according to law.

As to legal persons, the GRCL abide by the basic thoughts of civil law concerning the classification of legal persons, which fits the reform and development requirements of social organizations. The GRCL also replace "citizens" with "civil subjects" or "natural persons". This adjustment reflects the private law attributes of the GPCL. The GRCL further protect the rights of the fetus by adding a clause to grant and protect the rights of fetuses.

* *Dr., LL.M (Michigan), LL.M. (Cambridge)*; Professor and Dean, Shandong University, Law School. Chair for International Investment Law, Corporate Governance, Financial Regulation and International Commercial Arbitration.

The GRCL completely abolish the civil sanctions system. As a result, the civil liability rule returns to its true colors: the disputing parties are able to achieve a proper settlement for their dispute.

The GRCL also summarize the experience of juridical practice and accept judicial interpretations. Under the unified thinking of combining the civil statutes altogether, the GRCL focus on basic rules. The GRCL regard public order and good customs as the basic principles of civil law. This was not regulated by the GPCL. Meanwhile, it is also emphasized that the private law autonomy principle is subject to the principles of public order and good customs. These two principles must apply at the same time to build up a harmonious society and reflect the contemporary spirit of rule of law. The GRCL also state in Article 10 that judicial practice may be a source of our civil law. The GRCL equally protect private property, state property, collective property, and mixed property. The new rules especially endow the corporate capacity to rural collective economic organizations, cooperative economic organizations and self-governing mass organizations with the purpose of strengthening their legal status in law. The GRCL improve the efficacy system of civil juristic acts. In particular, the GRCL emphasize the core status of civil juristic acts, and define the civil juristic acts as an ideographical expression that brings out the change to civil rights and obligations, but do not require a "legality" essentially. The rules distinguish the applicable object of prescribed period for litigation and the applicable object during the scheduled period.

The article points out that although the renewed efforts for civil codification stress and strengthen the protection of private rights, the current political and legal system may present some political obstacles in realizing this rights-based legal ideology. Of the great importance is the lack of constitutional basis for the equal right entitlement. Given this backdrop, the codification of civil law is of little help to advance equal rights protection unless there would be a breakthrough in the Constitution.

This article focuses on some new or revised important rules codified in the GRCL. The new Civil Code absorbs and codifies a number of civil law principles. The so-called new principles, as discussed here, however are deviations of some basic civil law principles, which have been developed and embedded in civil societies and market economies for a long time. These so-called new civil law principles, even without being codified, have been and will be used. In this sense, there is indeed no breakthrough in the sense of doctrinal innovations. The most notable contribution of the GRCL is being part of the codification movement strengthening the rule of law, or more precisely, the rule by law, which reflects, if not redefines, many social and economic objectives in socialist China. Compared to a civil code itself, codifying the so-called new civil law principles into the GRCL are more like a decoration to old principles. In other words, it is more like a new bottle with old wine. To truly lift the face of and inject energy into China's civil law, the future civil code needs to change the traditional political and economic ideology thereby transferring powers from the Party-State to the people and strengthening the rule of law.

Principles in the Chinese Civil Code

*Thomas M.J. Möllers**

Abstract: *The General Rules of Civil Law (GRCL) will have a substantial influence on the development of Civil Law in the Peoples Republic of China in the coming years. Similarly, the general legal principles embedded in the GRCL will help to shape and concretize this redefined legal code. It is in this way that fundamental principles such as the freedom of contract and the absolute protection of particular legal interests have finally been incorporated into the legal framework in China. The consideration and implementation of such principles belong to a category of particularly challenging aspects of juridical work. Such fundamental principles are often not codified and must therefore first be deducted via the interpretation of more complex legal ideas. Once this has been done, it is up to the lawyers under the consideration of the lex superior doctrine to further outline and concretise these principles in order to avoid and resolve possible collisions. The following article shows by means of numerous examples how in its early stage, Chinese Civil Law can be inspired by and learn from German legal dogma. At the same time, the following article comprises a detailed comparison of the fundamental principles found in the GRCL and the German Civil Code (BGB).*

Keywords: Working with principles; legal principles; freedom to contract; legal idea; legal rule; legal doctrine; priority of norms; private autonomy; pacta sunt servanda; primacy of law.

---

* *Dr. iur. habil.;* Professor, University of Augsburg, Faculty of Law. Managing Director of the Center for European Legal Studies, Chair for Civil Law, Economic Law, European Law, Private International Law and Comparative Law. The Contribution was presented during the conference of the research institute RICE, also at the China University of Political Science and Law, the Gansu College, and the Lanzhou University. I would like to thank the participants for the stimulating discussions during these events.

I. On the legal relevance of legal principles

A lawyer does not only need to know and apply the law. A good lawyer knows the interplay between law, jurisdiction, and legal literature. Legal dogmatics is a combination of numerous written and unwritten rules which make the law understandable in the first place but which are indispensable for the profound understanding of the law. What are legal principles, though? How are the legal principles applied? The recently passed General Principles of Civil Law (GRCL) contain a shell thereof.

In the following, the legal principle will first be depicted and distinguished from the legal idea and the legal doctrine (I.). Then, four techniques to substantiate legal principles will be presented. The first one entails a reference to other more specific norms (II.). A second technique is the substantiation through induction and deduction (III.). Then, the methodology of the higher-ranking law will be described (IV.). Eventually, principles could be substantiated through balancing (V.).

In our society, having principles is usually a positive character trait for a person to have. If a person remains true to their principles, they are considered to be strong-willed, sincere, and straightforward. In this respect, politicians and representatives in election campaigns are very often prematurely assumed to put honest convictions aside in favour of securing power and influence; or acting opportunistically in the interests of the strongest lobby at the time, and against the interests of the sovereign people. According to Gandhi "politics without principles" even represents one of his famous seven deadly sins of modern society.[1] It is therefore hardly a new insight that both our man-made Basic Law (GG) and the ordinary law are permeated with numerous principles which are meant to ensure that the law is as straightforward as possible. However, it is all the more astonishing that only a few of these legal principles are set out in positive law. So, for example, there is as little explicitly recorded in writing on the principle in the law of obligations of freedom of contract[2] in the German Civil Code (BGB) as there is on the principle of contractual fidelity (pacta sunt servanda)[3]. However, no one seriously disputes the existence and applicability of these principles. Other states, however, have codified numerous principles.[4]

---

1 Mahatma Gandhi, Seven Social Sins, 43 Young India October 22, 361 (1925): "politics without principles".

2 The term is even referred to in the Motive zu dem Entwurfe eines Bürgerlichen Gesetzbuches für das Deutsche Reich (Statements on the Draft of a Civil Code for the German Reich), vol. 2, 2 (1896): "By virtue of the principle of freedom of contract, which governs the law of contractual obligations, the parties can determine their legal relationships and associations between themselves at their discretion with binding effect, insofar as there are no conflicting general or specific individual absolute legal provisions".

3 In contrast, the principle was even found in the original Article 77 of the Entwürfe eines Bürgerlichen Gesetzbuches für das Deutsche Reich (Draft of a Civil Code for the German Reich) (1888): "In order to conclude a contract, it is necessary for the contracting parties to declare their corresponding intentions to each other"; This Article 77 was then deleted by the second commission, see Commission's Report, 156, Benno Mugdan, Die gesamten Materialien des Bürgerlichen Gesetzbuchs für das Deutsche Reich, vol. 1, 688 (1899).

4 On pacta sunt servanda see for example fn. 28; on immorality see fn. 47.

1. Excerpt of legal principles in the GRCL: voluntariness and freedom to contract, equality and protection of physical integrity and property

Three principles of the GRCL have been chosen to provide an example of how to work out a structure with principles: In section 5 GRCL, the principle of the freedom to contract is phrased as the "principle of voluntariness". Hereto Professor Wei Shen stated in his contribution to the conference: "As the principle of voluntariness is rooted in the Western enlightenment conception of the individual, it is ironic that Chinese law should embrace a break with values rooted in Chinese family and collective traditions and it is similarly a milestone in the break with socialist values restricting freedom of economic action."

In Chinese law, one principle that is particularly stressed is the equality of the parties. It can be found in section 2 as well as in section 4 GRCL. In German law, equality is located in Art. 3 GG and as such is primarily a basic law and a right of defence against the state. Section 5 of the GPCL of 1986 still stated that "civil rights and interests of the citizens and legal entities" must be protected. The present section 3 GRCL phrases with more intensity that physical rights and property rights [...] may not be infringed by individuals or organisations.

2. Terms and Distinctions

a) Legal Principle (Rechtsprinzip)

A definition of a legal principle must contain three components: Legal principles or (often used synonymously) principles of law are initially only partly standardised, and often not set out in law at all. They are extracted from the legal system as the totality of the written and unwritten legal norms and are more than legal concepts. They allow a certain generalisation.[5] Principles form "the deep structure of the law".[6]

5 Jürgen Basedow, 200 AcP 446, 453 (2000). In detail, also Claus-Wilhelm Canaris, Die Feststellung von Lücken im Gesetz, 47 et seq (2nd ed. 1983).

6 Klaus Friedrich Röhl and Hans Christian Röhl, Allgemeine Rechtslehre, 283 (3rd ed. 2008).

They generally claim normative validity and lead to a presumption of conformity.[7] However, principles are frequently not classifiable and require further specification through legal rules or balancing. Or in the words of Bydlinski: "They are thus guiding principles and grounds of justification of a legal provision, but not the positive provision itself."[8] The Basic Law already contains those which are probably the best known: Fundamental rights are principles par excellence. The mere fact that legal principles dominate our highest-ranking codifications shows their enormous importance in reaching legally sound decisions, and thus forces legal scholars to discuss them.

b) Legal Concepts (Rechtsidee)

Legal concepts have a higher status than legal principles. They provide reasons for norms which formulate the requirements or prohibitions.[9] Such legal concepts, which are to some extent also referred to as values[10], are of a higher level of abstraction and frequently too general for them to be used to resolve a case. Legal concepts such as justice, expediency and legal certainty must therefore also be further specified to make it possible to have transparent, persuasive trains of thought and justification. Otherwise there is a risk that the concept is only used as an empty phrase.[11]

---

7 Klaus Friedrich Röhl and Hans Christian Röhl, Allgemeine Rechtslehre, 284 (3rd ed. 2008).

8 Franz Bydlinski, Juristische Methodenlehre und Rechtsbegriff, 132 (2nd ed. 1991).

9 Matthias Mahlmann, Rechtsphilosophie und Rechtstheorie, section 24, § 13 (3rd ed. 2015).

10 Wolfgang Fikentscher, Methoden des Rechts, vol. 4, 394 et seq. (1977).

11 This particularly applies for the concept of the "nature of the matter". See Heinrich Dernburg, Pandekten, vol. 1, 84 (7. ed. 1902); Heinrich Dernburg, System des römischen Rechts, vol. 1, section 32.2, 64 (8th ed. 1911); Andreas von Thur, Allgemeiner Teil des Bürgerliches Rechts, vol. 1, 42 (1910); Arthur Kaufmann, Analogie und „Natur der Sache“ (2nd ed. 1982); Friedrich Müller, Normstruktur und Normativität, 94 et seq. (1966); Karl Larenz, Methodenlehre der Rechtswissenschaft, 417 et seqq. (6th ed. 1991) with further citations; Claus-Wilhelm Canaris, Die Feststellung von Lücken im Gesetz, 100 (2nd ed. 1983).

c) Legal Doctrine (Rechtsinstitute)

Legal principles require further specification to be applicable for the specific case. A legal rule can exist in a legal doctrine developed by jurisprudence, such as the obligation to contract. A legal doctrine, in its application, is then eventually a rule in the sense of *Alexy* or a positive rule in the sense of *Bydlinski*.[12] In the interim, it is substantiated and, through the development of tangible, directly classifiable features, has also acquired a binding character[13] and apparent authority.[14]

3. Legal Obligation and the Prevention of Empty Phrases

a) Obligation to Induct and Substantiate

Some claim that legal principles are mere declarations of intent without legal relevance[15]. In the following, the opposite view is held. Legal principles, such as *pacta sunt servanda*, are legally significant. This is in accordance with the law in Germany. It is generally assumed that the BGB presupposes these principles as simply being obviously valid.[16] However, they need to be legally defined. Then, it needs to be outlined how they are applied. They need to be deducted in a first step and then substantiated in a second step.

---

12 See also Thomas M.J. Möllers, Juristische Methodenlehre, § 11 recital 12 et seqq. (2017).

13 Thus, for example, liability for apparent rights is established as a legal principle from sections 171, 172 BGB and section 405 BGB. This principle is then developed into the legal doctrine of agency by estoppel, Bundesgerichtshof [BGH] [Federal Supreme Court], October 15, 1987, III ZR 235/86, BGHZ 102, 60, 64; then without the doctrinal derivation: BGH, May 11, 2011, VIII ZR 289/09, BGHZ 189, 346 § 15 – use of a third-party eBay member's account.

14 BGH, January 20, 1983, VII ZR 32/82, BGHZ 86, 273, 274 et seq. – apparent authority.

15 William C Jones, 28 Harv. Int'l. L.J. 309 (1987).

16 Thus Werner Flume, DJT 135, 136 et seq. (1960); Werner Flume, Allgemeiner Teil des Bürgerlichen Rechts, Das Rechtsgeschäft, vol. 2, section 1.1, 1 (1965); agreeing Claus-Wilhelm Canaris, 200 AcP 273, 277 (2000); Reinhard Bork, Allgemeiner Teil des Bürgerlichen Gesetzbuchs, recital 99 (4th ed. 2016).

b) Preventing empty phrases

Section 6 GRCL uses the principle of "fairness" to determine rights and obligations of the parties. Section 7 GRCL mentions the principle of good faith. It was originally codified in section 4 GPCL and followed the German "good faith" of section 242 BGB. In Chinese law applying the principle of good faith is treated with respect because its vagueness is criticised. For this reason, it is not sufficient to use empty phrases. In the German law legal principles are in part derived from the "nature of the matter" (Natur der Sache). This was first introduced by *Dernburg*[17] and later accepted by the literature[18] and jurisdiction[19]. This is rejected because the term "nature of the matter" does not establish anything by itself.[20] Also legal ethical principles as for example "justice" and "fairness" need to be further substantiated to make comprehensible, persuasive thoughts and justifications possible.

II. Derivation and substantiation of legal principles through the priority of norms (lex specialis)

1. Lex specialis – the more specific norm precedes, section 11 GRCL

Section 11 GRCL determines that specific provisions precede.[21] The German law is also very aware of this principle. The rule *lex specialis derogat*

---

17 Heinrich Dernburg, Pandekten, vol. 1, 87 (4th ed. 1894); Heinrich Dernburg, System des römischen Rechts, vol. 1, 64 (8th ed. 1911); Andreas von Thur, Allgemeiner Teil des Bürgerliches Rechts, vol. 1, 42 (1910).

18 In detail Karl Larenz, Methodenlehre der Rechtswissenschaft 417 et seqq. (6th ed. 1991); Claus-Wilhelm Canaris, Die Feststellung von Lücken im Gesetz 100 (2nd ed. 1983).

19 BVerfG, February 20, 1952 (Az. 1 BvF 2/51), BVerfGE 1, 117, 131.

20 Critical: Horst Dreier, Zum Begriff der „Natur der Sache", 127 et seq. (1965); Klaus Friedrich Röhl and Hans Christian Röhl, Allgemeine Rechtslehre, 74 (3rd ed. 2008): "It turns out that the issue of the essence as well as the nature of the matter does not add any argument at any point"; Peter Raisch, Juristische Methoden, 178 (1995); Bernd Rüthers, Christian Fischer and Axel Birk, Rechtstheorie, recital 929 (9th ed. 2016).

21 See also Yuanshi Bu, ZChinR 183, 186 et seq. (2017).

legi generali is based on Roman law[22] and means that a specific law precedes the general law. The same rule can be found in Anglo American law: *Generalia specialibus non derogant*: A general rule cannot supersede a more specific rule.[23] The principle of *lex specialis* must be affirmed if a claim depends on requirements that are more restrictive and unfavourable.[24]

2. Selected examples

a) The principle of voluntariness and substantiation through specific provisions

The principle of voluntariness is derived from section 5 GRCL. It is substantiated in Chinese law. The principle of good faith according to section 7 GRCL is substantiated by section 119 GRCL insofar that a contract is legally binding and thus must be adhered to. In European law the principle of "pacta sunt servanda" is well-known. The counterpart to freedom of contract is the binding contract or contractual fidelity (pacta sunt servanda). The principle of a binding contract is not of Roman origin,[25] but was rather first developed for all types of contract by canon law, the late scholasticism,

22 For the original in Greek, see Mod. D. 1,4,4 as well as Pap. D. 48,19,41: nec ambigitur in cetero omni iure speciem generi derogare; see also Sebastiano Medici, De legibus, statutis, et consuetudine, 92 (Sebastiano Medici et al. eds., 1574): Lex specialis derogat generali.

23 Or literally: General provisions do not precede specific provisions; Oliver Jones and Francis Alan Roscoe Bennion, Bennion on Statutory Interpretation 281 (6th ed. 2013).

24 Ernst A. Kramer, Juristische Methodenlehre, 119 (5th ed. 2016) with reference to Hans Merz, Festschrift for Guhl, 87, 94 et seqq. (1950); note also Thomas M.J. Möllers, Juristische Methodenlehre, § 4 recital 134 (2017).

25 Roman law did not have any general option to be able to sue for contractual obligations. See in detail, Gerhard Kegel, Vertrag und Delikt, 3 et seq. (2002).

and the natural law[26] and German sources of law[27]. One can find the principle expressly in the Motive,[28] but not in the BGB, because the rule that the concurrence of wills is contractually binding was assumed to be known by the Second Commission and therefore deleted.

However, the principle of a binding contract has to be limited. This is why a civil law transaction is voidable if it has come into existence on the basis of a threat or deceit, sections 148–150 GRCL. Also in German law there is contractual justice by procedural fairness. Threat or bad faith do not automatically result in voidness but allow the contestation of the contract according to sections 119, 123, 142 BGB.

b) The protection of physical and proprietary rights and sections 107 et seqq. and sections 176 et seqq. GRCL

The protection of physical and proprietary rights as a general principle in section 3 GRCL is substantiated by numerous particular provisions: In sections 107 et seqq. GRCL there are numerous provisions which reinforce legally protected rights. The GRCL are not restricted to the legally protected rights of life, body, health and freedom in section 823 para. 1 BGB, but also explicitly protect human dignity, the right to privacy or data security, section 109 et seqq. GRCL. Here, the Chinese law is, without doubt, more modern than the version of the BGB from 1900. Up to the present day, the German legislator, for example, has failed to codify the general right of privacy despite several initiatives.[29]

---

26 See Christian Freiherr von Wolff, Grundsätze des Natur- und Völkerrechts, section 438 (1754): "When two or more jointly agree on one or more promises, it is a contract (pactum or pactio)." See Klaus-Peter Nanz, Die Entstehung des allgemeinen Vertragsbegriffs im 16.–18. Jahrhundert, 149 et seq. (1985); Helmut Coing, Europäisches Privatrecht, vol. 1, 397 et seq. (1985); in detail, Gerhard Kegel, Vertrag und Delikt, 3 et seq. (2002).

27 Sachsenspiegel, Leipziger Ausgabe, 1st book, Art. 7 (1595): "That which a man promises, so should he keep"; Glück, Ausführliche Erläuterungen der Pandekten, nach Hellfeld – ein Kommentar für meine Zuhörer, vol. 4, 279 et seq. (1786), with reference to the German legal rule: "A man's word is his bond." See also Friedrich Carl von Savigny, System des heutigen Römischen Rechts, vol. 3, 309 (1840).

28 Entwurf eines Bürgerlichen Gesetzbuches für das Deutsche Reich, section 77 (1888).

29 Thomas M.J. Möllers, Juristische Methodenlehre, § 7 recital 72 et seqq. (2017).

The legal consequence in section 120 GRCL is tort liability which in return is substantiated in sections 176 et seqq. GRCL: Not only the restitution of the original state but also the contractual penalty and alternative penalties can be comprised if it is stipulated by a law, section 179 GRCL. Such legal provisions exist as Wei Shen stated in his contribution to the conference: "Punitive damage, as the civil responsibility liability form of preventing and punishing the larger vicious violations through economic means, has been explicitly adopted by China's multiple single-line legislation. For example, Article 47 (Product Liability) of the Tort Liability Act, Article 55 (Consumers Fraud) of the Consumer Protection Act, and Article 148 (Food Safety Responsibility) of the Food Safety Law. The "General Principles of Civil Law" will formally put the punitive damages into one of the civil responsibility liability forms, which will likely lead to punitive damages being used more in future single-line legislation." The introduction of the punitive damages adds a deterrent effect to the claim for damages and thus renders them efficiently: It remains to be seen how rights as "human dignity" and "privacy" have to be interpreted, sections 109 et seq. GRCL. Foreign companies such as Apple, Google or Facebook and Chinese companies such as Alibaba, Tencent, and Baidu use their customers' personal data on a large scale. It is till unknown if the extensive basis of liability will lead to a liability risk that is difficult to gauge. Under a legal comparison, two further particularities should be pointed out: If the human dignity is worth protecting, a violation or exposure is quickly reached. In German law, this basic law is treated with special care.[30] The general right of privacy is called a "framework law"[31] and it is differentiated between social, private and intimate sphere. Moreover, a balancing with the other party's interests takes place.[32]

30 Prevailing view, BVerfG, June 3, 1987, 1 BvR 313/85, BVerfGE 75, 369, 380: "absolutely without a possibility to weigh up the choices (Güterabwägung)"; BVerfG, October 10, 1995, 1 BvR 1476/91 among others, BVerfGE 93, 266, 293: "the human dignity as the root of all basic rights is not open to balancing with any other individual basic right"; Michael Sachs and Wolfram Höfling, GG, § 1 Rn. 11 (7th ed. 2014); Jochen von Bernstorff, JZ 905 et seqq. (2013); Horst Dreier, GG (Horst Dreier ed., 3rd ed. 2013), Art. 1 I recital 46 with further references differing view Manfred Baldus, AöR 136, 529 et seqq. (2011).

31 Prevailing view among others Wolfgang Fikentscher and Andreas Heinemann, Schuldrecht, recital 1582, 1584 (10th ed. 2006).

32 See below V.1.c).

III. Substantiation through deduction of legal principles and the creation of new legal concepts

1. Induction and Deduction

Legal principles serve the development of law with already existing valuations. Figuratively speaking, legal principles link the existing law and the law that has yet to be developed. The combination of induction and deduction serves this purpose[33]. The literature of the deduction of legal principles also favours *Induction* which is the conclusion from the specific to the general.[34] According to *Canaris* the derivation of a thought comes from several legal provisions.[35] *Deduction* is the conclusion from the general to the specific. In the underlying context it describes how a general legal principle operates in the solution of a specific legal problem, which is from the principle to the rule. As well as the derivation of a general legal principle through induction is judicial development of the law, the legal rules and concepts obtained by deduction from the legal principles are development of the law.

Further substantiation is possible forming categories, subprinciples and similar factual conditions. The same procedure is applied to general stipulations trying to substantiate them with subprinciples, categories and similar factual conditions. Now, primarily pure case law is substantiated without such a legal basis.

Eventually, there is one last step to obtain a new legal sentence, e.g. a new basis for a claim, from a legal principle through development of the law. This is often accompanied by great uncertainty about how to justify them with legal dogmatics. A prime example in German law for this is the

---

33 More detailed Thomas M.J. Möllers, Juristische Methodenlehre, § 11 recital 19 et seqq. (2017).

34 In detail Aristoteles, Aristoteles' Erste Analytiken or: Lehre vom Schluss, chapter 23, 142 (Kirchmann ed. 1877); Francis Bacon, Novum Organum, Book I, Aphorismus CIV, 82 (1620).

35 For example Claus-Wilhelm Canaris, Die Feststellung von Lücken im Gesetz, 100, 97 et seq. (2nd ed. 1983): "A common legal thought is derived from several legal provisions and it is awarded the quality of a general legal one"; Neil MacCormick, Legal Reasoning and Legal Theory, 153 et seq., 232 et seq. (1978).

obligation to contract[36], the frustration of contract[37], and the contracts with protective effect to the benefit of third parties.[38] The jurisdiction has substantiated the newly developed legal rules by categories and similar factual conditions. As inherent to the judicial development, the approaches are experimental and the practical application can sometimes only be developed through a *trial and error* process.

2. Freedom to contract and binding effect of a contract

a) Freedom to contract according to sections 5, 7 GRCL

The freedom to contract is codified in section 5 GRCL with the wording that the civil legal relationship can be introduced, changed and terminated according to the will of the individual. The new GRCL substantiated the obligations to adhere to promises of section 7 GRCL insofar that a contract is legally binding, section 119 GRCL. This principle is known in German law as "pacta sunt servanda".

b) Freedom of contract as a consequence of freedom of the will under German Law

Private autonomy includes freedom of contract, but also freedom of ownership (section 903 BGB), freedom to marry (section 1297 BGB) and testamentary freedom, so the right to freely dispose of one's assets in the event

36 Reasoning on the basis of section 826 BGB RG, November 7, 1931, V 106/31, RGZ 133, 388, 392 – theater critic or for example BGH, December 2, 1974, II ZR 78/72, BGHZ 63, 282, 285 – compulsory admission to a monopoly organization. See for the newer view that derives an obligation to contract from a quasinegatory injunctive relief Karsten Schmidt, DRiZ 97, 98 (1977); Reinhard Bork, Julius von Staudingers Kommentar zum BGB, preliminary note on sections 145 et seqq. recital 2 (ed. 2015); Jan Busche, Münchener Kommentar BGB, before section 145 recital 21 (6th ed. 2012); Christian Armbrüster, BGB, before section 145 recital 29 (Walter Erman ed., 14th ed. 2014).

37 See for example BGH, February 25, 1993, VII 24/92, BGHZ 121, 378 recital 48.

38 Before RG, February 10, 1930, VI 270/29, RGZ 127, 218, 221 – Gas meter.

of death (section 1937 BGB).[39] Freedom of contract in turn includes freedom to conclude contracts, freedom of contractual partner, freedom of content, and generally freedom of form, but also freedom to amend and cancel.[40] The concept of freedom of contract was first introduced in the mid-19th century.[41] Freedom of contract is based on the intentions of the parties.[42] The parties can determine their legal relationships between themselves at their discretion, insofar as there are no conflicting legal provisions.

The parties are generally responsible for agreeing to the essentialia negotii, the essential components of the contract, such as the object of purchase and the purchase price. The price is not controlled. The parties may also conclude unreasonable contracts.[43] That corresponds with the liberal approach of *Adam Smith*, who described the market as the "invisible hand", on which supply and demand regulate themselves.[44] The underlying idea is that the conflict of interests between the parties lead to a correct result through the contract; one could refer to the "guaranteed correctness" of the negotiation.[45] *Hobbes* accurately stressed that it is the parties who are best

---

39 Motive zu dem Entwurfe eines Bürgerliches Gesetzbuches für das deutsche Reich, vol. 2, 2 (2nd ed. 1896).

40 Reinhard Bork, Allgemeiner Teil des Bürgerlichen Gesetzbuchs, section 661 (4th ed. 2016); Manfred Wolf and Jörg Neuner, Allgemeiner Teil des Bürgerlichen Rechts, section 10, § 33 et seq. (11th ed. 2016); Thomas M.J. Möllers, JuS 1191, 1192 (1999).

41 Friedrich Carl von Savigny, Das Recht des Obligationenrechts, vol. 2, sections 72–78 (1853); Bernhard Windscheid, Lehrbuch des Pandektenrechts, vol. 2, section 312, fn. 5 with further citations (8th ed. 1900); see Werner Scherrer, Die geschichtliche Entwicklung des Prinzips der Vertragsfreiheit, 33 et seq. (1948); Joachim Rückert, Naturrecht und Rechtsphilosophie in der Neuzeit, 135, 145 et seq. (Diethelm Klippel ed., 1997).

42 Motive zu dem Entwurfe eines Bürgerliches Gesetzbuches für das deutsche Reich, vol. 2, 126 (2nd ed. 1896): "Legal transaction in the sense of the Draft is a personal declaration of intent, aimed at emphasising a legal outcome, which occurs under the legal system as a result, because it is intended."

43 Oberlandesgericht [OLG] [Higher Regional Court] of Cologne, December 8, 2006, 19 U 109/06, MMR 2007, 446, 448: Purchase of a sugar beet harvester worth 60,000 euros in an eBay auction for 51 euros; agreeing, Marc-Philippe Weller, Die Vertragstreue, 170 (2009).

44 Adam Smith, Wealth of Nations, vol. III, book IV, chap. II (9th ed. 1799), Of Restraints upon the Importation from foreign Countries of such Goods as can be produced at Home, p. 181.

45 Walter Schmidt-Rimpler, 147 ACP 130, 149 et seq. (1941); Walter Schmidt-Rimpler, Festschrift for Raiser 3, 5 et seq. (1974); Manfred Lieb, 178 AcP 196, 206 (1978).

able to determine the value of the item.[46] This concept has been taken up by the BGB. For example, in addition to the conspicuous disparity between benefit and consideration as a further prerequisite to establish usury, section 138 para. 2 BGB requires that freedom of choice is impaired, such as with the exploitation of plight. This corresponds with the legal position in numerous other legal systems.[47] Thus only *procedural fairness* was to be ensured, guaranteed process, by protection against mistake or fraud (sections 119, 123 et seq., 142 et seq. BGB).[48]

c) The justification of a binding contract (pacta sunt servanda)

As the principle of a binding contract (pacta sunt servanda) cannot be taken directly from the law, one must derive it from the law indirectly by induction: Thus a person who offers to conclude a contract with another person is "bound by the offer" section 145 BGB. The contract and the contractual obligation follow from the deliberate statement to accept an offer. Without consensus, this leads to disagreement under sections 154 et seq. BGB. The mistake - the conflict of intention and declaration - is initially irrelevant for the binding effect. The contract is valid despite the mistake and only permits a challenge under sections 119, 142 BGB.[49] The binding contract can be discerned from the synallagmatic fulfilment obligations of the individual types of contract[50] or the general fulfilment obligations at the time of performance (section 271 BGB), the right of retention (section 273 BGB), and impossibility (section 275 BGB). Moreover, good faith (section 242 BGB) can be used to justify the obligation for contractual fidelity.[51] Moreover, under the 2001 reform of the law of obligations, freedom of contract and

46 Vividly, Thomas Hobbes, Leviathan, part I, chap. 15, 74 (2nd ed. 1886): "The value of all things contracted for, is measured by the appetite of the contractors: and therefore the just value is that which they be contented to give."

47 Art. 21 OR (Swiss Code of Obligations); Art. 282 port. cc (Portuguese código civil); Art. 388 Polish Civil Code of 23/04/1964.

48 On this procedural concept of fairness, see Konrad Zweigert and Hein Kötz, Einführung in die Rechtsvergleichung, 320 et seq. (3rd ed. 1996).

49 Sibylle Hofer, HKK-BGB, with section 145, § 10 (2003).

50 Such as from the contract of sale (section 433), rental agreement (section 535), contract for work (section 633) or contract for services (section 631 BGB).

51 BGH, December 17, 1982, V ZR 306/81, BGHZ 86, 167, 171 – increase in a ground rent in the absence of a contractual adjustment clause.

the binding contract can be established by sections 241, 311 para. 1 BGB.[52] The binding contract can be derived from the provisions cited by induction.

3. Private autonomy as self-determination for both parties

a) Self-determination of the individuals and mutual self-determination

With the presentation of the legal doctrine above, too much consideration was given to freedom of contract, and conversely self-determination was neglected. Self-determination is a prerequisite for the freedom of contract. The following wording is already contained in the Motiven zum BGB: "The legal system cannot allow free self-determination to be impaired in legal transactions in an unlawful way."[53] And the first sentence in Flume's work "Rechtsgeschäft" reads: "Private autonomy is the name given to the principle of self-organisation of legal relationships by the individual according to his/her will."[54] He continued verbatim: "For as far as self-determination reaches, there is no external control. The deliberate decision is valid because it is intended and the will of the individual is respected as such. Private autonomous organisation requires, insofar as it is recognised by law, no justification other than that the individual intends it."[55]

Self-determination is often only referred to in relation to one party.[56] However, the principle of self-determination obviously applies for both

---

52 Andreas Their, HKK-BGB, section 311 I, § 1 (2007); Marc-Philippe Weller, Die Vertragstreue, 170 (2009).

53 Motive zu dem Entwurfe eines Bürgerlichen Gesetzbuches für das Deutsche Reich (Statements on the Draft of a Civil Code for the German Reich), vol. 1, 204 (1888); in German it says: „Die Rechtsordnung kann nicht gestatten, daß die freie Selbstbestimmung auf rechtsgeschäftlichem Gebiete in wiederrechtlicher Weise beeinträchtigt wird.“

54 Werner Flume, Allgemeiner Teil des Bürgerlichen Rechts, vol. 2, 1 (4 ed. 1992); as above Werner Flume, Festschrift 100 Jahre DJT, vol. 1, 135, 136 et seq., 143 (1960); agreeing Claus-Wilhelm Canaris, 200 AcP, 273, 277 (2000); Reinhard Bork, Allgemeiner Teil des Bürgerlichen Gesetzbuchs, § 99 (4th ed. 2016); Joachim Rückert, HKK-BGB, with section 1 § 108 (2003) speaks of "drumbeat." See also BVerfG, May 13, 1986, 1 BvR 1542/84, BVerfGE 72, 155, 170.

55 Werner Flume, Festschrift 100 Jahre DJT, vol. 1, 135, 141 (1960).

56 Jan Busche, Münchener Kommentar BGB, section 145 Paragraph 6 and the evidence in section 12 fn. 65 (7th ed. 2015); Manfred Wolf and Jörg Neuner, Allgemeiner Teil des Bürgerlichen Rechts, section 10, § 30 (11th ed. 2016).

sides. Self-determination of both sides then also means protection against external control.[57] Flume rightly emphasises that the contract requires mutual self-determination and that an inequality of power or factual monopoly position leads to one-sided external control. The concept of mutual self-determination as part of private autonomy was met with approval.[58] Flume had already formulated the following in 1960:

"Insofar as individuals are provided the right to regulate legal relationships by mutual self-determination, that is by contract, in our legal system, it is based on the requirement that the individuals face one another with the power of self-determination, and do not enter into contracts by the power of one-sided external control instead of mutual self-determination. Compulsion and private autonomy are incompatible with one another. However, it is private autonomy's eternal dilemma that it is continually brought into question by an unequal distribution of power."[59]

b) Derivation of the principle of self-determination from the BGB and the constitution

One can now discern this principle from an indirect third-party effect of the fundamental rights. In the decision on the guarantee of relatives without assets, the BVerfG stressed that Art. 2 para. 1 GG guarantees the "self-determination of the individual in legal life"[60] as part of private autonomy. It also required such an understanding of private autonomy in several decisions, where there would have been a "structural inequality of bargaining

---

57 Norbert Reich, JZ 609 (1997).

58 Franz Jürgen Säcker, Münchener Kommentar BGB, Introduction Paragraph 37 (7th ed. 2015).

59 Werner Flume, Festschrift 100 Jahre DJT, vol. 1, 135, 143 (1960); similarly Karl Larenz, Schuldrecht, vol. 1, section 4, 41 (14. ed. 1987): "free self-determination of each of the two contracting parties".

60 BVerfG, October 19, 1993, 1 BvR 567 inter alia, BVerfGE 89, 214, 231 – guarantee agreements referring to Hans-Uwe Erichsen, HdB Staatsrecht, vol. 6, section 152 paragraph 58 et seq. (Hans-Uwe Erichsen ed. 1989), which in fn. 195, 197, again refers to Werner Flume (fn. 59).

power" or a "disrupted contractual parity".[61] In terms of a constitution-oriented (reinforcing) interpretation, there is nothing to preclude this.[62]

However, it is more convincing to interpret the principle of self-determination as part of the private autonomy of both parties and thus as a civil law legal principle. This principle can be found in the BGB in the intention theory of the 19th century, then standardised in section 133 ("to ascertain the true intention"), and the error rules (section 119 et seq.). Self-determination is also guaranteed in family and probate law.[63] Seen historically, the BGB did not only want to introduce freedom, but also an equal legal freedom[64] without differentiation between persons. Through European law the cancellation (section 312 BGB) was also added, which strengthened the self-determination of the consumer. Equal legal freedom thus means the equal use of freedom for all.

4. Deduction: The doctrinal legal justification of the various legal doctrines where the right of self-determination is absent

a) Obligation to contract and lack of self-determination

The obligation to contract can be justified from private autonomy itself: At a first glance, the obligation to contract is opposed to freedom of contract because one side loses the freedom to conclude contracts referred to above.[65] However, that is only applicable when one only considers the opposing party to the contract, the party refusing to accept, in isolation. Freedom of contract, however, is a conditioned freedom which is aimed at fulfilling mutual interests. If freedom of contract includes the self-determined decision of both sides, then private autonomy also allows the freedom to

---

61 Moreover, it referred to the welfare state principle (Art. 20 (1), 28 (1) Sentence 1 GG), see BVerfGE 89, 214, 231 et seq. (fn. 60) – guarantee agreements.

62 Thomas M.J. Möllers, Juristische Methodenlehre, section 7, § 73 (2017).

63 Sections 1821, 1822 in conjunction with 1643 BGB; section 1901 (1) Sentence 2 BGB; section 2064 BGB.

64 Joachim Rückert, HKK-BGB, with section 1, § 43 et seq. (2003), who speaks of a principle of equal legal freedom; agreeing Sibylle Hofer, Vertragsfreiheit am Scheideweg, 11 (2006).

65 Werner Flume, Allgemeiner Teil des Bürgerlichen Rechts, vol. 2, 611 (4th ed. 1992); Jörg Neuner, Privatrecht und Sozialstaat 287 (1999): "because it hereby involves the opposite of self-determined legal consequences".

form a contract and thus the right, under certain conditions, to force conclusion of a contract. Freedom of contract is impaired when there is no choice.[66] The reliance on the service clarifies the lack of self-determination, when there is an obligation to contract.[67] The self-determination of the party wishing to contract is severely restricted in the absence of alternatives, such that the self-determination of the other party is, by way of exception, restricted. The obligation to conclude a contract in this respect establishes a legal obligation which includes the obligation to give a declaration of intent aimed at the conclusion of a contract.[68]

b) Price controls under section 138 para. 1 BGB for contracts which intervene in the self-determined life with severe freedom-restricting consequences

Formally, the judgments on price controls for contracts[69] are not particularly convincing because the presumption of a reprehensible attitude in the event of a disparity between benefit and consideration only constitutes an apparent justification[70] and fiction[71]. In terms of content, such judgments are to be rejected because they contradict the BGB. The wording of section 138 para. 2 BGB also requires, with the need for a conspicuous disparity, exploitation of plight and therefore does not directly provide any general

66 Thus Josef Kohler, Lehrbuch der Rechtsphilosophie, 96 (1909); Jan Busche, Privatautonomie und Kontrahierungszwang, 125 et seq. (1999), in addition to the legally protected interests, mentions the dependence on the provider.

67 Lorenz Fastrich speaks of “existential dependence”, Richterliche Inhaltskontrolle im Privatrecht, 232 et seq. (1992). On dependence, see Walter Schmidt-Rimpler, 147 AcP 130, 157 fn. 34 (1941).

68 Christian Armbrüster, BGB, with section 145 paragraph 31 (Walter Erman ed., 14th ed. 2014).

69 BGH, November 26, 1997, VIII ZR 322/96, BB 1998, 393 – slot machine; BGH, November 10, 2016, IX ZR 119/14, ZIP 2017, 2479 recital 19 et seq. – immorality of a fee agreement, furthers comments Volker Römermann, EWiR 2017, 45 et seq. who criticises why exactly the quintuple shall justify immorality; BGH, July 10, 1986, III ZR 135/85, BGHZ 98, 174, 178; BGH, January 19, 2001, V ZR 437/99, BGHZ 146, 298, 302.

70 Helmut Koziol, 188 AcP 183, 207 (1988).

71 Theo Mayer-Maly, Das Bewußtsein der Sittenwidrigkeit, 12 (1971); Theo Mayer-Maly, Festschrift for Röhricht, 395, 400, 404 et seq. (1983); Werner Ebke, Festschrift for Westermann, 183, 193 (2008).

price controls. It is thereby fundamentally left to the contracting parties to determine the content and extent of the essential components of the contract (essentialia negotii) and to specify the price. Moreover, it would be systematically inconsistent if an unlawful threat or a fraudulent deception were "only" to lead to a right to void, but a particularly large disparity in benefit would lead ipso iure to invalidity under section 138 BGB.[72] Furthermore, it would be counterproductive if anyone were to be able to rely on judicial price control: The consequence would be a multitude of imprudent contracts being concluded.[73]

According to the view represented here, simple contracts of sale or contracts of service are not subject to the immorality and price control of section 138 BGB.[74] Instead of employing an immorality review of the relevant market, however, the breach of a duty to inform[75] or fault in conclusion of the contract (culpa in contrahendo) can intervene in such a case.[76] The BGH therefore correctly rejected immorality when a purchaser had acquired collectors' coins at a price of DM 20,000, and could then only resell them for the value of the metal at DM 2,250.[77] The market, and not the judge, thus fundamentally determines the reasonableness of the price.

Situations of imbalance can only be relevant when the consequences are exceptionally onerous and the self-determination is therefore massively impaired.[78] Contracts restrict the self-determined life when they act to severely

---

72 Rainald Maaß, NJW 3467, 3468 (2001); Thomas Fikenauer, Festschrift for Westermann 183, 205 (2008).

73 Horst Bartholomeyczik, 166 AcP 30, 62 (1966).

74 Also opposed, Theo Mayer-Maly, Festschrift for Larenz, 395, 398 et seq. (1983), Thomas Fikenauer, Festschrift for Westermann, 183 et seq. (2008), Joachim Rückert, HKK-BGB, with section 1 § 112 (2003).

75 Thus Reinhard Singer, JZ 195, 197 (2001) against the opinion of the BGH collector's coin (fn. 77).

76 BGH, December 22, 1999, VIII ZR 111/99, NJW 2000, 1254, 1255 – collector's coin.

77 BGH, December 22, 1999, VIII ZR 111/99, NJW 2000, 1254, 1255 – collector's coin. The hire purchase of pool/billiards equipment at 2.5 times the value was also not immoral, BGH, January 24, 1979, VIII ZR 16/78, WM 1979, 491, 492. See also above, III.2.b).

78 BVerfG, October 19, 1993, 1 BvR 567, 1044/89, BVerfGE 89, 214, 232 – Guarantee contract; Ritgen, JZ, 114, 119 (2002); Sibylle Hofer, Vertragsfreiheit am Scheideweg, 23 (2006); Josef Drexl, Die wirtschaftliche Selbstbestimmung des Verbrauchers, 208, 296 (1998); Claus-Wilhelm Canaris, Festschrift for Lerche,

restrict freedom. It is not justice, but rather injustice which is the standard for a legal intervention. The exploitation of a position of power or the restriction of freedom are also recognised as grounds for attribution within the general clause in section 138 BGB. After conclusion of the contact, one can include cases of loss of perspective[79] or the restriction of freedom in existential areas of life.[80] The case law here has already developed groups of cases. For transactions of existential importance, exceptionally, there is price control. In German Law, this is relevant for rent, the purchase of property, or wages.[81] Self-determination thus does not only refer to the exercise of a declaration of intent, but rather also the self-determined life, which should ensure that the wage is generally sufficient to live on, that tenancy law protects the tenant's social environment, and the purchase of a immorally inflated property does not drive the purchaser into the modern debtors' prison[82].

c) A freedom-restricting lack of equivalence as frustration of the contract

Also the legal doctrine of the frustration of contract is a weakening of the binding effect of the contract, that is, the principle of *pacta sunt servanda.* The doctrine of *clausula rebus sic stantibus* means that every contract is only binding for as long as the circumstances that were decisive for its signing have not changed fundamentally.[83] The requirements and groups of

---

873, 883 et seq. (1993); Manfred Wolf and Jörg Neuner, Allgemeiner Teil des Bürgerlichen Rechts, § 10 recital 30 (11th ed. 2016).

79 For a different view, however, Manfred Wolf and Jörg Neuner, Allgemeiner Teil des Bürgerlichen Rechts, section 10, § 55 et seq. (11th ed. 2016), which understands this as "immaterial property rights of the social principle".

80 Wolfgang Enderlein, Rechtspaternalismus und Vertragsrecht, 293 et seq. (1996).

81 Similar examples in Manfred Wolf and Jörg Neuner, Allgemeiner Teil des Bürgerlichen Rechts, section 46, § 52 (11th ed. 2016).

82 A debtors' prison was a private prison until the late Middle Ages and then a public prison for people who had not fulfilled their payment obligations, Steffen Breßler, Schuldknechtschaft und Schuldturm, 88, 115 et seq. (2004).

83 It can already be found in the Codex Maximilianeus bavaricus civilis [CMBC] and in the General State Laws for the Prussian States [ALR] and also in other codes, 4th part, chapter 15, § 12 CMBC: "and because […] all connections tacitly contain the clausulam sic stantibus"; 1st part, 5th title, sections 377-380 ALR; as

cases of frustration of contract were developed inductively within 80 years. Two key features are crucial: The background is, on the one hand, again the observation that courts cannot and should not review equivalence with frustration of contract. On the other hand, only in extreme circumstances, namely, situations which were not discernible for the contracting parties on conclusion of the contract and which massively disrupt the balance of the contract, an adjustment to the contract can be made.[84] Justice is thus specified as a legal concept through the principle of self-determination. This specifies the prerequisites of frustration of contract. The disruption may not fall within one of the contracting parties' areas of risk. In the event of a disruption of equivalence, it requires that the sphere of freedom is existentially impaired. It concerns cases which are simply incompatible with law and justice.[85] The disruptions of equivalence must therefore clearly be more than 50% of the market price[86] and again have severely restrictive impacts on freedom.

IV. Lex superior – Primacy of Law

1. The legal situation in Germany

a) The principle lex superior

In the 1930s, *Merkl* invented the hierarchy of the law[87] which stipulates that the legal system is built on different levels of legal provisions that are

---

well Art. 357 Polish Civil Code. In detail see Thomas M.J. Möllers, Juristische Methodenlehre, § 11 recital 37 (2017).

84 Bundestag document no. 14/6040, 176: "gross disparity with the creditor's interest in performance"; Claus-Wilhelm Canaris, JZ 499, 502 (2001). See BGH, February 25, 1993, VII 24/92, BGHZ 121, 378, 392 § 54: "when it concerns such a drastic change that adherence to the original provision would lead to an intolerable outcome which can plainly no longer be reconciled with law and justice, and adherence to the original contractual provision would therefore be unreasonable for the affected party". Similarly Marc-Philippe Weller, Die Vertragstreue, 298 et seq (2009).

85 Thus the formulation in Horst Eidenmüller, Jura 824, 829 (2001).

86 Devaluation by more than 60%, see BGH, September 18, 1992, V 116/91, BGHZ 119, 220, 222 – increase in the ground rent; on this group of cases see Hein Kötz, Vertragsrecht section 1014 et seq. (2nd ed. 2012).

87 Adolf Julius Merkl, Festschrift for Kelsen, 252, 272 et seqq (1931).

ranked in a super- and subordinate relationship. Insofar there is a hierarchy of provisions. The higher level is the reason for existence of the respective lower level and regulates the procedure as to how the lower provision comes into existence and, if needed, also its content. The doctrine of the hierarchy of the law has become prevailing.[88] The legal consequences of the hierarchical structure are considerable. If two provisions that are per se valid, but are derived from different sources and regulate the same legal question, create a direct contradiction, then this gives rise to a collision of provisions.[89] A collision arises when two different legal provisions regulate the same legal problem. If provisions collide, there is no balancing of the individual provisions. On the contrary, one rather applies an unambiguous priority rule. The higher-ranking law takes precedence over the lower-ranking law, Latin: *lex superior derogat legi inferiori*.[90] In modern times, this concept developed from the observation that the higher-ranking legislator is able to impede or abolish a contradicting law of the lower-ranking legislator.[91]

b) Higher rank of rules on competences

Germany is a federal constitutional state. According to the federal law the state law needs to be respected. Art. 31 GG is succinctly phrased: "Federal law precedes state law". Art. 31 GG derives from the states' self-conception

---

88 Hans Kelsen, Reine Rechtslehre, 228 et seqq. (2nd ed. 1960); Klaus F Röhl and Hans Christian Röhl, Allgemeine Rechtslehre, 308 et seq. (3rd ed. 2008); Bernd Rüthers, Christian Fischer and Axel Birk, Rechtstheorie, recital 272 et seqq. (9th ed. 2016); Franz Bydlinski, Juristische Methodenlehre und Rechtsbegriff, 201 (2nd ed. 1991); Ernst A. Kramer, Juristische Methodenlehre, 96 (5th ed. 2016); differing view for example Gunther Teubner, 2 Soziale Systeme, 229, 231 (1996): „terrific self-deception of the law".

89 BVerfG, June 4, 1969, 2 BvR 173/66 among others, BVerfGE 26, 116, 135; Klaus Stern, Das Staatsrecht der Bundesrepublik Deutschland, vol. 1, 720 (2. ed. 1984).

90 In the words of Adolf Julius Merkl, Festschrift for Kelsen, 252, 276 (1931): "A legal rule derogating another legal rule, while this other legal rule does not equally derogate it, is for this reason higher-ranking and the legal rule that is derogated is lower-ranking compared to the legal rule that derogates."

91 Lex superior tollat legem inferioris, see Sebastiano Medici, De legibus, statutis, et consuetudine, 90 (Sebastiano Medici et al. eds., 1574); see also Jan Schröder, Recht als Wissenschaft, 21 (2nd ed. 2012).

and is a classical lex superior principle.[92] Comparable rules can be found in Switzerland, Australia, Canada and indirectly also in the US Constitution.[93] Subsequently, the entire federal law precedes the entire state law. It would therefore generally be possible that a provision of the state constitution was considered void because it is inconsistent with an ordinance of the federal government. Art. 31 GG is, however, mostly superseded by *more specific* provisions, as for example the legislative power of sections 70 et seqq. GG.[94]

This conflict can also arise between the EU and the member states. Under certain conditions European law precedes the national law, which is called primacy of application. The result is that national law may not be applied.[95]

c) Primacy of the Constitution

A subsequent result is that ordinary law must be interpreted in light of the constitution because it is higher-ranking than ordinary law. The constitution-oriented and constitutional interpretation must be distinguished from the constitutional development of the law.[96]

2. The Primacy of Law in Chinese Law

a) The Primacy of Law according to Art. 95 Legislation Law

In Chinese law the principle of primacy is also known: it is codified in Art. 95 Legislation Law which is worded:[97]

---

92 It is insofar referred to ranking norms, see Peter M. Huber, GG, Art. 31 recital 7 (Michael Sachs and Peter M Huber eds., 7th ed. 2014); differing view Horst Dreier, GG, Art. 31 recital 18. (Horst Dreier ed., 3rd ed. 2015),

93 S. U.S. Const. art. 1, sec. 1; art 1, sec. 8 para. 18; art. 6 para. 2; U.S. Const. amend. X; Winfried Brugger, Einführung in das öffentliche Recht der USA, 31 et seqq. (2nd ed. 2001).

94 Besides Art. 70 et seqq., 84 para. 1 p. 4, 125a para. 1 p. 2 and Art. 142 GG; Peter M. Huber, GG, Art. 31 recital 5 ff. (Michael Sachs and Peter M. Huber eds., 7th ed. 2014).

95 Thomas M.J. Möllers, Juristische Methodenlehre, § 8 recital 4 et seqq. (2017).

96 Thomas M.J. Möllers, Juristische Methodenlehre, § 7 recital 37 et seqq. (2017); Thomas M.J. Möllers, Festschrift for Vedder, 721 et seqq. (2017).

97 This reference is owed to Jin Jing.

> "When local provisions and rules are inconsistent, the relevant organ will make a ruling in accordance with the following provisions on the scope of authority:
>
> (1) When a new general provision and an old special provision enacted by the same agency are inconsistent, the enacting agency shall make the ruling;
>
> (2) When local provisions and administrative rules are inconsistent regarding the same matter and the applicable provision cannot be determined, the State Council will issue an opinion and where the State Council finds that the local decree shall apply, the local decree shall be applied in the local jurisdiction; where the State Council deems that the administrative rule shall apply it shall request the Standing Committee of National People's Congress to make a ruling;
>
> (3) When there is an inconsistency on a matter between departmental rules or between departmental rules and local provisions the State Council will make a decision. When an administrative regulation enacted pursuant to authorization and a law are inconsistent and the applicable provision cannot be determined the Standing Committee of National People's Congress will make a ruling."

As well as in Germany, Europe and the USA it is recognised that the competences of different governmental authorities can conflict with each other, which can be solved by means of the hierarchy of norms.

b) Chinese Law and the Constitution, section 1 GRCL

In China, however, the question as to how to interpret the constitution has not been solved yet. For instance, it is hardly clarified if only the Standing Committee of the National People's Congress or the courts are allowed to interpret the constitution.[98] Also the question whether there is a hierarchy of several legal sources hardly seems to be clarified.[99] It is also not clear whether there is a constitutional interpretation in Chinese law.[100] The basic rights of the constitution are mainly perceived as mere agenda that are not legally binding and subsequently not enforceable either.[101]

---

98 For an overview see Hui Huang, Juristische Methodenlehre in China und Ostasien, 131, 152 (Yuanshi Bu ed. 2016).

99 To this Zhang, 1 Univ. Bologna L. Rev. 106, 117 (2016).

100 Sheng Zhang, China L.Science 110 et seqq. (2008); Hui Huang, Juristische Methodenlehre in China und Ostasien, 131, 152 (Yuanshi Bu ed. 2016).

101 One court dismissed a case regarding a fundamental rights violation, see Qi Yuling v. Chen Xiaoqi et al.: Dispute over Infringement of a Citizen's Basic Right to receive Education protected by Constitution Through Infringement of Right of Name, Supreme People's Court Gazette, 2001, Issue 5, 158-161 (齐玉苓诉陈晓琪等以侵犯姓名权的手段侵犯宪法保护的公民受教育的基本 权利纠纷案 «最高人民法院公报»2001年第5期，第158-161页).

If the constitution is understood as a legal system that describes the tasks of the People's Party is it clear that now basic rights must be searched for in another codification, namely the GRCL. In the current version of the GRCL, the basic rights cannot only be perceived as legal assets that private third parties may not harm. They can be perceived as basic rights that the government has to respect. This is suggested by the fact that no one may harm them, section 3 GRCL. A wording that the absolute legal assets may not be harmed is doubtful. Examining basic rights it is recognised that the infringement of a basic rights is legal if it can be justified. Basic rights are always limited by the basic rights of third parties. The claim to absoluteness is therefore excessive.

A second remarkable particularity is: in German law the constitution and therefore the basic rights are higher-ranking than the ordinary civil law. However, basic rights are directly applicable. In relation to Public Law and Criminal Law a certain priority is given to Civil Law. Among several claims the civil claim to damages is preceding, sections 187 GRCL. The relation of basic rights and ordinary law should therefore not be examined as a relation of constitution and private law, but within the GRCL.

V. Resolution of conflicts between principles through balancing – working with basic laws

1. No general principle of proportionality in the German BGB

a) Affirmation of a principle of proportionality in Civil Law

It is heavily debated if a principle of proportionality exists in Civil Law. The BGH states that the principle of proportionality "governs the entire Civil Law"[102] and the German Federal Labour Court (Bundesarbeitsgericht – BAG) even calls it a "superordinate legal principle of the private law."[103]

102 BGH, February 11, 1987, IVa ZR 194/85, BGHZ 100, 60, 64 – section 71 VVG; see also BGH, December 6, 1989, IVa ZR 249/88, BGHZ 109, 306, 312 – grave violation of piety.

103 BAG, June 6, 1980, 1 AZR 822/79, BAGE 33, 140 recital 110 – Labor Dispute Law.

Also a part of legal literature affirms the validity of the principle of proportionality for the Civil Law.[104] As the legislative branch is also bound by the constitutional order according to Art. 1 para. 3 GG under Civil Law, the principle of proportionality applies.[105] This shall also be valid for the jurisdiction of Civil Law.[106] Methodologically, the principle of proportionality is tried to be derived from section 242.[107] According to *Canaris,* under current law, a young person should not be obligated to pay the extremely high damages resulting from the destruction of an important artwork because such a claim violates the freedom of action and the prohibition of excessiveness, which also applies in Civil Law.[108]

b) Rejection of the principle of proportionality in Civil Law

The opposing view, however, criticises a general application of the principle of proportionality.[109] It emphasizes the autonomy of Civil Law: First,

104 Hans Hanau, Der Grundsatz der Verhältnismäßigkeit, 121 et seq. (2004), Michael Stürner, Der Grundsatz der Verhältnismäßigkeit im Schuldvertragsrecht, 442 (2010); Claudia Schubert, Münchener Kommentar BGB, section 242 recital 417 et seqq. (7th ed. 2016); Reiner Schulze, BGB, section 242 recital 33 (Reiner Schulze et al. eds., 9th ed. 2017), on abuse of rights respectively; Jörg Neuner, NJW 2000, 1822, 1824 for the non-transactional sector; for Public Law: Helmuth Schulze-Fielitz, GG Art. 20 (constitutional state) recital 197 (Horst Dreier ed., 3rd ed. 2015).

105 Manfred Wolf and Jörg Neuner, Allgemeiner Teil des Bürgerlichen Rechts, § 2 recital 2 (11th ed. 2016).

106 Claus-Wilhelm Canaris, JuS 161, 162 (1989).

107 Helmut Köhler, GRUR 82 (1996); Dirk Looschelders and Dirk Olzen, BGB, section 242 recital 277 et seqq. (Staudinger ed., revised ed. 2015).

108 Claus-Wilhelm Canaris, JZ 993, 1001 et seq. (1987); Claus-Wilhelm Canaris, JZ 494, 497 (1988).

109 Dieter Medicus, 192 AcP 35, 69 et seq. (1992); Detlef Merten, Festschrift for Schambeck, 349, 364 et seq. (1994); Christian Grüneberg, BGB, section 242 recital 54 (Otto Palandt ed., 77th ed. 2018); Marcus Bieder, Das ungeschriebene Verhältnismäßigkeitsprinzip als Schranke privater Rechtsausübung, 27 et seqq. (2007); Lorenz Kähler, Verhältnismäßigkeit, 210, 212 et seqq. (Matthias Jestaedt and Oliver Lepsius eds., 2015); For Public Law: Detlef Merten, HGR, vol. 3, § 68 recital 22 (2009).

according to this view, the legislator has already perfectly balanced the interests.[110] Second, the principle of proportionality would only be efficient to avert a public interference, but it would not be suitable among private persons because both parties could claim their basic rights.[111] Therefore, the principle of proportionality is not applicable or only strictly limited: As an expression of self-determination the parties can generally generate contracts at will. The objective principle of equivalence does not apply. The BGB deliberately decided against a price control, the "laesio enormis" is only applicable in rare cases.[112] Under Property Law the owner can make alterations at his or her will.[113] The owner may destroy the property without being prohibited from doing so.[114] Due to testamentary freedom the spouse or relatives can be excluded from the inheritance; only the claim to the legal portion of an estate is protected.

c) Own opinion

It can be agreed to the indirect effect of the basic rights under Civil Law, and that under Civil Law, the legislator is bound by the basic rights and therefore by the prohibition of excessiveness. This, however, does not result in the direct application of the basic rights under Civil Law.[115] Moreover, the just mentioned provisions are not eligible for generalisation[116] as they

---

110 Dieter Medicus, 192 AcP 35, 37 (1992); Ulrich Preis, Festschrift for Dietrich 429, 433 (1999).

111 Dieter Medicus, 192 AcP 35, 59 (1992); Ulrich Preis, Festschrift for Dietrich 429, 435, 438 (1999).

112 Also Thomas Raiser, Festschrift Deutscher Juristentag, vol. 1, 101, 129 et seqq. (1960); Franz Wieacker, Zur rechtstheoretischen Präzisierung des § 242 BGB, 38 (1956); Detlef Merten, HGR, vol. 3, § 68 recital 22 (2009); Lorenz Kähler, Verhältnismäßigkeit, 210, 225 (Matthias Jestaedt and Oliver Lepsius eds., 2015). Differing section 56 para. 1 sentence 2 VwVfG: "The consideration must be reasonable under the entire circumstances and materially connected to the contractual performance of the authority." See above III.2.b).

113 This principle has been carried on for hundreds of years.

114 Lorenz Kähler, Verhältnismäßigkeit, 210, 227 (Matthias Jestaedt and Oliver Lepsius eds., 2015).

115 Günter Dürig, Festschrift for Nawiasky 157, 176 et seqq. (1956); BVerfG, January 15, 1958, 1BvR 400/51, BVerfGE 7, 198, 206 et seq.

116 Detlef Merten, HGR, vol. 3, § 68 recital 22 (2009); Lorenz Kähler, Verhältnismäßigkeit 210, 217 et seqq. (Matthias Jestaedt and Oliver Lepsius eds., 2015).

only relate to the defence of rights or the extent of enforcement. The reference to section 242 BGB is not convincing either, because this provision under the tradition of the Roman legal *bonas fides*[117] only aims at certain obligations within a creditor-debtor relation without forcing a balancing of all the interests affected.[118] Randomly correcting legal provisions with the principle of proportionality exceed the limits of permissible development of the law: The "art vandal", who intentionally destroys a valuable painting, is liable because the ownership of the injured person is clear. Moreover, the culprit is adequately protected by Bankruptcy Law.[119]

Establishing a balance of interests is incumbent upon the legislator.[120] The legislator can clearly establish a better balance of interests than an examination of the proportionality by the courts.[121] The examination of proportionality and its criteria of suitability, necessity and proportionality in the narrow sense would restrict the private autonomy in a manner contrary to the system.[122] Opposing interests are imminent to synallagmatic contracts as for instance the purchase and service contract: One party wants to buy low, the other party wants to sell high. The judge is generally not interested in whether the bottle of Coca Cola is sold for 50 Cents or 5 Euros. Therefore, the individual generally does not have to act respecting any fiduciary duties or in the best interests of the other party, but may pursue only his or her own interests. Thus, Civil Law allows a right to excessiveness within the boundaries of section 138 and section 242 BGB and does not

---

117 Martin Joseph Schermaier, Good Faith in European Contract Law 63, 66 (Reinhard Zimmermann and Simon Whittacker eds., 2000).

118 Lorenz Kähler, Verhältnismäßigkeit, 210, 221 (Matthias Jestaedt and Oliver Lepsius eds., 2015).

119 Opposing Claus-Wilhelm Canaris, JZ 993, 1001 et seq. (1987); Claus-Wilhelm Canaris, JZ 494, 497 (1988); the following authors: Thilo Ramm, JZ 489, 491 et seq. (1988); Dieter Medicus, 192 AcP 35, 66 et seq. (1992); Ulrich Preis, Festschrift for Dietrich, 429, 460 (1999); Gerald Spindler, BGB, section 823 recital 0.12 (Heinz Georg Bamberger and Herbert Roth eds., 3rd ed. 2012); Dirk Looschelders and Dirk Olzen, BGB, section 242 recital 278 (Julius von Staudinger ed., revised ed. 2015); Lorenz Kähler, Verhältnismäßigkeit, 210, 215 (Matthias Jestaedt and Oliver Lepsius eds., 2015).

120 Klaus Stern, Das Staatsrecht der Bundesrepublik Deutschland, vol. III/1, 1578 (Klaus Stern ed. 1988); Konrad Hesse, Grundzüge des Verfassungsrechts der Bundesrepublik Deutschland, recital 355 (20th ed. 1999).

121 Ulrich Preis, Festschrift for Dietrich, 429, 448 (1999).

122 Marcus Bieder, Das ungeschriebene Verhältnismäßigkeitsprinzip als Schranke privater Rechtsausübung 39 et seqq. (2007).

perform a content review. In terms of a *presumption rule,* a refutable presumption for the validity of privately autonomous agreements applies.[123]

The legislator introduced the proportionality test when General Terms and Conditions and their one-sided shaping power impair the other party's self-determination: Clauses according to section 307 para. 1 BGB, for instance, are void if they "unreasonably disadvantage" the other party.[124] Shaping powers, such as the termination of a contract, must be exercised proportionately.[125] Here, the prohibition of the legally abusive exercise of a law under section 242 BGB is in effect.

The Constitutional Law, and thus also the proportionality control, must always be considered especially if the Constitutional Law *directly affects the Civil Law*. Decisions in the legal matters Lüth[126] or Lebach[127] illustrate that injunctive relief or damage claims under Civil Law must be limited. The general right of privacy, for example, must also be protected by the protection obligation of the State under Civil Law. However, this can be opposed by the freedom of opinion. Therefore, comprehensive balancing must be performed.[128] The above-mentioned art vandal may, however, not claim that the liability for damages restricts his or her life planning in the long term if he or she caused the damage on the basis of self-determination. It would be absurd if the culprit who acted deliberately would not be held liable only because he or she caused particularly high damages.[129]

123 Ulrich Preis, Festschrift for Dietrich, 429, 440 (1999) and above III.3.b).

124 Ulrich Preis, Festschrift for Dietrich, 429, 440 (1999).

125 BGH, February 17, 1955, II ZR 316/53, BGHZ 16, 317, 322 et seqq. on section 140 HGB. Compare also section 133 para. 2 HGB.

126 BVerfG, January 15, 1958, 1 BvR 400/51, BVerfGE 7, 198 – Lüth.

127 BVerfG, June 5, 1973, 1 BvR 536/72, BVerfGE 35, 202 – Lebach.

128 BGH, October 26, 1951, I ZR 8/51, BGHZ 3, 270, 280 et seqq. – Constanze I; BGH, June 21, 1966, VI ZR 261/64, BGHZ 45, 296, 307 et seqq. – Hellfire; Gottfried Schiemann, HKK-BGB, sections 823, 830, 840, 842-853 recital 122 (2013); Hartwig Sprau, BGB, section 823 recital 95 et seqq. (Otto Palandt ed., 77th ed. 2018).

129 Differing view Claus-Wilhelm Canaris, JZ 993, 1001 et seq. (1987); Claus-Wilhelm Canaris, JZ 494, 497, fn. 108 (1988).

2. Principle of proportionality in Chinese Civil Law?

The GRCL were not aware of the principle of proportionality; it was, however, at least debated in Public Law[130]. Ultimately, the principle of proportionality can only be transferred to Civil Law if the legislator establishes corresponding regulations as is the case in the dispositive Contract Law and the inspection of the General Terms and Conditions according to sections 309 et seqq. BGB. Apart from that, deducing a general principle of proportionality from section 6 GRCL must be handled with care. Instead, the freedom of contract must be properly determined. The obligations would have to be substantiated in detail through the Chinese Contract Law[131] as explained above.

VI. Summary

1. The General Rules of Chinese Law (GRCL) of 2017 contain numerous legal principles of the General Part, as for instance legal transactions or the Law of Minors. Additionally, there are general legal principles such as the freedom to contract or the protection of absolute legal assets. Legal principles must be differentiated from the legal idea and the legal rule. Legal ideas such as justice, practicality, and legal security are highly abstract which renders them (useless) empty phrases in the resolution of cases. Legal rules or legal principles, however, can be subsumed.
   The Civil Code, which was influenced by the Pandectics of the 19th century[132], trains the German jurist in systematic thinking, the legal dogmatics, and principles related thereto. For the development of

---

130 Yuanshi Bu, Einführung in das Recht Chinas, 45 (2008) with further references.

131 See also Yuanshi Bu, Einführung in das Recht Chinas, 102 et seqq. (2008).

132 As for instance Anton Friedrich Justus Thibaut, System des Pandektenrechts, vol. 3, (5th ed. 1846); Georg Friedrich Puchta, Pandekten (5th ed. 1850); Bernhard Windscheid, Lehrbuch des Pandektenrechts, vol. 3 (7th ed. 1891); Heinrich Dernburg, Pandekten, vol. 3 (4th ed. 1894); Ferdinand Regelsberger, Pandekten, vol. 1 (1893); Reinhard Zimmermann, HKK-BGB, before section 1 recital 6 et seqq. (Matthias Schmoeckel et al. eds., 2003).

law[133], but also for a better understanding, consolidated legal dogmatics with legal principles are needed.[134] Legal principles are not only non-binding ideas. Legal principles create meaning by means of their interaction and allow for a certain degree of generalisation. Legal principles generally claim normative validity and result in a presumption of conformity. They cannot be subsumed and need to be further substantiated.

2. In a first step, legal principles must be derived from the current law. In a second step, the rules must be substantiated. The legal sentence *lex specialis derogat legi generali* serves this purpose.

3. Further necessary substantiation has to be performed by balancing or induction and deduction. The aim is to establish legal rules as regulations with similar factual conditions.
   In Civil Law, the *freedom to contract* is an important legal principle which can be derived indirectly from several provisions of the BGB. Individual legal rules, as for example, the obligation to contract, the price control, or the doctrine of frustration of contracts seem to contradict this principle. Neither an accuracy check, nor a social principle, nor the influence of the constitution are able to explain the obligation to contract, the price control, or the doctrine of frustration of contracts. These legal principles can rather be established by the principle of self-determination which is part of the private autonomy.

4. Further substantiation is possible through the principle *lex superior derogat legi inferiori*. This principle is for instance applicable to several governmental authorities as with regard to central power and province. It is, however, questionable, to what extent the basic rights of the constitution must be considered.

5. The collision of principles can also be used to substantiate principles. *Balancing,* which the principle of proportionality (section 6 GRCL) is based on, can be used for this purpose. However, balancing in German

133 On the function of general legal principles to fill gaps see above I.1.

134 Legal dogmatics is descriptively compared to grammar, without which the language, here the legal provisions, cannot be understood, Maximilian Herberger, Dogmatik, 37 et seq., 74 et seqq., 119, 257 et seqq. (1981) with detailed references on Roman law; Nils Jansen, ZEuP 750, 754 (2005).

law is a domain of Public Law. Examining the basic rights, the sophisticated legal dogmatics, differentiates between scope of protection, infringement, justification, and exceptions for restrictions of basic rights. Details are, however, disputed because of the allocation of the burden of argumentation and justification: Using the fundamental freedoms generally does not require justification but attempting to restrict them does.
The principle of proportionality, however, is only restrictively applicable in Civil Law.

6. If the work with legal principles is correctly understood, principles can be directly derived from the valuations of the legislation and the law. Applying the customs according to section 10 GRCL is therefore generally not necessary.

The Law of Natural Persons in the New General Rules of Civil Law: Innovations, Debates and Prospects

*Hongjie Man**

Abstract: *Chapter II of the General Rules of Civil Law (GRCL) is a development of Chapter II of the General Principles of Civil Law (GPCL), in terms of the regulations concerning natural persons. The concept of "natural persons" has been introduced to replace the former term "citizen (natural person)" in the GPCL. In the section "Capacity for Civil Rights and Capacity for Civil Conduct", the interests of fetuses are generally protected, while the age limit for limited capacity for civil conduct is lowered to eight, instead of ten years in the GPCL. In the section on guardianship, the law does not make a distinction between parental custodianship, minor guardianship and adult guardianship. Comparatively, the new law emphasizes the principle of autonomy and best interests of the ward, and a supportive principle in adult guardianship, while enhancing the responsibility of public authorities in terms of the protection of wards. Durable power of attorney in adult and testamentary guardianship are also introduced into the new law. However, from an academic point of view, the new law's regulations are too conservative in the reform of the capacity of civil conduct, which shall be supportive to natural persons without full capacity. In the section on guardianship, the confusion in the concepts mentioned above has a negative impact on the effectiveness and accuracy of the mechanism. The autonomy of the adult is not fully and feasibly respected in the case of the selection of a guardian and the subsequent decision-making in his or her personal affairs. The provisions for the tasks of a guardian are not instructive and practical enough for the parties and the judge. Furthermore, the outdated concepts of "individual business" and "lease holding farm household" should have been abandoned in the new law.*

Keywords: Citizen (Natural Person), Natural Person, Legal Capacity, Guardianship.

---

* *Dr., LL.M. (Shandong)*; Associate Professor and Assistant Dean, Shandong University, Faculty of Law. Chair for Civil Law, Health Law and Human Rights Law.

On March 15, 2017, the General Rules of the Civil Law of the People's Republic of China (GRCL) were adopted at the 5th Session of the 12th National People's Congress (NPC), and became effective on October 1, 2017. Within the 11 chapters and 206 articles, Chapter II (Art. 13 to Art. 56) provides the regulations concerning natural persons. As the other parts of the GRCL, this part is a development of Chapter II of the General Principles of Civil Law (GPCL). In this article, the author will make a comparison between the two legislations mentioned above. In doing so, he will further explore the pros and cons of the GRCL, and will make suggestions on the explanation and future modification of the law.

I. An Overview

Chapter II of the GRCL is titled "Natural Persons". Diverging from this, the title of Chapter II in the GPCL is "Citizen (Natural Person)". The use of the term "citizen" when referring to natural persons is the outcome of the Soviet law's influence upon contemporary Chinese law. The GRCL have now abandoned the term of the "citizen" in civil law, which shows that not only Chinese citizens but also foreigners shall enjoy equal status as a legal subject.

Chapter II of the GRCL consists of four sections, namely "Section 1 Capacity for Civil Rights and Capacity for Civil Conduct", "Section 2 Guardianship", "Section 3 Declarations of Missing Persons and Death", and "Section 4 Individual Businesses and Lease Holding Farm Households". In contrast to the GPCL, it does not have a section on partnership between individuals.[1] In the four remaining sections, there are 44 articles, 23 articles more than in the GPCL.

1. Capacity for Civil Rights and Capacity for Civil Conduct

a) Capacity for Civil Conduct and its Beginning and Ceasing

The first section treats the capacity for civil rights and capacity for civil conduct. It continues to use the terms of "capacity for civil rights" and "capacity for civil conduct", which are similar to the "legal capacity" and "capacity to contract" used in the German Civil Code (Bürgerliches Gesetzbuch – BGB). Art. 13 GRCL states that commencing at the time of birth and ceasing at the time of death, a natural person has the capacity for civil rights, may enjoy civil rights and shall assume civil obligations in accordance with the law. Art. 14 GRCL further claims that the capacity for civil rights of natural persons is equal. The only difference is that Art. 13 & Art. 14 CRCL use "natural person" to replace the term "citizen" used in GCPL.

Art. 15 GRCL is a new regulation concerning the proof of birth and death time. Birth/death certificates are the principal evidence, in the absence of which, the date recorded on the household registration or any other valid identity registration shall apply. The article also mentions that if there is any other evidence sufficient to overturn the aforesaid date, the date supported by such evidence shall prevail, which means that such proof can also be overruled by other evidence accepted by the court.

b) The Protection of the Fetus

For the first time in Chinese civil law Art. 16 GRCL provides protection for the fetus. It stipulates that where a fetus is involved in inheritance, acceptance of gifts or any other protection of his/her interests, the fetus shall be deemed as having the capacity for civil rights. However, if the fetus is

1 Section 5 of Chapter II of the General Principles of Civil Law (1986) (GPCL).

born dead, the capacity for civil rights shall be deemed as non-existent since the beginning.

c) Capacity for Civil Conduct

Similarly to the GPCL, the GRCL contain three types of capacity for civil conduct, e.g., full capacity, limited capacity and non-capacity. The age of majority is 18 (Art. 17 GRCL). A major has full capacity, and the minor aged over 16 whose main source of income is his/her job shall be deemed as a person of full capacity (Art. 18 GRCL), which is derived directly from Art. 11 GPCL.

However, the GRCL lowers the age for limited capacity from ten[2] to eight (Art. 19 GRCL). This article further stipulates that a minor with limited capacity shall be represented in the performance of civil juristic acts by his/her legal guardian or shall obtain consent or the acknowledgement from such a guardian. "Acknowledgement" was added, in order to be coordinated with Art. 47 of the Contract Law.[3] Furthermore, in accordance with Art. 47 of the Contract Law, Art. 12 GRCL allows such minors to independently perform any civil juristic act that has a nature of pure profit for the minor or the performance of which is compatible with his/her age and intelligence.

As for the adult without full capacity, Arts. 21 and 22 GRCL use the expression "adult who is unable to realize the consequences of his/her conduct" to replace the phrase "mental patient" of Art. 13 GPCL.

Art. 24 GRCL is the declaration of limited or no capacity. An interested person or an organization concerned may apply to a People's Court for determining that an adult is of limited or no capacity for civil conduct, because he/she is not or not fully aware of the consequences of his/her conduct. In addition, upon the application of the person with limited or no capacity, an interested person, or an organization concerned, the court may declare the recovery of full or limited capacity, judging from the intelligence or mental condition of the person involved. The organizations mentioned in this article include residents' committees, villagers' committees, schools, medical

2 Art. 12 Para. 1 GPCL.

3 Art. 47 Contract Law of the People's Republic of China (1999)
Contracts concluded by persons with limited capacity for civil conduct shall be valid by the acknowledgement of the legal agent. However, a pure profit contract or a contract compatible with his/her age, intelligence and mental condition shall be valid and does not need the acknowledgement of the legal agent.

institutions, and women's federations, federations of persons with disabilities, elderly organizations and civil affairs authorities.

d) Domicile

For the domicile of natural persons, Art. 25 GRCL is very similar to Art. 15 GPCL, except that the former version accepts the residence recorded in other valid identity registers, in addition to the household register, as a proof of residence.

2. Guardianship

The title of Chapter 2 of Section 2 is Guardianship. In accordance with the GPCL, this section includes not only guardianship for minors, but also the guardianship (custodianship) for adults with limited or no capacity for civil conduct.

a) Guardianship for Minors

As the counter part of Art. 16 GPCL, Art. 27 GRCL stipulates that parents are the predominant guardians of their minor children. If both parents of a minor are deceased or have no guardianship competence, the persons and organizations below should take on the responsibility as the guardian: (1) Grandparents or maternal grandparents; (2) Older brothers or sisters; or (3) Any other individual or organization that is willing to act as the guardian of the minor, subject to the consent of the residents' committee, the villagers' committee, or the civil affairs authority at the place of the minors' domicile. However, there are still differences in two aspects.

Firstly, the new law requires the potential guardians to take on the responsibility in a sequence line, which was not required by the GPCL.

Secondly, in the GPCL, other relatives or friends with a close relationship to the minor, after the grandparents and elderly siblings, who are willing to accept the responsibility of guardianship, could assume the guardianship with the approval of the units of the minor's parents or of the neighborhood or village committee of the locality in which the minor is domiciled. In the new law, there is no approval requirement for close relatives. The new law allows any other individual or organization that is willing to act as the guardian of the adult, subject to the consent of the residents' committee, the villagers committee, or the civil affairs authority at the place of the domicile of the adult. Among the approval bodies, the parents' unit was taken away, whilst the civil affairs authority was added in.

b) Adult Guardianship

For adults with limited or no capacity of civil conduct, the following persons with guardianship competence can act as the guardian in the sequence below: (1) The adult's spouse; (2) The adult's parents or children; (3) The adult's close relatives; or (4) Any other individual or organization that is willing to act as the guardian of the adult, subject to the consent of the residents' committee, the villagers' committee, or the civil affairs authority at the place of the domicile of the adult. Contrary to the General Principles, the adult's unit was not the authority body any more.

Furthermore, Art. 33 GRCL for the first time allows an adult with full capacity for civil conduct, in prior consultation with his/her close relatives, or other individuals or organizations who are willing to act as his/her guardian, to determine his/her guardian in writing. The agreed guardian shall perform the guardianship duties when such an adult entirely or partially loses his/her capacity for civil conduct. Therefore, an adult with full capacity may use an "advanced directive" or "living will", to appoint a guardian in case he/she loses his/her capacity. Guardian by advanced directive was firstly promulgated by the amendment to the Law on the Protection of Rights and Interests of the Elderly in 2015.[4] The adult who makes the advanced directive is not bound by the sequence line within the potential guardians. It is also possible to appoint another natural person or organization rather than the relatives.

4 Art. 26 Law on the Protection of Rights and Interests of the Elderly (2012) *An elderly person with full capacity for civil activities may select his/her own guardian within his/her close relatives, or persons or organizations with close relationship, who is willing to assume the guardian's responsibility. The selected guardian shall assume the guardianship once the elderly person lost capacity for civil activities partly or entirely. If the elderly person does not select the guardian in advance, his/her guardian shall be confirmed according to law, in case of lack of capacity for civil activities partly or entirely.*

c) Selection of Guardian

According to Art. 27 and Art. 29 GRCL, potential guardians, such as the spouse, parents, grandparents, elder siblings, or other close relatives may assume the guardianship automatically, in line with the sequence. Other natural persons or organizations must first obtain consent from the authorities.

To resolve the possible disputes concerning the selection of a guardian, Art. 31 GRCL further states that if there are disputes on the determination of a guardian, the residents' committee, the villagers' committee, or the civil affairs authority at the place where the ward resides may appoint a guardian. In the GPCL, Arts. 16 and 17 authorize the unit (of the ward or of the ward's parents), as well as the residents' committee and villagers' committee to appoint the guardian. If a party concerned disagrees with the appointed guardian, it may apply to a People's Court to appoint a new guardian, which is the same in Arts. 16 and 17 GPCL. Beside this path, the new law allows the concerned party the right to apply to a court for appointing a guardian, without referring to the above-mentioned authorities.

Beside the "traditional" way of guardian selection, the new law gives two advanced approaches. One is the advanced directive model for adults, as mentioned in Section 1.2.3. The other way is appointing by will. Art. 29 GRCL allows the parents of a ward to appoint a guardian through a will when the parents act as the guardian. This seems to be applicable to the guardianship not only for minors, but also for adults.

In order to protect the interests of the ward during the period of dispute, the residents' or the villagers' committee, organizations stipulated by law or the civil affairs authority shall act as the temporary guardian, as required by Art. 31 Para. 3 GRCL.

In the appointing of the guardian, according to Art. 31 Para. 2 GRCL, the decision-making bodies shall respect the true will of the ward and appoint a guardian within the scope of persons legally qualified for guardianship under the principle of "benefiting the ward to the greatest extent".

d) Public Guardian

When there are no qualified guardians, Arts. 16 and 17 GPCL require that the units of the minor's parents or the units of the adult, the residents' committee, the villagers' committee and the civil affairs authority shall assume the guardianship. Art. 31 GRCL stipulates that the civil affairs authority, or the residents' committee or villagers' committee that fulfill the conditions of performing guardianship can assume the guardianship.

e) Duties and Responsibility of the Guardian

Concerning the duty and responsibility of a guardian, the GRCL have more enriched provisions than the GPCL. In the latter, there is only one provision, i.e. Art. 18, which requires that a guardian shall carry out the duties of a guardian and protect the person, property and other legitimate rights and interests of his ward. Art. 18 GPCL also stipulates that a guardian is protected by law in his exercise, according to the law of his guardianship rights. Only in the interest of the ward, the guardian can dispose the ward's property. In case the guardian fails to perform his/her duty or violates the legitimate rights and interests of the ward, he/she shall be held responsible, and liable for the caused loss.

Comparatively, in the new law this aspect is phrased longer. Besides Art. 34 GRCL, which is quite similar to the previous law, Art. 35 GRCL requires a guardian to perform the duties of guardianship under the principle of "benefiting the ward to the greatest extent". Moreover, the last two paragraphs of this article stipulate that the guardian shall respect the will of the ward to the most. The guardian of a minor shall, in making the decision related to the ward's interests, respect the true will of the ward according to the ward's age and mental condition. The guardian of an adult shall respect the true will of the ward to the greatest extent, protect and assist the ward in the performance of civil legal acts that are compatible with the ward's intelligence and mental health, and shall not interfere with the affairs with which the ward is able to deal.

f) Revocation of Guardianship

In the GPCL, there is only one sentence relating to the revocation of guardianship. Art. 18 Para. 3 GPCL authorizes the court to revoke a guardian's status in response to a petition by a relevant person or unit. No further criterion is provided by that law. In the GRCL, Art. 36 outlines the criterion for the revocation of guardianship, including one has to: (1) Perform acts that seriously damage the physical or mental health of the ward; (2) Be indifferent in the performance of duties of guardianship, or unable to perform duties of guardianship, and refuse to delegate part or all of the guardianship duties to others, causing difficulties or danger for the ward; (3) Perform other acts that seriously infringe upon the legitimate rights and interests of the ward.

Under any of the above circumstances, upon the application of an individual or organization concerned, the court may revoke the guardianship and disqualify the guardian, establish temporary guardianship, and appoint another guardian under the principle of "benefiting the ward to the greatest extent". The persons or organizations who may file an application include: other persons legally qualified for guardianship in accordance with the law, residents' committees, villagers' committees, schools, medical institutions, women's federations, associations of persons with disabilities, minors protection organizations, elderly organizations. If individuals and organizations other than civil affairs authorities provided for in the preceding clause fail to apply in time to a people's court for disqualification of guardianship, the civil affairs authorities shall do so instead.

When the guardianship is revoked, it does not stop the former guardian's duty to support the ward, in case the former guardian has legal responsibility to do so (Art. 37 GRCL).

g) Restoration of Guardianship

After the revocation of guardianship, Art. 38 GRCL allows the court to restore the guardianship in case the former guardian, who shows repentance, and has not committed any deliberate offence to the ward by respecting the will of the ward. In this case, the guardianship appointed by the court terminates simultaneously.

h) Termination of Guardianship

Art. 39 GRCL is a new provision for the termination of guardianship. The criterions for termination include: (1) The ward obtains or reinstates full capacity for civil conduct; (2) The guardian has lost his/her guardianship competence; (3) Either the ward or the guardian has deceased; (4) Other circumstances determined by the people's court as termination of guardianship. After the termination of guardianship, another guardian shall be determined in accordance with the law if guardianship is still needed.

3. Declarations of Missing Persons and Death

a) Declaration of Missing Persons

Art. 40 GRCL contains the same requirements for the declaration of missing persons, meaning the person has to stay non-contactable for at least 2 years. Furthermore Art. 41 GRCL stipulates that the time during which the whereabouts of a natural person became unknown shall be calculated from the first day when the natural person is non-contactable. During a war, such time shall be calculated from the day when the war ends or from the day on which the natural person's unknown whereabouts are confirmed by relevant authorities.

b) Administration of Property

When declared missing, the property of a missing person shall be under the administration of his/her spouse, adult offspring, parents or other persons who are willing to serve as a custodian of the property.

In the case of a dispute over administration, or in the absence of the above proper administrators with competence, the court shall appoint an administrator instead.

Art. 43 GRCL requires the administrator to adequately manage the property and safeguard the property rights and interests of the missing person. Any tax, debt and other due charges owed by the missing person shall be paid by the custodian with the property of the missing person.

Concerning the liability of the administrator, the same article stipulates that if the administrator causes losses to the property under administration due to deliberate offence or gross negligence, the administrator shall be liable for compensation.

c) Change of Administrator

Art. 44 GRCL is developed from Art. 35 of the Opinions of the Supreme People's Court on Several Issues concerning the Implementation of the General Principles of the Civil Law of the People's Republic of China (For

Trial Implementation).[5] According to this article, if the administrator does not perform his/her duties, infringes upon the interests of the missing person, or loses competence, the interested person of the missing person may apply to a court for the change of the administrator. In addition, the administrator may apply to terminate his/her status as administrator, as long as he/she "has a justified reason". In case of a change of administrator, the new administrator may request the previous administrator to hand over the property under administration and report the situation of the property.

d) Declaration of Death

For the criterion of declaration of death Art. 46 GRCL states: (1) The natural person's whereabouts have been unknown for four years; and (2) the natural person's whereabouts have been unknown for two years due to an accident in which he/she was involved. Furthermore, if a natural person's whereabouts became unknown due to an accident and it is impossible for such person to survive as proved by relevant authorities, the application for declaration of death is not subject to the aforesaid provision of two years.

Art. 47 GRCL includes the regulations from the Opinions of the Supreme People's Court on Several Issues concerning the Implementation of the General Principles of the Civil Law of the People's Republic of China (For Trial Implementation), stating that if there are claims for both the declaration of death and the declaration of a missing person, the court shall declare the death if both the claims meet the criterion.

Art. 48 GRCL is the regulation for the date of death, which shall be based on the date of the judgment for the declaration of death, or if the death is declared due to the person's unknown whereabouts caused by an accident, the date on which the accident occurred shall be deemed the date of death of the person.

Art. 49 GRCL emphasizes that the declaration of death shall not affect the validity of the civil juristic acts performed by the natural person if he/she in fact is still alive.

5 Opinions of the Supreme People's Court on Several Issues concerning the Implementation of the General Principles of the Civil Law of the People's Republic of China (For Trial Implementation) (1988) («最高人民法院关于贯彻执行«中华人民共和国民法通则»若干问题的意见（试行）»), effective on Jan. 26, 1988.

e) Revocation of Declaration of Death

When a natural person who has been declared dead reappears, the court shall revoke the death declaration upon the application of the person or that of an interested person (Art. 50 GRCL).

After the revocation of the declaration of death, the marriage will automatically resume on the date of the revocation, unless the spouse remarries or gives written notice to the marriage registration authority of the reluctance to recover the marriage (Art. 51 GRCL). Meanwhile, if someone else adopted their children, the adoption relationship shall not be invalidated on the ground that such adoption has not been consented by such person (Art. 52 GRCL).

The person has the right to request the return of property by succession. If the property cannot be returned, he/she can request compensation. If the interested persons conceal the truth and cause the wrongful declaration of death, they shall return the property and shall be liable for the resulting loss (Art. 53 GRCL).

4. Individual Businesses and Lease Holding Farm Households

The GRCL renders individual businesses and lease holding farm households as civil subjects, who have the same status as an individual natural person.

a) Individual Businesses

In the GRCL, Art. 54 allows natural persons who are engaged in industrial and commercial business, to register as individual industrial and commercial households, who may have a trading name. Comparatively, in the GPCL, a citizen can be engaged in industrial or commercial businesses by approval, within the scope permitted by law (Art. 26 GPCL).

b) Lease Holding Farm Households

Lease holding farm households are the members of the rural collective economic organizations, who obtain the right of rural land contract management according to the law and engage in household contract management (Art. 55 GRCL). Similarly, in the GPCL, Art. 27 permits this.

c) Capacity for Liability

In the GPCL, the debts of individual businesses and lease holding farm households shall, where such enterprises are individually operated, be settled with the property of the individual. Where debts are made by a household operated business, they shall be settled with the property of the household (Art. 29 GPCL).

In the GRCL, the debts of an individual business shall be borne firstly by personal property. Only if the household operates the business, the debt shall be borne by the household property. If it is unable to distinguish between personal property and household property, the debt shall be borne by the household property (Art. 56 Para. 1 GRCL). On the contrary, the debts of lease holding farm households shall be borne by the household. Only if the business is in fact operated by part of the rural household, the debt shall be borne by the property of such part of the rural household (Art. 56 Para. 2 GRCL).

II. Innovations

There are some important developments in the GRCL concerning natural persons.

1. The Replacement of "Citizen (Natural Person)"

As mentioned above, the GRCL replaced the term "citizen (natural person)" with "natural person". The use of "citizen" in modern Chinese law was due to the Soviet tradition starting from the 1950s. However, it can further be traced back to the French Civil Code and even to the Roman law. Art. 8 French Civil Code states that every French person enjoys civil rights. Art. 11 French Civil Code states that an alien enjoys the same civil rights that are or will be granted to French persons by treaties of the nation to which the alien belongs. Therefore, in the French Civil Code, there is a distinction in terms of civil law status between French "citizens" and non-citizens. Back to the Roman law, there was a distinction between the law of the Roman citizens (*jus civile*) and of other people (*jus gentium*). However, in the later stage, influenced by the Stoics morality, the jurists "sized the notion of a law of nature, and proceeded to identify it with the *jus gentium*"[6], to apply to all free persons. The BGB on the other hand, has a wider scope of allocation and considers its laws applicable to all persons. Art. 1 BGB states that "the legal capacity of a human being begins with the completion of birth." The new GRCL follow the way of the German Civil Code's model and uses the term of "natural person" to be able to distinguish from "legal person". Accordingly, the provisions for the application scope of civil law changed. Art. 8 GPCL regulates that unless otherwise stipulated by law, the laws of the People's Republic of China shall apply to civil activities carried out within the territory of the People's Republic of China. Also unless otherwise stipulated by law, the provisions of this Law with regard to citizens apply to foreign nationals and stateless persons within the territory of the People's Republic of China. On the contrary, only the first sentence remains in Art. 12 GRCL, which means that all the civil activities, including those by aliens and people without nationality, shall be regulated by civil law. Moreover, by the use of "otherwise stipulated by law", the alien's civil law status can be adjusted by the treaties and principle of reciprocity. Although some scholars pointed out that there should be a difference between "civil and military staff, lay persons and priests, citizens and aliens" in terms of capacity of civil activities,[7] the majority of scholars has agreed to this change.

6 William Alexander Hunter, Introduction to Roman Law 3 (William Maxwell & Son eds., 1880).

7 Xu Guodong, *Four Questions in the Drafting of General Rules of Civil Law* ("我国民法总则制定中的四个问题"), 2 Jinan Journal (Philosophy and Social Science), 57, 66–68 (2017).

2. The Protection of the Fetus

The protection of the fetus is one of the most significant developments of the GRCL.[8] In the GPCL, citizens have civil legal capacity and, according to the law, enjoy civil rights and bear civil obligations, commencing at the time of birth and ceasing at the time of death (Art. 9 GPCL). Generally speaking, no protection was provided to the fetus before birth. The only exception was Art. 28 of the Law on Succession, which states that in the division of legacy, the share of the fetus shall be reserved. If the fetus is born dead, the share reserved shall be succeeded according to the law. In the drafting of the GRCL, the legislator deemed it necessary to protect the interests of the fetus. In the explanation of the GRCL on June 28, 2016, the legislator explained "the capacity for civil rights of the natural person starts from birth, in principle, the unborn fetus does not have the capacity for civil rights. However, in order to protect the rights in succession or concerning the acceptance of gifts, it is necessary to provide the fetus a certain degree of capacity for civil rights in order to protect its interests. Therefore, the draft made a clear provision based on the Law of Succession: where a fetus is involved in inheritance, the acceptance of gifts or any other protection of his/her interests, the fetus shall be deemed as having the capacity for civil rights. However, if the fetus is born dead, the capacity for civil rights shall be deemed as non-existent since the beginning."[9] Professor Wang Liming, the Chairperson of the China Civil Law Society stated in an interview: "This provision aims to provide protection for the interests of the fetus from two aspects. On the one hand, from the point of view of succession, it guarantees the reserved share for the fetus. On the other hand, in case of tort liability,

---

8 See Li Jianguo, Vice-Chairman of the Standing Committee of the National People's Congress, Statement on the Draft of the General Rules of Civil Law of the People's Republic of China at the 5th Session of the 12th National People's Congress (8 Mar. 2017) (关于«中华人民共和国民法总则（草案）»的说明—2017年3月8日在第十二届全国人民代表大会第五次会议上), Official Website of the Central Government of the P. R. China, (中国中央人民政府网站): http://www.gov.cn/xinwen/2017-03/09/content_5175399.htm#1, (last visited May 27, 2017).

9 Statement on the Draft of the General Rules of Civil Law of the People's Republic of China (关于«中华人民共和国民法总则（草案）»的说明), http://www.npc.gov.cn/npc/lfzt/rlyw/2016-07/05/content_1993422.htm (last visited May 27, 2017).

the fetus may claim compensation independently towards the wrongful conduct to the fetus before birth that caused congenital defect."[10] This is a significant theoretical change in Chinese civil law in terms of the recognition of civil law status for the fetus.[11] The last sentence in Art. 16 GRCL indicates that there is a resolutive condition for the capacity of civil rights, if the fetus is born dead.

3. Capacity for Civil Conduct

In the regulation for civil activities, there are two major developments.

a) The Age Limit of Limited Capacity of Minors

The GRCL lower the age for limited capacity from ten to eight. The reasoning is that "with the development of society and economy, and with the improvement of living and educational levels, the minors' psychological and physiological maturity and cognitive ability have improved. It will be beneficial to lower the age limit appropriately, in order to allow the minors to conduct civil activities which are in accordance with their age and intelligence, to respect the minors' self-consciousness, and to protect their interests."[12] In the drafts presented to the Standing Committee of the NPC for review, the age limit was six years. "It is in accordance with the regulation of the Law on Compulsory Education that minors above the age of six shall receive the compulsory education."[13] However, in the last draft presented to the NPC, the age limit changed to eight.

---

10 Wang Liming, A Reading of the 10 Highlights of the General Rules (Draft) ("民法总则草案十大亮点解读"), http://www.npc.gov.cn/npc/xinwen/lfgz/2016-06/28/content_1992355.htm (last visited May 27, 2017).

11 Yang Zhen, *Review on the "Natural Person" (Chapter 2) of the General Principles of the Civil Code* ("民法总则"自然人"立法研究"), 5 Jurist 20, 23–24 (2016).

12 Wang Liming, A Reading of the 10 Highlights of the General Rules (Draft) ("民法总则草案十大亮点解读"), http://www.npc.gov.cn/npc/xinwen/lfgz/2016-06/28/content_1992355.htm (last visited May 27, 2017).

13 Wang Liming, A Reading of the 10 Highlights of the General Rules (Draft) ("民法总则草案十大亮点解读"), http://www.npc.gov.cn/npc/xinwen/lfgz/2016-06/28/content_1992355.htm (last visited May 27, 2017).

b) Adult Without Full Capacity

As mentioned above, Arts. 21 and 22 GRCL use the expression of "adult who is unable to realize the consequences of his/her conduct" to replace the phrase of "mental patient". It is not only an alternation of wording for political correctness in order to avoid discrimination of persons with mental disorders, but also an extension of the coverage to those people suffering mental disability due to reasons other than mental disorders, such as dementia. China is an aging society. In 2015, the population aged 65 or above amounted to 144,340,000, which was more than 10 % of the whole population. A report released in 2016 predicted that by the year 2040, there will be more than 24,000,000 senior people suffering from Alzheimer's disease.[14] For those people and others whose intelligence ability gets weak and becomes unstable due to aging, the extension of the scope of limited capacity provides an essential mechanism to protect their interests. The Law on the Protection of Rights and Interests of the Elderly amended in 2015 allows an "elderly person" (defined to be a person over 60 years of age) with full capacity to appoint a legal guardian in advance of losing capacity. The GRCL's change is a follow-up of this statute.

4. Guardianship

In the guardianship part, the GRCL provide some new regulations and mechanisms to protect the interest of the ward.

a) Respect of Autonomy

The new law expresses the principle of protection of the ward's interests and respect of the ward's autonomy. Art. 35 GRCL requires the guardian of a minor to perform the duties of guardianship and respect the true will of the ward according to the ward's age and mental condition. The guardian of an adult is required to perform the duties of guardianship and to respect the

---

14 It is reported there will be more than 20 million Alzheimer's disease patients by 2020, see Zhou Weiwe, Report Says there will be more than 20 Million Alzheimer's Patients in China in 2020 (周围围：报告称2020年中国老年痴呆症患者将超2000万), http://news.youth.cn/gn/201505/t20150507_6620622.htm (last visited May 27, 2017).

true will of the ward to the greatest extent. It shows the legislator's aim to protect and respect the autonomy of the ward, in accordance with their cognitive ability. Especially for the adult ward, their will shall be respected by the guardian to the greatest extent possible.

In addition to the foresaid, Art. 30 GRCL stipulates that in the case of a guardian determined by agreement, the true will of the ward shall be respected. Art. 31 Para. 2 GRCL requires the residents' committee, the villagers' committee, the civil affairs authority or the People's Court to respect the true will of the ward, and appoint a guardian within the scope of persons legally qualified for guardianship under the principle of "benefiting the ward to the greatest extent". This means the will of the ward shall be respected not only in their activities, but also in the selection of the guardian.

b) Supportive Principle in Adult Guardianship

Art. 35 GRCL requires the guardian of an adult to protect and assist the ward in the performance of civil legal acts that are compatible with the ward's intelligence and mental health, and shall not interfere with the affairs with which the ward is able to deal. This means that the adult guardianship is based on a supportive principle. The guardian shall assist the ward in case of need, and the ward has the right to deal with civil activities which he/she is intelligently and mentally able to understand.

c) Social Bodies as Guardians

In the GPCL, in case there are no suitable guardians from the family, the "unit" of the minor's parents or the adult ward shall assume the responsibility of a guardian. "Unit" was a conception with Chinese characteristics at the time of the drafting of the GPCL in the 1980s. A unit does not only mean an employer such as a company, it is also the provider of welfare to its members, and even their families, for housing, healthcare and pension. In case of need, the unit is ready to take on the responsibility as the guardian to the ward. However, after the promulgation of the GPCL, Chinese society has witnessed a dramatic change in social structure and economy. In current Chinese economy, employment is mostly controlled by the market. With the establishment of the social welfare system, housing, healthcare, pension, education, etc., are covered by social security. There is no such thing as a “unit” anymore that is able and willing to provide guardianship to its members or their family. Practically, the courts seldom appoint units as guardians. The new law abolished the units’ status as guardian. Furthermore, it allows other persons and organizations to assume the guardianship with the permission of the resident’s committee or villager’s committee. It gives room to the individuals and organizations, such as lawyers or NGOs for social welfare, to act as the guardian in the future.

d) Guardianship by Advanced Directive and Testamentary Guardianship

Following the development in the Law on the Protection of Rights and Interests of the Elderly, the new law allows adults to appoint a guardian by advance directive. This provision was influenced by the “durable power of attorney” system in the reform of guardianship law, such as the Japanese law.

Art. 29 GRCL allows parents assuming guardianship to appoint a guardian for their children. It not only can apply in guardianship for minors, but also in guardianship for adults.[15]

e) Revocation of Guardianship

The new law stipulates the revocation of guardianship, in order to prevent the ward from being abused by the guardian. Art. 36 GRCL authorizes a wide range of persons and organizations to initiate the procedure of revocation. The civil affair authorities are given the power of “watchdog” in case there is no concerned person or organization to file the claim.

III. Debates and Problems

Although the new law has quite a few developments in the above aspects, there are still some debates from a theoretical and practical point of view.

15 Zhang Rongshun ed. (张荣顺主编), A Reading of the General Rules of Civil Law of the People’s Republic of China («中华人民共和国民法总则解读»), 89 (China Legal Publishing House, 2017).

1. The Inequality in the Capacity for Civil Conduct

Traditionally, the capacity for civil conduct is a mechanism for the protection of persons with limited or no understanding and knowledge of the consequences of civil conduct. By declaring the conduct null and void, it prevents the person's interests from being abused and infringed. At the same time, it gives protection to the security of transaction and the interests of third parties. In doing so, it deprives minors and adults of their capacity because they are considered to have no control of their conduct due to a deficiency of cognitive ability. However, this is incompatible with the present universal understanding of human equality in terms of such cognitive ability. The Convention on the Rights of Persons with Disabilities passed by the General Assembly of the United Nations in 2006 (CRPD) requires the equal recognition of legal status.[16] Art. 12 CRPD stipulates that "1. States Parties reaffirm that persons with disabilities have the right to recognition everywhere as persons before the law. 2. States Parties shall recognize that persons with disabilities enjoy legal capacity on an equal basis with others in all aspects of life. 3. States Parties shall take appropriate measures to provide access by persons with disabilities to the support they may require in exercising their legal capacity. […] 5. Subject to the provisions of this article, States Parties shall take all appropriate and effective measures to ensure the equal right of persons with disabilities to own or inherit property, to control their own financial affairs and to have equal access to bank loans, mortgages and other forms of financial credit, and shall ensure that persons with disabilities are not arbitrarily deprived of their property." China was an active party in the drafting of the CRPD, which was signed by the Chinese government in 2007 and ratified by the NPC in 2008. Therefore, China bears a duty to ensure the equal rights of disabled persons in terms of legal capacity for civil conduct, to the maximum extent of their cognitive ability. In the drafting of the new law, some scholars suggested that there should be only two categories of capacity for civil conduct, namely full capacity and limited capacity.[17] Minors and adults who do not

---

16 Art. 12 Convention on the Rights of Persons with Disabilities passed by the General Assembly of the United Nations in 2006 is entitled "Equal recognition before the law".

17 Zhu Guangxin, *The Legislative improvement of Capacity for Civil Conduct: An Analysis on the General Rules of Civil Law (Draft)* ("民事行为能力制度的立法完善——以«中华人民共和国民法总则（草案）»为分析对象"), 6 Contemporary Law Review 3, 8 (2016).

have full cognitive ability shall have limited capacity, which should be adjusted according to their cognitive ability at any different time, for different legal issues. Unfortunately, the legislator chose to stay in the paradigm of the GPCL, which completely deprives persons without the capacity for civil conduct of the possibility of taking part in legal transactions.

The other problem is the overlap of regulations in terms of the legal effect of capacity. The dominant purpose of the capacity for civil conduct mechanisms is the criterion of judgement for the extent to which an individual can effectively engage in civil conduct. Arts. 19–22 GRCL are the regulations for the range of civil conduct that can be performed by the person with limited or no capacity. In Chapter VI "Civil Juristic Acts", Art. 144 GRCL stipulates that civil juristic acts by persons of no capacity for civil conduct are invalid, whilst Art. 145 GRCL stipulates that effectiveness of civil juristic acts by persons with limited capacity shall be judged by the nature of the act and the consent or acknowledgement of his/her legal agent. This overlapped and illogical structure was considered to be another example of the Soviet influence upon Chinese law, which showed that Soviet law did not value the autonomy principle much in the construction of the juristic act.[18] In the BGB on the contrary, all the regulations concerning the capacity to contract are put into the division of legal transaction, which is not only more logical, but also focuses more on the true purpose of the mechanism of legal capacity.

2. Guardianship

The guardianship part is more controversial in the drafting of the law. Most scholars in this field suggested taking more innovative steps to meet the standards required by international human rights norms, and follow the trend of the modification of guardianship law that happened in other countries such as Germany and Japan. However, the legislator took a more conservative path.

18 Zhu Guangxin, *The Legislative improvement of Capacity for Civil Conduct: An Analysis on the General Rules of Civil Law (Draft)* ("民事行为能力制度的立法完善——以«中华人民共和国民法总则（草案）»为分析对象"), 6 Contemporary Law Review 3, 8 (2016).

a) The Confusing Concept of "Guardianship"

Same as in the GPCL, the concept of "guardianship" is somehow confusing and a mixture of different things. Firstly, it is a combination of parental custodianship and guardianship by a person other than a parent. Art. 26 GRCL states that parents are obligated to foster, educate and protect their minor children. Art. 27 Para. 1 GRCL further defines that parents are guardians of their minor children. Then Art. 27 Para. 2 states that if both parents of a minor are deceased or have no guardianship competence, other persons or organizations can take on the guardianship. It is a weird and puzzling mixture of parental custodianship, guardianship and a parent's duty to support their children. As pointed out by scholars, the parental custodianship is based on the hypotheses that the "state should trust parents" and that "parents, more than any other persons or organizations, are concerned with their children's best interests".[19] On the contrary, the theoretical fundament of guardianship is characterized by non-trust.[20] In the latter condition, the law and public authority set up more supervision and restriction on guardianship. The legislator wasted the opportunity to abandon the "umbrella definition" of guardianship in the GRCL, and did not make any progress in this aspect.

Another problem is that the law does not recognize the difference between guardianship for minors and guardianship for adults. As in the GPCL, the GRCL still treat the adult with limited or no capacity for civil conduct the same as minors. However, the difference between these two mechanisms is obvious. The modern adult guardianship law is based on supportive and protective principles. The main purpose of adult guardianship is to support and assist the person under guardianship to handle personal affairs, not only in the person's best interest, but in also respecting the person's free will. It is not the law's intention to restrict or deprive individuals of their capacity, as it did in the abolished interdiction system in Germany and other civil countries. The ignorance of this difference results in the incompatibility of quite a few specific regulations. For instance, Art. 29 GRCL allows

19 Liu Zhengfeng, *Neglected Differences: Blind Zones of the Debate over the Narrow versus Broad Legislative Pattern of Guardianship in the General Part of China's Civil Law Drafts* ("被忽视的差异——«民法总则（草案）»'大小监护'立法模式之争的盲区"), 1 Modern Law Science 181, 184 (2017).

20 Liu Zhengfeng, *Neglected Differences: Blind Zones of the Debate over the Narrow versus Broad Legislative Pattern of Guardianship in the General Part of China's Civil Law Drafts* ("被忽视的差异——«民法总则（草案）»'大小监护'立法模式之争的盲区"), 1 Modern Law Science 181, 186 (2017).

the parents of a ward to appoint a guardian through a will. In the first and second draft, this article stated, "Parents of a minor may appoint a guardian through a will." However, in the third draft, this clause was modified to the current wording, in order to include adult guardianship. By nature, it is a continuation of the parents' custodianship of children. However, by enlarging the scope of application, it is wrongfully applicable to adult guardianship. The question is, why the parents' will shall prevail over the adult ward's autonomy and best interests?

b) Lack of Respect of Autonomy in Adult Guardianship

As mentioned above, the respect of autonomy is the most precious virtue of adult guardianship. However, due to the conservative attitude towards an innovative change of guardianship law, the GRCL keep many regulations that are not in favor of and even against respecting autonomy. Take Art. 28 GRCL as an example. It states that any of the following persons with guardianship competence may assume the responsibility of the guardian of an adult with limited or no capacity for civil conduct in sequence below. That means that, in the selection of a guardian for the adult, the court must follow the sequence line among the family members and relatives. This requirement is neither feasible in practice, nor reasonable in theory. On the one hand, in an aging society, one of the most important issues concerning adult guardianship is to provide suitable guardians for senior persons whose cognitive ability is fading. If a senior person is facing the aging problem, usually his/her spouse is in a similar situation too. It may not be the best for the ward to have his or her spouse as the guardian. On the other hand, it is not in accordance with the autonomy principle if the sequence is compulsory, which can be binding not only to the court, but also to the ward. Comparatively, Art. 1897 BGB authorizes the custodianship court to appoint "as custodian a natural person who is suited to take care of the affairs of the person under custodianship from a legal point of view within the group of tasks determined by the court and to take care of his person to the extent necessary." This means that the only criterion for the selection of a custodian is that he/she must be "suited" and there is no restriction concerning the scope and sequence of the natural persons who can be appointed as custodian.

Furthermore, Art. 30 GRCL states qualified persons of guardianship may agree to determine a guardian. In the case of a guardian determined by agreement, the true will of the ward shall be respected. Although there is a requirement to respect the will of the ward, the ward is regarded to as a passive audience, instead of part of the decision-making body. The potential guardian has the possibility to launch the procedure and reach the agreement.

c) Ambiguous Orientation of the Tasks of Guardian

Traditionally in legal theory in China, the task of guardianship is to supplement the capacity of the ward, to help the ward to conclude civil juristic acts.[21] The GRCL did not change this understanding and orientation. Art. 34 GRCL stipulates that the guardian of a ward has the duties to perform civil legal acts on behalf of the ward and to protect personal rights, property rights and other legitimate rights and interests of the ward. Therefore, the main duty of the guardian is to act as the legal agent of the ward.[22] However, in modern guardianship, the role of the guardian is more than just a legal agent. Besides handling property issues, the guardians shall assist the ward to make decisions in personal and medical affairs, such as marriage, invasive treatment, or sterilization. In the modification process in the 1990s, more detailed provisions concerning the duties of guardianship were added to the BGB. However, the new GRCL keep silent in these aspects.

Furthermore, the new law does not give expressive direction as to the range of the guardian's tasks, i.e. what kind of affairs the guardian can interfere with. Art. 1897 Para. 2 BGB indicates that a custodian may be appointed only for groups of tasks in which the custodianship is necessary. In the appointment of a guardian, the court shall decide the group of tasks for an individual guardian, according to the need and situation of the ward. The Japanese Civil Code, on the other hand, uses a different model. There are three types of mechanisms available for persons with difficulties in cognitive ability, namely guardianship, curatorship and assistance. In each mechanism, there is a certain group of tasks for the "guardian". The new Chinese law does not provide any systematic regulation for the tasks. On one hand, there is no restriction to the power of a guardian to protect some essential interests and values of the ward. On the other hand, there is no definite

21 Xie Huaishi, An Abstract of the General Part of Civil Law («民法总则讲要»), 86 (Peking University Press, 2007).

22 Art. 23 GRCL:
"The guardian of a person without or with limited capacity for civil conduct is his/her legal agent."

boundary to guarantee the ward's freedom to deal with other issues which are in compliance with his/her remaining cognitive ability.

3. Individual Business and Lease Holding Farm Household – Outdated Concepts

Individual business and lease holding farm households were inventions of the GPCL. After the reform commencing from the late 1970s, the GPCL used the term of "individual business" to encourage urban residents to be engaged in industrial and commercial businesses, rather than being hired by state-owned enterprises. In the past 30 years, this private section became a very important part of the economy. However, the promulgation of the Law on Individual Enterprise, the Law on Partnership Enterprise and other commercial laws has made these clauses in the GPCL less useful in practice. Although there are a few modifications of phrasing in the new law, there is no material change. Replaced by the commercial law regulations, it is hard to justify the necessity of the provision.

In the agricultural industry, lease holding farm households are still an important sort of participant. However, they are much more like an organization than a natural person by nature and therefore should not be included in this section for natural persons.

IV. Prospects

According to the legislative plan, after the promulgation of the GRCL, the specific provisions of the Civil Code, including property law, contract law, tort liability law, family law and law of succession, will be promulgated. The codification of the Civil Code is planned to be finished by 2020.[23] Based on the discussions above, the author has the following suggestions to the natural person part in the coming Civil Code.

23 Zhang Mingqi, *The Legislation of the General Rules of Civil Law* ("«中华人民共和国民法总则»的制定"), 2 China Legal Science 5, 23 (2017).

1. Two- stage Capacity for Civil Conduct

A two-stage capacity model, i.e., limited capacity and full capacity, shall replace the current three-stage model, in order to respect the free will of persons without full capacity, and enable them to take part in civil activities, which are compatible with their cognitive abilities.

Additionally, to avoid the overlap of regulations concerning the effect of civil activities conducted by a person with limited ability, it would be more harmonious to move these regulations into the section for juristic acts.

2. Differentiation of Parental Custodianship, Guardianship for Minors and Custodianship for Adults

As discussed above, there are three different mechanisms with different theoretical basis and principles. The future Civil Code should abolish the umbrella definition of guardianship and differentiate accordingly.

As the author suggested, the nature of guardianship as a mechanism to protect the wards, besides supplementing their legal capacity, makes it illogical to have all the regulations in the general part of the Civil Code. It may be a good solution to have a provision for human beings out of the general part.[24] However, the Chinese legislator has been quite clear that the Civil Code will have a pandectic structure with some modifications. In this case, it would be better to relocate the guardianship section into the new Family Law, than placing it in the general part.

3. An Overhaul of Adult Guardianship

In accordance with the CRPD, adult guardianship law shall guarantee the equal legal status and capacity of persons with a handicap or other cognitive problems, and provide them with necessary assistance when needed. Therefore, adult guardianship law in the coming Civil Code shall have the following merits:

- Recognition of the priority of an authorized representative.

---

24 Man Hongjie, *Three Basic Questions concerning the Adult Guardianship in the General Principles of Civil Law (Draft)* ("关于«民法总则(草案)»成年监护制度三个基本问题"), 1 Legal Forum 38, 40 (2017).

- Taking the free will and the best interests of the ward, instead of the relationship of family or blood, as the decisive element in the selection of a guardian.
- Detailing the regulations of the guardian's tasks and authorities, not only for property management, but also for personal and health care issues. More specifically, the law should draw very clear boundaries and restrictions for the guardian's power in making such decisions.
- Introducing the supervision of guardianship. Persons other than the guardian or pubic authorities can be appointed as supervisor of the guardian, to safeguard the guardian to perform his/her duties properly, and take over the responsibility as guardian for the good of the ward in case of need.

V. Summary

In this article, the author made a comparison between the GRCL and the GPCL. The author was very pleased to witness the innovations in the new law. For instance, the terminology of "citizen (natural person)" being replaced by "natural person", and the protection of fetus which was for the first time manifested in the civil law, and is one of the most significant developments of the GRCL. Besides, in the regulation for civil activities, the GRCL lowered the age for limited capacity from ten to eight (Art. 19). In the guardianship part, the new law emphasized the principle of autonomy and best interests of the ward, and a supportive principle in adult guardianship, while enhancing the responsibility of public authorities in terms of protection of the ward.

In the meantime, we have to admit that there are quite a few unsatisfactory regulations in the new law. The author has put forward several suggestions for future modifications of the law. For instance, a two-stage capacity model, i.e. limited capacity and full capacity, shall replace the current three-stage model. In addition, an overhaul of the adult guardianship system, which should be in accordance with the requirements of human rights protection, seems to be necessary and inevitable.

In conclusion, the promulgation and implementation of civil law is a remarkable move for the codification of Chinese civil law, and may draw much attention from scholars interested in comparative private law research.

Comment: Natural Persons in German Civil Law

*Raphael Koch**
*Finn Mrugalla***

Abstract: *Quite different from Chinese law, the law of natural persons in German civil law has not undergone major changes in recent times. The new provisions of the General Rules of Civil Law (GRCL) are largely similar to the corresponding provisions in the German BGB (German Civil Code). Many similarities regarding the legal capacity of human beings can be found. However, there are still important differences in detail. The jurisdiction of the Federal High Court of Justice [Bundesgerichtshof] [BGH] and the Federal Constitutional Court [Bundesverfassungsgericht] [BVerfG] has created a much more detailed system for the protection of unborn life than Chinese law, especially regarding the legal status of a not yet conceived person and the legal capacity beyond death. The German and Chinese systems of capacity also differ in minor aspects, e.g. regarding the age limits for incapacity to contract and limited capacity to contract. The most crucial and important differences between the German and the Chinese law of natural persons concern the representation of persons incapable of contracting. First, contrary to the GRCL, representation of persons incapable of contracting is not regulated in the General Part of the BGB (1st Book of BGB) but in the fourth book, the Family law. Secondly, German family law contains a more sophisticated system of representation. It focuses on the reasons for the need of representation and on the interest of the person incapable of contracting – contrary to the provisions in the GRCL which only govern this to a rough extent. Finally, German law also includes a more strict control through the family court.*

Keywords: Natural Person, Legal Capacity, Capacity to act, Capacity to contract, Guardianship, Responsibility for tort.

---

* *Dr. iur. habil., LL.M. (Cambridge), EMBA*; Professor, University of Augsburg, Faculty of Law. Chair for Civil Law, Law of Civil Procedure, Corporate and Company Law, European Private Law and International Procedural Law.

** Academic Assistant, University of Augsburg, Faculty of Law. Chair for Civil Law, Law of Civil Procedure, Corporate and Company Law, European Private Law and International Procedural Law.

I. Introduction

In the German BGB (German Civil Code), the regulations concerning the legal position of a natural person are found mainly in the General Part (Book 1) and in the Family Law (Book 4). The General Part does not only contain provisions on legal capacity (section 1 BGB [Civil Code]), majority (section 2 BGB), residence (sections 7-11 BGB) and the right to a name (section 12 BGB) but also on legal transactions (sections 104 et seq. BGB) which also refer to natural persons. The rules on the representation of legally incapable persons are, however, located in Family Law and cover parental custody for minors (sections 1626 et seq. BGB), guardianship for minors (sections 1773 et seq. BGB) and legal custodianship persons for persons of full age (sections 1896 et seq. BGB). On the other hand the responsibility for tort is regulated in tort law (sections 827 and 828 BGB) which is part of the Law of Obligations (Book 2 of the BGB).

II. Recent development of the right of natural persons in German civil law

While family law has been subject to constant change since 1900 (due to changing social circumstances), the General Part and the Law of Property (Sachenrecht), which is regulated in Book 3, have remained essentially unchanged since coming into force in 1900.[1]

After the unification of the German Empire in 1871 the German legislator sought the codification of civil law at the end of the nineteenth century. He intended a coherent system to regulate all spheres of human life from birth through business to family affairs and death or inheritance in a uniform codification for the entire Empire.[2]

General provisions, in particular with regard to legal subjects and legal transactions, which should also apply to the following four books (especially the Law of Obligations), were put in a general section.[3] This system of regulation and the provisions of the general section remained largely unchanged until today. The recent change process, which was largely caused by the harmonization and/or unification of the law within the European Union, mainly affects the second book of the BGB (Law of Obligations), especially consumer contracts.[4]

In this respect, it is from a German perspective very interesting to see how this area of civil law, which has almost remained unchanged in Germany for the last 100 years, is developing in other country's legal systems.

---

1 Franz Jürgen Säcker, Münchener Kommentar BGB, Einleitung para. 17 (7th ed. 2015); Christian Grüneberg, Palandt Bürgerliches Gesetzbuch Einleitung para. 10-12 (77th ed. 2018); Heinrich Honsell, Staudinger BGB Einleitung para. 105 (ed. 2013).

2 Comp. Heinrich Honsell, Staudinger BGB Einleitung para. 19-30 (ed. 2013); Manfred Wolf and Jörg Neuner, Allgemeiner Teil des Bürgerlichen Rechts, § 11 para. 1-5 (11th ed. 2016).

3 Dieter Leipold, BGB I Einführung und Allgemeiner Teil § 3 para. 2–4 (8th ed. 2015); Christian Grüneberg, Palandt Bürgerliches Gesetzbuch Einleitung para. 6 (77th ed. 2018).

4 Christian Grüneberg, Palandt Bürgerliches Gesetzbuch Einleitung para. 10-11 (77th ed. 2018); Franz Jürgen Säcker, Münchener Kommentar BGB, Einleitung para. 22 (7th ed. 2015).

III. The natural person in the BGB

German civil law distinguishes between legal subjects and legal objects. The legal subjects are divided into natural and legal persons. Furthermore there are also legal entities which are not legal subjects, but are in some situations essentially treated as such e.g. partnerships under the HGB (Commercial Code).[5]

Natural persons within the meaning of the Civil Code are all human beings, see section 1 BGB. Functionally, this fulfils the same purpose as the concept of the "natural person" in the General Rules of Civil Law in Chinese law.

1. Legal capacity

One who can be the bearer of rights and obligations has legal capacity.[6] Every human being is legally capable, legal capacity and being a human being are inextricably linked.[7]

a) Beginning of legal capacity

A human being is legally capable from the completion of the birth on, section 1 BGB. On the one hand it is required that the person is born alive, but on the other hand it is, in contrast to other legal systems, not essential that the person has lived for a certain time before being legally capable.[8] For the

---

5 Haimo Schack, BGB-Allgemeiner Teil para. 82 (15th ed. 2016), Rn. 82a; Dieter Leipold, BGB I Einführung und Allgemeiner Teil § 30 para. 3-4 (8th ed. 2015).

6 Jürgen Ellenberger, Palandt Bürgerliches Gesetzbuch Abschnitt 1. Personen para. 1 (77th ed. 2018); Jochem Schmitt, Münchener Kommentar BGB, section 1 para. 6 (7th ed. 2015); Dieter Leipold, BGB I Einführung und Allgemeiner Teil § 30 para. 1 (8th ed. 2015).

7 Ernst Wolf, Anfang und Ende der Rechtsfähigkeit des Menschen, 50, 82-83 (Ernst Wolf and Hans Naujoks eds., 1955).

8 Gerhard Hohloch, Erman BGB Art 7 EGBGB para. 4 (15th ed. 2017); Rainer Hausmann, Staudinger BGB Art. 7 EGBGB para. 30-31 (ed. 2013).

proof that a person has lived, it is sufficient that any vital function like heartbeat or breathing was noticeable.[9]

b) End of legal capacity

Legal capacity ends exclusively with the death of the person. Even though this is not mentioned explicitly, this was considered by the legislator to be self-evident.[10] Furthermore this can be derived from the law based on several aspects: E.g. the existing rights and obligations of the deceased are passed onto the heir at the moment of death (see section 1922 BGB), employment ends with the death of the employee (see section 613 BGB), marriage and property regime end with the death of a spouse (section 1371 BGB) and, subject to contrary agreement, partnerships are dissolved by the death of one partner (section 727 BGB).

The controversy regarding death only concerns the exact entry of death, because a man's cardiac and brain death must be distinguished. Using the methods of modern medicine, it is often possible both to revive patients of cardiac death and to keep a brain dead person alive artificially. In today's German practice, brain death is adopted as a time of death, for example, in organ transplantation. In detail, however, this is still discussed controversially in the literature.[11]

If a person is not proven dead, but still lost, the provisions of the Disappearance Act [VerschG] apply, which is not part of the BGB. Sections 3 to 7 of the Disappearance Act regulate the various types of disappearance (for example due to war, at sea or destruction of an aircraft). If the person who was lost is declared missing after the expiry of the required time, sections 13 et seq., section 9 VerschG contain the refutable presumption that he died. However, this does not remove the legal capacity, which is done exclusively by the actual death.[12]

---

9 Manfred Wolf and Jörg Neuner, Allgemeiner Teil des Bürgerlichen Rechts, § 11 para. 5 (11th ed. 2016); Jochem Schmitt, Münchener Kommentar BGB, section 1 para. 6 (7th ed. 2015).

10 Prot. I, S. 4; VI, S. 106.

11 Norbert Habermann, Staudinger BGB Vorbemerkungen zu section 1 VerschgG para. 3-8 (ed. 2013).; Manfred Wolf and Jörg Neuner, Allgemeiner Teil des Bürgerlichen Rechts, § 11 para. 9-10 (11th ed. 2016).

12 Haimo Schack, BGB-Allgemeiner Teil para. 24-26 (15th ed. 2016).

Finally, the loss of legal capacity by deprivation or entry into a religious order does also not exist under German law.[13]

c) Protection of unborn life

The legal capacity of a human being begins with the completion of birth, see above. German law, however, contains a few exceptions in which the already conceived but not yet born foetus (Latin: *nasciturus*) is protected as well. These exceptions are found, on one hand, in criminal law, which punishes the termination of pregnancy in section 218 of the Penal Code, but on the other hand also in civil law.

Similar to Art. 16 of the General Rules, section 1923, para. 2 BGB contains a provision which gives the already conceived but not yet born human being the legal capacity to inherit under the condition that he is born alive.[14] The *nasciturus* can also be the beneficiary of a contract to the benefit of a third party according to section 331, para. 2 BGB.[15] On the contrary to Art. 16 General Rules, German law does not specifically regulate the acceptance of gifts by a *nasciturus*. Nevertheless, this does not mean that the rights of an unborn person are limited to the mentioned cases. Based on these provisions it is acknowledged that there is a superordinate principle in German law that the *nasciturus* has to be treated as legally capable in obligation, property and succession law matters if it is to his sole benefit, e.g. donations according to section 516 BGB.[16]

Furthermore the *nasciturus* is protected under the principles of tort law in sections 823 et seq. BGB. In addition to a claim based on the physical integrity of the mother, the unborn child can also file a separate claim for damages, e.g. in accordance with section 823, para. 1 BGB.[17]

---

13 Norbert Habermann, Staudinger BGB Vorbemerkungen zu section 1 VerschG para. 1 (ed. 2013).

14 Jan Lieder, Erman BGB section 1923 para. 3 (15th ed. 2017); Dietmar Weidlich, Palandt Bürgerliches Gesetzbuch section 1923 para. 6 (77th ed. 2018).

15 Manfred Wolf and Jörg Neuner, Allgemeiner Teil des Bürgerlichen Rechts, § 11 para. 19 (11th ed. 2016).

16 Jochem Schmitt, Münchener Kommentar BGB, section 1 para. 33-36 (7th ed. 2015, Bernd Kannowski, Staudinger BGB section 1 para. 16 (ed. 2013).

17 Gerhard Wagner, Münchener Kommentar BGB, section 823 para. 204 (7th ed. 2017); Rüdiger Wilhelmi, Erman BGB section 823 para. 22 (15th ed. 2017).

More difficult and controversially discussed are those cases in which a child is born ill, but the only alternative would have been a termination of pregnancy ("wrongful life"). A claim not to be born because one is handicapped is contrary to German and European basic rights, especially considering the high value of human life and human dignity. Consequently, the Bundesgerichtshof [BGH] [Federal High Court of Justice] has rejected claims for damages against the doctors or the parents in these cases.[18]

d) Legal status of the *nondum conceptus*

While the already conceived but not yet born *nasciturus* is granted protection of his integrity and under some aspects even of his assets, a person who is not even conceived (Latin: *nondum conceptus*) may only acquire rights in exceptional cases. For example, a not yet conceived person can already be appointed as heir in such a way that the person only becomes an heir after another heir has first been heir (subsequent heir), sections 2101, para. 1, 2106, para. 2, 2109, para. 1, Nr. 1 BGB. Alternatively a legacy can be turned to a not yet conceived person, sections 2162, 2178 BGB, which comes into existence when the person is born.[19]

e) Legal capacity beyond death?

Normally the legal capacity of a person ends with his death, see above. From the essential content of human dignity, Art. 1, para. 1 GG (Basic Law), however, claims for the protection of the person beyond death can be derived. Especially concerning the breach of a person's privacy or disturbance of the peace of the dead, the right to their own image as well as proprietary interest of the general right of privacy of the deceased, the courts accept injunctive reliefs or claims for damages, which can each be enforced by the heirs.[20]

---

18 Gerhard Wagner, Münchener Kommentar BGB, section 823 para. 207-208 (7th ed. 2017); Manfred Wandt, Gesetzliche Schuldverhältnisse, § 16 para. 10-11 (8th ed. 2017).

19 Bernd Kannowski, Staudinger BGB section 1 para. 24-25 (ed. 2013).

20 Hartwig Sprau, Palandt Bürgerliches Gesetzbuch section 823 para. 89-90 (77th ed. 2018); Manfred Wolf and Jörg Neuner, Allgemeiner Teil des Bürgerlichen Rechts, § 11 para. 26-29 (11th ed. 2016).

Under this point of view it appears that legal capacity can exist beyond death.

2. Capacity to act

German civil law distinguishes the concept of legal capacity from the capacity to act. The capacity to act means the capacity to carry out legal acts and to respectively establish claims and duties because of own actions. This capacity to act is split into the capacity to contract (sections 104 et seq. BGB) and the responsibility for tort (sections 827, 828 BGB).[21]

a) Capacity to contract

While a human being under German law always has legal capacity, the capacity to contract is not necessarily given. The BGB, however, assumes that all human beings principally have capacity to contract and only regulates the exceptions in sections 104 et seq. BGB.

(i) Incapacity to contract

A person who is not yet seven years old is always incapable to contract, section 104 Nr. 1 BGB. This is similar to the requirement of an age of eight years in Art. 20 of the General Rules. The exact age limits for incapacity of minors and respectively the age of majority can be discussed under various points of view but in the end it is just a decision of the legislator and not one of the fundamental aspects of a country's law. More interesting is the case of those who are incapable to contract due to a state of pathological mental disturbance, which prevents the free exercise of will, unless the state by its nature is a temporary one, section 104 Nr. 2 BGB. It has to be inves-

---

21 Manfred Wolf and Jörg Neuner, Allgemeiner Teil des Bürgerlichen Rechts, § 12 para. 1 (11th ed. 2016); Jürgen Ellenberger, Palandt Bürgerliches Gesetzbuch Abschnitt 1. Personen para. 3 (77th ed. 2018).

tigated carefully if the state of pathological mental disturbance is only temporary and if it affects only certain areas of life with their respective legal transactions. Legal transactions that are not affected by this limited incapacity to contract are still valid.[22]

The second group of incapacity to contract especially concerns people of full age who suffer from significant dementia such as Alzheimer's disease.[23] Until 2050 approximately 38% of the German population will be older than 60 years (2013: 27%).[24] This process of an aging population will automatically increase the number of people suffering from Alzheimer's disease and will lead to growing numbers of legal custodianship cases in Germany. Dealing with these cases and the interest of the persons involved will be one of the major challenges in family law for future generations.

(ii) Limited capacity to contract

A person who has reached the age of seven but not full age yet, which is according to section 2 BGB 18 years, is not completely incapable to contract anymore, but still has limited capacity to contract, section 106 BGB.

(iii) Consequences of incapacity to contract and limited capacity to contract

According to section 105, para. 1 BGB any declaration of intent (e.g. as part of any contract) of a person incapable of contracting is void. The same applies for declarations of intent that have been made in a state of unconsciousness or temporary mental disturbance, section 105, para. 2 BGB.

The purpose of section 105, para. 1 BGB with respect to the incapacity to contract of minors is sometimes questionable as the legal consequence is that even a legally or economically benefical legal transaction (or contract)

---

22 Jochem Schmitt, Münchener Kommentar BGB, section 104 para. 13, 16-19 (7th ed. 2015); Jürgen Ellenberger, Palandt Bürgerliches Gesetzbuch section 104 para. 4-6 (77th ed. 2018).

23 Hans-Friedrich Müller, Erman BGB section 104 para. 3 (15th ed. 2017); Jürgen Ellenberger, Palandt Bürgerliches Gesetzbuch section 104 para. 5 (77th ed. 2018).

24 Bundeszentrale für politische Bildung [http://www.bpb.de/nachschlagen/zahlen-und-fakten/soziale-situation-in-deutschland/61541/altersstruktur] (Last visited 20th April 2018).

is void.[25] This problem becomes even more evident if adults who are incapable of contracting are involved. According to the UN Convention on the Rights of Persons with Disabilities these persons shall take part in daily life on equal basis. Treating disabled persons of full age like those who are younger than seven years would violate these principles.

For this reason transactions that can be effected with funds of low value are regarded as valid with regard to performance and (if agreed) consideration, as soon as performance has been effected and consideration rendered according to section 105a BGB. The intention of this rule is to offer mentally disabled persons of full age the opportunity to take part in daily life with respect to their human dignity and a self-determined way of life as long as there are no serious threats for their property and assets.[26]

In all other cases, persons incapable to contract need to be represented by a legal representative.

A person with limited capacity to contract needs the consent of a legal representative to contract, section 107 BGB. Any contract which is made without the necessary consent is only effective subject to the ratification of the legal representative, section 108, para. 1 BGB. If the legal representative refuses the request to declare his ratification, the contract is void, see section 108, para. 2 BGB.

The BGB furthermore contains with sections 110 and 107 BGB prescriptions that are similar to Art. 19, sentence 2 of the General Rules. A contract entered by a minor without the approval of the legal representative is deemed effective if the minor effects the performance under the contract with means that were given to him for this purpose or free disposal or if the contract offers him only legal benefits.[27]

Compared to section 110 BGB, Art. 19 General Rules is slightly more general as it refers to the age and intelligence of the minor and not just the means he needs to effect the performance. The advantage of a provision that refers to the age of a person like Art. 19, sentence 2 General Rules is the possibility to respect individual skills and mental maturity of a person. On the other hand it might cause serious problems to prove respectively whether something is compatible with the age or intelligence of a person or

25 Comp. Claus-Wilhelm Canaris, Verstöße gegen das verfassungsrechtliche Übermaßverbot im Recht der Geschäftsunfähigkeit und im Schadensrecht, JZ 993-1004 (1987).

26 Jürgen Ellenberger, Palandt Bürgerliches Gesetzbuch, section 105a para. 1 (77th ed. 2018).

27 Section 107 BGB refers only to legal and not economic benefits.

not. In the long term, this will lead to legal uncertainty in an unpredictable number of cases.

To avoid this uncertainty section 112 BGB requires the ratification of the family court in advance of independent operation of business by a minor instead of the fixed age limit of 16 years in Art. 18, sentence 2 General Rules for contracts of minors whose main income is their job.

(iv) Legal representative of persons incapable of contracting

Persons without capacity to contract need to be represented by a legal representative in order to contract. The same applies to persons with limited capacity to contract in most cases (see above). The German legislator has developed a much more differentiated system of representation.

The legal representatives of minors are his/her parents, sections 1626, 1629 BGB. In general the parents represent the child jointly, unless one parent exercises sole custody or the decision has been transferred to him by the family court, section 1629, para. 1 BGB.

If the parents are unable or unentitled to represent a minor, e.g. because they are dead, guardianship has to be ordered by the family court of its own motion under sections 1773 et seq. BGB. For persons of full age the regulations on guardianship do not apply.

For persons of full age who cannot in whole or in part take care of their affairs due to a mental illness or a physical, mental or psychological handicap, the custodianship court (which is part of the local courts[28]) may appoint a custodian for him, section 1896, para 1, sentence 1 BGB.

Incapacity to contract is often the reason behind the appointment of a custodian, but it is not an essential requirement.[29] It is also possible to appoint a custodian only for those groups of tasks where it is necessary because the person cannot take care of his affairs, see section 1896, para. 1, sentence 1 BGB ([…] can not in whole […]).

However the appointment of custodianship against the free will of the person of full age is illegal, section 1896, para. 1a BGB. This does of course not apply if the person of full age is not capable to create a free will.[30]

---

28 Section 23c GVG, section 271 FamFG.

29 Isabell Götz, Palandt Bürgerliches Gesetzbuch Einf. v. section 1896 para. 13 (77th ed. 2018).

30 Isabell Götz, Palandt Bürgerliches Gesetzbuch Einf. v. section 1896 para. 4 (77th ed. 2018).

The German provisions on guardianship and custody contain much more detailed and differentiated regulations in relation to the person who is to become guardian or custodian than the Chinese equivalent. Whereas Art. 27 and 28 of General Rules give a fixed order who shall become the guardian/custodian, the German provisions are a lot more flexible.

In particular, the German provisions for the appointment of a custodian for a person of full age are significantly different from Art. 28 General Rules.

Under German law the custodian must be suited to take care of the affairs of the person under custodianship and take care of him to the extent necessary, section 1897, para. 1 BGB. The will of the ward has priority for the appointment of the custodian. According to section 1897, para. 4 BGB the suggestion or rejection of a person as custodian by the ward has to be taken into account (comparable to Art. 33 General Rules). But in contrast to Art. 33 General Rules the family court has to approve that the suggestion of a person as custodian is not inconsistent with the best interest of the person of full age, section 1897, para. 4, sentence 1 BGB. If the person of full age has not suggested any person as custodian, the custodian is selected by the custodianship court. For it's decision the court has to take into account family and other personal ties, section 1897, para. 5 BGB.

As a result, the appointment of the custodian is always performed through the custodianship court with regard to the interests and the will of the ward and not according to a fixed order as in Art. 28 General Rules for which Art. 31 General Rules merely provides an exception for disputes on the determination of the guardian. At first glance, the difference between these approaches does not seem to be that important because in practice German and Chinese law will mostly lead to the same result. Usually the family court chooses the closest relative as custodian or guardian. But, when looking more closely, there is a huge difference regarding the concept of guardianship/custodianship.

While the Chinese system with its fixed orders is much simpler, the German system always refers to the interest of the person of full age to provide a maximum of self-determination and respect of their free will. Therefore the requirements and standards for custodianship are relatively high under German law and ensure frequent control by the custodianship court to protect the free will and the freedom of the affected persons.

b) Responsibility for tort

The German BGB distinguishes not only between legal capacity and capacity to contract but also the responsibility for torts. According to the BGB, claims for damages may not only result from a breach of duty arising from an obligation but also from tort (sections 823 et seq. BGB). Therefore, in these cases the responsibility for damages is the equivalent to the capacity to contract.

Sections 827 and 828 BGB have similar content to the sections regarding the capacity to contract. For example a person who has not reached the age of seven (= incapable to contract, section 104 Nr. 1 BGB) is not responsible for damages caused to another person, section 828, para. 1 BGB. On the other hand the responsibility of a person between seven and eighteen years is determined under consideration of his capability to recognise and understand his responsibility, section 828, para. 3 BGB.

An exemption of this is if the minor has caused the damage unintentionally in an accident involving a motor vehicle, a railway or suspension railway, section 828, para. 2 BGB. In these cases the minimum age for responsibility is ten years because children who are younger are usually not capable of judging the risks of traffic properly.[31]

A difference between the incapacity to contract and the responsibility for tort is found in section 827 BGB. Contrary to section 104 Nr. 2 BGB, the state of pathological and mental disturbance which excludes the responsibility for tort can be only a temporary one if it is not induced by alcoholic beverages or similar means.

In addition to the provisions on the responsibility for tort, the BGB also contains an interesting exception for the requirement of responsibility for tort in section 829 BGB. For the reasons of equity, a person which is not responsible for damages he caused under sections 827 and 828 BGB still has to pay compensation for damages if compensation can not be obtained from a third party and if the compensation does not deprive the ressources needed for reasonable maintenance and to discharge his statutory maintenance duties. (For this reason section 829 BGB is called the "Millionaire Section".[32])

---

31 Gerhard Wagner, Münchener Kommentar BGB, section 828 para. 5 (7th ed. 2017).

32 Gerhard Wagner, Münchener Kommentar BGB, section 829 para. 2 (7th ed. 2017).

3. Summary

To sum up, many parallelisms between the German BGB and the Chinese General Rules can be found. One difference that has to be considered is that the BGB has already been in force since 1st January 1900. Within the last 117 years the courts and literature could influence the changes, development of usage and interpretation in many ways, e.g. the protection of the *nasciturus* under tort law. The future will show if the new Chinese regulations will adapt the German law respectively develop in a similar way or go a different way.

One of the most important basic principles of German private law, and especially of the BGB, is the doctrine of privity to contract, which follows from Article 1 of the GG (Basic Law) and the basic right of Personal freedoms according to Art. 2 GG.[33] This principle is only restricted where the protection of one of the parties involved is necessary, for example the protection of minors, consumers or persons of full age without the capacity to contract.

Regarding the incapacity to contract and limited capacity to contract, German and Chinese law are largely similar. Huge differences occur, however, as far as legal representation is concerned. With the provisions on guardianship, custodianship and legal curatorship the BGB contains a differentiated model, each with its own procedural rules, in order to meet the interests of the parties involved and to respect freedom of persons as far as possible. These differentiated institutes of German family law are codified in more than 150 sections of the German Civil Code. Although the number of provisions is not an indicator for quality (sometimes less is more), it still shows that a more detailed codification is required than 14 sections in the General Rules.

Furthermore it should be discussed if guardianship is a suitable content of a General Part of a Civil Code at all. In German and Roman civil law, the concept of a general part of a civil code was to regulate the general matters in a general part that refers to all special parts of the code, which contain the exceptions of the general assumptions. Aslong as the incapacity to contract of persons of full age is still the exception it should be part of the section on family law and not of the general part. Time will show if the Chinese legislator will adapt this solution or find a different way to handle this conflict of interest.

---

33 Manfred Wolf and Jörg Neuner, Allgemeiner Teil des Bürgerlichen Rechts, § 10 para. 27–41 (11th ed. 2016).

Klassifizierung der juristischen Personen im Sinne des Allgemeinen Teils des chinesischen Zivilgesetzbuchs: Reformen und Probleme

*Tong Zhang**

Zusammenfassung: *Hinsichtlich der Klassifizierung juristischer Personen folgt der im Jahr 2017 erlassene Allgemeine Teil des chinesischen Zivilgesetzbuchs, die sog. General Rules of Civil Law (GRCL), dem roten Faden der General Principles of Civil Law (GPCL). Nach ihrem Errichtungszweck und ihren Funktionen werden juristische Personen in wirtschaftliche, nicht wirtschaftliche und spezielle juristische Personen eingeteilt. Dieses Klassifikationsmodell greift nicht einfach nur das alte Modell auf, vielmehr gelingen ihm Innovation und der Durchbruch. Selbstverständlich ist das Klassifikationsmodell der GRCL auch auf Kritik gestoßen. Wie die einschlägigen Regeln in der Praxis umgesetzt werden, bleibt noch abzuwarten.*

Stichwörter: Begriffsentwicklung der juristischen Person, juristische Personen, wirtschaftliche juristische Person, nicht wirtschaftliche juristische Personen.

---

* *Dr., LL.M. (Frankfurt a. M.)*; Professorin, Chinesische Universität für Politikwissenschaft und Recht. Lehrstuhl für Bürgerliches Recht, Handelsrecht, Europarecht und Rechtsvergleichung.

I. Einleitung

Das System der juristischen Personen übt großen Einfluss auf Politik, Wirtschaft und Gesellschaft aus. Da in diesem komplexe Probleme wie die Verkehrssicherheit und der Schutz Dritter eine Rolle spielen, gibt es in fast allen Rechtsordnungen einen Typenzwang bezüglich juristischer Personen,[1] ebenso im chinesischen Recht. Diese Typen sind sehr kompliziert und sie lassen sich nach verschiedenen Maßstäben klassifizieren. Weil juristische Personen nach dem Gesetz fiktive Personen sind, werden sie in den verschiedenen Ländern der Welt unterschiedlich klassifiziert. Beispielsweise können sie in wirtschaftliche und nicht wirtschaftliche juristische Personen, in Vereine und Stiftungen oder in juristische Personen des öffentlichen Rechts und des Privatrechts eingeteilt werden. Eine Einteilung ist aus folgenden zwei praktischen Gründen von Bedeutung: Erstens sind je nach Typ die Voraussetzungen für die Errichtung unterschiedlich. In einem Verein etwa können sich mehrere Personen zusammenschließen und Vermögen auf diesen übertragen, wenn das Gesetz dies nicht ausdrücklich verbietet. Eine Stiftung hingegen ist definiert als einem bestimmten Zweck dienendes Vermögen. Zweitens unterscheiden sich je nach Typ auch die Organ- und die Verwaltungsstruktur.

Mit der wirtschaftlichen und gesellschaftlichen Entwicklung Chinas sind inzwischen immer neuere Formen juristischer Personen entstanden, welche nicht mehr von der Klassifikation der 1986 in Kraft getretenen GPCL um-

---

1 *Wolf/Neuner*, Allgemeiner Teil des Bürgerlichen Rechts, 10. Aufl. 2012, S. 149.

fasst sind. Es ist daher für die umfassende Vertiefung der Reform des Zivilrechts und die Förderung der sozialistischen Marktwirtschaft von großer Bedeutung, die alte Klassifikation an den neuesten Entwicklungsstand des Systems sozialer Organisationen anzupassen.

Am 15. März 2017 verabschiedete der Nationale Volkskongress den Allgemeinen Teil des chinesischen Zivilgesetzbuchs (ZGB), die GRCL.[2] In diesem werden in drei verschiedenen Kapiteln natürliche Personen, juristische Personen bzw. Organisationen ohne Rechtspersönlichkeit geregelt. Dabei bilden die juristischen Personen einen wesentlichen Teil der Zivilrechtssubjekte, weshalb sie auch bei der Kodifikation des ZGB und allgemein bei der zivilrechtlichen Gesetzgebung in China eine wichtige Rolle spielen.

Im Gegensatz zu den GPCL im Allgemeinen wurden die Regeln über die juristischen Personen im Speziellen nicht nur oft erheblichen Änderungen unterworfen, sondern auch am heftigsten kritisiert. Die größte Auseinandersetzung bestand darin, ob juristische Personen in wirtschaftliche und nicht wirtschaftliche juristische Personen oder in Vereine und Stiftungen eingeteilt werden sollten. In den GRCL ist schließlich die wesentliche Klassifikationsmethode übernommen worden, nämlich die Einteilung in wirtschaftliche und nicht wirtschaftliche juristische Personen. Die nicht wirtschaftlichen juristischen Personen werden wiederum in Institutionen, soziale Organisationen, Spenden-Einrichtungen und staatliche Organe unterteilt. Diese Klassifizierung stellt nicht nur einen Durchbruch dar und innoviert die begriffliche Systematisierung juristischer Personen in den GRCL, sondern wahrt zugleich die legislative Kontinuität und Stabilität.

In dieser Arbeit werden zunächst der historische Hintergrund und die Klassifikation juristischer Personen in den GPCL vorgestellt. Hierauf werden Reform und Innovation bei der Klassifizierung juristischer Personen in den GRCL erläutert. Schließlich wird diese kritisiert und die möglichen mit ihr einhergehenden Probleme werden aufgezeigt.

II. Klassifizierung der juristischen Personen in den GPCL

1. Arten der juristischen Personen in den GPCL

In den GPCL werden juristische Personen in vier Typen eingeteilt, in Unternehmen, staatliche Organe, Institutionen und soziale Organisationen.

2 Die GRCL sind am 1.10.2017 in Kraft getreten.

Die letzten drei Typen werden auch als Nicht-Unternehmen bezeichnet. Die Unternehmen werden im zweiten, die Nicht-Unternehmen im dritten Titel des dritten Kapitels geregelt.

Wegen des langjährigen Einflusses des sozialistischen Systems auf das chinesische Zivilrecht wurde nicht die traditionelle zivilrechtliche Klassifikation verwendet, sondern die juristischen Personen werden nach Befugnissen oder Eigentumsarten eingeteilt.

a) Die Unterteilung juristischer Personen in Unternehmen und Nicht-Unternehmen

Juristische Personen werden in Unternehmen und Nicht-Unternehmen eingeteilt, je nachdem, ob sie einen wirtschaftlichen Geschäftsbetrieb haben oder nicht.

b) Die Unterteilung juristischer Personen nach dem Kriterium des Auslandsbezugs

Juristische Personen können eingeteilt werden in solche mit und solche ohne Auslandsbezug. Erstere können folgendermaßen weiter unterteilt werden: Chinesisch-ausländische Joint Ventures, Unternehmen mit Auslandskapital sowie chinesisch-ausländische Unternehmenskooperationen.

c) Die Unterteilung juristischer Personen in staatseigene Unternehmen, Unternehmen im Kollektiveigentum und private Unternehmen

Juristische Personen ohne Auslandsbezug werden ferner unterteilt in staatseigene Unternehmen, Unternehmen im Kollektiveigentum und private Unternehmen.

d) Die Unterteilung juristischer Personen in staatliche Organe, Institutionen und soziale Organisationen

Nicht-Unternehmen werden in staatliche Organe, Institutionen und soziale Organisationen eingeteilt, wobei sich die Voraussetzungen der Errichtung und die Befugnisse jeweils unterscheiden.

(i) Staatliche Organe

Staatliche Organe dienen der staatlichen oder öffentlichen Verwaltung und sind mit einem eigenen Budget ausgestattet.

(ii) Institutionen

Unter Institutionen versteht man die nicht der staatlichen Verwaltung, sondern der Öffentlichkeit dienenden Einrichtungen, die staatlich, durch die Provinzen oder kommunal finanziert werden und deren Zweck nicht auf einen wirtschaftlichen Geschäftsbetrieb gerichtet ist, wie z. B. Schulen, Krankenhäuser und Rundfunkanstalten.

(iii) Soziale Organisationen

Unter sozialen Organisationen versteht man staatliche Körperschaften, die nicht zu den staatlichen Organen oder Institutionen zählen und deren Zweck nicht auf einen wirtschaftlichen Geschäftsbetrieb gerichtet ist, z. B. Stiftungen, Assoziationen und Forschungsanstalten.

2. Hintergrund der Klassifizierung juristischer Personen in den GPCL

a) Politische Aufgabe: Qualifizierung der Unternehmen als juristische Personen

Obwohl die zivilrechtliche Gesetzgebung als grundlegendes Projekt des Rechtsstaates gilt und das Zivilgesetzbuch eher wissenschaftlich geprägt ist, ist nicht zu übersehen, dass die legislativen Entscheidungen im Zivilrecht eng mit dem politischen Hintergrund verbunden sind.

Vor 1949 wurden in China das deutsche BGB und das japanische Zivilgesetzbuch als Vorbilder herangezogen. Dies führte zur Übernahme der Einteilung juristischer Personen in Vereine und Stiftungen im Entwurf eines Zivilgesetzes am Ende der Qing-Dynastie und im Zivilgesetzbuch während der Zeit der Republik China (1912–1949). Allerdings übernahm die Volksrepublik China diese Klassifikation nicht, sondern teilte aus bestimmten Gründen die juristischen Personen in Unternehmen, offizielle (staatliche) Organe, Institutionen und soziale Organisationen ein. In den GPCL finden sich jedoch nur die grundsätzlichen Vorschriften zum jeweiligen Typ einer juristischen Person. Weitere spezielle Regelungen finden sich in den einschlägigen speziellen Gesetzen sowie Verwaltungsverordnungen.[3]

Obwohl beim Entwurf der GPCL zivilrechtliche Traditionen gewahrt wurden, berücksichtigte der Gesetzgeber die veränderten realen Verhältnisse in China durch die Fortführung bestimmter wesentlicher Begrifflichkeiten kommunistischer Prägung. Hinter der Bildung des Systems juristischer Personen steckte der dringende politische Wunsch, eine Grundlage für die Reform der staatseigenen Unternehmen zu schaffen. Im Oktober 1984 wurde beim Beschluss über die Reform des Wirtschaftssystems in der dritten Plenarsitzung des 12. Zentralkomitees auf Folgendes hingewiesen: „Es muss sein, dass Unternehmen zu relativ eigenständigen wirtschaftlichen Einheiten werden, dass sie zu sozialistischen Warenproduzenten und Betreibern werden, die selbstständig arbeiten und Verantwortung für Gewinne und Verluste tragen können, und dass sie zu juristischen Personen werden, die bestimmte Rechte und Verpflichtungen haben."[4] Aus der bereits vor Erlass der GPCL bestehenden Kategorie des „Unternehmens" als Ausgangpunkt der Gesetzgebung folgt logisch die Gegenüberstellung der Kategorie des „Nicht-Unternehmens". So teilte die Kommission für legislative Angelegenheiten des Ständigen Ausschusses des Nationalen Volkskongresses beim Entwurf der GPCL die vier Typen juristischer Personen in diese zwei Kategorien ein. Auch nach Ansicht von *Gu Angran* sind die juristischen Personen der GPCL in zwei Kategorien einzuteilen: Einerseits die Unternehmen, andererseits die offiziellen Organe, Institutionen und sozialen Organisationen.[5] Dies entspricht der Einteilung juristischer Personen in der endgültigen Fassung der GPCL.

---

3 Z. B. finden sich Regelungen zu Unternehmen hauptsächlich im 2005 in Kraft getretenen Gesellschaftsgesetz («公司法») und Regelungen zu Institutionen und sozialen Organisationen in drei allesamt 1998 vom Staatsrat verabschiedeten Verordnungen: Vorübergehende Verordnung über die Eintragung und Verwaltung der Institutionen («事业单位登记管理暂行条例») bzw. vorübergehende Verordnung über die Eintragung und Verwaltung der privaten Nicht-Unternehmen («民办非企业单位登记管理暂行条例») bzw. vorübergehende Verordnung über die Eintragung und Verwaltung der sozialen Organisationen («社会团体登记管理条例»).

4 Beschluss über die Reform des Wirtschaftssystems in der dritten Plenarsitzung des 12. Zentralkomitees im Oktober 1984.

5 *Gu Angran*, Überblick über die General Principles of the Civil Law und ihre Hauptprobleme – Rede im Rahmen des Kurses des Obersten Volksgerichtshofs über die General Principles of the Civil Law vom 28.7.1986, in: Notizen über die Gesetzgebung, 2006, S. 228.

b) Prägende Wirkung der sowjetischen Gesetzgebung

Die GPCL wurden durch die sowjetische Gesetzgebung geprägt. Nach dem sowjetischen Zivilgesetzbuch können juristische Personen im Staatseigentum, im Privateigentum und im genossenschaftlichen Eigentum stehen. Der sowjetische Gesetzgeber war der Meinung, dass der größte Teil des Wirtschaftslebens öffentlich und daher vom Staat zu kontrollieren sei. Eine Einmischung Privater sollte nur in eng begrenzten Ausnahmefällen stattfinden. Daher konnten etwa die von privaten Personen eingerichteten Stiftungen nicht als juristische Personen anerkannt werden.

c) Prägende Wirkung des chinesischen Verwaltungsstils

Bei der Klassifizierung juristischer Personen in den GPCL wurde der aus dem „Einrichtungs- und Personalmanagement" des Staatsrates stammende Maßstab mechanisch übernommen, nach dem juristische Personen in Unternehmen und Nicht-Unternehmen (staatliche Organe, Institutionen und soziale Organisationen) eingeteilt wurden. [6] Dieser ist durch den planwirtschaftlichen Verwaltungsstil geprägt, was zu einem großen Defizit an Typen von juristischen Personen führte, da Stiftungen und Organisationen für religiöse Aktivitäten nicht berücksichtigt wurden. Die nicht mit der sozialen Entwicklung Schritt haltende Klassifizierung hatte zur Folge, dass die Grenze zwischen juristischen Personen des öffentlichen Rechts und juristischen Personen des Privatrechts verschwamm, was Wissenschaft und Praxis seit langem heftig kritisierten.

d) Grund für die Ablehnung des Begriffs der Stiftung

Der Begriff der Stiftung wurde neben den politischen auch aus folgenden Gründen nicht in die GPCL übernommen: Erstens gab es damals schon den Begriff der Institution, der funktional den Begriff der Stiftung miteinschließt. Der Unterschied besteht lediglich darin, dass Institutionen in der Regel durch den Staat eingerichtet werden, während Stiftungen eher die von privaten Stiftern eingerichteten Non-Profit-Organisationen sind. Zweitens gab es damals keine durch Private oder sog. „soziale Kräfte" eingerichteten

6 *Sun Xianzhong*, Analyse zum Vermögen der Stiftungen und der Zugehörigkeit des religiösen Vermögens, 4 Chinesische Rechtswissenschaft, S. 78 (1990).

Non-Profit-Organisationen, weshalb die Kategorie der Stiftung nicht erforderlich war. Nicht zuletzt ist der Begriff „Stiftung als juristische Person" sowohl schwer verständlich[7] als auch missverständlich[8] und konnte sich folglich nicht in die sozialistische Ideologie integrieren.

III. Reform der Klassifizierung juristischer Personen durch die GRCL

1. Debatte über die Klassifizierung der juristischen Personen

In den Sitzungen der Kommission für legislative Angelegenheiten des Ständigen Ausschusses und des Gesetzeskomitees des Nationalen Volkskongresses wurde dieses Thema vielfach besprochen. Die kurz nach Beginn der Reform- und Öffnungspolitik beschlossenen GPCL von 1986 werden den heutigen politischen, gesellschaftlichen, wirtschaftlichen und kulturellen Bedürfnissen in China nicht mehr gerecht. Deshalb kam man bei der Kodifizierung des Zivilrechts überein, dass das bisherige Klassifikationsmodell durch die GRCL von 2017 reformiert werden müsse. Die Meinungen, wie juristische Personen zu klassifizieren seien, gehen allerdings auseinander. Im Gesetzgebungsprozess wurden drei Möglichkeiten erörtert: Erstens eine traditionelle Klassifizierung in Vereine und Stiftungen, zweitens die Schaffung der Begriffe wirtschaftlicher und nicht wirtschaftlicher juristischer Personen oder drittens die Einteilung in Unternehmen, staatliche Organe, Institutionen, religiöse Anstalten und Stiftungen unter Aufgabe der Dichotomie.

Der chinesische Handelsrechtsverbund machte 2015 den Vorschlag, nicht Vereine und Stiftungen, sondern wirtschaftliche und nicht wirtschaftliche juristische Personen als wesentliche Klassifizierung in das ZGB zu

7 *Hua Xuan*, Gespräch zwischen Jiang Ping und Wang Zejian: Wie regelt man das chinesische Zivilgesetzbuch?, Southern Weekend v. 27.4.2017.

8 In den Modernen Chinesischen Wörterbüchern des Redaktionsbüros des Sprachenforschungsinstituts der chinesischen Akademie der Sozialwissenschaft definiert die Stiftungen als „Monopolisten oder ihre Gruppen in einer Kapitalgesellschaft, die viele Unternehmen, Banken und Gesellschaften kontrollieren", 2011, S. 124.

übernehmen. Außerdem sei ein Gesetz über die nicht wirtschaftlichen juristischen Personen auszuarbeiten. Folgende Argumente wurden für diesen Vorschlag vorgetragen:[9]

Zunächst wurden die Begriffe des Vereins und der Stiftung als juristische Person nicht in die GPCL aufgenommen. Innerhalb der letzten dreißig Jahre seit der Verabschiedung der GPCL sind in der Praxis jedoch einige besondere Arten von nicht wirtschaftlichen juristischen Personen entstanden. Neben den Institutionen gibt es private Nicht-Unternehmen (private Institutionen), soziale Organisationen und Stiftungen. Diese besonderen Arten sind in der vorübergehenden Verordnung über private Nicht-Unternehmen von 1998, der Verordnung über die Eintragung der sozialen Organisationen von 1998 und der Verordnung über das Stiftungsmanagement von 2004 geregelt. Obwohl es die Kategorie der Stiftung als juristische Person nicht gab, entwickelten sich nicht wirtschaftliche juristische Personen in der Praxis, was zeige, dass die Einführung dieser Kategorie überflüssig sei. Vielmehr solle die traditionelle Klassifikation juristischer Personen nach den GPCL, die die Unternehmen in den Mittelpunkt stellt, fortgeführt und weiterentwickelt werden.

Ferner würden sich die Formen der Stiftung und des Vereins als juristische Personen in der Praxis annähern. Zudem sei sogar eine Mischform aus beiden entstanden. Die rechtlichen Unterschiede würden also immer kleiner werden.

Außerdem wird auf das US-amerikanische Recht verwiesen, das bei juristischen Personen ebenfalls nicht zwischen Vereinen und Stiftungen, sondern wirtschaftlichen und nicht wirtschaftlichen juristischen Personen unterscheidet. An dieser amerikanischen Gesetzgebung könne man sich orientieren. Gleichzeitig könne ein spezielles Gesetz als „Basisgesetz“ für nicht wirtschaftliche juristische Personen erlassen werden.

Darüber hinaus sei die Klassifizierung in wirtschaftliche und nicht wirtschaftliche juristische Personen eines der drängendsten Probleme der Praxis. Die Klassifizierung sei nicht nur von theoretischer Bedeutung, da sich die Kategorie der nicht wirtschaftlichen juristischen Personen mit den schon bestehenden Typen juristischer Personen, wie sozialen Organisationen, Stiftungen und privaten Nicht-Unternehmen (privaten Institutionen), decken könne.

---

9 Kurzbericht über die Aussprache über die GRCL am 28.10.2015, in: Sammlung des legislativen Hintergrundes und der Auseinandersetzungen über die GRCL, 2017, S. 523.

Schließlich würden Gesetzgebungsressourcen gespart, wenn neben der Klassifizierung im ZGB ein Gesetz über nicht wirtschaftliche juristische Personen erlassen würde. Dies wäre auch im Interesse der Vereinigung der Vorschriften über nicht wirtschaftliche juristische Personen. Gegenwärtig existieren jeweils unterschiedliche Gesetze zu privaten Nicht-Unternehmen (privaten Institutionen), sozialen Organisationen und Stiftungen. Dies hat zur Folge, dass es zu bestimmten Fragen oft mehrere ähnliche Regelungen gibt, was eine Verschwendung legislativer Ressourcen bedeute und oftmals zu Chaos führe. Sollte eine Gesetzgebung zu nicht wirtschaftlichen juristischen Personen nicht möglich sein, könne man alternativ eine allgemeine Vorschrift über nicht wirtschaftliche juristische Personen in das ZGB aufnehmen und der Staatsrat könne gleichzeitig eine dazugehörige Verordnung verabschieden.

Nicht zuletzt müsse der Begriff der nicht wirtschaftlichen juristischen Person im ZGB definiert werden, wenn man diese Klassifizierung einführen will. Dafür sei die Definition anhand des Merkmals des „wirtschaftlichen Geschäftsbetriebs“ in das ZGB zu übernehmen, wodurch dieses eine handelsrechtliche Dimension erhalte.

2. Legislative Orientierung bei den GRCL

In den letzten zwanzig Jahren haben die durch soziale Kräfte errichteten, nicht wirtschaftlichen Organisationen einen Boom erlebt. Das hat dazu geführt, dass die traditionelle Klassifizierung juristischer Personen in den GPCL überholt war. Die Regelung der nicht wirtschaftlichen Organisationen war demnach eine dringende Aufgabe. Schon beim vierten Entwurf des ZGB von 2002 trat dieses Problem zutage. *Gu Angran* sagte hierzu: „Neben dem Problem der zivilrechtlichen Subjekte ist noch eines bezüglich der Klassifizierung juristischer Personen zu lösen. In den GPCL werden juristische Personen in Unternehmen, staatliche Organe, Institutionen und soziale Organisationen unterteilt, aber zurzeit gibt es immer mehr Mischformen wie Privatschulen, Schulen durch Joint Ventures und private Krankenhäuser, die den vier bestehenden Typen juristischer Personen in den GPCL nur schwer zuzuordnen sind. Deshalb muss man sich darüber Gedanken machen, wie man die Vorschriften über zivilrechtliche Subjekte und die Klassifizierung juristischer Personen reformieren kann.“[10]

---

10 *Gu Angran*, Erklärungen zum Entwurf des ZGB der Volksrepublik China vom 23.12.2002, in: Notizen über Gesetzgebungen, 2006, S. 358.

Erheblich beeinflusst wurden die Vorschriften der GRCL über juristische Personen durch den „Beschluss über einige wichtige Fragen zur allseitigen Vertiefung der Reformen", der in der dritten Plenarsitzung des 12. Zentralkomitees im Oktober 2013 gefasst wurde. Im Beschluss findet sich folgender Hinweis: „Die Dynamik der sozialen Organisationen ist anzuregen. Die Beziehungen zwischen Regierung und Gesellschaft sollen richtig geregelt werden. Man muss die Trennung zwischen Regierung und Gemeinschaft beschleunigen und die sozialen Organisationen antreiben, ihre Rechte und ihre Verantwortung klarzustellen, sich dem Gesetz entsprechend zu verwalten und zu betätigen."[11] Durch diesen Beschluss wurde die Entwicklung der nicht wirtschaftlichen Organisationen zu einem präzedenzlosen politischen Höhepunkt. Offenbar war die Ausarbeitung der GRCL nicht nur rechtlich eine wichtige Aufgabe, sondern auch eine wesentliche politische Obliegenheit.

Deswegen war eine wichtige Frage beim Entwurf der GRCL, wie die nicht wirtschaftlichen juristischen Personen, die in den letzten zwanzig Jahren in der Praxis entstanden sind, in die Klassifizierung juristischer Personen zu integrieren seien. Schon vor dem Entwurf der GRCL wurde der Begriff der „nicht wirtschaftlichen juristischen Personen"[12] verwendet. Aber bei der Kodifizierung der GRCL galt es, die praktischen Erfahrungen der letzten zwanzig Jahre mit nicht wirtschaftlichen juristischen Personen zusammenzufassen.

Die Unterscheidung zwischen wirtschaftlichen und nicht wirtschaftlichen juristischen Personen wurde aus den folgenden drei Gründen als wesentliche Klassifikation in die GRCL aufgenommen: Erstens spricht dafür der historische Ursprung der Begriffe in den GPCL. Zweitens sollten die

---

11 Beschluss über einige wichtige Fragen zur allseitigen Vertiefung der Reformen in der dritten Plenarsitzung des 12. Zentralkomitees im Oktober 2013.

12 Z. B. lautet Abs. 2 der Verordnung über die Verwaltung der Stiftungen («基金会管理条例»): „Die Stiftungen im Sinne dieser Verordnung bedeuten die kraft dieser Verordnung errichteten nicht wirtschaftlichen juristischen Personen, die mit Vermögen, das von natürlichen Personen, juristischen Personen oder anderen Organisationen gestiftet wird, dem Gemeinwohl dienen." Die überarbeitete Fassung des Gesetzes über die Förderung privater Schulen («民办教育促进法») nimmt eine Klassifizierung in wirtschaftliche und nicht wirtschaftliche private Schulen vor. S. § 19 Abs. 1 dieses Gesetzes: „Die Gründer der privaten Schulen können sich selbst entscheiden zwischen wirtschaftlichen privaten Schulen und nicht wirtschaftlichen privaten Schulen. Aber sie dürfen nicht die wirtschaftlichen privaten Schulen errichten, die Pflichtschulbildung übernehmen."

Probleme der nicht wirtschaftlichen juristischen Personen in der Praxis gelöst werden. Drittens war die Aktualisierung des Systems der juristischen Personen eine politische Aufgabe der Regierungspartei bei der Gesetzgebung.[13]

3. Innovationen in den GRCL

Die GRCL behalten die ursprünglichen Typen aus den GPCL bei, schaffen jedoch zugleich eine neue Klassifikation nach Errichtungszweck und Funktion. „Wirtschaftliche juristische Personen" und „nicht wirtschaftliche juristische Personen" stellen die grundlegende Klassifikation dar. Außerdem werden in einem einzelnen Kapitel die „speziellen juristischen Personen" geregelt.[14] Im Einzelnen enthalten die GRCL bei der Klassifizierung juristischer Personen die folgenden Reformen und Innovationen:

a) Festlegung der grundlegenden Typen juristischer Personen

Durch die Klassifizierung in wirtschaftliche und nicht wirtschaftliche juristische Personen lässt sich die gesamte Wirklichkeit juristischer Personen erfassen. Sie legt den grundlegenden Status nach den GRCL fest.

Welche Klassifizierung von juristischen Personen im ZGB sinnvoll ist, hängt von zwei Faktoren ab: Einerseits von den Bedürfnissen der Praxis, andererseits von der Integrierbarkeit in das bestehende gesetzliche System und von den Gesetzgebungskosten. Diese Aspekte sind bei der Gesetzge-

---

13 *Wang Yong*, Klassifizierung der juristischen Personen: Kommentar zur Entscheidung der GRCL, 3 Chinesische und Ausländische Rechtswissenschaft, S. 613 (2017).

14 Im Vergleich zum zweiten Entwurf der GRCL wurde dem dritten Entwurf, der vom Nationalen Volkskongress als endgültiges Gesetz beschlossen wurde, neben den wirtschaftlichen und nicht wirtschaftlichen juristischen Personen die speziellen juristischen Personen hinzugefügt. Die staatlichen Organe, die im zweiten Entwurf den nicht wirtschaftlichen juristischen Personen zugeordnet waren, finden sich nunmehr im Kapitel „Spezielle juristische Personen". Spezielle juristische Personen können in staatliche Organe, Selbstverwaltungsorganisationen der Volksbasis, ländliche kollektive ökonomische Organisationen sowie wirtschaftliche Genossenschaften unterteilt werden.

bung des ZGB zu beachten. Vor allem ist Rücksicht zu nehmen auf die Einheitlichkeit des Systems juristischer Personen und es ist eine effiziente Regelungstechnik zu verwenden, indem man die wichtigsten Regelungen „vor die Klammer zieht". Beim Entwurf der GRCL wurde auf das Vor-die-Klammer-Ziehen großen Wert gelegt. Der Vize-Vorsitzende des Ständigen Ausschusses des Nationalen Volkskongresses, Li Jianguo, sagte: „Der Entwurf des Allgemeinen Teils des ZGB nimmt die GPCL als Grundlage. Und mit dem Vor-die-Klammer-Ziehen werden die allgemein geltenden und grundlegenden zivilrechtlichen Regeln in den Entwurf aufgenommen."[15]

Bei der gesetzgeberischen Technik des Vor-die-Klammer-Ziehens werden allgemeine Regeln in den GRCL verankert. Sie bilden auch die allgemeinen Regeln über handelsrechtliche Subjekte und sind damit auch für das Handelsrecht Allgemeiner Teil anwendbar. Hierdurch wird eine Vereinheitlichung des Zivil- und Handelsrechts realisiert.

Die GRCL gelten sowohl für das Zivil- als auch für das Handelsrecht. Die wirtschaftlichen juristischen Personen sind nämlich ökonomische Organisationen; die nicht wirtschaftlichen juristischen Personen beinhalten alle Formen von sozialen Organisationen und sind identisch mit den Nicht-Unternehmen (ausgenommen staatliche Organe). Dadurch definieren die GRCL ein sehr klares System juristischer Personen als Rechtssubjekte, welches das Zivilrecht und das Handelsrecht vereinheitlicht. Manche Rechtswissenschaftler glauben, dass mit dieser Klassifikation zwei praktische Vorteile auf einmal erzielt werden können. Zum einen wird eine wichtige Differenzierung vorgenommen. Zum anderen werden durch die Kategorie der wirtschaftlichen juristischen Personen die handelsrechtlichen Subjekte festgelegt und eine mögliche Grundlage für die spätere Schaffung eines Allgemeinen Teils des Handelsrechts oder eines Handelsgesetzbuches gelegt.[16] Der Gesetzgeber ist auch der Auffassung, dass diese Klassifikation nicht nur alle traditionellen Typen juristischer Personen wie z. B. Institutionen und soziale Organisationen, sondern auch neue Formen wie Stiftungen und

15 *Li Jianguo*, Erklärungen über den Entwurf der GRCL der Volksrepublik China vom 8.3.2017 im 12. Nationalen Volkskongress, in: Sammlungen des legislativen Hintergrundes und Auseinandersetzungen über die GRCL, 2017, S. 6.

16 *Wang Yong*, Klassifizierung der juristischen Personen: Kommentar zur Entscheidung der GRCL, 3 Chinesische und Ausländische Rechtswissenschaft, S. 618 (2017).

Anstalten für öffentliche Dienste erfasst und damit der tatsächlichen Situation in China entspricht.[17]

Die Unterscheidung zwischen juristischen Personen, ihrer Eintragung sowie ihrer Verwaltung wird erleichtert.

Meist gilt für wirtschaftliche juristische Personen das relativ lockere Maßregelprinzip, während für nicht wirtschaftliche juristische Personen das relativ strikte Genehmigungsprinzip gilt. Das Maßregelprinzip, auch Prinzip der Eintragung genannt, bezieht sich auf die gesetzlichen Anforderungen für die Gründung von juristischen Personen. Solange diese Bedingungen erfüllt sind, kann der Gründer bei der Eintragungsbehörde die Eintragung ins Handelsregister beantragen. Wenn bei der Prüfung durch die Eintragungsbehörde festgestellt wird, dass die gesetzlichen Anforderungen erfüllt sind, ist eine juristische Person einzutragen, was diese zur Entstehung bringt. Das chinesische Gesellschaftsrecht übernimmt dieses Prinzip für die Gründung einer Gesellschaft mit beschränkter Haftung. Das Genehmigungsprinzip bedeutet, dass juristische Personen erst nach Genehmigung durch die staatliche Verwaltung gegründet werden dürfen. Dieser Grundsatz gilt für Kontrolle und Verwaltung von juristischen Personen in speziellen Branchen, z. B. bei der Gründung von sozialen Organisationen.

Nach Ansicht der Legislative unterscheiden sich die Verwaltungsstrukturen nicht wirtschaftlicher und wirtschaftlicher juristischer Personen. Durch diese Klassifikation könnte daher die Verwaltungsstruktur sozialer Organisationen besser geleitet und kontrolliert werden.[18]

b) Definition und Grundmerkmale wirtschaftlicher und nicht wirtschaftlicher juristischer Personen

In den GRCL werden alle juristischen Personen, deren Zweck auf einen wirtschaftlichen Geschäftsbetrieb gerichtet ist, als wirtschaftliche juristische Personen definiert.

§ 76 GRCL definiert wirtschaftliche juristische Personen folgendermaßen: „Juristische Personen, deren Zweck auf einen wirtschaftlichen Geschäftsbetrieb gerichtet ist, sind wirtschaftliche juristische Personen. Dazu

17 *Li Shishi*, Erklärungen über den Entwurf der GRCL der Volksrepublik China in der 21. Sitzung des 12. Ständigen Ausschusses des Nationalen Volkskongresses, in: Sammlungen des legislativen Hintergrundes und Auseinandersetzungen über die GRCL, 2017, S. 11.

18 *Xie Hongfei*, Levels und Standards der Klassifizierung der juristischen Personen in den GRCL, 4 SJTU Law Review, S. 43 (2016).

gehören Gesellschaften mit beschränkter Haftung, Aktiengesellschaften und andere Unternehmen." Dieser Paragraf ist nicht nur eine einfache technische Regel, sondern vor allem von normativer Bedeutung. Denn dieser Paragraf setzt sich mit dem Wort „wirtschaftlich" auseinander. Eine juristische Person ist auf einen wirtschaftlichen Geschäftsbetrieb gerichtet, wenn sie auf Gewinnerzielung und -ausschüttung gerichtet ist. Die GRCL gelten derzeit für alle wirtschaftlichen juristischen Personen, unabhängig davon, ob es sich um unternehmerische oder nicht-unternehmerische wirtschaftliche juristische Personen handelt.

Juristische Personen sollen nach rechtswissenschaftlich wesentlichen Merkmalen klassifiziert werden. Bei chinesischen juristischen Personen ist es ein grundlegender Unterschied, ob sie auf einen wirtschaftlichen Geschäftsbetrieb gerichtet sind oder nicht. Denn dies ist maßgeblich für den Umfang der Rechts- und Geschäftsfähigkeit einer juristischen Person sowie ihrer Rechte und Pflichten, insbesondere im Steuerrecht.

In den GPCL werden juristische Personen in Unternehmen und Nicht-Unternehmen (einschließlich der staatlichen Organe, Institutionen und sozialen Organisationen) eingeteilt. Dabei sind Unternehmen mit den wirtschaftlichen juristischen Personen, Nicht-Unternehmen mit den nicht wirtschaftlichen juristischen Personen gleichzusetzen. Die Einteilung in den GRCL in wirtschaftliche und nicht wirtschaftliche juristische Personen entspricht im Grundsatz der Klassifikation der GPCL. Der Unterschied besteht jedoch darin, dass der Begriff „unternehmerisch" durch den Begriff „wirtschaftlich" ersetzt wurde. Die neue Terminologie ist nicht nur logischer, sondern auch leichter handhabbar.[19] Das chinesische Gesellschaftsrecht gilt als vergleichsweise ausgereift. Jedoch fehlt es den anderen Typen wirtschaftlicher juristischer Personen (z. B. den nicht in Gesellschaften umgewandelten staatseigenen Unternehmen, den kollektiveigenen Unternehmen, Unternehmen mit ausländischem Kapital und Unternehmen mit Joint-Stock-System) an vergleichbar umfangreichen Regelungen. Mit den allgemeinen Regelungen zu wichtigen Aspekten in den GRCL wurde ein einheitlicher Maßstab für Gerichtsentscheidungen geschaffen und Spielraum für spezielle Gesetzgebung hinsichtlich unternehmerischer, wirtschaftlicher juristischer Personen belassen.

Erwähnenswert sind zudem die Vorschriften über nicht wirtschaftliche juristische Personen in den GRCL. Unter nicht wirtschaftliche juristische

19 *Zhao Xudong*, Durchbruch und Innovation des Klassifikationssystems im Entwurf der GRCL, 14 Chinesischer NPC, S. 18 (2016).

Personen fallen Institutionen, soziale Organisationen, Stiftungen und Anstalten für soziale Dienste.

Nicht wirtschaftliche juristische Personen werden entweder zur Förderung des Gemeinwohls oder zu anderen nicht wirtschaftlichen Zwecken, etwa zum gegenseitigen Nutzen der Mitglieder gegründet. Hintergrund ist in letzterem Fall ein gemeinsames Interesse der Mitglieder, wie z. B. bei Zünften, Gewerkschaften und Alumni-Verbänden.

Was versteht man unter einer nicht wirtschaftlichen juristischen Person? Gemäß § 87 GRCL ist eine nicht wirtschaftliche juristische Person eine juristische Person, die für das Gemeinwohl oder zu anderen nicht wirtschaftlichen Zwecken errichtet wird und keine Profite an Investoren, Gründer oder Mitglieder verteilt. Nach dieser Definition schließt ein wirtschaftlicher Geschäftsbetrieb nicht aus, dass es sich um eine nicht wirtschaftliche juristische Person handelt, sie darf nur ihre Gewinne nicht an ihre Investoren, Gründer oder Mitglieder verteilen. Demgemäß lassen sich nicht wirtschaftliche juristische Person derzeit in zwei Typen unterteilen: Zum einen in juristische Personen für das Gemeinwohl, wie z. B. die China Charity Federation, die Red Cross Society of China, die Environmental Protection Association, Damen- und Kinderorganisationen und alle Arten von Stiftungen; zum anderen in juristische Personen für andere nicht wirtschaftliche Zwecke, wie z. B. die Handelskammer, Zünfte, wissenschaftliche Verbände und Klubs. Dem Gesetzgeber war bei Erlass der §§ 87 ff. GRCL wichtig, mehr nicht wirtschaftliche juristische Personen in das ZGB einzubeziehen.

In den GRCL werden „Spenden-Einrichtungen" als eine neue Form der nicht wirtschaftlichen juristischen Personen definiert.[20]

In den GRCL werden die durch gespendetes Vermögen im Interesse des Gemeinwohls errichteten Stiftungen und Anstalten für soziale Dienste als „Spenden-Einrichtungen" bezeichnet. Darüber hinaus wird zum ersten Mal festgelegt, dass auch die kraft Gesetzes errichteten Organisationen für religiöse Aktivitäten die Befugnisse von Spenden-Einrichtungen erhalten können.

Nach der Definition in § 92 GRCL sind die Spenden-Einrichtungen mit den Stiftungen im Sinne des deutschen Rechts identisch. Es unterscheidet sich lediglich die Bezeichnung. Nach Ansicht der Wissenschaft wurde ein

---

20 § 92 GRCL:
Die durch Spenden errichteten, dem Gemeinwohl dienenden Stiftungen und Anstalten für soziale Dienste, die die Voraussetzungen der juristischen Person erfüllen und kraft Gesetz in das Registerbuch eingetragen worden sind, gelten als Spenden-Einrichtungen.

anderer Begriff aus dem Grund verwendet, dass den meisten chinesischen Bürgern der Begriff „Stiftung“ wenig vertraut sei und dieser daher leicht als eine Form wirtschaftlicher Unternehmen missverstanden werden könne, während der Begriff „Spenden-Einrichtung“ wahrscheinlich auf höhere Akzeptanz stoßen werde.[21] In China fallen unter den Begriff der Spenden-Einrichtung Stiftungen im allgemeinen Sinn, Anstalten für soziale Dienste[22] und Organisationen für religiöse Aktivitäten.

c) Neue Regelungen über spezielle juristische Personen

In China kommt es oft vor, dass Staatsorgane, Dorfkomitees und Nachbarschaftskomitees mit anderen Rechtssubjekten Verträge schließen. Würde ihnen der Status als juristische Person verwehrt, wäre es für sie schwierig, am Rechtsverkehr teilzunehmen. Auch würde die Sicherheit des Rechtsverkehrs darunter leiden. Durch das System der „speziellen juristischen Personen“ wird ihnen der Status einer juristischen Person zuerkannt, damit sie sich am Rechtsverkehr beteiligen und selbstständig Verantwortung übernehmen können. Zum ersten Mal in der chinesischen Gesetzgebung werden in den GRCL Dorf- und Nachbarschaftskomitees als juristische Personen anerkannt. Zum ersten Mal wird auch ländlichen kollektiven ökonomischen Organisationen der Status juristischer Personen zuerkannt. Um dem Umstand Rechnung zu tragen, dass es in den meisten ländlichen Gebieten Chinas keine ländlichen kollektiven ökonomischen Organisationen gibt, wird geregelt, dass die Dorfkomitees die Befugnisse der ländlichen kollektiven ökonomischen Organisationen ausüben. Im Einzelnen gibt es folgende Arten von speziellen juristischen Personen in den GRCL:

(i) Staatliche Organe

Staatliche Organe werden kraft Verfassungsrecht und einschlägiger Rechtsverordnungen eingerichtet, um die Aufgaben der öffentlichen Verwaltung wahrzunehmen. In diesem Punkt unterscheiden sie sich von anderen juristischen Personen.

---

21 *Jiang Ping*, Auseinandersetzung über das System der juristischen Personen, 1998, S. 50; *Liu Kaixiang*, Allgemeiner Teil des ZGB, 2008, S. 178.

22 Gemeint sind private Nicht-Unternehmen.

(ii) Ländliche kollektive ökonomische Organisationen

Die ländlichen kollektiven ökonomischen Organisationen haben eine besondere chinesische Prägung. Gemäß Verfassungs- und Sachenrecht üben sie als Vertreter der Bauern das Eigentumsrecht am kollektiveigenen Land und das Recht auf Selbstbestimmung über den wirtschaftlichen Geschäftsbetrieb aus.

(iii) Selbstverwaltungsorganisationen der Volksbasis

Die Selbstverwaltungsorganisationen der Volksbasis, wie z. B. Dorf- und Nachbarschaftskomitees, unterliegen besonderen Regelungen sowohl hinsichtlich Gründung, Änderung und Auflösung als auch hinsichtlich Haftung und Ausübung von Befugnissen, weshalb es erforderlich ist, sie als spezielle juristische Personen anzuerkennen.

(iv) Wirtschaftliche Genossenschaften in Gemeinden und Dörfern

Die Angebot- und Marketing-Genossenschaften sind etwa im Innenverhältnis zwischen den Mitgliedern von gegenseitigem Nutzen oder von allgemeinem Nutzen. Nach außen tätigen sie wirtschaftliche Geschäfte. Auch sie sind in den GRCL als juristische Personen anerkannt.

IV. Bewertung der Klassifizierung juristischer Personen in den GRCL

1. Bedeutung der neuen Klassifizierung

Die Klassifizierung der juristischen Personen gilt als wichtiges Thema bei der Kodifizierung des ZGB. Es gibt eine Reihe von Klassifikationsmethoden und –maßstäben. Die GRCL beschränken sich jedoch auf die grundlegende Unterscheidung zwischen wirtschaftlichen und nicht wirtschaftlichen juristischen Personen. Derzeit gibt es in fast allen Rechtsordnungen einen Typenzwang in Bezug auf juristische Personen, um ein Gleichgewicht zwischen der Vereinigungsfreiheit der Bürger und dem Interesse des Staates sowie der Gesellschaft zu schaffen. Für jeden Typ einer juristischen Person gelten spezielle Regelungen, insbesondere unterscheiden sich die Rechte und Pflichten der Gründer und der Mitglieder. Die chinesische Gesetzgebung hinsichtlich juristischer Personen gilt es weiter zu verbessern. Reformbedarf besteht insbesondere bei der Kategorisierung von Privatschulen, privaten Krankenhäusern und privaten Altersheimen, die derzeit keiner der Kategorien zweifelsfrei zuordenbar sind. Es ist unvermeidbar, dass die Rechtsposition juristischer Personen und ihrer Mitglieder durch die Entscheidung des Gesetzgebers zugunsten einer bestimmten Klassifizierung sowie durch Anerkennung bzw. Nicht-Anerkennung juristischer Personen beeinflusst werden. Dies ist der Hauptgrund für die heftigen Auseinandersetzungen über die Klassifizierung juristischer Personen.

Eine der wichtigsten Aufgaben des ZGB liegt darin, die Gesellschaft durch die Systematisierung der juristischen Personen zu motivieren und zu organisieren. Durch die Vorschriften über die juristischen Personen wird natürlichen Personen das Recht gewährt, juristische Personen zu errichten, die ebenso wie natürliche Personen als Rechtssubjekte anerkannt werden. Im Vergleich zu einer einzelnen natürlichen Person hat die juristische Person mehr Kraft, um schwierige Aufgaben zu bewältigen, die durch Einzelpersonen nicht zu meistern sind. Eine juristische Person endet zudem nicht per se mit dem Tod des Gründers, sondern kann im Gegenteil eine längere Lebensdauer als eine natürliche Person haben. Hierin zeigt sich die große Bedeutung der juristischen Personen, welche auch dazu beiträgt, dass die Klassifikation als ein umstrittenes Thema bei der Kodifizierung des Zivilrechts gilt. Das System der juristischen Personen bewirkt vor allem, dass die Vereinigungsfreiheit der Bürger, insbesondere hinsichtlich nicht wirtschaftlicher juristischer Personen, umfassend und effektiv gewährleistet wird.[23]

Im Grundsatz reagieren die GRCL auf die dringenden Bedürfnisse im chinesischen Rechtsleben und sie könnten großen Einfluss auf die zukünftige Entwicklung von Gesellschaft und Wirtschaft haben. Eine der positivsten Veränderung ist die umfassende Gewährleistung der Vereinigungsfreiheit der Bürger.

Die nicht wirtschaftlichen juristischen Personen umfassen Vereine und Stiftungen im Sinne traditioneller juristischer Personen. Natürlichen Personen wird so die Möglichkeit gegeben, alle Arten von nicht wirtschaftlichen juristischen Personen zu errichten, um sich entweder für das Gemeinwohl einzusetzen oder um eigene Werte zu verwirklichen. Die natürliche Person

23 *Xie Hongfei*, Rechtsnatur der juristischen Personen im ZGB, 6 Chinesische und Ausländische Rechtswissenschaft, S. 1525 (2015).

kann sich dabei entweder persönlich dem Gemeinwohl widmen oder sich durch die Errichtung einer Spenden-Einrichtung dafür engagieren. Daher haben die GRCL nicht nur dazu beigetragen, die Gesellschaft zu organisieren und zu motivieren, sondern auch dazu, dass die Gesellschaft nicht ausschließlich marktwirtschaftlich bestimmt wird. Es ist absehbar, dass sich durch das Inkrafttreten der GRCL die gesellschaftliche Motivation, Selbstorganisation und Selbstverwaltung weiterentwickeln werden. Ebenfalls dürfte sich die gesellschaftliche Fähigkeit zur Innovation und sozialen Integration erhöhen. Jedoch werden die nicht wirtschaftlichen juristischen Personen in den GRCL nur in den Grundzügen geregelt, weshalb für die Praxis unterstützende spezielle Gesetze und Verordnungen erforderlich sind. Denkbar wäre hierbei eine einheitliche Gesetzgebung bezüglich nicht wirtschaftlicher juristischer Personen.

2. Kritik an der Klassifizierung juristischer Personen in den GRCL

Neben der oben genannten positiven Beurteilung haben die GRCL auch Kritik hervorgerufen.

a) Fehlende Umsetzung des Prinzips der Vereinheitlichung des Zivil- und Handelsrechts

Die gewählte Klassifikationsmethode missachtet die Verzahnung von allgemeinen und speziellen Gesetzen, verwechselt die unterschiedliche Bedeutung von zivilrechtlichen und handelsrechtlichen Subjekten und hält hartnäckig an den alten Regeln der GPCL fest. Dies hat zur Folge, dass die Harmonie innerhalb des Privatrechts, innerhalb der GRCL, sowie innerhalb des Kapitels über juristische Personen gestört und die Wissenschaftlichkeit der GRCL beeinträchtigt wird.

Die Einheit von Zivil- und Handelsrecht gilt sowohl bei der Gesetzgebung als auch in der Wissenschaft traditionell als wichtiges und lohnenswertes Prinzip. Bisher gibt es auch noch keine Tendenzen für ein eigenständiges Handelsgesetzbuch, so dass die Einheit von Zivil- und Handelsrecht als Maxime der Gesetzgebung erhalten bleiben sollte.

Gesetzgebungstechnisch sind der Inhalt der GRCL vor die Klammer gezogene Regelungen. Es sollten in den GRCL nicht die verschiedenen Typen juristischer Personen geregelt werden, sondern die Gemeinsamkeiten der schon bestehenden juristischen Personen. Es stellt sich sodann die Frage, ob das Prinzip der Vereinheitlichung von Zivil- und Handelsrecht allein durch die Unterscheidung zwischen wirtschaftlichen und nicht wirtschaftlichen juristischen Personen ausreichend gewahrt wird. Dies ist zu verneinen. Im Gegenteil verkörpert die Unterscheidung zwischen wirtschaftlichen und nicht wirtschaftlichen juristischen Personen gerade die Trennung zwischen Zivil- und Handelsrecht. Denn nach traditionellen zivilrechtlichen Theorien gilt die juristische Person im Zivilrecht als nicht wirtschaftlich und im Handelsrecht als wirtschaftlich. Auch die Bestimmung des Maßstabs „wirtschaftlich“ bereitet Schwierigkeiten: Der Zweck vieler Privatschulen zum Beispiel kann entweder als wirtschaftlicher oder nicht wirtschaftlicher angesehen werden, deshalb werden sie mitunter verschiedenen Typen juristischer Personen zugeordnet.[24]

Statistiken zufolge gibt es in China derzeit mehr als 150.000 Privatschulen mit Millionen von Schülern und mehr als 12.000 private Krankenhäuser, die fast die Hälfte aller Krankenhäuser landesweit ausmachen. Nach dem Inkrafttreten der GRCL haben die Anteilseigner von Privatschulen und Krankenhäusern folgende Handlungsoptionen: Bei Errichtung einer wirtschaftlichen juristischen Person können erwirtschaftete Profite verteilt werden. Bei Errichtung einer nicht wirtschaftlichen juristischen Person ist dies konsequenterweise nicht möglich. Dieses scheinbar gerechte System ist in der Praxis allerdings schwierig umzusetzen.[25] Es bleibt auch abzuwarten, ob sich die Klassifizierung in wirtschaftliche und nicht wirtschaftliche juristische Personen negativ auf Anstalten für öffentliche Dienste auswirkt.

b) Mangelnde Praktikabilität und wissenschaftliche Defizite der Vorschriften über wirtschaftliche juristische Personen

Gemäß § 73 Abs. 2 GRCL können wirtschaftliche juristische Personen in Gesellschaften mit beschränkter Haftung, Aktiengesellschaften und andere Unternehmen eingeteilt werden. Für viele Unternehmen, mit Ausnahme insbesondere der Eigenbetriebe ohne Rechtspersönlichkeit und der Personengesellschaften, greifen jedoch schon die bestehenden Regelungen für

24 *Li Yongjun*, Systembildung der juristischen Personen aufgrund der Klassifizierung in Vereine und Stiftungen, 5 Academic Journal of the East China University of Political Science and Law, S. 36 (2016).

25 *Xie Hongfei*, Innovation und Einfluss des Systems der juristischen Personen in den GRCL, Economic Information Daily v. 11.4.2017.

Unternehmen, z. B. das Gesellschaftsrecht, das Gesetz über chinesisch-ausländische Aktien-Joint-Ventures, das Gesetz über chinesisch-ausländische kooperative Unternehmen und das Gesetz über ausschließlich in ausländischem Eigentum stehende Unternehmen. Dazu zählen außerdem das Gesetz über staatseigene industrielle Unternehmen, die Verordnung über ländliche kollektiveigene Unternehmen und die Verordnung über private Unternehmen. Die wirtschaftlichen juristischen Personen bzw. die Unternehmen sind also bereits durch spezielle Rechtsverordnungen geregelt. Aufgrund des Vorrangs spezieller Gesetze bleibt kaum Raum für die Anwendung der Regeln über wirtschaftliche juristische Personen in den GRCL. Hinzu kommt, dass die Vorschriften der GRCL über wirtschaftliche juristische Personen die einschlägigen Vorschriften des Gesellschaftsrechts in weitem Umfang lediglich übernehmen. Unter diesen Umständen machen Vorschriften über wirtschaftliche juristische Personen in den GRCL keinen Sinn.

c) Fehlende Differenzierung zwischen juristischen Personen des öffentlichen Rechts und des Privatrechts

Im Kapitel über die nicht wirtschaftlichen juristischen Personen in den GRCL werden diese in staatliche Organe, Institutionen, Spenden-Einrichtungen und soziale Organisationen eingeteilt. Dabei ist bemerkenswert, dass die privaten Nicht-Unternehmen nicht in den GRCL erwähnt werden. Daher wird zu Recht angenommen, dass Institutionen im Sinne der GRCL sowohl öffentliche als auch private Institutionen (also private Nicht-Unternehmen) umfassen. Im Vergleich zu § 2 der vorübergehenden Verordnung über die Eintragung und Verwaltung der Institutionen ist der Begriff der Institution in den GRCL weiter gefasst. Es werden nämlich außer den staatlichen Organen auch die übrigen drei Typen von juristischen Personen sowohl aus dem öffentlichen Recht als auch aus dem Privatrecht umfasst, was zu einer fließenden Grenze zwischen den juristischen Personen des öffentlichen Rechts und des Privatrechts führt. Diese fehlende Differenzierung bewirkt, dass der Begriff der nicht wirtschaftlichen juristischen Person eine chaotische Mischung darstellt. Insbesondere wird durch die Einbeziehung der Organisationen für religiöse Aktivitäten und der sozialen Organisationen die Tatsache kaschiert, dass diese eigentlich durch speziellere Gesetze reguliert werden.[26]

d) Mangelnde Systematik

Die Kategorie der wirtschaftlichen juristischen Personen wurde weniger heftig kritisiert als die der nicht wirtschaftlichen juristischen Personen. Der Gesetzgeber hat diese Kritik berücksichtigt, indem er die Vorgabe getroffen hat, die Reform des Systems sozialer Organisation weiter voranzutreiben, ohne dabei die wirtschaftlichen juristischen Personen zu vernachlässigen.

Im März 2016 wurde das Wohltätigkeitsgesetz erlassen, nach dem es drei Formen von Wohlfahrtsorganisationen (also nicht wirtschaftlichen sozialen Organisationen) gibt: Stiftungen, soziale Gruppen und Anstalten für öffentliche Dienste. Die Wohlfahrtsorganisation ersetzt nun die vorherige Bezeichnung „privates Nicht-Unternehmen“. Im August 2016 hat das Ministerium für Zivile Angelegenheiten die Verordnung über die Eintragung und Verwaltung der Anstalten für öffentliche Dienste und die Verordnung über die Eintragung und Verwaltung der privaten Nicht-Unternehmen (überarbeiteter Entwurf) bekannt gegeben. Gleichzeitig wurden Stellungnahmen zur Reform des Verwaltungssystems von privaten Nicht-Unternehmen und der Förderung der gesunden Entwicklung der sozialen Organisationen durch das Ministerium für Zivile Angelegenheiten angekündigt. Im August wurde eine Verordnung vom Zentralkomitee der Kommunistischen Partei Chinas sowie vom Büro des Staatsrates bekannt gegeben, in der Eintragung und Überprüfung von Wohltätigkeitsorganisationen geregelt sind. So wird etwa für bestimmte Typen von sozialen Organisationen die direkte Eintragung und die vorherige Überprüfung durch die Behörde vorgeschrieben.

Diese Rechtsverordnungen hatten auf jeden Fall einen großen Einfluss auf das Verfahren zum Erlass der GRCL, da die direkte Eintragung und die vorherige Überprüfung durch die Behörde in diesen vorgeschrieben werden. Die Kommunistische Partei sowie das Büro des Staatsrats haben außerdem Leitlinien bekannt gegeben, in denen definiert wurde, wo die Verwaltung der sozialen Organisationen noch zu reformieren ist und für

---

26 *Zhang Gu*, Kontrolle oder Autonomie ist wirklich ein Problem! – Kommentar über das Kapitel der juristischen Personen im Entwurf der GRCL, 4 Rechtswissenschaft der Jiaotong-Universität, S. 68 (2016).

welche Teilbereiche eine Regelung im künftigen ZGB noch nicht infrage kommt. Wird hierdurch die Stabilität und Autorität des ZGB beeinträchtigt? Und ist es sinnvoll, diese Regeln größtenteils in das ZGB aufzunehmen, obwohl sie eigentlich in speziellere Gesetze gehören?

V. Fazit

Die GRCL bringen in vielen Bereichen Innovationen und sind durch unser Zeitalter geprägt. Besonders fördern sie die Vielfalt und Offenheit des Systems privatrechtlicher Subjekte und sie reformieren durchgreifend die Typen juristischer Personen sowie ihre Errichtungsgrundlagen.

Die Einführung der Klassifizierung in wirtschaftliche und nicht wirtschaftliche juristische Personen befriedigt gesellschaftliche und wirtschaftliche Entwicklungsbedürfnisse und deckt erfolgreich den Bedarf nach Typenvielfalt bei juristischen Personen, der durch den Boom von Unternehmen und sozialen Organisationen entstanden ist. Darüber hinaus fungieren die GRCL durch ihre Regeln über wirtschaftliche juristische Personen nicht nur als Allgemeiner Teil des Zivilrechts, sondern auch des Handelsrechts.[27] Die Antwort auf die Forderung nach einer Reform der sozialen Organisation ist: Die GRCL übernehmen von den GPCL die grundlegende Einteilung in Unternehmen und andere juristische Personen für Organisationen mit und ohne Rechtspersönlichkeit. Je nach Errichtungszweck und Befugnissen werden juristische Personen fortan in wirtschaftliche und nicht wirtschaftliche juristische Personen eingeteilt. Gleichzeitig wurden spezielle juristische Personen und Organisationen ohne Rechtspersönlichkeit geschaffen. Die Einteilung in wirtschaftliche und nicht wirtschaftliche juristische Personen steht im Einklang mit der Reform der Institutionen, wodurch die verschiedenen Verwaltungsstrukturen vereinheitlicht werden konnten. Die Einführung der speziellen juristischen Personen befriedigt den Bedarf nach speziellen Formen bestimmter Organisationen unter den derzeitigen politischen und wirtschaftlichen Umständen. Dies wird begünstigen, dass sich die speziellen juristischen Personen in Richtung der normalen juristischen

27 *Wang Yong*, Klassifizierung der juristischen Personen: Kommentar zur Entscheidung der GRCL, 3 Chinesische und Ausländische Rechtswissenschaft, S. 618 (2017).

Personen entwickeln und dass die Rechte und Interessen ihrer Mitglieder besser geschützt werden.[28] Die Selbstverwaltungsorganisationen der Volksbasis, die ländlichen kollektiven ökonomischen Organisationen und die wirtschaftlichen Genossenschaften besitzen nun Rechtspersönlichkeit, was für die Umsetzung der Reform und die Modernisierung der Verwaltungsstrukturen auf Volksebene von erheblicher Bedeutung ist. Die Qualifizierung staatlicher Organe als spezielle juristische Personen legt die Grundlage für die zukünftige Reform ihrer Befugnisse und ihrer Teilnahme am Rechtsverkehr.

Die Kodifizierung des ZGB, insbesondere hinsichtlich der Vorschriften über juristische Personen, gilt als wichtiger Schritt nicht nur zur umfassenden Förderung der Rechtsstaatlichkeit, sondern auch zur Verbesserung des staatlichen Verwaltungssystems und zur Modernisierung der gesellschaftlichen Organisationsfähigkeit. Die GRCL schaffen die Grundlage für die Ausarbeitung des ZGB. Zusammenfassend kann man sagen, dass die Vorschriften über juristische Personen einen Reformerfolg darstellen und eine mögliche rechtsstaatliche Richtung für die weitere Reform deuten. Trotz der geäußerten Kritik und der damit verbundenen Auseinandersetzungen befindet man sich dank der GRCL auf der „Schnellstraße" in Richtung ZGB.

28 *Long Weiqiu*, Suche nach dem Verständnis des neuen Systems juristischer Personen in den GRCL, Vorwort, in: Auslegung der GRCL der Volksrepublik China und Anleitung zur Anwendung, 4. Aufl. 2017.

Neuere Entwicklungen bei der Rechtsfähigkeit wirtschaftlicher Einheiten und bei der „Juristischen Person“

*Michael Kort**

Zusammenfassung: *Die Kategorisierung von Rechtsträgern in natürliche Personen und juristische Personen im deutschen Recht gerät dort an ihre Grenzen, wo der deutsche Gesetzgeber Wirtschaftseinheiten, insbesondere Personen- und Personenhandelsgesellschaften, schon von Gesetzes wegen ermöglicht, (teilweise) selbst Träger von Rechten und Pflichten zu sein. Diese Wirtschaftseinheiten nehmen daher eine Sonderstellung ein. Insgesamt neigt die Rechtsprechung der vergangenen Jahre dazu, diese Wirtschaftseinheiten immer weiter an die juristischen Personen anzunähern und bestehende Unterschiede zu diesen zu beseitigen. So wurde etwa der Außen-GbR vom BGH Rechtsfähigkeit zugesprochen. Ähnliche Annäherungen gibt es im Bereich der Wohnungseigentümergemeinschaft und der Vorgesellschaften. Der nachfolgende Beitrag zeichnet diese Entwicklung nach und beschäftigt sich mit den daraus resultierenden Folgen und rechtlichen Fragen.*

Stichwörter: Juristische Person; Gesamthandsgemeinschaft; Rechtsfähigkeit; Vorgesellschaft; Verbrauchereigenschaft von Wirtschaftseinheiten.

* *Dr. iur. habil.;* Professor, Universität Augsburg, Juristische Fakultät. Lehrstuhl für Bürgerliches Recht, Wirtschaftsrecht, Gewerblichen Rechtsschutz und Arbeitsrecht.

I. Einleitung

Das deutsche Zivilrecht und das deutsche Wirtschaftsrecht unterscheiden bei den „Personen" zwischen den natürlichen Personen und den juristischen Personen. Diese Zweiteilung findet sich im Bürgerlichen Gesetzbuch bereits seit dem Jahr 1900. Charakteristisch für beide Gruppen von Personen (natürliche Personen und juristische Personen) ist deren Rechtsfähigkeit, gemeint als die Fähigkeit, Träger von Rechten und Pflichten sein zu können. Das BGB definiert indessen nicht die Rechtsfähigkeit, sondern setzt sie voraus.[1]

II. Natürliche Person

Die natürliche Person wird in § 1 BGB angesprochen. Demgemäß beginnt die Rechtsfähigkeit des Menschen mit der Vollendung der Geburt. Zugleich macht diese Norm deutlich, dass unter einer natürlichen Person nur ein Mensch zu verstehen ist. Freilich schließt das nicht aus, dass der Gesetzgeber auch anderen Einheiten Rechtsfähigkeit zubilligt. So wäre es möglich,

1 *Mansel*, in: Jauernig, BGB, 16. Aufl. 2015, § 1 Rn. 1.

auch höheren Arten von Tieren oder zumindest Primaten (Teil-) Rechtsfähigkeit zuzuerkennen.[2] Dem stünde die deutsche Verfassung (das Grundgesetz) nicht entgegen.[3] Auch wäre es möglich, bestimmten Teilen künstlicher Intelligenz (KI), etwa lernfähigen (Software-) Agenten oder künstlichen neuronalen Netzen, (Teil-) Rechtsfähigkeit zuzuerkennen.[4] Hierbei handelt es sich freilich um „Zukunftsmusik“, die bislang weder vom deutschen Gesetzgeber noch von der deutschen Rechtsprechung thematisiert worden ist.

III. Juristische Person

Was die juristische Person (des Privatrechts) betrifft, so findet sich weder im BGB noch in anderen zivil- und wirtschaftsrechtlichen Gesetzen eine Definition dafür, was eigentlich darunter zu verstehen ist. Grund für diese Scheu des Gesetzgebers, die juristische Person zu definieren, ist u.a. der in Deutschland bereits im 19. Jahrhundert bestehende Theorienstreit, ob die juristische Person – anders als die natürliche Person – bloße Fiktion ist (Fiktionstheorie) oder es sich um eine „reale“ Verbandspersönlichkeit handelt (Theorie der realen Verbandspersönlichkeit). Zutreffend besteht heute weitgehende Einigkeit, dass dieser Theorienstreit für die praktische Rechtsanwendung unerheblich ist.[5]

Unter der juristischen Person ist im deutschen Zivil- und Wirtschaftsrecht letztlich eine Zusammenfassung von Personen oder Sachen zu einer rechtlich geregelten und zweckgebundenen Organisation, der die Rechtsordnung Rechtsfähigkeit verliehen hat und die dadurch als Träger eigener Rechte und Pflichten verselbständig ist, zu verstehen.[6]

Die systematische Gleichstellung von natürlichen und juristischen Personen am Beginn des BGB zeigt, dass es – wie bei natürlichen Personen – auch bei juristischen Personen um eine vollständige „Rechtsfähigkeit“ der juristischen Person geht: Nach dem BGB ist die juristische Person umfassend Träger von Rechten und Pflichten.

---

2 *Behme*, in: beck-online Großkommentar BGB, Stand 1.12.2017, § 1 Rn. 35.1.

3 *Behme*, in: beck-online Großkommentar BGB, Stand 1.12.2017, § 1 Rn. 36.1.

4 Dazu umfassend *Mayinger*, Die künstliche Person, 2017, S. 166 ff.; ferner *Behme*, in: beck-online Großkommentar BGB, Stand 1.12.2017, § 1 Rn. 37.

5 *Mansel*, in: Jauernig, BGB, 16. Aufl. 2015, vor § 21 Rn. 2.

6 *Schöpflin*, in: Bamberger/Roth, Beck'scher Online-Kommentar BGB, Stand 1.11.2017, § 21 Rn. 1 m.w.N.

IV. Keine deutliche Unterscheidbarkeit der Juristischen Person von anderen, bloß teilrechtsfähigen Einheiten

Indessen beweist die Geschichte des deutschen Zivil- und Wirtschaftsrechts seit 1900, dass die Auffassung, man könne klar zwischen (wirtschaftlichen) Einheiten, denen umfassend Rechtsfähigkeit zukommt und die damit „Juristische Personen" sind, und solchen Einheiten, denen keine Rechtsfähigkeit zukommt und die damit keine juristischen Personen sind, unterscheiden, unzutreffend ist.

Insbesondere zeigt das deutsche Gesellschaftsrecht bereits seit der Konzeption des deutschen Handelsgesetzbuches (HGB), das ebenso alt wie das deutsche BGB ist, dass es in Deutschland – wie in vielen anderen Gesellschaftsrechtsordnungen in Europa und außerhalb von Europa – eine „Grauzone" wirtschaftlicher Einheiten gibt, denen zwar nicht die volle Rechtsfähigkeit zukommt und die deshalb im eigentlichen Sinne der Definition der juristischen Person keine juristischen Personen sind, die aber doch umfassend Träger von Rechten und Pflichten sind.

V. Personenhandelsgesellschaften (OHG; KG) und Juristische Personen (GmbH; AG)

Das gilt in Deutschland insbesondere für die offene Handelsgesellschaft (OHG) und die Kommanditgesellschaft (KG), die gemäß § 124 HGB Träger von Rechten und Pflichten sind.[7] Hiermit zeigte sich bereits früh im deutschen Gesetzesrecht, dass es wirtschaftliche Einheiten gibt, die in annähernd derselben Weise Träger von Rechten und Pflichten sein können wie die juristische Person. Bereits der Blick in § 124 HGB zeigt, dass es in Deutschland gerade keine strikte Zweiteilung in juristische Personen, die umfassend Träger von Rechten und Pflichten sind, und anderen Wirtschaftseinheiten, die nicht umfassend, sondern nur teilweise Träger von Rechten und Pflichten sind, gibt, sondern eine Grauzone bzw. ein Kontinuum.

---

7 Dazu *Roth*, in: Hopt, HGB, 38. Aufl. 2018, § 124 Rn. 1 f.

VI. Haftungsrechtliche Bedeutung der Registereintragung bei Juristischen Personen

Dennoch bestehen gewisse Unterschiede zwischen den in Form der „Gesamthand“ konstituierten, sogenannten Personenhandelsgesellschaften (OHG; KG) und den eigentlichen juristischen Personen im Gesellschaftsrecht (insbesondere GmbH und AG). Die Gesellschaft mit beschränkter Haftung (GmbH) und die Aktiengesellschaft (AG) werden erst durch einen Formalakt, nämlich die Handelsregistereintragung, zur juristischen Person.

Im Gegensatz zu anderen (teil-) rechtsfähigen Wirtschaftseinheiten entstehen juristische Personen des Privatrechts im deutschen Recht nicht schon durch einen privatautonomen Akt, etwa den Abschluss eines Gesellschaftsvertrags zwischen den Gesellschaftern, sondern es bedarf in der Regel zusätzlich eines Formalakts, etwa der Eintragung in das Vereinsregister oder das Handelsregister.

Staatliche Institutionen, die das Vereinsregister bzw. das Handelsregister führen, sind in Deutschland nach dem System der Normativbestimmungen verpflichtet eine Eintragung vorzunehmen, wenn die wirtschaftliche Einheit die rechtlichen „Spielregeln“ für den Erwerb der Rechtsfähigkeit erfüllt hat. Zwar wird die Einhaltung dieser Normativbestimmungen teilweise von staatlicher Stelle – etwa von dem Handelsregistergericht – überprüft, jedoch besteht bei den meisten wirtschaftlichen Einheiten, die juristische Personen werden wollen, kein Ermessensspielraum der öffentlichen Hand (des Registerrichters) bei der Eintragung.

Das früher in Deutschland bestehende Konzessionssystem, nach dem die Eigenschaft als juristische Person von einer staatlichen Verleihung oder einer Genehmigung abhing, die ihrerseits einen Ermessensspielraum der öffentlichen Hand voraussetzte, gibt es in Deutschland – in eingeschränkter Form – nur noch für die sogenannten wirtschaftlichen Vereine, für die Stiftung und für den Versicherungsverein auf Gegenseitigkeit.[8]

Im deutschen Gesellschaftsrecht spielt die Unterscheidung zwischen den juristischen Personen und den sogenannten Gesamthandsgemeinschaften wie der OHG und der KG vor allem haftungsrechtlich eine Rolle,[9] denn anders als die Gesellschafter der Personenhandelsgesellschaft haften die Gesellschafter der juristischen Person, also der GmbH und der AG, so gut wie

8 *Schöpflin*, in: Bamberger/Roth, Beck'scher Online-Kommentar BGB, Stand 1.11.2017, § 21 BGB Rn. 8.

9 Dazu *Koch*, in: Hüffer/Koch, AktG, 12. Aufl. 2016, § 1 Rn. 4.

nie gegenüber den Gläubigern der juristischen Person, also im Außenverhältnis.

VII. Verfassungsrechtlicher Schutz der Juristischen Person und anderer Einheiten

In der deutschen Verfassung (dem Grundgesetz) sind auch juristische Personen (neben natürlichen Personen) in besonderer Weise geschützt. Sie können – insbesondere in ihrem Verhältnis gegenüber dem Staat – Träger von Grundrechten sein, wie Art. 19 Abs. 3 GG deutlich macht. Der in Art. 19 Abs. 3 GG benutzte Begriff der „Juristischen Person" erstreckt sich jedoch, wie eine Auslegung dieses Begriffs deutlich macht, nicht nur auf die eigentlichen juristischen Personen wie die AG und die GmbH, sondern auch auf sonstige Einheiten, die teilweise oder vollständig Träger von Rechten und Pflichten sein können, so etwa auf die OHG und die KG.[10]

VIII. Teilrechtsfähigkeit der Außen-GbR und des nicht eingetragenen Vereins

Die Rechtsprechung in Deutschland ist dadurch gekennzeichnet, dass nicht nur der OHG und der KG als Personenhandelsgesellschaften und damit Gesamthandsgemeinschaften über § 124 HGB hinaus Rechtsfähigkeit nach außen zugebilligt wird und sie damit immer stärker der juristischen Person angenähert werden, sondern auch andere wirtschaftliche Einheiten, bei denen man früher nicht angenommen hat, dass sie ihrerseits (Teil-) Rechtsfähigkeit haben, durch die Rechtsprechung – insbesondere des deutschen Bundesgerichtshofs (BGH) – immer mehr eine (Teil-) Rechtsfähigkeit nach außen zugebilligt worden ist. Das gilt insbesondere für die Gesellschaft bürgerlichen Rechts, soweit sie im Geschäftsverkehr nach außen tätig ist (Außen-GbR) sowie für den nicht im Vereinsregister eingetragenen, also eigentlich nicht rechtsfähigen, Verein.[11]

---

10 *Remmert*, in: Maunz/Dürig, Grundgesetz-Kommentar, 81. EL September 2017, Art. 19 Rn. 37 ff.

11 BGH, Urt. v. 16.1.2001 (Az. XI ZR 113/00), NJW 2001, 1065; dazu *Schöpflin*, in: Bamberger/Roth, Beck'scher Online-Kommentar BGB, Stand 1.11.2017, § 21 BGB Rn. 7; kritisch zum Begriff der Teilrechtsfähigkeit *Wertenbruch*, in: Ebenroth/Boujong/Joost/Strohn, HGB, 3. Aufl. 2014, § 105 Rn. 13.

Insgesamt betrachtet geht die Entwicklung der Rechtsprechung damit immer stärker in die Richtung, diejenigen wirtschaftlichen Einheiten, die keine juristischen Personen sind, der juristischen Person anzunähern, indem sie immer stärker als Träger eigener Rechte und Pflichten angesehen werden.

Allerdings darf man angesichts der Beobachtungen dieses Phänomens nicht vergessen, dass gerade in Hinblick auf die Haftung der in der wirtschaftlichen Einheit verbundenen Personen nach wie vor gewisse Unterschiede zwischen juristischen Personen und anderen wirtschaftlichen Einheiten mit (Teil-) Rechtsfähigkeit bestehen.

IX. Wohnungseigentümergemeinschaft

Eine Tendenz in Hinblick auf die Annäherung solcher wirtschaftlicher Einheiten, denen früher keine (Teil-) Rechtsfähigkeit zugebilligt wurde, an die juristische Person findet sich auch im Recht der Gemeinschaft der Wohnungseigentümer. 2005 hatte der Bundesgerichtshof (BGH) entschieden, dass die Gemeinschaft der Wohnungseigentümer als solche rechtsfähig ist.[12] Während vor dieser Anerkennung der Rechtsfähigkeit der Gemeinschaft der Wohnungseigentümer die einzelnen Wohnungseigentümer gemeinsam verpflichtet waren und gesamtschuldnerisch hafteten, ist seit der BGH-Entscheidung von 2005 Vertragspartner und Haftungsschuldner in gemeinschaftsbezogenen Angelegenheiten die Gemeinschaft der Wohnungseigentümer selbst als rechtsfähiger Verband, dessen Verwaltungsvermögen den Gläubigern haftet.[13]

Einige Zeit nach der Entscheidung des BGH hat der deutsche Gesetzgeber in § 10 Abs. 6 WEG ausdrücklich der Gemeinschaft der Wohnungseigentümer als Verband eine eigene Rechtsfähigkeit zuerkannt und damit die Rechtsprechung in Gesetzesform gegossen.[14]

X. Vorgesellschaft

Eine weitere Entwicklung der Annäherung bislang nicht rechtsfähiger wirtschaftlicher Einheiten an die juristische Person findet sich auch im Recht der GmbH und der AG. Nach § 11 Abs. 1 Satz 1 GmbHG und § 41 Abs. 1

---

12 BGH, Urt. v. 16.1.2001 (Az. XI ZR 113/00), NJW 2001, 2061.

13 *Falkner*, in: beck-online Großkommentar WEG, Stand 1.3.2018, § 10 Rn. 192.

14 *Falkner*, in: beck-online Großkommentar WEG, Stand 1.3.2018, § 10 Rn. 417.

Satz 1 AktG entsteht die GmbH bzw. die AG erst mit dem Formalakt der Eintragung in das Handelsregister als juristische Person. Vor dieser Eintragung besteht die Gesellschaft „als solche“ (also als juristische Person) nicht.

Deshalb und wegen Überlegungen zum Haftungssystem bei der GmbH und der AG wurde früher vertreten, dass die Gemeinschaft der Gründungsgesellschafter vor der Eintragung der GmbH bzw. der AG in das Handelsregister nicht selbständig Träger von Rechten und Pflichten sein könne bzw. jedenfalls nicht in einem Ausmaß Träger von Rechten und Pflichten sein könne, das dem Ausmaß der Rechte und Pflichten der eingetragenen juristischen Person gleichkam.

Dem hat der BGH in einer Entscheidung aus dem Jahr 1981[15] und seitdem in ständiger Rechtsprechung ein neues Konzept entgegengesetzt, nach dem die wirtschaftliche Einheit der (Gründungs-) Gesellschafter im GmbH-Recht sowie im Aktienrecht bereits vor der Eintragung der GmbH und der AG als „Vorstufe“ der eingetragenen juristischen Person anzusehen ist und gleichsam „Embryonalstadium“ der später eingetragenen Gesellschaft ist.

Zwar ist in diesem Zusammenhang in der Regel nur von einer „Teilrechtsfähigkeit“ der Vorgesellschaft – im Gegensatz zur Rechtsfähigkeit der juristischen Person, also der eingetragenen Gesellschaft – die Rede.[16] Berücksichtigt man allerdings, wie weitgehend und in wie vielen Aspekten die Rechtsprechung des BGH in den letzten Jahrzehnten die Vorgesellschaft mit der eingetragenen GmbH bzw. mit der eingetragenen AG gleichgestellt hat, so lassen sich in Hinblick auf den Umfang der Rechte und Pflichten der Vorgesellschaft gegenüber dem Umfang der Rechte und Pflichten der eingetragenen GmbH bzw. AG nur noch wenige Unterschiede ausmachen.

Unterschiede bestehen freilich nach wie vor in Hinblick auf die Haftung der (Gründungs-) Gesellschafter gegenüber der Haftung der Gesellschafter der eingetragenen Gesellschaft, auf die hier nicht näher eingegangen werden kann.

---

15 BGH, Urt. v. 9.3.1981 (Az. II ZR 54/80), BGHZ 80, 129; dazu *Fastrich*, in: Baumbach/Hueck, GmbHG, 21. Aufl. 2017, § 11 Rn. 6.

16 Dazu *C. Jaeger*, in: Ziemons/Jaeger, Beck'scher Online-Kommentar GmbHG, Stand 1.2.2018, § 11 Rn. 16.

XI. Verbrauchereigenschaft wirtschaftlicher Einheiten

Abschließend soll aus der Fülle der Rechtsprechung zur Rechtsstellung von wirtschaftlichen Einheiten noch ein neueres Urteil des BGH vom 30.03.2017[17] genannt werden. Der BGH macht in dieser Entscheidung deutlich, dass eine Gesellschaft bürgerlichen Rechts, deren Gesellschafter eine natürliche Person und eine juristische Person sind, nicht Verbraucher im Sinne des § 13 BGB sein kann, und zwar unabhängig davon, ob die Außen-GbR lediglich zu privaten Zwecken und nicht gewerblich oder selbständig beruflich tätig ist.

Das deutsche Recht grenzt den Verbraucher, auf den im Grundsatz das deutsche Verbraucherschutzrecht Anwendung findet, in § 13 BGB von dem Unternehmer, der gerade kein Verbraucher ist, und in § 14 BGB geregelt ist, ab.

§ 14 Abs. 1 BGB bezeichnet als Unternehmer eine natürliche Person, eine juristische Person oder eine rechtsfähige Personengesellschaft, die bei Abschluss eines Rechtsgeschäfts in Ausübung einer gewerblichen oder selbständigen beruflichen Tätigkeit handelt. § 14 Abs. 2 BGB unternimmt den verunglückten, nämlich in tautologischer Weise erfolgenden Versuch, eine „rechtsfähige Personengesellschaft" zu definieren.

Personengesellschaften, die nicht juristische Personen sind, können zwar, wie sich aus der BGH-Entscheidung vom 30.3.2017 indirekt ergibt, im Grundsatz „Verbraucher" sein; im Gegensatz dazu können juristische Personen nicht „Verbraucher" im Sinne von § 13 BGB sein.

Jedoch kann eine Personengesellschaft nicht Verbraucher sein, wenn ihr eine Person als Gesellschafter angehört, die ihrerseits eine juristische Person ist. Damit kann der Fall eintreten, dass jemand als natürliche Person i. S. des Verbraucherbegriffs des § 13 BGB Gesellschafter einer Außen-GbR wird, die ihrerseits – wegen der Eigenschaft eines ihrer Gesellschafter als juristische Person – nicht dem Verbraucherbegriff unterliegt. Damit unterfällt die natürliche Person (allerdings nur beim Handeln der Außen-GbR, nicht aber bei eigenem Handeln) nicht mehr dem Verbraucherbegriff des § 13 BGB und damit dem Schutz des Verbraucherrechts. Das ist aber, wie der BGH zutreffend deutlich macht, nur Folge der privatautonomen Entscheidung der natürlichen Person, einer solchen Außen-GbR als Gesellschafter anzugehören.

---

17 BGH, Urt. v. 30.3.2017 (Az. VII ZR 269/15), NZG 2017, 696, mit Anm. *Linardatos* = DStR 2017, 1336, mit Anm. *Beck*; dazu *Wied*, GWR 2017, 223; *Pfeiffer*, LMK 2017, 390452.

XII. Fazit

Insgesamt betrachtet zeigt sich, dass die deutsche zivilrechtliche Rechtsprechung sehr stark dazu neigt, wirtschaftliche Einheiten, die ganz oder teilweise Träger von Rechten und Pflichten sind, der juristischen Person anzunähern.

Civil Juristic Acts: History, Comparison and Issues (Summary)

*Yongqiang Chen**

One important aspect of the inheritance and development of the General Rules of Civil Law (GRCL) from the General Principles of Civil Law (GPCL) is the system of civil juristic acts (Chapter 6). According to the new GRCL a civil juristic act means an act performed by a civil subject through expression of intention to initiate, change or terminate civil legal relationship (Art. 133). Chapter 6 is divided into four sections. The first is "General Stipulations", including 4 articles (Article 133 to Article 136). The second is "Declaration of Intent", which includes 6 articles (Article 137 to Article 142). The third and largest part is "Validity of Civil Juristic Acts". This section comprises 15 articles (Article 143 to Article 157). The fourth is "Conditions and Duration of Civil Juristic Acts" (Article 158 to Article 160).

The GRCL have made 14 major changes in this part, especially deleting the requirement of legality, increasing autonomy and equality, distinguishing between declaration of intent and juristic act, clearing the rules for interpreting the intent, and so on.

The second part of the essay makes a comparison between Chinese civil law and German civil law in the field of civil juristic acts. It contains differences in the framework and in the specific system and rules. In the respect of framework, there exist three major differences. As for the specific provisions, there exist 12 distinctions.

The logic, innovation and characteristic of China's civil juristic acts legislation is fully elaborated in the third part of the essay. Firstly, the GRCL retouches the phrase "juristic acts" with "civil" instead of the traditional term of "juristic acts". The word "civil" should differentiate it from other acts in the fields such as criminal acts and administrative acts. Secondly, Chinese law creates "civil acts" as a super-ordinate concept to unify the concept of lawful acts and unlawful acts. Civil juristic acts are defined as lawful acts.

* *Dr.*; Professor, Jiliang University, Faculty of Law. Chair for Civil Law, Philosophy of Law, Anglo American law, and Property Law.

Thus, new questions emerge. Why can a lawful juristic act possibly be invalid? The use of the term of "civil juristic acts" cannot avoid such a contradiction. The paper then discusses the word "invalid". "Invalidity" means that the effect expected by parties does not take place and there is no binding force between parties. Then, how to define the meaning of the word "lawful"? In light of the most generalized concept of "lawful", i.e., violation of laws, illegal juristic acts can possibly become valid. Illegal juristic acts without corresponding capacity could be juristic acts with pending validity and become valid through consent or confirmation.

Since an illegal act can be valid, defining the element of legitimacy as requirement of civil juristic acts will cause a new logical contradiction: why can an illegal juristic act lead to a consequence of a valid civil juristic act? If illegality is limited to compulsory stipulation, only acts not abiding by compulsory stipulations are illegal. However, must juristic acts not abiding by compulsory stipulations be invalid? The answer is still "No".

Nevertheless, the interpretation system constructed by juristic acts and civil juristic acts is still full of contradictions. The GRCL finally abandon the element of legality and the concept of civil acts, but continues to use the term of "civil juristic acts". In the author's opinion, the functions of the word "civil" are not only to distinguish public law and private law, but also to carry the value of fairness of private law. Therefore, Chinese civil law is different from German civil law, which emphasizes the value of autonomy.

The fourth part of the essay elaborates the system of validity of civil juristic acts. There are some unique aspects of the GRCL regarding validity. Firstly, the new civil code stipulates both the valid conditions and the invalid situations of civil juristic acts. The positive provisions of the valid should not be deemed as unnecessary just because the negative provisions of the invalid are provided. That is because the court still needs positive valid conditions to admit the validity of a contract, rather than using the negative invalid conditions. Secondly, the mandatory provisions in the first paragraph of Article 153 GRCL come from Article 52 para. 5 of China's Contract Law (1999). The judicial interpretation of the contract law divides mandatory provisions into mandatory provisions on management and on effectiveness. In violation of the mandatory provisions on management, the contract is not invalid, but the contract is invalid if it violates the mandatory provisions on effectiveness. Thus, the mandatory provisions of Chinese law are wider than the statutory prohibitions of German law.

Whether a provision is mandatory on management or on effectiveness depends on the balance between the legal interests protected by the provisions and protected by the juristic acts. If the interests protected by the provisions should be given a higher evaluation, the juristic acts may be invalid. However, unlike academic studies, the Chinese legal practice usually does not use the balance of legal interests to evaluate whether mandatory provisions affect the validity of contracts. Instead, "public interests" or "public order and good customs" are often used as a standard to judge whether the violation of the mandatory provisions leads to the invalidity of a juristic act. This makes violating mandatory provision meaningless. Therefore, the use of mandatory provisions should according to its purpose and balance of legal interests be an independent ruling. It should not rely on public order and good customs.

In conclusion, the provisions of GRCL on civil juristic acts inherit the traditional term “civil juristic act", and demonstrate the idea of equality of private law. The GRCL remove the requirement of legality and resume the autonomous function of juristic acts. As for mandatory provisions that lead to the invalidity of contracts, the provisions in Chinese civil law are more extensive. On the stage of civil law codification around the world, Chinese law has the defects of being extensive and not elaborate. The advantage however is that the code is more flexible, and easy to evolve along with development of time.

Das „erhebliche Missverständnis" im chinesischen Zivilgesetzbuch

*Tianfan Wang**

Zusammenfassung: *§ 88 Abs. 1 des taiwanesischen Zivilgesetzbuches (TWN-ZGB) wurde nach dem Vorbild des § 119 Abs. 1 BGB geschaffen. In § 88 Abs. 1 Hs. 1 TWN-ZGB folgt auf die Regelung des Inhaltsirrtums der Satz „wenn anzunehmen ist, dass er sie bei Kenntnis der Sachlage und bei verständiger Würdigung des Falles nicht abgegeben haben würde". Die Position dieses Zusatzes im TWN-ZGB und seine wissenschaftliche Auslegung unterscheiden sich jedoch vom deutschen BGB. Dies führt in der Praxis zu Problemen.*

Ein „erhebliches Missverständnis" im chinesischen Zivilrecht ist ein Irrtum des Erklärenden. Der Gesetzgeber der General Principles of Civil Law der Volksrepublik China (GPCL) soll das Wort „Missverständnis" aus dem russischen Recht übernommen haben, ohne dieses jedoch zu definieren, was in der Praxis zu Unstimmigkeiten führt. Grund dafür ist vor allem die Diskrepanz zwischen der Bedeutung des Wortes „Missverständnis" im chinesischen Sprachgebrauch und der theoretischen Bedeutung der Irrtumsanfechtung im traditionellen Zivilrecht. Der Gesetzgeber der seit Oktober 2017 geltenden General Rules of Civil Law der Volksrepublik China (GRCL) hat jedoch die Chance verpasst, einen durch eine Definition konturierten Begriff zu benutzen.

Stichwörter: Irrtumsanfechtung, Erhebliches Missverständnis, Irrtumsbegriff

* *Dr.*; Dozentin, Beihang Universität. Lehrstuhl für Bürgerliches Recht, Handelsrecht und Rechtvergleichung.

I. Einleitung

„Erhebliches Missverständnis“ bedeutet im chinesischen Zivilrecht nach h. M. einen Irrtum des Erklärenden.[1] Das Gesetz definiert diesen Begriff jedoch nicht. Dies bereitet rechtliche Schwierigkeiten. Das Problem ist mangels aussagekräftiger wissenschaftlicher Untersuchungen immer noch nicht ganz gelöst, weshalb die Praxis in dieser Frage keine Unterstützung durch die Wissenschaft erfährt. Aus diesem Grund sind ausländische Erfahrungen wichtige Referenzen für den Gesetzgeber und die Justiz bei der Diskussion der Irrtumsanfechtung im Hinblick auf das chinesische Zivilgesetzbuch (ZGB). Doch bei der Anlehnung an das ausländische Recht ist Vorsicht geboten, da diese zu noch größeren Problemen führen kann. Die vorliegende Arbeit geht von den Regelungen über das erhebliche Missverständnis in den GPCL und den versuchsweise durchgeführten Ansichten des Obersten Volksgerichtshofs der Volksrepublik China zu einigen Fragen der Anwendung der *General Principles of Civil Law*[2] (OVG-Ansichten GPCL) aus, um die mögliche Anlehnung an ausländisches Recht im chinesischen Gesetzgebungsprozess zu untersuchen. Die Prüfung einer Anlehnung an

1 *Wang Liming* u. a., Bürgerliches Recht («民法»), 6. Aufl. 2015, S. 114.

2 最高人民法院关于贯彻执行«中华人民共和国民法通则»若干问题的意见（试行）.

ausländisches Recht wird am Beispiel des TWN-ZGB vorgenommen. Schließlich werden die chinesischen Regelungen analysiert.

II. Irrtumsanfechtung im TWN-ZGB

1. Geschichte der Gesetzgebung und Rechtsübernahme

§ 88 Abs. 1 TWN-ZGB wurde nach dem Vorbild des deutschen § 119 Abs. 1 BGB geschaffen.

> **§ 88 Abs. 1 Zivilgesetzbuch der Republik China (1930)**
>
> Wer bei der Abgabe einer Willenserklärung über deren Inhalt im Irrtum war oder wenn anzunehmen ist, dass er sie bei Kenntnis der Sachlage und bei verständiger Würdigung des Falles nicht abgegeben haben würde, kann die Erklärung anfechten, vorausgesetzt, dass der Erklärende für den Irrtum oder die Unkenntnis nicht schuldig ist.

Aus der Gesetzgebungsgeschichte ist bekannt, dass das TWN-ZGB das von 1929–1931 erlassene Zivilgesetzbuch der Republik China ist, dessen Hauptquelle der Entwurf des Zivilgesetzes der Qing-Dynastie war.[3] Dieser Entwurf umfasste fünf Abschnitte.[4] §§ 181–184 regelten die „Anfechtbarkeit wegen Irrtums“.[5]

> **§ 181 Entwurf des Zivilgesetzes der Qing-Dynastie**
>
> Wer bei der Abgabe einer Willenserklärung über deren Inhalt im Irrtum war oder eine Erklärung dieses Inhalts überhaupt nicht abgeben wollte, kann die Erklärung anfechten, wenn anzunehmen ist, dass er sie bei Kenntnis der Sachlage und bei verständiger Würdigung des Falles nicht abgegeben haben würde.
>
> Als Irrtum über den Inhalt der Erklärung gilt auch der Irrtum über solche Eigenschaften der Person oder der Sache, die als wesentlich angesehen werden.[6]

---

3 *Pan Weihe*, Geschichte des modernen chinesischen Zivilgesetzes («中国近代民法史»), 1982, S. 118.

4 *Pan Weihe*, Korrektur und Interpretation von Chinas vergangenem Zivilgesetzentwurf («中国历次民律草案校释»), 1982, Inhaltsübersicht.

5 *Pan Weihe*, Korrektur und Interpretation von Chinas vergangenem Zivilgesetzentwurf («中国历次民律草案校释»),1982, S. 177 f.

6 § 182
Der vorstehende Artikel gilt auch für eine Willenserklärung, welche durch die zur Übermittlung verwendete Person unrichtig übermittelt worden ist.

Diese Regelungen scheinen eine wörtliche Übernahme der §§ 119 ff. BGB zu sein. Das ist, auch aus heutiger Sicht, ein gewagter Schritt. Der Grund hierfür könnte der Berater des Gesetzgebers, Matsuoka Yoshimasa,[7] gewesen sein, der auch ein wichtiger Verfasser des Allgemeinen Teils und des Vermögensrechts in besagtem Entwurf war. Er empfahl dem Gesetzgeber der Qing-Dynastie, zahlreiche Regelungen aus dem deutschen BGB zu übernehmen, das seiner Ansicht nach ein Vorbild für ein chinesisches Zivilgesetzbuch war. Deswegen war der Entwurf des Zivilgesetzes der Qing-Dynastie dem BGB ähnlicher als dem japanischen Zivilgesetzbuch. Aufgrund des Sturzes der Qing-Dynastie im Jahre 1911 trat der Entwurf nicht in Kraft. Trotzdem ist es der erste Versuch einer Gesetzgebung in der Geschichte des chinesischen Zivilrechts.

Im Entwurf des Zivilgesetzes der Republik China, der von 1925–1926 erarbeitet wurde und geschichtlich der zweite Entwurf ist,[8] ist der Irrtum in

---

§ 183
Die Anfechtung muss in den Fällen der §§ 181, 182 unverzüglich erfolgen, nachdem der Anfechtungsberechtigte von dem Anfechtungsgrund Kenntnis erlangt hat. Die Anfechtung ist ausgeschlossen, wenn seit der Abgabe der Willenserklärung zwei Jahre verstrichen sind.
§ 184
Ist eine Willenserklärung nach § 179 nichtig oder auf Grund der §§ 181, 182 angefochten, so hat der Erklärende, einem anderen oder dem Dritten den Schaden zu ersetzen, den der andere oder der Dritte dadurch erleidet, dass er auf die Gültigkeit der Erklärung vertraut. Die Schadensersatzpflicht tritt nicht ein, wenn der Beschädigte den Grund der Nichtigkeit oder der Anfechtbarkeit kannte oder infolge von Fahrlässigkeit nicht kannte (kennen musste).

7 Die Hintergründe der Beauftragung von Matsuoka Yoshimasa für den Entwurf des Allgemeinen Teils und des Eigentumsrechts ergeben sich aus der Gesetzessammlung der Qing-Dynastie («大清法规大全»), Bd. 1, 1911, welche auf S. 11 folgenden Abschnitt enthält: „1. Konzentrieren wir uns auf das weltweit am meisten verbreitete Gesetz. Die Kommunikationen über das Meer sind heutzutage sehr häufig. [...] Wenn wir einer Klage begegnen, folgt der Andere den verbreiteten Regeln, und wir den alten. Die Diskrepanz dazwischen ist absolut riesig. […] Wir sollten die kommenden Regeln adaptieren, um beiderseitige Interessen auszubalancieren und Gerechtigkeit widerfahren zu lassen. 2. Wissenschaften sind universell, nicht nur für eine bestimmte Nation. Die Regelungen über juristische Personen und das Recht der Schuldverhältnisse (des japanischen Zivilgesetzbuches) wurden von allen Ländern angenommen, da sie sehr präzise sind. Deshalb sind diese Regelungen natürlich für uns nutzbar".

8 *Pan Weihe*, Korrektur und Interpretation von Chinas vergangenem Zivilgesetzentwurf («中国历次民律草案校释»), 1982, S. 363 f.

§§ 117–120 im Abschnitt 3 des Allgemeinen Teils „Rechtsgeschäfte“ geregelt.[9] Die Regelungen über die Irrtumsanfechtung sind nahezu identisch mit denen des Entwurfs des Zivilgesetzes der Qing-Dynastie.[10] Jedoch hat der Gesetzgeber in § 117 den Zusatz „wenn anzunehmen ist, dass er sie bei Kenntnis der Sachlage […] nicht abgegeben haben würde“ nicht mehr als Kriterium der Erheblichkeit des Irrtums bestimmt, wie dies im deutschen BGB oder im Entwurf des Zivilgesetzes der Qing-Dynastie der Fall ist, sondern als eine besondere Art des Irrtums. Auch dieser Entwurf trat jedoch nicht in Kraft.

§ 117 Entwurf des Zivilgesetzes der Republik China (1925)

Wer bei der Abgabe einer Willenserklärung über deren Inhalt im Irrtum war, kann die Erklärung anfechten. Als Irrtum über den Inhalt der Erklärung gilt auch der Irrtum über solche Eigenschaften der Person oder der Sache, die im Verkehr als wesentlich angesehen werden.

Der vorstehende Absatz gilt auch wenn anzunehmen ist, dass er sie bei Kenntnis der Sachlage und bei verständiger Würdigung des Falles nicht abgegeben haben würde.

Während der Zeit der Nanjinger Nationalen Regierung erließ der Legislativ-Yuan das Zivilgesetzbuch der Republik China von 1930, das in Taiwan bis

---

9 § 119
Die Anfechtung muss in den Fällen der §§ 117, 118 unverzüglich erfolgen, nachdem der Anfechtungsberechtigte von dem Anfechtungsgrund Kenntnis erlangt hat. Die Anfechtung ist ausgeschlossen, wenn seit der Abgabe der Willenserklärung drei Jahre verstrichen sind.
§ 120
Ist eine Willenserklärung nach § 115 nichtig oder auf Grund der §§ 117, 118 angefochten, so hat der Erklärende, einem anderen oder dem Dritten den Schaden zu ersetzen, den der andere oder der Dritte dadurch erleidet, dass er auf die Gültigkeit der Erklärung vertraut. Die Schadensersatzpflicht tritt nicht ein, wenn der Beschädigte den Grund der Nichtigkeit oder der Anfechtbarkeit kannte oder infolge von Fahrlässigkeit nicht kannte (kennen musste).
Pan Weihe, Korrektur und Interpretation von Chinas vergangenem Zivilgesetzentwurf («中国历次民律草案校释»), 1982, S. 378f.

10 Tatsächlich wollte der Gesetzgeber damals für den Entwurf des Zivilgesetzes der Qing-Dynastie eine größere Revision einleiten und Zivilgewohnheiten untersuchen. Aufgrund der Washingtoner Konferenz drängte die damalige chinesische Regierung jedoch auf Wiederherstellung der Konsulargerichtsbarkeit. Die Konferenz beschloss, Truppen aus allen Ländern nach China zu schicken, um die Justiz zu untersuchen. Daher erfolgte diese Gesetzgebungsarbeit "eilig". Zur weiteren Information: *Huang Yuansheng*, Gesetzlicher Wandel und Rechtsprechung in der frühen Republik China («民初法律变迁与裁判»), 2000, S. 381.

heute noch gültig ist.[11] Die Irrtumsregelungen in diesem Gesetzbuch sind in §§ 88–91 enthalten[12] und ähneln den Regelungen der §§ 119–122 BGB stark. Die oben genannten Änderungen durch den ersten Entwurf von 1925 blieben jedoch erhalten.

Aus der Geschichte der Gesetzgebung kann gefolgert werden, dass das BGB die Regelungen über die Irrtumsanfechtung in jedem chinesischen zivilrechtlichen Gesetzesentwurf einschließlich des Zivilgesetzbuchs der Republik China von 1930 stark beeinflusst hat. Trotzdem unterscheiden sich die Irrtumsregelungen des BGB von denen des heutigen TWN-ZGB in zweierlei Hinsicht. Zum einen begründet der Gesetzgeber durch den Zusatz in § 88 Abs. 1 TWN-ZGB „wenn anzunehmen ist, dass er sie bei Kenntnis der Sachlage und bei verständiger Würdigung des Falles nicht abgegeben haben würde" eine weitere Art des Irrtums neben dem Inhaltsirrtum. Zum anderen ist Voraussetzung für die Anfechtung, dass den Erklärenden kein Verschulden trifft. An dieser Stelle soll nur der erste Aspekt thematisiert

---

11 Taiwanesische Abteilung für Justizverwaltung, Zusammenstellung der historischen Dokumente der Gesetzgebung des Zivilgesetzes der Republik China («中华民国民法制定史料汇编»), 1976.

12 § 88
Wer bei der Abgabe einer Willenserklärung über deren Inhalt im Irrtum war oder wenn anzunehmen ist, dass er sie bei Kenntnis der Sachlage und bei verständiger Würdigung des Falles nicht abgegeben haben würde, kann die Erklärung anfechten. Vorausgesetzt ist, dass der Erklärende für den Irrtum oder die Unkenntnis nicht schuldig ist. Als Irrtum über den Inhalt der Erklärung gilt auch der Irrtum über solche Eigenschaften der Person oder der Sache, die im Verkehr als wesentlich angesehen werden.
§ 89
Eine Willenserklärung, welche durch die zur Übermittlung verwendete Person oder Einrichtung unrichtig übermittelt worden ist, kann unter der gleichen Voraussetzung angefochten werden wie nach § 88 eine irrtümlich abgegebene Willenserklärung.
§ 90
Die Anfechtung in den Fällen der §§ 88, 89 ist ausgeschlossen, wenn seit der Abgabe der Willenserklärung ein Jahr verstrichen ist.
§ 91
Ist eine Willenserklärung auf Grund der §§ 88, 89 angefochten, so hat der Erklärende, wenn die Erklärung einem anderen gegenüber abzugeben war, diesem, andernfalls jedem Dritten den Schaden zu ersetzen, den der andere oder der Dritte dadurch erleidet, dass er auf die Gültigkeit der Erklärung vertraut. Die Schadensersatzpflicht tritt nicht ein, wenn der Beschädigte den Grund der Nichtigkeit oder der Anfechtbarkeit kannte oder infolge von Fahrlässigkeit nicht kannte (kennen musste).

werden: Ist die Abänderung gegenüber der deutschen Regelung unbeabsichtigt? Fügt sie sich in das System anderer zivilrechtlicher Regelungen ein? Führt sie zu Schwierigkeiten in der Praxis?

2. Das Merkmal „wenn anzunehmen ist, dass er sie bei Kenntnis der Sachlage […] nicht abgegeben haben würde" im TWN-ZGB

a) Lehre und Rechtsprechung

In § 88 Abs. 1 Hs. 1 TWN-ZGB folgen nach dem Inhaltsirrtum die Worte „oder wenn anzunehmen ist, dass er sie bei Kenntnis der Sachlage und bei verständiger Würdigung des Falles nicht abgegeben haben würde". Voraussetzung für die Anfechtung ist nach § 88 Abs. 1 Hs. 2 TWN-ZGB zudem, dass „der Erklärende für den Irrtum oder die Unkenntnis nicht schuldig ist". Legt man die Norm systematisch aus, so scheint es dass die „Unkenntnis" mit den Worten „wenn anzunehmen ist, dass […] nicht abgegeben haben würde" gleichzusetzen ist. Interessanterweise gibt es im Entwurf des Zivilgesetzes der Qing-Dynastie keine solche Überschneidung. Denn dort wurden die Regelungen der §§ 119 ff. BGB übersetzt und übernommen. Im Entwurf des Zivilgesetzes der Republik China von 1925 wurden die Regelungen jedoch überraschend geändert und in § 117 S. 3 Folgendes hinzugefügt: *„Der vorstehende Absatz gilt auch wenn anzunehmen ist, dass er sie bei Kenntnis der Sachlage und bei verständiger Würdigung des Falles nicht abgegeben haben würde."* Das bedeutet, dass durch den Satz „wenn anzunehmen ist, dass […] nicht abgegeben haben würde" eine eigenständige Anfechtungsgrundlage neben Inhaltsirrtum und Eigenschaftsirrtum begründet wird. Die Gründe für diese Änderung sind heutzutage nicht mehr rekonstruierbar. Dennoch ist der Satz noch kodifiziert. Was ist seine genaue Bedeutung?

Ein großer Teil des taiwanesischen Schrifttums hält den Satz „wenn anzunehmen ist, dass […] nicht abgegeben haben würde" für eine Beschreibung des Erklärungsirrtums und damit den Fall, dass „der Erklärende fehlerhaft erklärt, was er nicht will“[13] oder dass „der Erklärende eine nicht gewollte Art und Weise der Erklärung benutzt hat“.[14] Eine andere Ansicht geht davon aus, dass dieser Satz nicht den Erklärungsirrtum, sondern eine zusätzliche Irrtumsart, die „Unkenntnis“, darstellt; mithin den Fall, dass der Erklärende „keinerlei Vorstellung vom Inhalt seiner Erklärung“[15] hat. Wieder andere Autoren sind zwar der Ansicht, dass der Satz „wenn anzunehmen ist, dass […] nicht abgegeben haben würde“ den Fall der „Unkenntnis“[16] bzw. das „Fehlen des subjektiven Geschäftswillens“[17] meint, diese verwenden bei der Erläuterung aber Beispiele wie das Sichverschreiben oder das Sichversprechen.

Die Ansicht der Rechtsprechung ist ebenfalls unklar. Der Oberste Gerichtshof Taiwans war in der Entscheidung 59 Tai-Oberst 3080[18] der Meinung, dass der Satz „wenn anzunehmen ist, dass […] nicht abgegeben haben würde“ das Fehlen des Geschäftswillens meint. Jedoch verstand das Gericht in der Entscheidung 60 Tai-Oberst 1108[19] diesen Satz als „Unkenntnis“. In der Entscheidung 81 Tai-Oberst 322 vertrat das Gericht schließlich die Ansicht, dass mit diesem Satz der Erklärungsirrtum gemeint sei: „Der Erklärende kennt die objektive Bedeutung seiner Erklärung, benutzt jedoch ein

---

13 *Wu Xueyi*, Allgemeiner Teil des chinesischen Zivilrechts («中国民法总论»), 1934, S. 402.

14 *Wang Zejian*, Allgemeiner Teil des Zivilrechts («民法总论»), 2014, S. 414 ff.

15 *Hu Changqing*, Allgemeiner Teil des chinesischen Zivilrechts («中国民法总论»), 1997, S. 241.

16 *Zheng Yubo*, Allgemeiner Teil des Zivilrechts («民法总则»), 2003, S. 343.

17 *Shi Qiyang*, Allgemeiner Teil des Zivilrechts («民法总则»), 1983, S. 252.

18 Der Satz „wenn anzunehmen ist, dass er sie bei Kenntnis der Sachlage und bei verständiger Würdigung des Falles nicht abgegeben haben würde“ in § 88 Abs. 1 TWN-ZGB bedeutet, dass der Erklärende hinsichtlich der Erklärung keine Kenntnis hat. Der Erklärende hat objektiv gehandelt, was nach normativer Auslegung von Dritten als Willenserklärung verstanden werden könnte. Dem Erklärenden fehlt jedoch der Geschäftswille. Er weiß nicht, dass seine Handlung eine Willenserklärung konstituiert. (59年台上字第3080号判决, 1970.9.18).

19 In dem Urteil wollte der Berufungskläger wegen Unkenntnis von Landnutzungskategorien anfechten. Die Landesregierung muss angemeldete Landnutzungskategorien jedoch veröffentlichen. Deshalb kann man sich diesbezüglich nicht gemäß § 88 Abs. 1 TWN-ZGB (Fn. 12) auf Unkenntnis berufen. Bei Unkenntnis der Landnutzungskategorien liegt Fahrlässigkeit vor, weshalb der Berufungskläger die Erklärung nicht nach § 88 Abs. 1 TWN-ZGB anfechten konnte. (60年台上字第1108号判决,1971.3.26).

falsches Mittel. Das falsche Erklärungsmittel verursacht die Abweichung vom Geschäftswillen."[20] Die theoretische Uneinigkeit verstärkt sich mit der Entscheidung 83 Tai-Oberst 2960,[21] in der das Gericht den Satz gleichzeitig in zwei verschiedenen Hinsichten versteht, nämlich zum einen als Erklärungsirrtum und zum anderen als Erfordernis der Anfechtbarkeit bei der „Unkenntnis" als eigene Art eines beachtlichen Irrtums.

b) Diskussion: Eine eigene Art des Irrtums oder ein Maßstab für die Erheblichkeit des Irrtums?

Geht man zum deutschen BGB zurück, ist es klar, dass die Worte „wenn anzunehmen ist, dass er sie bei Kenntnis der Sachlage […] nicht abgegeben haben würde" keine eigene Art des Irrtums darstellen, sondern das Erfordernis der Erheblichkeit des Irrtums betreffen.[22] Diese Bedingung umfasst eine subjektive und eine objektive Komponente. In subjektiver Hinsicht ist erforderlich, dass der Erklärende bei Kenntnis der Sachlage die Erklärung nicht abgegeben haben würde. Objektiv verlangt die Erheblichkeit als normativer Maßstab die „verständige Würdigung des Falles" durch eine „vernünftige Person".

Die gegenwärtigen taiwanesischen Regelungen werfen jedoch noch einige Fragen auf. In welchem Verhältnis stehen die „Unkenntnis" und der Erklärungsirrtum? Nach Ansicht der Rechtsprechung und eines Teils des Schrifttums gibt es zwischen den beiden Begriffen keinen Unterschied. Sie

---

20 81年台上322号判决,1992.2.24.

21 Das Urteil betont die konzeptionelle Verschiedenheit von Irrtum und Unkenntnis. „Unkenntnis" bedeutet, dass der Erklärende keine Vorstellung vom Inhalt der Erklärung hat, während ein Irrtum nicht nur keine Vorstellung, sondern eine positive Fehlvorstellung voraussetzt. Die Erklärung ist bei Unkenntnis jedoch anfechtbar wie bei einem Irrtum, was aus dem Zusatz in § 88 Abs. 1 Hs. 1 TWN-ZGB folgt: „wenn anzunehmen ist, dass er sie bei Kenntnis der Sachlage und bei verständiger Würdigung des Falles nicht abgegeben haben würde". § 88 Abs. 1 Hs. 1 Alt. 1 TWN-ZGB regelt den Inhaltsirrtum, § 88 Abs. 1 Hs. 1 Alt. 2 TWN-ZGB den Erklärungsirrtum. Der Berufungsbeklagte in diesem Urteil unterlag bei seiner Willenserklärung einem Inhaltsirrtum nach § 88 Abs. 1 Hs. 1 Alt. 1 TWN-ZGB. (83年台上字第2960号判决,1994.11.23).

22 *Armbrüster*, in: MünchKomm BGB, 7. Aufl. 2015, § 119 Rn. 137; *Flume,* Allgemeiner Teil des BGB, Bd. 2, 4. Aufl. 1992, § 21/3, S. 419; *Larenz/Wolf,* Allgemeiner Teil des BGB, 9. Aufl. 2004, §36 Rn. 32; *Medicus,* Allgemeiner Teil des BGB, 10. Aufl. 2010, Rn. 746.

sollen bedeuten, dass „der Erklärende keinerlei Vorstellungen über die Erklärung hat".[23] Nach anderer Ansicht sind Sichverschreiben oder Sichversprechen gerade keine Fälle der „Unkenntnis", weshalb diese vom typischen Erklärungsirrtum zu unterscheiden sei.[24] Beide Ansichten gehen davon aus, dass die Rechtsfolge der „Unkenntnis" wie bei einem Inhaltsirrtum die Anfechtbarkeit der Erklärung ist. In der Entscheidung 83 Tai-Oberst 2960 vertritt der Oberste Gerichtshof Taiwans die Meinung, dass der Erklärende im Falle der „Unkenntnis" keinerlei Vorstellung vom Inhalt der Erklärung habe, während ein Irrtum eine positive Fehlvorstellung voraussetze. Jedoch soll nach Ansicht des Gerichts in beiden Fälle dieselbe Rechtsfolge, nämlich die Anfechtbarkeit, greifen.[25]

Wenn man sich über den Inhalt seiner Erklärung keine konkrete Vorstellung macht, gibt es nach der herrschenden Lehre zum BGB keine Diskrepanz zwischen Erklärtem und Gewolltem. Daher ist die „Unkenntnis" im deutschen Recht eben kein Erklärungsirrtum, bei ihr scheidet eine Anfechtung generell aus.

Ist es möglich, den Satz „wenn anzunehmen ist, dass [...] nicht abgegeben haben würde" als Erklärungsirrtum zu verstehen, obwohl die grammatikalische Auslegung ein solches Verständnis nicht trägt? Damit eröffnet sich noch ein anderes Problem: Die Erheblichkeit des Irrtums ist nach § 88 Abs. 1 TWN-ZGB dann keine Voraussetzung für eine Anfechtung. Ist diese Voraussetzung überhaupt notwendig? Dabei muss die aktuelle Funktion der Voraussetzung der Erheblichkeit berücksichtigt werden. In der deutschen Rechtsprechung wird die Irrtumsanfechtung häufig mithilfe des Merkmals der Erheblichkeit eingeschränkt. Die Ermittlung der subjektiven Umstände beim Irrenden ist dabei jedoch oft schwierig. Deshalb ist der normative Maßstab bedeutsam. Nach diesem ist eine Anfechtung ausgeschlossen, wenn die Erklärung „auf subjektivem Eigensinn oder törichten Anschauungen beruht"[26], der Irrtum

23 *Zheng Yubo,* Allgemeiner Teil des Zivilrechts («民法总则»), 2003, S. 343; die Unkenntnis als fehlendes Erklärungsbewusstsein, qualifizierend *Shi Qiyang,* Allgemeiner Teil des Zivilrechts («民法总则»), 1983, S. 252.

24 *Hu Changqing,* Allgemeiner Teil des chinesischen Zivilrechts («中国民法总论»), 1997, S. 241.

25 Das Gericht ordnet die Unkenntnis als Inhaltsirrtum ein. (83年台上字第2960号判决,1994.11.23).

26 *Larenz/Wolf,* Allgemeiner Teil des Bürgerlichen Rechts, 9. Aufl. 2004, §36 Rn. 32.

„geringfügig" [27] ist, den Erklärenden „wirtschaftlich nicht schlechter stellt" [28] oder wenn bei wirtschaftlicher Betrachtung nur eine minimale Abweichung zwischen Wille und Erklärung gegeben ist, etwa wenn ein Preisunterschied von nur wenigen Cent bei einem Geschäft über mehrere hundert Euro vorliegt. [29] Manche Autoren sind der Meinung, dass das Erfordernis der Erheblichkeit die Verkehrssicherheit gefährde, da es die Relevanz des Erklärungsirrtums im Anschluss an Savigny lediglich am Rande einschränkt.[30] Bemerkenswert ist, dass diese Kritik die Schwelle des Erfordernisses erhöhen möchte, um den Umfang der Anfechtung einzuschränken.

Obwohl es im TWN-ZGB keine entsprechende Vorschrift gibt, wendet der Oberste Gerichtshof Taiwans, gestützt auf den Grundsatz von Treu und Glauben, einen solchen Maßstab[31] an.[32] In der Entscheidung *79 Tai-Oberst 2348*[33] heißt es, dass die Anfechtung „nach Treu und Glauben" ausgeschlossen ist, auch wenn „die tatsächliche Fläche des Landrechts 19.922 m^2 ist und zwischen ihr und der Geeigneten (20.049 m^2) eine Diskrepanz von 0.127 m^2 besteht"[34]. Das Prinzip von Treu und Glauben zu bemühen, ist für die Gerichte eine praktische Lösung. Ob es auch eine gute Lösung ist, ist aber noch umstritten.

27 *Larenz/Wolf*, Allgemeiner Teil des Bürgerlichen Rechts, 9. Aufl. 2004, §36 Rn. 32.

28 *Wolf/Neuner*, Allgemeiner Teil des BGB, 10. Aufl. 2012, § 41 Rn. 33.

29 *Faust,* Bürgerliches Gesetzbuch Allgemeiner Teil, 4. Aufl. 2014, § 21 Rn. 6; *Armbrüster*, in: MünchKomm BGB, 7. Aufl. 2015, § 119 Rn. 137.

30 *Kramer,* in: MünchKomm BGB, 5. Aufl. 2006, § 119 Rn. 7.

31 In 83 Tai-Oberst 2960 (83年台上字第2960号判决, 1994.11.23) wird die Formulierung „wenn anzunehmen ist, dass er sie bei Kenntnis der Sachlage und bei verständiger Würdigung des Falles nicht abgegeben haben würde" als subjektive Komponente der Erheblichkeit der Unkenntnis verstanden.

32 *Chen Ziqiang*, Grundproblem des Irrtums («意思表示错误之基本问题»), 52 Chengchi Law Review, S. 311 ff. (1994).

33 In diesem Fall wird die Diskrepanz für die Messung von Land zwischen subjektiv Gewolltem und objektiv Erklärtem unter dem Gesichtspunkt der Sachmängelhaftung diskutiert.

34 79年台上字第2348号判决, 1990.

III. Das „erhebliche Missverständnis" im chinesischen Zivilrecht

1. Ursprung des „erheblichen Missverständnisses" und Rechtstransplantation

Nach h. M. ist das „erhebliche Missverständnis" in § 59 Abs. 1 S. 1 GPCL genauso zu handhaben wie die Irrtumsanfechtung.

> **§ 59 GPCL**
>
> Bei den folgenden Zivilhandlungen hat eine Seite das Recht, beim Volksgericht oder beim Schiedsorgan die Änderung oder Aufhebung zu verlangen:
>
> 1. wenn der Handelnde in Bezug auf den Inhalt der Handlung einem **erheblichen Missverständnis** unterlag;
>
> 2. wenn sie deutlich ungerecht sind.
>
> Aufgehobene Zivilhandlungen sind vom Beginn der Handlung an unwirksam.

Weshalb wählt der Gesetzgeber das Wort „Missverständnis" (误解) anstelle des Wortes „Irrtum" (错误)? Diese Frage muss historisch untersucht werden. Bislang gibt es kein eindeutiges Material hierzu. In wichtigen historischen Referenzmaterialien über den Hintergrund der Gesetzgebung der GPCL wird jedoch erwähnt, dass man sich während des Ausarbeitungsprozesses der GPCL an vielen einflussreichen ausländischen Zivilgesetzbüchern, wie etwa dem französischen *Code Civil,* dem japanischen und dem sowjetischen Zivilgesetzbuch, orientierte.[35] Bei genauerer Betrachtung der damaligen Übersetzungen dieser Zivilgesetzbücher bemerkt man, dass im

35 Oberstes Volksgericht Gruppenkurse, Vorlesungen zu den GPCL («民法通则讲座»), 1986, S. 9.

Falle des BGB, des französischen *Code Civil,* des japanischen und des taiwanesischen Zivilgesetzbuches das Wort „Irrtum",[36] im Falle des sowjetrussischen Zivilgesetzbuches von 1922[37] und des Zivilgesetzbuches der Russischen Sozialistischen Föderativen Sowjetrepublik von 1964 hingegen das Wort „Missverständnis"[38] benutzt wurde. Außerdem werden in den Übersetzungen der sowjetischen Lehrbücher,[39] welche signifikante Auswirkungen auf die chinesische Rechtswissenschaft und Rechtsprechung hatten, ebenfall die Begriffe „erhebliches Missverständnis" oder „schwerwiegendes Missverständnis" verwendet, wenn es um eine entsprechende Norm[40] oder deren Erläuterung geht. Die Erörterung des „erheblichen Missverständnisses" in den Lehrbüchern zu den GPCL gleicht derjenigen in den sowjetischen Lehrbüchern.[41] Diese ist, genauer betrachtet, überraschenderweise wiederum ähnlich zu § 119 BGB nach dem Verständnis der herrschenden Lehre in Deutschland. Beispielsweise werden meistens mögliche

---

36 *Ma Yuming*, Code Civil (Code Napoléon) («法国民法典»), Übersetzung, 1982, S. 222 f.; Institut für Rechtwissenschaft der Akademie für Sozialwissenschaften Shanghai, Bürgerliches Gesetzbuch der Bundesrepublik Deutschland («德意志联邦共和国民法典») Übersetzung, 1984, S. 25; Juristische Fakultät der Universität Peking, Referenzmaterial-Japanisches ZGB («民法参考资料日本民法典»), 1982, S. 95; *Hu Changqing*, Vergleich der Zivilgesetze in verschiedenen Ländern (Allgemeine Regeln) (各国民法条文比较（总则编）), 1982, S. 97f.

37 § 32 des sowjetrussischen Zivilgesetzbuches (1922); Zentrale Volksregierung Gesetzgebungsausschuss, Zusammenstellung des Zivilrechts, Bd. 1 Sowjetunion (民法资料汇编（第一辑苏联部分）), 1953, S. 9; *Zheng Hua*, Sowjetrussisches ZGB («苏俄民法典»), Übersetzung, 1956, S. 12.

38 § 57 des sowjetrussischen ZGB (1964). Institut für Rechtwissenschaft der Chinesischen Akademie für Sozialwissenschaften, («苏俄民法典»), 1980, S. 21.

39 *Brasov*, Das sowjetische Zivilrecht I («苏维埃民法（上）»), in das Chinesische übersetzt durch die Juristische Fakultät der Renmin-Universität, 1954, S. 154; *Genkin/Bratus*, Das sowjetische Zivilrecht I («苏维埃民法（第1册）»), in das Chinesische übersetzt durch die Juristische Fakultät der Renmin-Universität, 1956, S. 288; *Gràbbanov*/Korneyev, Zivilrecht der Russischen Sozialistischen Föderativen Sowjetrepublik I («苏联民法（上册）»), in das Chinesische übersetzt durch das Institut für Rechtwissenschaft der Chinesischen Akademie für Sozialwissenschaften, 1984, S. 232 f.

40 § 32 des Sowjetrussischen Zivilgesetzbuches (1922) und § 57 des Zivilgesetzbuches der Russischen Sozialistischen Föderativen Sowjetrepublik (1964).

41 Oberstes Volksgericht Gruppenkurse, Vorlesungen zu den GPCL («民法通则讲座»), 1986, S. 152 f.; Tong Rou, Kurzkommentar GPCL («中华人民共和国民法通则简论»), 1987, S. 137 ff.; Tang Dehua/Zhou Xianqi/Chen Wenhao, Einführungen in die GPCL («中华人民共和国民法通则讲话»), 1986, S. 64 f.; *Chen Xingde/Zhang Yuxi*, Einführung in die GPCL («民法通则讲话»), 1987, S. 74 f.

Gegenstände eines Irrtums dargelegt: der Gegenstand der Willenserklärung, mithin Eigenschaften einer Sache wie Art, Qualität, Spezifikationen und Menge des Gegenstandes. Es wird in vielen sowjetischen Lehrbüchern dargelegt, dass (1) ein bloßer Motivirrtum grundsätzlich unbeachtlich ist[42] und (2) wegen Irrtums angefochten werden kann, wenn anzunehmen ist, dass der Irrende die Erklärung „bei Kenntnis der Sachlage und verständiger Würdigung des Falles nicht abgegeben haben würde".[43] Das Erfordernis der Erheblichkeit des Irrtums wird hier wie im deutschen BGB vorausgesetzt, dessen Einfluss auf Russland und China im Rahmen der Rechtsgeschäftslehre signifikant gewesen ist.[44] Ferner wird die Definition des „Missverständnisses" durch § 71 OVG-Ansichten GPCL erläutert. Die unbeabsichtigte Änderung von „Irrtum" zu „Missverständnis" bleibt in den GRCL bestehen. Ist dies eine wohlüberlegte Entscheidung?

Die Probleme entsprechen im Wesentlichen denjenigen, welche bei § 88 Abs. 1 TWN-ZGB dargestellt wurden.

2. Probleme des „erheblichen Missverständnisses" im chinesischen Zivilrecht

In der traditionellen zivilrechtlichen Lehre hat das „Missverständnis" eine ganz andere Bedeutung als der „Irrtum". Ein „Missverständnis" betrifft die Perspektive des Erklärungsempfängers, ein „Irrtum" die Perspektive des Erklärenden. Ein Irrtum liegt vor, wenn es Abweichungen zwischen Wille und Erklärung gibt, deren auszulegender Inhalt dem Erklärenden zurechenbar

---

42 *Brasov*, Das sowjetische Zivilrecht I («苏维埃民法（上）»), in das Chinesische übersetzt durch die Juristische Fakultät der Renmin-Universität, 1954, S. 154; *Genkin/Bratus*, Das sowjetische Zivilrecht I («苏维埃民法（第1册）»), in das Chinesische übersetzt durch die Juristische Fakultät der Renmin-Universität, 1956, S. 289.

43 *Brasov*, Das sowjetische Zivilrecht I («苏维埃民法（上）»), in das Chinesische übersetzt durch die Juristische Fakultät der Renmin-Universität, 1954, S. 154; *Genkin/Bratus*, Das sowjetische Zivilrecht I («苏维埃民法（第1册）»), in das Chinesische übersetzt durch die Juristische Fakultät der Renmin-Universität, 1956, S. 289; Oberstes Volksgericht Gruppenkurse, Vorlesungen zu den GPCL («民法通则讲座»), 1986, S. 153.

44 *Gianmaria*, Return to the codification: the experiences of the civil codifications in the east European countries and Russia after the transformation of the economic system, in das Chinesische übersetzt durch XueJun, 6 Peking University Law Journal, S. 692 ff. (2004).

ist. Dagegen soll der Gegenstand des Missverständnisses die Willenserklärung des Erklärenden sein. Gemäß § 71 OVG-Ansichten GPCL ist Gegenstand des Missverständnisses aber keine Willenserklärung der anderen Partei.

§ 71 OVG-Ansichten GPCL

Wenn irrige Vorstellungen des Handelnden über die Natur der Handlung, über den oder die Beteiligten auf der anderen Seite oder über Art, Qualität, Spezifikationen und Mengen des Handlungsgegenstandes dazu führen, dass die Ergebnisse der Handlung seinem Willen widersprechen und größere Schäden herbeiführen, kann dies als erhebliches Missverständnis angesehen werden.

Das Merkmal „erhebliches Missverständnis" ist weder in den GPCL noch im Vertragsgesetz der Volksrepublik China von 1999 definiert. Der Gesetzgeber und die Rechtswissenschaft orientieren sich insoweit direkt an Russland und indirekt an Deutschland. Deshalb führt das Fehlen einer Definition des Merkmals in der Praxis zu Unsicherheiten. Wenn man die relevante Rechtsprechung der chinesischen Gerichte untersucht, wird deutlich, dass ein „erhebliches Missverständnis", obwohl sehr viele Kläger ihren Anspruch darauf stützen, meistens als etwas anderes als einen „Irrtum" angesehen wird. Zudem verstehen die Gerichte „erhebliches Missverständnis" oft synonym zum Begriff „deutlich ungerecht"[45] (wie etwa in § 138 Abs. 2 BGB).

Obwohl nach h. M. der chinesischen Wissenschaftler das „erhebliche Missverständnis" dasselbe ist wie der traditionelle zivilrechtliche „Irrtum", ist die Anzahl der Gerichtsentscheidungen, die dieser Ansicht folgen, sehr gering.[46] Oft verstehen die Gerichte das „Missverständnis" im wörtlichen

---

45 S. Zhang Wenyuan v. Zhang Quanming u. a. (张文元诉张全明等合同纠纷案), Volksgerichtshof des Bezirks Beijing-Pinggu, (2011) Min Chu Zi No. 5822 ((2011)民初字第5822号); Hu Mou v. Yi Mou (胡某诉易某买卖合同纠纷案), Höherer Volksgerichtshof Shanghai, (2008) Hu Gao Min Yi (Min) Zai Zhong Zi No. 10 ((2008)沪高民一（民）再终字第10号). Manager eines Bauunternehmens v. Unternehmen für Bau und Installation u. a., Volksgericht der Provinz Jilin in Dunhua, (2006) Dun Min Chu Zi No.193 ((2006) 敦民初字第193号). Das Durchsuchen der Datenbank „pkulaw.cn" nach Rechtsprechung zum „erheblichen Missverständnis" ergibt über 20.000 Treffer. In den meisten Entscheidungen geht es jedoch nur um die Wirksamkeit des jeweiligen Vertrages ohne die Definition des Merkmals zu diskutieren.

46 S. China Construction Bank Datong New Road Branch v. Shanxi Provincial Highway Bureau Datong Zweig und Shanxi Provincial Communications Abteilung (中国建设银行大同市新建路支行与山西省公路局大同分局、山西省交通厅借

Sinne als einen Irrtum des Erklärungsempfängers über die Erklärung. Darunter fällt vielfach das Missverständnis über die Rechtsfolgen der Erklärung.

Noch größer ist jedoch die Zahl der Entscheidungen, in denen Gerichte das „erhebliche Missverständnis" weder i. S. e. „Irrtums" noch eines wirklichen „Missverständnisses",[47] sondern im Sinne seiner alltäglichen sprachlichen Bedeutung verstehen. In vielen solchen Fällen vertreten die Kläger die Ansicht, es liege ein „erhebliches Missverständnis" vor. Tatsächlich haben diese Fälle mit der Irrtumsanfechtung oder dem theoretischen Missverständnis meist aber nichts zu tun. Da die Gerichte auf solche Rechtsansichten nicht eingehen, werden diese Fälle hier nicht weiter erörtert.

Es gibt viele Fälle, in denen nach der Ansicht der Wissenschaft eine Willenserklärung aufgrund „Irrtums" anfechtbar wäre. Die Gerichte verstehen das „Missverständnis" aber als etwas anderes als einen „Irrtum", sodass der Empfänger, wenn der Erklärende bei ihm keine fehlerhafte Vorstellung verursacht, vor Gericht nicht anfechtungsberechtigt ist.[48]

> „In dem Widerspruch der Volksstaatsanwaltschaft der Provinz Anhui erklärt diese deutlich, dass in diesem Fall das ‚Missverständnis' des Klägers von der Immobilien Entwicklung Corporation verursacht wurde. Es besteht ein kausaler Zusammenhang

---

款担保合同纠纷上诉案), Oberster Volksgerichtshof der Volksrepublik China, Zweite Zivilkammer, in: dies., Anleitungen zur Zivil- und Handelsrechtsprechung («民商事审判指导»), 2004 No. 2, S. 270; Duyang Tujia und Miao Autonome Grafschaft, Versorgung und Vermarktung von Assoziierten Genossenschaften des Nativen Produkts v. Chongqing Longxi Bau (Gruppe) Co., Ltd, (酉阳土家族苗族自治县供销合作社联合社土产果品公司与重庆隆西建设（集团）有限公司建设工程施工合同纠纷抗诉案) Vermittlung des Obersten Volksgerichtshofs der Volksrepublik China, 2014.7.24 (最高人民法院调解书2014年7月24日).

47 S. Sun Yanhua v. China Joint Property Insurance Company Shanghai Branch, Volksgerichtshof des Bezirks Shanghai-Luwan, (2005) Lu Min Yi (Min) Chu Zi No. 1868 ((2005)卢民一（民）初字第1868号); Wei Lu v. Lanxi Stadt Bo Yuan Metal Co., Ltd, (2013) Zhe Jin Shang Zhong No. 154 ((2013) 浙金商终第154号); Xinjiang Machinery Chemical Metalle, Mineralien und Leichtindustrie Import und Export Corporation v. Urumqi Hengxiang Handelsentwicklung Co., Ltd, Oberster Volksgerichtshof der Volksrepublik China, (1999) Jing Zhong Zi No. 43 ((1999) 经终字第43号).

48 S. Yan Yuehua v. Zhao Tiejun, Zhejiang Shengzhou Volksgericht, (2012) Shao Sheng Gan Shang Chu Zi No.181 ((2012) 绍嵊甘商初字第181号); Ma'anshanDakang Industrie und Handel Development Co., Ltd v. Ma'anshan Immobilien Entwicklung Corporation und Ma'anshan Immobilien Entwicklung Corporation Abteilung für Immobilienverwaltung, Höheres Volksgericht Anhui, (2007) Ma Min Yi Zai Zhong Zi No.15 ((2007) 马民一再终字第15号).

> zwischen dem Missverständnis des Klägers und dem Verhalten der Immobilien Entwicklung Corporation."[49]
>
> „Das ‚Missverständnis' des Erklärungsempfängers ist nicht durch den Erklärenden verursacht worden, deshalb liegt kein ‚erhebliches Missverständnis' vor."[50]

Die genannten Unstimmigkeiten ergeben sich vor allem aus der Diskrepanz zwischen der Bedeutung des Wortes „Missverständnis" im chinesischen Sprachgebrauch und der theoretischen Bedeutung der Irrtumsanfechtung im traditionellen Zivilrecht.

Leider bleibt in § 147 GRCL das Wort „Missverständnis" nach wie vor ohne Definition erhalten. Der Gesetzgeber hat die Chance verpasst, einen konturierten Begriff zu benutzen und die Regelung der Irrtumsanfechtung für die Praxis klar zu formulieren.

> **§ 147 GRCL**
>
> Der Handelnde ist berechtigt, beim Volksgericht oder beim Schiedsorgan das Rechtsgeschäft anzufechten, wenn das Rechtsgeschäft auf einem erheblichen Missverständnis basiert.

Nach der Stellungnahme des Stellvertretenden Vorsitzenden des Ständigen Ausschusses des Nationalen Volkskongresses, Li Jianguo, sollen die GPCL wirksam bleiben, auch nachdem die GRCL in Kraft treten. Sind die Regelungen der GRCL mit denen der GPCL unvereinbar, sollen erstere vorrangig gelten. Wenn in den GRCL eine bestimmte Regelung fehlt, gelten die Vorschriften der GPCL weiterhin. Dies wird zu einem neuen Problem führen, denn in den GRCL gibt es die Vorschrift über das „erhebliche Missverständnis". Folglich sind die GPCL insofern und zwar theoretisch zusammen mit OVG-Ansichten GPCL nicht mehr wirksam. Das „erhebliche Missverständnis" wird derzeit aber nur in § 71 OVG-Ansichten GPCL konkretisiert. Wie werden die Gerichte entscheiden, wenn sie nur die GRCL anwenden dürfen? Wird der Oberste Gerichtshof der Volksrepublik China wieder Ansichten zur Anwendung der GRCL erlassen?

---

49 Ma'anshan Dakang Industrie und Handel Development Co., Ltd v. Ma'anshan Immobilien Entwicklung Corporation und Ma'anshan Immobilien Entwicklung Corporation Abteilung für Immobilienverwaltung, Höheres Volksgericht Anhui, (2007) Ma Min Yi Zai Zhong Zi No.15 ((2007)马民一再终字第15号).

50 Yan Yuehua v. Zhao Tiejun, Zhejiang Shengzhou Volksgericht, (2012) Shao Sheng Gan Shang Chu Zi No.181 ((2012) 绍嵊甘商初字第181号).

IV. Fazit

Das gegenwärtige TWN-ZGB ist das vom Legislativ-Yuan der Nationalregierung erlassene Zivilgesetzbuch der Republik China von 1930, dessen Grundlage der Entwurf des Zivilgesetzes der Qing-Dynastie ist. In § 88 Abs. 1 Hs. 1 TWN-ZGB folgt auf den Inhaltsirrtum der Zusatz „wenn anzunehmen ist, dass er sie bei Kenntnis der Sachlage und bei verständiger Würdigung des Falles nicht abgegeben haben würde“. Nach systematischer Auslegung scheint es so als sei dieser Zusatz mit dem Begriff der „Unkenntnis“ gleichzusetzen. Die taiwanesische Lehre ordnet den Zusatz als Erklärungsirrtum bzw. als „Unkenntnis“ ein. Die Ansicht der Rechtsprechung ist ebenfalls unklar. Das Tatbestandsmerkmal der „Unkenntnis“ ist grundlegend von einem „Irrtum“ zu unterscheiden, da bei ersterer eine Anfechtung generell ausscheidet. Versteht man den Ausdruck „wenn anzunehmen ist, dass […] nicht abgegeben haben würde“ als Erklärungsirrtum, fällt die Erheblichkeit des Irrtums als Tatbestandsvoraussetzung im TWN-ZGB weg. Deshalb leitet der Oberste Gerichtshof Taiwans die Erheblichkeit als Voraussetzung aus dem Grundsatz von Treu und Glauben ab. Ob dies eine gute Lösung ist, ist aber noch umstritten.

Das „erhebliche Missverständnis“ bedeutet nach h. M. einen Irrtum des Erklärenden. Der Gesetzgeber der GPCL soll sich bei dem Begriff „Missverständnis“ an Russland orientiert haben. Das Fehlen einer Definition dieses Begriffs führt in der Praxis zu Verwirrung. In der Tat verstehen die Gerichte das „Missverständnis“ nicht im Sinne von „Irrtum“, sondern gemäß seiner alltäglichen sprachlichen Bedeutung. Die praktischen Unstimmigkeiten ergeben sich vor allem aus der Diskrepanz zwischen der Bedeutung des Wortes „Missverständnis“ im chinesischen Sprachgebrauch und der theoretischen Bedeutung der Irrtumsanfechtung im traditionellen Zivilrecht. Der Gesetzgeber der GRCL hat aber die Chance verpasst, einen konturierten und definierten Begriff zu kodifizieren. Dies wird künftig weitere Probleme verursachen.

Das Verbot des Selbstkontrahierens nach § 168 Abs. 1 GRCL aus rechtsvergleichender Perspektive

*Qiangzhi Hu**

Zusammenfassung: *In § 168 Abs. 1 des am 15.3.2017 neu erlassenen Allgemeinen Teils zum künftigen chinesischen Zivilgesetzbuch, den sog. General Rules of Civil Law (GRCL) wird das Verbot der Selbstkontraktion geregelt. Die genaue Historie dieser Vorschrift sowie der Normzweck und etwaige Rechtsfolgen sollen herausgearbeitet werden. Daneben wird dahingehend auch das Verbot des In-Sich-Geschäftes im deutschen Recht, das in § 181 Alt. 1 Bürgerliches Gesetzbuch (BGB) verankert ist, erörtert. Zudem werden die Regelungen im Internationalen Privatrecht, welche das Verbot des Selbstkontrahierens normieren, genauer Art. 2.2.7 der UNIDROIT-Grundregeln für Internationale Handelsverträge 2010 (PICC) und Art. 3:205 der Grundregeln des Europäischen Vertragsrechts (PECL) dargestellt. Eine anschließende Rechtsvergleichung soll Lösungsansätze hinsichtlich der sich im Chinesischen Recht eröffnenden Problematik bieten.*

Stichwörter: Selbstkontrahieren, Verbot, In-Sich-Geschäft, Rechtsvergleichung

* Doktorandin, Ruhr-Universität Bochum, Juristische Fakultät.

I. Einleitung

In dem am 15.3.2017 neu erlassenen Allgemeinen Teil des zukünftigen chinesischen Zivilgesetzbuches, den sog. *General Rules of Civil Law* (GRCL), wird das Verbot des Selbstkontrahierens in § 168 Abs. 1 geregelt. Diese Regelung wurde neu in die GRCL eingeführt und hat keine Vorgängervorschrift in den *General Principles of Civil Law* von 1986 (GPCL) und dem Vertragsgesetz von 1999 (VG). Zudem sind in den GRCL die Rechtsfolgen eines Verstoßes gegen diese Vorschrift nicht geregelt. Zu ermitteln sind daher der Gesetzgebungshintergrund dieser Vorschrift sowie deren Normzweck und Rechtsfolgen. Die angewandte Forschungsmethode ist die Rechtsvergleichung. Miteinander verglichen werden § 168 Abs. 1 GRCL, § 181 Alt. 1 des Bürgerlichen Gesetzbuches (BGB), Art. 2.2.7 der UNIDROIT-Grundregeln für Internationale Handelsverträge 2010 (PICC) und Art. 3:205 der Grundregeln des Europäischen Vertragsrechts (PECL).

II. Verbot des Selbstkontrahierens nach § 168 Abs. 1 GRCL

§ 168 Abs. 1 Hs. 1 GRCL verbietet dem Vertreter, im Namen des Vertretenen ein Rechtsgeschäft mit sich selbst vorzunehmen. Das chinesische Recht enthält somit ein Verbot des Selbstkontrahierens (zi ji dai li, 自己代理[1]),[2] welches ebenso wie das Verbot der Doppelvertretung[3] (shuang fang dai li,

1 Auch „zi wo qi yue, 自我契约“, *Shi Shangkuan* (史尚宽), Allgemeiner Teil des Zivilrechts («民法总论»), 2002, S. 534; *Hu Changqing* (胡长清), Allgemeiner Teil des chinesischen Zivilrechts («中国民法总论»), 1998, S. 311, *Zhu Qingyu* (朱庆育), Allgemeiner Teil des Zivilrechts («民法总论»), 2. Aufl. 2016, S. 350; *Chi Ying* (迟颖), Übersetzungswerk von Flume, Das Rechtsgeschäft («法律行为论»), 2013, S. 972; *Shao Jiandong* (邵建东), Übersetzungswerk von Medicus, Allgemeiner Teil des BGB («德国民法总论»), S. 723, Rn. 955.

2 *Wang Liming* (王利明), Das Zivilrecht («民法»), 2. Aufl. 2010, S. 134; *Liang Huixing* (梁慧星), Allgemeiner Teil des Zivilrechts («民法总论»), 4. Aufl. 2010, S. 228; *Zhu Qingyu* (朱庆育), Allgemeiner Teil des Zivilrechts («民法总论»), 2. Aufl. 2016, S. 350; *Zhang Junhao* (张俊浩), Kapitel 9: Stellvertretung bei den Zivilrechtsgeschäften, in: Zhang Junhao (张俊浩编), Theorien der Zivilrechtswissenschaft («民法学原理»), 1997, S. 270.

3 *Shi Shangkuan* (史尚宽), Allgemeiner Teil des Zivilrechts («民法总论»), 2002, S. 534; *Wang Liming* (王利明), Das Zivilrecht («民法»), 2. Aufl. 2010, S. 135; *Liang Huixing* (梁慧星), Allgemeiner Teil des Zivilrechts («民法总论»), 4. Aufl. 2010, S. 228.

双方代理) bzw. Mehrvertretung[4] (duo fang dai li, 多方代理) zu den Beschränkungen der Vertretungsmacht gehört.[5] Eine Ausnahme vom Verbot des Selbstkontrahierens sieht § 168 Abs. 1 Hs. 2 GRCL vor, wenn der Vertretene dem Selbstkontrahieren zugestimmt hat.

1. Gesetzgebung des Verbots des Selbstkontrahierens nach § 168 Abs. 1 GRCL

Das bestehende chinesische Recht kannte vor Erlass der GRCL das Verbot des Selbstkontrahierens zwar nicht als eine allgemeine Regelung für die Stellvertretung, rechtshistorisch war dieses Verbot aber sowohl in § 106 des Zivilgesetzbuchs der Republik China (1912–1949)[6] als auch in § 56 des ersten Entwurfes des Zivilgesetzbuches der Volksrepublik China vom 5.10.1955[7] enthalten. Zudem enthielten § 49 des zweiten Entwurfes eines Zivilgesetzbuches der Volksrepublik China vom 24.10.1955[8] und § 7

---

4 *Zhu Qingyu* (朱庆育), Allgemeiner Teil des Zivilrechts («民法总论»), 2. Aufl. 2016, S. 350.

5 *Shi Shangkuan* (史尚宽), Allgemeiner Teil des Zivilrechts («民法总论»), 2002, S. 534; *Wang Liming* (王利明), Das Zivilrecht («民法»), 2. Aufl. 2010, S. 134 f.; *Liang Huixing* (梁慧星), Allgemeiner Teil des Zivilrechts («民法总论»), 4. Aufl. 2010, S. 228.

6 § 106 Zivilgesetzbuchs der Republik China (1929)
Der Vertreter kann ohne Zustimmung des Vertretenen das Rechtsgeschäft zwischen dem Vertretenen und ihm selbst nicht vornehmen, er kann auch nicht als Vertreter einer Dritten das Rechtsgeschäft mit dem Vertretenen vornehmen, es sei denn, dass das Rechtsgeschäft nur die Tilgung von Verbindlichkeiten zum Inhalt hat.

7 § 59 Erster Entwurf des Zivilgesetzbuches der Volksrepublik China (1955)
Der Vertreter kann nicht im Namen des Vertretenen das Rechtsgeschäft mit sich selbst oder mit einer von ihm vertretenen Dritten vornehmen, außer der Vertretene hat ihm seine Zustimmung gegeben.
Hierzu He Qinhua (何勤华编), Übersicht über die Entwürfe des Zivilgesetzbuches der Volksrepublik China I («新中国民法典草案总览(上卷)»), 2003, S. 10.

8 § 49 Zweiter Entwurf des Zivilgesetzbuches der Volksrepublik China (1955)
Der Vertreter kann nicht im Namen des Vertretenen das Rechtsgeschäft mit sich selbst oder mit einem von ihm vertretenen Dritten vornehmen, außer der Vertretene hat ihm seine Zustimmung gegeben.
Hierzu He Qinhua (何勤华编), Übersicht über die Entwürfe des Zivilgesetzbuches der Volksrepublik China I («新中国民法典草案总览(上卷)»), 2003, S. 19.

Abs. 1 Nr. 1 Alt. 2 Wirtschaftsvertragsgesetz von 1981 (WVG)[9] eine vergleichbare Regelung. Die GPCL sowie das VG haben jedoch – trotz entsprechender Vorschläge – auf die Aufnahme dieser Regelung verzichtet.[10]

Bei der Ausarbeitung der GRCL war die Vorschrift über das Verbot des Selbstkontrahierens in jedem gesetzgeberischen Entwurf enthalten.[11] Der einzige Unterschied zwischen den Entwürfen und der endgültigen Fassung des § 168 Abs. 1 GRCL besteht in den Ausnahmefällen. In den Entwürfen war zusätzlich eine Ausnahme für den Fall vorgesehen, dass das Selbstkontrahieren durch spezielle gesetzliche Regelungen erlaubt wird. § 168 Abs. 1 GRCL hat diese Ausnahme nicht übernommen, weil es eine solche Regelung im bestehenden chinesischen Recht nicht gibt. [12] Auch § 148 Abs. 1 Nr. 4 Gesellschaftsgesetz (GesG)[13] und § 32 Abs. 2 Personengesellschaftsgesetz (PersG)[14] sehen lediglich die Zustimmung des Ver-

---

9 § 7 Abs.1 Nr. 1 Alt. 2 WVG (1981)
Die folgenden Wirtschaftsverträge sind unwirksam: [...] 3. die Verträge, die vom Vertreter ohne Vertretungsmacht bzw. im Namen des Vertretenen mit sich selbst oder mit einer von ihm vertretenen Dritten abschlossen wurden.

10 *Fang Xinjun* (方新军), Erfolg und Mängel des Rechtsinstituts der „Stellvertretung“ im Kapitel 7 der GRCL des Zivilrechts ("民法总则第七章'代理'制度的成功与不足"), Schulzeitung der Ostchinesischen Universität für Politikwissenschaft und Recht («华东政法大学学报») 2017 Heft 3, 35, 39.

11 § 124 Abs. 1 Entwurf vom 29.1.2016; § 148 Abs. 1 Entwurf vom 5.7.2016; § 163 Abs. 1 Entwurf vom 18.11.2016; § 172 Abs. 1 Entwurf vom 27.12.2016.

12 *Ma Xinyan* (马新彦), Gesetzgebungsuntersuchung der Stellvertretung in den GRCL des Zivilrechts ("民法总则代理立法研究"), Die Rechtswissenschaftler («法学家») 2016 Heft 5, 121, 128; *Fang Xinjun* (方新军), Erfolg und Mängel des Rechtsinstituts der „Stellvertretung“ im Kapitel 7 der GRCL des Zivilrechts ("民法总则第七章'代理'制度的成功与不足"), Schulzeitung der Ostchinesischen Universität für Politikwissenschaft und Recht («华东政法大学学报») 2017 Heft 3, 35, 39–40.

13 § 148 Abs. 1 Nr. 4 GesG (2014)
Die Vorstandsmitglieder und das leitende Managementpersonal dürfen die folgenden Handlungen nicht vornehmen: [...] 4. gegen die Gesellschaftssatzung verstoßen oder ohne Zustimmung der Gesellschafter- bzw. Hauptgesellschafterversammlung einen Vertrag mit dieser Gesellschaft abzuschließen oder mit dieser Gesellschaft handeln.

14 § 32 Abs. 2 PersG (2006)
Der Geschäftspartner darf nicht mit dieser Personengesellschaft handeln, es sei denn, dies ist durch Geschäftsvereinbarung vereinbart worden oder alle Geschäftspartnern haben zugestimmt.

tretenen vor, enthalten aber keine originäre gesetzliche Erlaubnis des Vertreters zur Selbstkontraktion.[15] Gäbe es in der Zukunft eine ausdrückliche gesetzliche Erlaubnis, so ließe sich diese nach § 11 GRCL, der den Vorrang spezieller Regelungen vor allgemeineren kodifiziert, als lex specialis behandeln.[16]

Die GRCL regeln zwar das Verbot des Selbstkontrahierens in § 168 Abs. 1 GRCL, sehen aber keine Rechtsfolgen für einen Verstoß dagegen vor. Nur für das Gesellschaftsrecht und das Personengesellschaftsrecht wurde ausdrücklich geregelt, dass die Gesellschaft bzw. Personengesellschaft den Gewinn des Vorstandsmitgliedes (§ 149 Abs. 2 GesG[17]) oder Geschäftspartners (§ 99 S. 1. Hs. 2 PersG[18]) erhält, den dieser aus dem In-sich-Geschäft bzw. der Mehrfachvertretung gezogen hat.

In § 168 Abs. 1 GRCL sind nur die Einwilligung oder Genehmigung des Vertretenen als Ausnahme für das Verbot des Selbstkontrahierens geregelt. Nach Auffassung der Literatur besteht in der Praxis jedoch ein Bedürfnis nach weiteren Ausnahmefällen. Diese Rechtsfortbildung über den Wortlaut hinaus kann durch teleologische Reduktion (mu di xing xian suo, 目的性限

15 Hier ist eine umgekehrte Gesetzesauslegung vorzunehmen, s. auch *Fang Xinjun* (方新军), Erfolg und Mängel des Rechtsinstituts der „Stellvertretung“ im Kapitel 7 der GRCL des Zivilrechts ("民法总则第七章'代理'制度的成功与不足"), Schulzeitung der Ostchinesischen Universität für Politikwissenschaft und Recht («华东政法大学学报») 2017 Heft 3, 35, 39–40.

16 *Geng Lin/Cui Jianyuan* (耿林/崔建远), Konstruktion des Rechtsinstituts der Stellvertretung in den GRCL des Zivilrechts ("民法总则应当如何设计代理制度"), Die Rechtsanwendung («法律适用»), 2016 Heft 5, 51, 58; *Fang Xinjun* (方新军), Erfolg und Mängel des Rechtsinstituts der „Stellvertretung“ im Kapitel 7 der GRCL des Zivilrechts ("民法总则第七章'代理'制度的成功与不足"), Schulzeitung der Ostchinesischen Universität für Politikwissenschaft und Recht («华东政法大学学报») 2017 Heft 3, 35, 40; s. zum Lex-specialis-Grundsatz insbesondere auch *Möllers* in diesem Band, S. 62 ff.

17 § 148 Abs. 2 GesG (2014)
Die Gesellschaft bekommt die Gewinne des Vorstandsmitgliedes oder leitenden Managementpersonals, welche er verstoßend gegen den Abs. 1 der Vorschrift erworben hat.

18 § 99 S. 1. Hs. 2 PersG (2006)
Hat der Geschäftspartner durch ein Handeln mit dieser Personengesellschaft gegen das Gesetz oder eine Geschäftsvereinbarung verstoßen, bekommt die Personengesellschaft den Gewinn des Geschäftspartners, welchen dieser aus dem selbstkontrahierten Handel erworben hat.

缩) oder teleologische Extension (mu di xing kuo zhang, 目的性扩张) erreicht werden.[19]

2. Konzeption und Normzweck des Verbotes des Selbstkontrahierens nach § 168 Abs. 1 GRCL

Die wissenschaftliche Auseinandersetzung mit dem Verbot des Selbstkontrahierens im chinesischen Recht ist heute in den meisten Lehrbüchern[20] und wissenschaftlichen Beiträgen zu finden.[21] Mit dem Erlass der GRCL wurde dieses Thema auch in einigen jüngeren Beiträgen aufgegriffen.[22] Zugleich ist das Verbot des Selbstkontrahierens gelegentlich auch in der Rechtsprechung thematisiert worden.[23]

---

19 *Wang* Zejian (王泽鉴), Allgemeiner Teil des Zivilrechts («民法总则»), 2009, S. 440.

20 Wie etwa *Wang Liming* (王利明), Das Zivilrecht («民法»), 2. Aufl. 2010, S. 134-135; *Liang Huixing* (梁慧星), Allgemeiner Teil des Zivilrechts («民法总论»), 4. Aufl. 2010, S. 228; *Zhu Qingyu* (朱庆育), Allgemeiner Teil des Zivilrechts («民法总论»), 2. Aufl. 2016, S. 350; *Long Weiqiu* (龙卫球), Allgemeiner Teil des Zivilrechts («民法总论»), 2001, S. 671-672.

21 Z. B. *Shi Shangkuan* (史尚宽), Allgemeiner Teil des Zivilrechts («民法总论»), 2002, S. 534-537; *Hu Changqing* (胡长清), Allgemeiner Teil des chinesischen Zivilrechts («中国民法总论»), 1998, S. 311-313; *Wang Zejian* (王泽鉴), Allgemeiner Teil des Zivilrechts («民法总则»), 2009, S. 440-444.

22 Z. B.: *Geng Lin/Cui Jianyuan* (耿林/崔建远), Konstruktion des Rechtsinstituts der Stellvertretung in den GRCL des Zivilrechts ("民法总则应当如何设计代理制度"), Die Rechtsanwendung («法律适用») 2016 Heft 5, , 51–61; *Fang Xinjun* (方新军), Erfolg und Mängel des Rechtsinstituts der „Stellvertretung“ im Kapitel 7 der GRCL des Zivilrechts ("民法总则第七章'代理'制度的成功与不足"), Schulzeitung der Ostchinesischen Universität für Politikwissenschaft und Recht («华东政法大学学报») 2017 Heft 3, 35, 35–48; *Xie Hongfei* (谢鸿飞), Grundgedanken und wichtige Rechtsinstitute zur Gesetzgebung der Stellvertretung ("代理部分立法的基本理念和重要制度"), Schulzeitung der Ostchinesischen Universität für Politikwissenschaft und Recht («华东政法大学学报») 2016 Heft 5, 64–74; *Ma Xinyan* (马新彦), Gesetzgebungsuntersuchung der Stellvertretung in den GRCL des Zivilrechts ("民法总则代理立法研究"), Die Rechtswissenschaftler («法学家») 2016 Heft 5, 121–138.

23 Z. B.: Mittleres Volksgericht (MVG) Heilongjiang in Daqing, Urt. v. 1.12.1999, (2002) qing jing chu zi Nr. 70; Volksgericht (VG) Zhejiang in Deqing, Urt. v. 28.09.2009, (2009) hu de shang chu zi Nr. 743; MVG Hunan in Changsha, Urt. v. 25.4.2012, (2012) chang zhong min san zhong zi Nr. 1573; Oberster

Das Verbot des Selbstkontrahierens stützt sich im chinesischen Recht auf folgende Erwägungen: Zunächst wird darauf verwiesen, dass es beim Selbstkontrahieren nur eine Partei, den Vertreter, gebe, was der Struktur eines Vertrags widerspreche.[24] Gerade weil beim Selbstkontrahieren der Vertreter die einzige Partei ist, sei der Prozess der Einigung eigentlich nur ein Gedankenspiel des Vertreters, sodass das durch Selbstkontrahieren zustande gekommene Rechtsgeschäft von außen nicht erkennbar sei.[25] Außerdem wird angenommen, dass der Vertreter, der im Namen des Vertretenen mit sich selbst einen Vertrag abschließt, von Natur aus den Vertrag zugunsten seiner eigenen Interessen ausgestalten und die Interessen des Vertretenen beeinträchtigen würde.[26]

Der ersten Erwägung wird der Ausnahmefall der Zustimmung des Vertretenen entgegengehalten. Das heißt, dass das selbstgestaltete Rechtsgeschäft rechtsgültig ist, wenn der Vertretene schon vorher dem Selbstkontrahieren des Vertreters zustimmt; jedoch handelt auch bei einer solchen Selbstkontraktion nur eine Partei, nämlich der Vertreter. Hier zeigt sich, dass es von der Deutung des Gesetzes abhängt, ob das Selbstkontrahieren als ein Rechtsgeschäft angesehen werden kann.[27] Auch das Argument der mangelnden Erkennbarkeit des In-sich-Geschäfts ist nicht überzeugend. Denn bei nicht formbedürftigen Rechtsgeschäften kann ein Dritter das In-sich-Geschäft des Vertreters meistens erkennen, beispielsweise wenn der

---

Volksgerichtshof, Urt. v. 18.11.2013, (2013) min shen zi Nr. 1485; Oberes Volksgericht Shanghai, Urt. v. 10.11.2016, (2016) hu min shen Nr. 2233.

24 *Hu Changqing* (胡长清), Allgemeiner Teil des chinesischen Zivilrechts («中国民法总论»), 1998, S. 311; *Zhang Junhao* (张俊浩), Kapitel 9: Stellvertretung bei den Zivilrechtsgeschäften, in: Zhang Junhao (张俊浩编), Theorien der Zivilrechtswissenschaft («民法学原理»), 1997, S. 271.

25 *Geng Lin/Cui Jianyuan* (耿林/崔建远), Konstruktion des Rechtsinstituts der Stellvertretung in den GRCL des Zivilrechts ("民法总则应当如何设计代理制度"), Die Rechtsanwendung («法律适用») 2016 Heft 5, 51, 58.

26 *Hu Changqing* (胡长清), Allgemeiner Teil des chinesischen Zivilrechts («中国民法总论»), 1998, S. 312; *Shi Shangkuan* (史尚宽), Allgemeiner Teil des Zivilrechts («民法总论»), 2002, S. 534; *Mei Zhongxie* (梅仲协), Das Wesentliche des Zivilrechts («民法要义»), 1998, S. 144, Rn. 162; *Wang Liming* (王利明), Das Zivilrecht («民法»), 2. Aufl. 2010, S. 134; *Long Weiqiu* (龙卫球), Allgemeiner Teil des Zivilrechts («民法总论»), 2001, S. 671; *Zhang Junhao* (张俊浩), Kapitel 9: Stellvertretung bei den Zivilrechtsgeschäften, in: Zhang Junhao (张俊浩编), Theorien der Zivilrechtswissenschaft («民法学原理»), 1997, S. 271.

27 *Hu Changqing* (胡长清), Allgemeiner Teil des chinesischen Zivilrechts («中国民法总论»), 1998, S. 312.

Vertreter vor einem anderen das Rechtsgeschäft vorgenommen hat oder der betroffene Handel in das Rechnungsbuch eingetragen worden ist.[28] Beachtlich hingegen ist der Interessenkonflikt, denn das Verbot des Selbstkontrahierens zielt gerade auf den Schutz der Interessen des Vertretenen.[29] Das Selbstkontrahieren birgt die Gefahr des Interessenkonflikts vor allem dann, wenn die Vollmacht im Interesse des Vertretenen erteilt wurde und der Vertreter somit in dessen Interesse handeln muss.[30] Obwohl es bisher noch keine Anwendungsfälle gegeben hat, sind doch auch Fälle denkbar, in denen die Erteilung der Vollmacht vor allem dem Interesse des Vertreters dient. Dann ist ein Interessenkonflikt seltener. Auch dann können dem berechtigten Interesse des Vertreters beim Vertragsschluss freilich Grenzen gezogen sein. Dies hat aber meist nur Auswirkungen im Innenverhältnis.

3. Rechtsfolgen des Verstoßes gegen das Verbot des Selbstkontrahierens nach § 168 Abs. 1 GRCL

Bei der Diskussion über die Rechtsfolgen des Verstoßes gegen das Verbot des Selbstkontrahierens steht hauptsächlich die Wirksamkeit des Vertrages

---

28 *Shi Shangkuan* (史尚宽), Allgemeiner Teil des Zivilrechts («民法总论»), 2002, S. 535.

29 *Hu Changqing* (胡长清), Allgemeiner Teil des chinesischen Zivilrechts («中国民法总论»), 1998, S. 312; *Shi Shangkuan* (史尚宽), Allgemeiner Teil des Zivilrechts («民法总论»), 2002, S. 534; *Mei Zhongxie* (梅仲协), Das Wesentliche des Zivilrechts («民法要义»), 1998, S. 144, Rn. 162; *Wang Liming* (王利明), Das Zivilrecht («民法»), 2. Aufl. 2010, S. 134; *Long Weiqiu* (龙卫球), Allgemeiner Teil des Zivilrechts («民法总论»), 2001, S. 671; *Zhang Junhao* (张俊浩), Kapitel 9: Stellvertretung bei den Zivilrechtsgeschäften, in: Zhang Junhao (张俊浩编), Theorien der Zivilrechtswissenschaft («民法学原理»), 1997, S. 271.

30 *Zhang Junhao* (张俊浩), Kapitel 9: Stellvertretung bei den Zivilrechtsgeschäften, in: Zhang Junhao (张俊浩编), Theorien der Zivilrechtswissenschaft («民法学原理»), 1997, S. 270.

im Vordergrund. Die Meinungen dazu sind geteilt, zum Teil wird die Unwirksamkeit,[31] die schwebende Unwirksamkeit[32] bzw. die schwebende Wirksamkeit des Rechtsgeschäfts, also dessen Anfechtbarkeit,[33] angenommen. Die chinesische Rechtsprechung vertritt bisher den Standpunkt, dass ein Selbstkontrahieren wegen Verletzung der Interessen des Vertretenen unwirksam ist.[34] In der Rechtswissenschaft besteht ebenso Einigkeit, dass das Selbstkontrahieren nicht die Interessen der Allgemeinheit, sondern die des Vertretenen gefährdet. Jedoch folgert die Literatur daraus, dass das Selbstkontrahieren gestattet werden soll, wenn der Vertretene es erlaubt.[35]

---

31 MVG Heilongjiang in Daqing, Urt. v. 1.12.1999, (2002) qing jing chu zi Nr. 70; MVG Hunan in Changsha, Urt. v. 25.4.2012, (2012) chang zhong min san zhong zi Nr. 1573; a. A. VG, Urt. v. 28.9.2009, (2009) hu de shang chu zi Nr. 743 (hier war das Selbstkontrahieren insoweit unwirksam, als der Vertretene es nicht genehmigte).

32 *Wang Liming* (王利明), Das Zivilrecht («民法»), 2. Aufl. 2010, S. 134; *Zhang Junhao* (张俊浩), Kapitel 9: Stellvertretung bei den Zivilrechtsgeschäften, in: Zhang Junhao (张俊浩编), Theorien der Zivilrechtswissenschaft («民法学原理»), 1997, S. 270–271.

33 *Geng Lin/Cui Jianyuan* (耿林/崔建远), Konstruktion des Rechtsinstituts der Stellvertretung in den GRCL des Zivilrechts ("民法总则应当如何设计代理制度"), Die Rechtsanwendung («法律适用») 2016 Heft 5, 51, 58; *Liang Huixing* (梁慧星), Allgemeiner Teil des Zivilrechts («民法总论»), 4. Aufl. 2010, S. 228; *Xie Hongfei* (谢鸿飞), Grundgedanken und wichtige Rechtsinstitute zur Gesetzgebung der Stellvertretung ("代理部分立法的基本理念和重要制度"), Schulzeitung der Ostchinesischen Universität für Politikwissenschaft und Recht («华东政法大学学报») 2016 Heft 5, 64, 70.

34 MVG Heilongjiang in Daqing, Urt. v. 1.12.1999, (2002) qing jing chu zi Nr. 70; MVG Hunan in Changsha, Urt. v. 25.4.2012, (2012) chang zhong min san zhong zi Nr. 1573; a. A. VG, Urt. v. 28.9.2009, (2009) hu de shang chu zi Nr. 743 (hier war das Selbstkontrahieren insoweit unwirksam, als der Vertretene es nicht genehmigte).

35 *Shi Shangkuan* (史尚宽), Allgemeiner Teil des Zivilrechts («民法总论»), 2002, S. 535; *Hu Changqing* (胡长清), Allgemeiner Teil des chinesischen Zivilrechts («中国民法总论»), 1998, S. 312–313; *Mei Zhongxie* (梅仲协), Das Wesentliche des Zivilrechts («民法要义»), 1998, S. 144, Rn. 162; *Wang Liming* (王利明), Das Zivilrecht («民法»), 2. Aufl. 2010, S. 134; *Zhang Junhao* (张俊浩), Kapitel 9: Stellvertretung bei den Zivilrechtsgeschäften, in: Zhang Junhao (张俊浩编), Theorien der Zivilrechtswissenschaft («民法学原理»), 1997, S. 270–271; *Long Weiqiu* (龙卫球), Allgemeiner Teil des Zivilrechts («民法总论»), 2001, S. 671.

Insofern können für das Selbstkontrahieren die Regeln über die Vertretung ohne Vertretungsmacht entsprechend angewendet werden.[36]

Dies wird unter Verweis auf den erforderlichen Interessenausgleich und die Effektivität des Rechtsverkehrs kritisiert und stattdessen die Anfechtbarkeit des In-sich-Geschäfts durch den Vertretenen vorgeschlagen.[37] Diese Ansicht stützt sich vor allem auf den Grundsatz der Förderung des Handels (gu li jiao yi, 鼓励交易).[38] In Fällen, in denen die Interessen des Vertretenen nicht verletzt werden, wäre die Effektivität des Rechtsverkehrs erheblich gemindert, wenn es jedes Mal einer Genehmigung des Vertretenen bedürfte.[39] Außerdem solle der Vertretene die Risiken der Vertretung tragen, wozu auch die Folgen des Selbstkontrahierens seines Vertreters zählen.[40] Es wird daher angenommen, dass die Anfechtbarkeit des In-sich-Geschäfts

---

36 *Geng Lin/Cui Jianyuan* (耿林/崔建远), Konstruktion des Rechtsinstituts der Stellvertretung in den GRCL des Zivilrechts ("民法总则应当如何设计代理制度"), Die Rechtsanwendung («法律适用») 2016 Heft 5, 51, 58; *Shi Shangkuan* (史尚宽), Allgemeiner Teil des Zivilrechts («民法总论»), 2002, S. 535.

37 *Geng Lin/Cui Jianyuan* (耿林/崔建远), Konstruktion des Rechtsinstituts der Stellvertretung in den GRCL des Zivilrechts ("民法总则应当如何设计代理制度"), Die Rechtsanwendung («法律适用») 2016 Heft 5, 51, 58; *Liang Huixing* (梁彗星), Allgemeiner Teil des Zivilrechts («民法总论»), 4. Aufl.2010, S. 228; *Xie Hongfei* (谢鸿飞), Grundgedanken und wichtige Rechtsinstitute zur Gesetzgebung der Stellvertretung ("代理部分立法的基本理念和重要制度"), Schulzeitung der Ostchinesischen Universität für Politikwissenschaft und Recht («华东政法大学学报») 2016 Heft 5, 64, 70.

38 *GENG Lin/CUI Jianyuan* (耿林/崔建远), Konstruktion des Rechtsinstituts der Stellvertretung im GRCL des Zivilrechts ("民法总则应当如何设计代理制度"), Die Rechtsanwendung («法律适用»), 2016 Heft 5, 51, 58; *XIE Hongfei* (谢鸿飞), Grundgedanken und wichtige Rechtsinstitute zur Gesetzgebung der Stellvertretung ("代理部分立法的基本理念和重要制度"), Schulzeitung der Ostchinesischen Universität für Politikwissenschaft und Recht, («华东政法大学学报»), 2016 Heft 5, 64, 70.

39 *Xie Hongfei* (谢鸿飞), Grundgedanken und wichtige Rechtsinstitute zur Gesetzgebung der Stellvertretung ("代理部分立法的基本理念和重要制度"), Schulzeitung der Ostchinesischen Universität für Politikwissenschaft und Recht («华东政法大学学报») 2016 Heft 5, 64, 70.

40 *Geng Lin/Cui Jianyuan* (耿林/崔建远), Konstruktion des Rechtsinstituts der Stellvertretung in den GRCL des Zivilrechts ("民法总则应当如何设计代理制度"), Die Rechtsanwendung («法律适用») 2016 Heft 5, 51, 58.

als Lösung der Selbstkontraktion angemessener ist, als die Unwirksamkeit bzw. schwebende Unwirksamkeit des Rechtsgeschäfts.[41]

Beiden Ansichten zur Unwirksamkeit bzw. Anfechtbarkeit ist nicht zu folgen. Eine anfängliche Unwirksamkeit ist nicht sachgerecht, weil es – wie bereits das Schrifttum erkannt hat – nicht um Interessen der Allgemeinheit geht und ein gesetzlicher Unwirksamkeitsgrund fehlt.[42] Die Überlegung, dass ein Selbstkontrahieren als anfechtbares Rechtsgeschäft anzusehen ist, lässt sich ebenfalls nicht mit dem geltenden Recht vereinbaren. Die herkömmliche Auffassung von der Funktion der Anfechtung geht dahin, dass es sich um ein Rechtsinstitut handelt, das vor allem der Beseitigung von Willensmängeln dient und somit die Privatautonomie schützt.[43] Zur Vermeidung einer Interessenkollision trägt die Anfechtung nach ihrem Grundkonzept nicht bei. Zudem lässt sich die Anfechtbarkeit des Selbstkontrahierens rechtsdogmatisch auch kaum rechtfertigen: der Vertretene bestellt einen Vertreter, weil er davon ausgegangen ist, dass sein Vertreter in seinem Interesse seinen Willen bilden und das Vertretergeschäft mit einem Dritten abschließen wird.[44] Ferner gilt es zu bedenken, dass im geltenden chinesischen Recht die Anfechtung klageweise geltend gemacht werden muss (§§ 147 ff. GRCL) und die Aufhebung des In-sich-Geschäfts dadurch erheblich erschwert würde.[45] Auch der Schutz des Rechtsverkehrs rechtfertigt

---

41 *Geng Lin/Cui Jianyuan* (耿林/崔建远), Konstruktion des Rechtsinstituts der Stellvertretung in den GRCL des Zivilrechts ("民法总则应当如何设计代理制度"), Die Rechtsanwendung («法律适用») 2016 Heft 5, 51, 59.

42 *Shi Shangkuan* (史尚宽), Allgemeiner Teil des Zivilrechts («民法总论»), 2002, S. 535; *Hu Changqing* (胡长清), Allgemeiner Teil des chinesischen Zivilrechts («中国民法总论»), 1998, S. 312–313; *Mei Zhongxie* (梅仲协), Das Wesentliche des Zivilrechts («民法要义»), 1998, S. 144, Rn. 162; *Wang Liming* (王利明), Das Zivilrecht («民法»), 2. Aufl. 2010, S. 134; *Zhang Junhao* (张俊浩), Kapitel 9: Stellvertretung bei den Zivilrechtsgeschäften, in: Zhang Junhao (张俊浩编), Theorien der Zivilrechtswissenschaft («民法学原理»), 1997, S. 270–271; *Long Weiqiu* (龙卫球), Allgemeiner Teil des Zivilrechts («民法总论»), 2001, S. 671.

43 *Zhu Qingyu* (朱庆育), Allgemeiner Teil des Zivilrechts («民法总论»), 2. Aufl. 2016, S. 231; *Zeng Xiangsheng* (曾祥生), Untersuchung des Anfechtungsrechts («撤销权制度研究»), 2010, S. 10.

44 *Zhang Junhao* (张俊浩), Kapitel 9: Stellvertretung bei den Zivilrechtsgeschäften, in: Zhang Junhao (张俊浩编), Theorien der Zivilrechtswissenschaft («民法学原理»), 1997, S. 270.

45 S. ausführlich *Xue Jun* (薛军), Ausübungsweise des Anfechtungsrechts für anfechtbare Rechtsgeschäfte ("论可撤销法律行为撤销权行使的方法"), Zeitschrift der Rechtswissenschaftler («法学家») 2016 Heft 5, 45–56.

die Anfechtbarkeit nicht. Ein Selbstkontrahieren ist grundsätzlich verboten, da die Gefahr besteht, dass die Interessen des Vertretenen vom Vertreter beeinträchtigt werden.[46] Diese generelle Gefahr wiegt schwerer als die Beeinträchtigungen des Rechtsverkehrs, zumal der Vertretene das In-Sich-Geschäft zulassen kann, wenn er es für förderlich hält.

Daher ist die stärkere gesetzliche Kontrolle berechtigt. Die schwebende Unwirksamkeit beugt dieser Gefahr besser vor als die Anfechtbarkeit und schützt die Interessen des Vertretenen effektiver. Das In-sich-Geschäft geht, wie schon festgestellt, über das Ziel des Vertretenen bei der Stellvertretung hinaus. Der Vertreter hat in dieser Situation eigentlich keine Vertretungsmacht. Somit ist das Selbstkontrahieren konsequent nach den Vorschriften über die Vertretung ohne Vertretungsmacht gemäß §§ 171 ff. GRCL bzw. §§ 48 ff. VG zu behandeln. Diese Herangehensweise scheint auch dogmatisch passender, weil das Selbstkontrahierungsverbot Teil des Stellvertretungsrechts ist.

4. Ausnahmen vom Verbot des Selbstkontrahierens nach § 168 Abs. 1 GRCL

a) Wirksames Selbstkontrahieren

Der Gesetzgeber hat in § 168 Abs. 1 GRCL das Selbstkontrahieren mit Einwilligung oder Genehmigung des Vertretenen für ausnahmsweise wirksam erklärt. Das ist angesichts des Grundsatzes der Privatautonomie zu begrüßen. Rechtstheoretisch wurden darüber hinaus noch weitere Ausnahmen er-

46 *Hu Changqing* (胡长清), Allgemeiner Teil des chinesischen Zivilrechts («中国民法总论»), 1998, S. 312; *Shi Shangkuan* (史尚宽), Allgemeiner Teil des Zivilrechts («民法总论»), 2002, S. 534; *Mei Zhongxie* (梅仲协), Das Wesentliche des Zivilrechts («民法要义»), 1998, S. 144, Rn. 162; *Wang Liming* (王利明), Das Zivilrecht («民法»), 2. Aufl. 2010, S. 134; *Long Weiqiu* (龙卫球), Allgemeiner Teil des Zivilrechts («民法总论»), 2001, S. 671; *Zhang Junhao* (张俊浩), Kapitel 9: Stellvertretung bei den Zivilrechtsgeschäften, in: Zhang Junhao (张俊浩编), Theorien der Zivilrechtswissenschaft («民法学原理»), 1997, S. 271.

örtert: erstens für das Selbstkontrahieren zur Erfüllung einer Verbindlichkeit[47] und zweitens für den Fall, dass dem Vertretenen lediglich ein rechtlicher Vorteil entsteht.[48]

Das Selbstkontrahieren bei der Erfüllung von Verbindlichkeiten entfaltet nach deutschem, japanischem sowie taiwanesischem Recht ausnahmsweise Wirksamkeit, weil allein die Erfüllung der Verbindlichkeiten kein neues Rechtsverhältnis begründet und dem Vertretenen kein Nachteil entsteht.[49] Problematisch ist allerdings, ob die Erfüllung von Verbindlichkeiten ein selbständiges Rechtsgeschäft ist und bejahendenfalls, welche Fallkonstellationen als Erfüllung von Verbindlichkeiten im Sinne der Norm gelten sollen.[50] Der taiwanesischen Rechtsdogmatik zufolge kann die Erfüllung einer Verbindlichkeit an Erfüllung statt nicht durch Selbstkontrahieren erfolgen, weil dabei ein neuer Vertrag zustande kommt.[51] Etwas anderes gilt für die Aufrechnung, denn es gibt hier keinen neuen Interessenausgleich.[52] Nach japanischem Recht ist die Erfüllung einer Verbindlichkeit typischerweise ein Eintragungsauftrag bzw. eine notarielle Beurkundung.[53] Jedoch kennt das japanische Recht kein Abstraktionsprinzip. Somit sind Eintragung und

---

47 *Ma Xinyan* (马新彦), Gesetzgebungsuntersuchung der Stellvertretung in den GRCL des Zivilrechts ("民法总则代理立法研究"), Die Rechtswissenschaftler («法学家») 2016 Heft 5, 121, 128.

48 *Ma Xinyan* (马新彦), Gesetzgebungsuntersuchung der Stellvertretung in den GRCL des Zivilrechts ("民法总则代理立法研究"), Die Rechtswissenschaftler («法学家») 2016 Heft 5, 121, 129; *Xie Hongfei* (谢鸿飞), Grundgedanken und wichtige Rechtsinstitute zur Gesetzgebung der Stellvertretung ("代理部分立法的基本理念和重要制度"), Schulzeitung der Ostchinesischen Universität für Politikwissenschaft und Recht («华东政法大学学报») 2016 Heft 5, 64, 71.

49 *Wang Liming* (王利明), Das Zivilrecht («民法»), 2. Aufl. 2010, S. 442; *Hu Changqing* (胡长清), Allgemeiner Teil des chinesischen Zivilrechts («中国民法总论»), 1998, S. 313; *Shi Shangkuan* (史尚宽), Allgemeiner Teil des Zivilrechts («民法总论»), 2002, S. 536.

50 *Ma Xinyan* (马新彦), Gesetzgebungsuntersuchung der Stellvertretung in den GRCL des Zivilrechts ("民法总则代理立法研究"), Die Rechtswissenschaftler («法学家») 2016 Heft 5, 121, 128.

51 *Wang Liming* (王利明), Das Zivilrecht («民法»), 2. Aufl. 2010, S. 442; *Shi Shangkuan* (史尚宽), Allgemeiner Teil des Zivilrechts («民法总论»), 2002, S. 536.

52 *Shi Shangkuan* (史尚宽), Allgemeiner Teil des Zivilrechts («民法总论»), 2002, S. 536; *Hu Changqing* (胡长清), Allgemeiner Teil des chinesischen Zivilrechts («中国民法总论»), 1998, S. 313.

53 *Qu Tao* (渠涛), Grundriss des Zivilrechts I, Allgemeiner Teil des Zivilrechts («民法讲义 I 民法总则»), 2015, S. 231.

Beurkundung keine selbständigen Rechtsgeschäfte, so dass es sich nicht um ein eigenständiges Selbstkontrahieren handelt.[54] Zudem wird die Meinung vertreten, dass der Vertretene in der Realität in jede Erfüllung einer Verbindlichkeit einwilligen würde, sodass diese Ausnahme als Fall der Zustimmung eingeordnet werden könne.[55]

Der andere Ausnahmefall betrifft die für den Vertretenen lediglich rechtlich vorteilhaften Rechtsgeschäfte. In der Sache geht es meist um die Rechtsgeschäfte von Minderjährigen. Nach § 19 GRCL muss bei einem Rechtsgeschäft eines Minderjährigen grundsätzlich dessen gesetzlicher Vertreter handeln. Ein In-sich-Geschäft liegt vor, wenn der gesetzliche Vertreter zugleich Geschäftsgegner ist, wie z. B. bei der Schenkung (§§ 185 ff. VG). In diesem Fall widerspräche es dem Schutzzweck des Verbots des Selbstkontrahierens, die Schenkung für unwirksam zu erklären.[56]

b) Als Selbstkontrahieren anzusehende Rechtsgeschäfte

Wenn der Vertreter unter Umgehung des Verbotes des Selbstkontrahierens mit einem Untervertreter einen Vertrag abschließt, so liegt auch in diesem Fall ein Selbstkontrahieren vor, weil sich der Vertragsinhalt nur nach dem Willen des Vertreters richtet.[57]

Eine ähnliche Konstellation ist der Vertragsabschluss zwischen Ehegatten. Daher ist der Wohnungskaufvertrag nach einer Entscheidung des Mittleren Volksgerichts der Provinz Hunan[58] wegen Selbstkontrahierens unwirksam, wenn der Ehemann als Vertreter des Wohnungsverkäufers mit seiner Ehefrau einen Wohnungskaufvertrag schließt. Diese Entscheidung

54 *Ma Xinyan* (马新彦), Gesetzgebungsuntersuchung der Stellvertretung in den GRCL des Zivilrechts ("民法总则代理立法研究"), Die Rechtswissenschaftler («法学家») 2016 Heft 5, 121, 128.

55 *Ma Xinyan* (马新彦), Gesetzgebungsuntersuchung der Stellvertretung in den GRCL des Zivilrechts ("民法总则代理立法研究"), Die Rechtswissenschaftler («法学家») 2016 Heft 5, 121, 128.

56 *Ma Xinyan* (马新彦), Gesetzgebungsuntersuchung der Stellvertretung in den GRCL des Zivilrechts ("民法总则代理立法研究"), Die Rechtswissenschaftler («法学家») 2016, 121, 129.

57 *Shi Shangkuan* (史尚宽), Allgemeiner Teil des Zivilrechts («民法总论»), 2002, S. 535.

58 MVG Hunan in Changsha, Urt. v. 25.4.2012, (2012) chang zhong min san zhong zi Nr. 1573.

ist zu begrüßen. Es handelt sich zwar formal nicht um Selbstkontrahieren, der Interessenkonflikt zwischen Vertreter und Vertretenem und die Gefahr der Interessenbeeinträchtigung zu Lasten des Vertretenen liegen aber faktisch in gleicher Weise vor.

III. Verbot des Selbstkontrahierens nach § 181 Alt. 1 BGB

Im deutschen Recht ist das Selbstkontrahieren unter dem Oberbegriff des „In-sich-Geschäfts" in § 181 Alt. 1 BGB geregelt, wonach der Vertreter nicht im Namen des Vertretenen ein Rechtsgeschäft mit sich selbst schließen darf.[59] Als In-sich-Geschäft ist daneben die sog. Mehrvertretung von § 181 Alt. 2 BGB erfasst. Ausnahmen für das Verbot des In-sich-Geschäfts gelten nach § 181 BGB im Falle der Gestattung des In-sich-Geschäfts durch den Vertretenen und bei der Erfüllung einer Verbindlichkeit.

1. Zur Gesetzgebungsgeschichte des Verbotes des Selbstkontrahierens nach § 181 Alt. 1 BGB

Das Verbot des Selbstkontrahierens war in Deutschland bereits im gemeinen Recht des 19. Jahrhunderts enthalten.[60] Bei der Erarbeitung des Bürgerlichen Gesetzbuchs hat die erste Kommission im Entwurf von 1874 ein Selbstkontrahieren indes grundsätzlich zugelassen, sofern keine besondere Vorschrift für ein Verbot eines solchen In-sich-Geschäfts bestand.[61] Wegen der mangelnden Berücksichtigung von Interessenkollisionen wurde diese

---

59 *Rüthers/Stadler,* Allgemeiner Teil des BGB, 18. Aufl. 2014, S. 465, Rn. 54; *Flume*, Allgemeiner Teil des Bürgerlichen Rechts, Bd. 2: Das Rechtsgeschäft, 4. Aufl.1992, S. 809; *Brox/Walker*, Allgemeiner Teil des BGB, 40. Aufl. 2016, S. 257, Rn. 584; MüKo/*Schubert*, 7. Aufl. 2015, § 181 BGB, Rn. 1; BeckOK/*Schäfer*, 42. Aufl. 2017, § 181 BGB, Rn. 1.

60 RG, Urt. v. 23.11.1881 (Az. I 82/81), RGZ 6, 11, 15; RG, Urt. v. 18.10.1882 (Az. I 335/82), RGZ 7, 119, 120; BeckOGK/*Fröhler*, § 181 BGB, Rn. 37; *Kiehnle*, AcP 212 (2012), 875, 893.

61 RG, Urt. v. 13.5.1909 (Az. IV 248/08), RGZ 71, 162, 165; *Mugdan*, Die gesammelten Materialien zum Bürgerlichen Gesetzbuch für das Deutsche Reich, Bd. 1, 1899, S. 476; BeckOGK/*Fröhler*, § 181 BGB, Rn. 39; *Kiehnle*, AcP 212 (2012), 875, 893.

Regelung heftig kritisiert. Die Vorkommission hat daher das In-sich-Geschäft in ihrem Vorschlag grundsätzlich verboten, ausgenommen waren die Fälle der Gestattung durch den Vertretenen und der Erfüllung einer Verbindlichkeit.[62] Diesen Vorschlag übernahm die zweite Kommission mit der Begründung, dass In-sich-Geschäfte mit der Verkehrssicherheit sowie den Bedürfnissen des Rechtsverkehrs unvereinbar seien.[63] Diese Regelung entspricht im Wesentlichen dem heutigen § 181 BGB.

2. Konzeption und Normzweck des Verbotes des Selbstkontrahierens nach § 181 Alt. 1 BGB

Das Verbot des Selbstkontrahierens dient in erster Linie dem Schutz des Vertretenen vor Kollisionen zwischen seinen Interessen und denen des Vertreters; das wurde bereits vom Gesetzgeber deutlich zum Ausdruck gebracht.[64] Dies wird auch von der Literatur hervorgehoben.[65] Es geht um die Prävention von Interessenkonflikten. Daher hängt das Verbot des Selbstkontrahierens nach § 181 Alt. 1 BGB nicht von einem konkreten Interessenkonflikt bzw. einer tatsächlichen Interessenverletzung des Vertretenen ab.[66] Die Norm ist somit eine formale Ordnungsvorschrift.[67] Neben der

---

62 Jakobs/Schubert (Hrsg.), Die Beratung des Bürgerlichen Gesetzbuchs, Bd. 2, 1985, S. 922; BeckOGK/*Fröhler*, § 181 BGB, Rn. 40; *Kiehnle*, AcP 212 (2012), 875, 894.

63 RG, Urt. v. 20.3.1908 (Az. II 586/07), RGZ 68, 172, 175; *Mugdan*, Die gesammelten Materialien zum Bürgerlichen Gesetzbuch für das Deutsche Reich, Bd. 1, 1899, S. 759; BeckOGK/*Fröhler*, § 181 BGB, Rn. 41; *Kiehnle*, AcP 212 (2012), 875, 894.

64 *Mugdan*, Die gesammelten Materialien zum Bürgerlichen Gesetzbuch für das Deutsche Reich, Bd. 1, 1899, S. 759.

65 *Rüthers/Stadler*, Allgemeiner Teil des BGB, 18. Aufl. 2014, S. 465, Rn. 55; *Brox/Walker*, Allgemeiner Teil des BGB, 40. Aufl. 2016, S. 258, Rn. 586; MüKo/*Schubert*, 7. Aufl. 2015, § 181 BGB, Rn. 2; BeckOK/*Schäfer*, 42. Aufl. 2017, § 181 BGB, Rn. 2.

66 MüKo/*Schubert*, 7. Aufl. 2015, § 181 BGB, Rn. 3; BeckOK/*Schäfer*, 42. Aufl. 2017, § 181 BGB, Rn. 3; *Rüthers/Stadler*, Allgemeiner Teil des BGB, 18. Aufl. 2014, S. 467, Rn. 60; *Flume*, Allgemeiner Teil des Bürgerlichen Rechts, Bd. 2: Das Rechtsgeschäft, 4. Aufl.1992, S. 811; *Hübner*, Allgemeiner Teil des Bürgerlichen Gesetzbuchs, 2. Aufl. 1996, S. 547, Rn. 1322.

67 MüKo/*Schubert*, 7. Aufl. 2015, § 181 BGB, Rn. 3; Jauernig/*Mansel*, 16. Auflage 2015, § 181 BGB, Rn. 6; BeckOK/*Schäfer*, 42. Aufl. 2017, § 181 BGB, Rn. 3;

Vermeidung von Interessenkonflikten bezweckt sie die Sicherheit des Rechtsverkehrs,[68] was sich bereits aus den Gesetzesmaterialien ergibt.[69]

Darüber hinaus dient § 181 Alt. 1 BGB dem Gläubigerschutz vor verborgenen Vermögensverschiebungen.[70] Das bestätigt § 35 Abs. 2 GmbHG, wonach § 181 Alt. 1 BGB auch für das Selbstkontrahieren in einer Ein-Personen-GmbH Anwendung findet. Ein solches Selbstkontrahieren durch den Gesellschafter-Geschäftsführer mit der GmbH hat keine Interessenkollision zwischen dem Vertreter und der Vertretenen zu Folge,[71] schützt aber die Gläubiger vor einer Überführung der Vermögensgegenstände aus dem GmbH-Vermögen in das Privatvermögen des Gesellschafter-Geschäftsführers.[72] § 181 Alt. 1 BGB kann den Gläubigerschutz indes nicht hinreichend verwirklichen, weil der Gesellschafter-Geschäftsführer von dem Verbot des Selbstkontrahierens leicht befreit werden kann, wenn in der Satzung einer Ein-Personen-GmbH eine Gestattung solcher Geschäfte enthalten ist oder in dieser das Rechtsgeschäft rückwirkend genehmigt wird.[73] Gefahren für die Gläubiger können auch bestehen, wenn es um die Erfüllung einer Verbindlichkeit als Ausnahmefall nach § 181 a. E. BGB geht (z. B. der Vertreter tilgt seine eigene Forderung vor allen anderen Gläubigern).[74]

Zusammenfassend ist festzuhalten, dass das Verbot des Selbstkontrahierens im deutschen Recht vor allem der Prävention von Interessenkollisionen und daneben der Sicherheit des Rechtsverkehrs dient. Dem Gläubigerschutz kann § 181 Alt. 1 BGB nicht hinreichend Rechnung tragen.

Hübner, Allgemeiner Teil des Bürgerlichen Gesetzbuchs, 2. Aufl. 1996, S. 547, Rn. 1322.

68 MüKo/*Schubert*, 7. Aufl. 2015, § 181 BGB, Rn. 3; BeckOK/*Schäfer*, 42. Aufl. 2017, § 181 BGB, Rn. 3; *Schiemann*, in: Staudinger, Eckpfeiler des Zivilrechts, 2014, S. 308, Rn. 219.

69 *Mugdan*, Die gesammelten Materialien zum Bürgerlichen Gesetzbuch für das Deutsche Reich, Bd. 1, 1899, S. 759.

70 MüKo/*Schubert*, 7. Aufl. 2015, § 181 BGB, Rn. 3, 30, 90; BeckOK/*Schäfer*, 42. Aufl. 2017, § 181 BGB, Rn. 3, 36a; *Hübner*, Allgemeiner Teil des Bürgerlichen Gesetzbuchs, 2. Aufl. 1996, S. 548, Rn. 1326.

71 MüKo/*Schubert*, 7. Aufl. 2015, § 181 BGB, Rn. 30; *Hübner*, Allgemeiner Teil des Bürgerlichen Gesetzbuchs, 2. Aufl. 1996, S. 548, Rn. 1326.

72 MüKo/*Schubert*, 7. Aufl. 2015, § 181 BGB, Rn. 30; BeckOK/*Schäfer*, 42. Aufl. 2017, § 181 BGB, Rn. 3; *Hübner*, Allgemeiner Teil des Bürgerlichen Gesetzbuchs, 2. Aufl. 1996, S. 548, Rn. 1326.

73 MüKo/*Schubert*, 7. Aufl. 2015, § 181 BGB, Rn. 30.

74 *Hübner*, Interessenkonflikt und Vertretungsmacht, 1977, S. 17.

3. Rechtsfolgen des Verstoßes gegen das Verbot des Selbstkontrahierens nach § 181 Alt. 1 BGB

Einhellig wird im deutschen Recht vertreten, dass das Verbot des Selbstkontrahierens nicht nur das rechtliche Dürfen des Vertreters, sondern auch sein rechtliches Können beschränkt.[75] Der Vertreter hat für ein In-sich-Geschäft keine Vertretungsmacht.[76] Somit finden auf ein gegen § 181 Alt. 1 BGB verstoßendes Rechtsgeschäft die Regeln der Vertretung ohne Vertretungsmacht gem. §§ 177 ff. BGB entsprechende Anwendung.[77] Das Vertretergeschäft ist schwebend unwirksam und wird erst mit der Genehmigung des Vertretenen wirksam.[78]

4. Ausnahmen vom Verbot des Selbstkontrahierens nach § 181 Alt. 1 BGB

Für die Anwendung des § 181 Alt. 1 BGB ist nur eine formale Personenidentität erforderlich. Das hat den Vorteil der Rechtssicherheit.[79] Neben den beiden vom Gesetz vorgesehenen Ausnahmefällen – der Gestattung des In-sich-Geschäfts und der Erfüllung einer Verbindlichkeit – bedarf es weiterer Einschränkungen, weil eine solch rigorose formale Anknüpfung in manchen Interessenlagen nicht sachgerecht ist.[80] Daher wird das Verbot des

---

75 BeckOK/*Schäfer*, 42. Aufl. 2017, § 181 BGB, Rn. 2, 29; *Brox/Walker*, Allgemeiner Teil des BGB, 40. Aufl. 2016, S. 258, Rn. 589.

76 MüKo/*Schubert*, 7. Aufl. 2015, § 181 BGB, Rn. 2, 65; *Brox/Walker*, Allgemeiner Teil des BGB, 40. Aufl. 2016, S. 258, Rn. 589.

77 MüKo/*Schubert*, 7. Aufl. 2015, § 181 BGB, Rn. 56; BeckOK/*Schäfer*, 42. Aufl. 2017, § 181 BGB, Rn. 29; *Schiemann*, in: Staudinger (Hrsg.), Eckpfeiler des Zivilrechts, 2014, S. 309, Rn. 222; *Hübner*, Allgemeiner Teil des Bürgerlichen Gesetzbuchs, 2. Aufl. 1996, S. 551, Rn. 1333; *Rüthers/Stadler*, Allgemeiner Teil des BGB, 18. Aufl. 2014, S. 466, Rn. 56.

78 Ein selbstkontrahiertes einseitiges Rechtsgeschäft ist aber nach § 180 S. 1 BGB nichtig, dies wird hier nicht ausgeführt.

79 MüKo/*Schubert*, 7. Aufl. 2015, § 181 BGB, Rn. 3; BeckOK/*Schäfer*, 42. Aufl. 2017, § 181 BGB, Rn. 3; *Schiemann*, in: Staudinger, Eckpfeiler des Zivilrechts, 2014, S. 308, Rn. 219.

80 *Schiemann*, in: Staudinger, Eckpfeiler des Zivilrechts, 2014, S. 309, Rn. 221; *Hübner*, Allgemeiner Teil des Bürgerlichen Gesetzbuchs, 2. Aufl. 1996, S. 547, Rn. 1323; *Flume*, Allgemeiner Teil des Bürgerlichen Rechts, Bd. 2: Das Rechtsgeschäft, 4. Aufl.1992, S. 812.

Selbstkontrahierens teleologisch reduziert und ein In-Sich-Geschäft in weiteren Fallgruppen zugelassen, soweit dabei eine Interessenkollision nicht ersichtlich ist.[81] Umgekehrt greift § 181 Alt. 1 BGB analog ein, wenn formal zwar keine Personenidentität vorliegt, wie sie für das Selbstkontrahieren erforderlich ist, materiell eine solche aber doch gegeben ist und die rechtsgeschäftliche Konstellation diese lediglich umgeht.[82]

a) Wirksames Selbstkontrahieren

Ein Selbstkontrahieren ist nach deutschem Recht wirksam, wenn es vom Vertretenen gestattet wurde oder wenn es ausschließlich der Erfüllung einer Verbindlichkeit dient (§ 181 BGB). Der von § 181 BGB bezweckte Schutz der Interessen des Vertretenen ist in diesen Fällen entbehrlich. Der Vertretene kann auf diesen Schutz durch Gestattung des Selbstkontrahierens verzichten.[83] Diese muss dem Vertreter vor der Vornahme des Vertretergeschäfts erteilt werden[84] und ist nicht formbedürftig. Sie kann sowohl ausdrücklich als auch konkludent erklärt werden.[85] Bei der Erfüllung einer Verbindlichkeit fehlt ein Interessenkonflikt, da die Verpflichtung des Vertretenen bereits durch das vorherige Eingehen einer Verbindlichkeit entstanden ist und diese ohnehin erfüllt werden muss,[86] sofern sie wirksam, einredefrei und fällig ist.[87]

---

81 MüKo/*Schubert*, 7. Aufl. 2015, § 181 BGB, Rn. 5; Jauernig/*Mansel*, 16. Auflage 2015, § 181 BGB, Rn. 7; BeckOK/*Schäfer*, 42. Aufl. 2017, § 181 BGB, Rn. 18; *Rüthers/Stadler*, Allgemeiner Teil des BGB, 18. Aufl. 2014, S. 467, Rn. 59.

82 *Schiemann*, in: Staudinger, Eckpfeiler des Zivilrechts, 2014, S. 309, Rn. 221.

83 *Hübner*, Allgemeiner Teil des Bürgerlichen Gesetzbuchs, 2. Aufl. 1996, S. 547, Rn. 1321.

84 MüKo/*Schubert*, 7. Aufl. 2015, § 181 BGB, Rn. 65.

85 MüKo/*Schubert*, 7. Aufl. 2015, § 181 BGB, Rn. 71; HK-BGB/*Dörner*, 9. Aufl. 2017, § 181 BGB, Rn. 7; *Rüthers/Stadler*, Allgemeiner Teil des BGB, 18. Aufl. 2014, S. 466, Rn. 57.

86 *Rüthers/Stadler*, Allgemeiner Teil des BGB, 18. Aufl. 2014, S. 466, Rn. 58; *Hübner*, Allgemeiner Teil des Bürgerlichen Gesetzbuchs, 2. Aufl. 1996, S. 547, Rn. 1321; *Brox/Walker*, Allgemeiner Teil des BGB, 40. Aufl. 2016, S. 259, Rn. 591.

87 *Rüthers/Stadler*, Allgemeiner Teil des BGB, 18. Aufl. 2014, S. 466, Rn. 58; *Hübner*, Allgemeiner Teil des Bürgerlichen Gesetzbuchs, 2. Aufl. 1996, S. 547, Rn. 1321.

Die Ausnahmen vom Verbot des Selbstkontrahierens sind von Rechtsprechung und Literatur erweitert worden. Die wichtigste Fallgruppe bilden die lediglich rechtlich vorteilhaften Rechtsgeschäfte.[88] Wenn das Selbstkontrahieren dem Vertretenen lediglich rechtliche Vorteile bringt, besteht weder eine Gefahr des Interessenkonflikts noch ist der Vertretene schutzbedürftig.[89] § 181 Alt. 1 BGB ist teleologisch zu reduzieren und findet daher keine Anwendung.[90] Eine wesentliche Fallgruppe ist der Abschluss eines Schenkungsvertrags von Eltern mit ihren minderjährigen Kindern, § 181 Alt. 1 BGB.[91] Dadurch ist die Bestellung eines Ergänzungspflegers nach §§ 1629 Abs. 2, 1795 Abs. 2, 1909 BGB entbehrlich. Diese teleologische Reduktion knüpft vor allem an den Minderjährigenschutz an. Daher lässt die h. M. das Selbstkontrahieren zu, wenn das Rechtsgeschäft rechtlich neutral ist (§ 107 BGB).[92]

Einschränkungen sind aber erforderlich, wenn die Erfüllung des Schenkungsvertrags für den Minderjährigen rechtlich nachteilhaft ist (z. B. Erwerb einer Eigentumswohnung[93]). Im deutschen Recht wird in diesem Fall § 181 a. E. BGB dahingehend angewendet, dass eine Selbstkontraktion trotz der bloßen Erfüllung einer Verbindlichkeit nicht zulässig ist. § 181 Alt. 1 BGB greift ein, weil die Gefahr der Benachteiligung des Vertretenen besteht.[94]

---

88 BGH, Urt. v. 27.9.1972 (Az. IV ZR 225/69), BGHZ 59, 236, 240; BGH, Urt. v. 25.4.1985 (Az. IX ZR 141/84), BGHZ 94, 232, 235; BGH, Urt. v. 8.6.1989 (Az. IX ZR 234/87), BGH NJW 1989, 2542.

89 BeckOK/*Schäfer*, 42. Aufl. 2017, § 181 BGB, Rn. 19; *Brox/Walker*, Allgemeiner Teil des BGB, 40. Aufl. 2016, S. 258 f., Rn. 592.

90 HK-BGB/*Dörner*, 9. Aufl. 2017, § 181 BGB, Rn. 13; *Rüthers/Stadler,* Allgemeiner Teil des BGB, 18. Aufl. 2014, S. 466, Rn. 59.

91 BGH, Urt. v. 27.9.1972 (Az. IV ZR 225/69), BGHZ 59, 236, 240; BGH, Urt. v. 25.4.1985 (Az. IX ZR 141/84), BGHZ 94, 232, 235; BGH, Urt. v. 8.6.1989 (Az. IX ZR 234/87), BGH NJW 1989, 2542.

92 MüKo/*Schubert*, 7. Aufl. 2015, § 181 BGB, Rn. 29; BeckOK/*Schäfer*, 42. Aufl. 2017, § 181 BGB, Rn. 19.

93 BGH, Urt. v. 9.7.1980 (Az. V ZB 16/79), BGHZ 78, 29, 34.

94 BGH, Urt. v. 9.7.1980 (Az. V ZB 16/79), BGHZ 78, 29, 34; MüKo/*Schubert*, 7. Aufl. 2015, § 181 BGB, Rn. 29, 87; HK-BGB/*Dörner*, 9. Aufl. 2017, § 181 BGB, Rn. 12; *Brox/Walker*, Allgemeiner Teil des BGB, 40. Aufl. 2016, S. 258 f., Rn. 592.

b) Selbstkontrahieren i. S. v. § 181 Alt. 1 BGB

Das Selbstkontrahieren knüpft formal an der Personenidentität von Vertreter und Geschäftspartner an. § 181 Alt. 1 BGB wird im deutschen Recht aber auch auf Fälle angewandt, in denen die Personenidentität umgangen wird. Eine weite Auslegung oder analoge Anwendung des § 181 Alt. 1 BGB knüpft aber nicht an das Vorliegen eines Interessenkonflikts an, sondern nur an der Umgehung der Personenidentität.[95] Dem ist zu folgen, weil es trotz Interessenkonflikts kein Selbstkontrahieren i. S. v. § 181 Alt. 1 BGB ist, wenn z. B. der Vertreter mit dem Vertretenen einen Bürgschaftsvertrag zur Sicherung der Schuld des Vertreters abschließt und dieser Vertrag offensichtlich nur zu Gunsten des Vertreters ist.[96] Eine typische Fallgruppe für die Ausdehnung des § 181 BGB ist die Bestellung eines Untervertreters durch den Vertreter, mit dem er das Rechtsgeschäft im Namen des Vertretenen abschließen kann und somit die formale Personenidentität, an die § 181 Alt. 1 BGB anknüpft, vermeidet.[97] § 181 Alt. 1 BGB findet insofern analoge Anwendung.[98]

IV. Verbot des Selbstkontrahierens nach Art. 2.2.7 PICC und Art. 3:205 PECL

1. Regelungskonzept

Unabhängig von den Regelungen des nationalen Rechts bestehen regionale bzw. internationale Regeln, die auf eine Rechtsvereinheitlichung zielen. Eine einheitliche Rechtsanwendung für Handelsverträge streben insbesondere die PICC an. In Europa hat eine Expertengruppe zudem die PECL erarbeitet. Beide Regelwerke enthalten Bestimmungen, die dem Verbot des

95 *Rüthers/Stadler*, Allgemeiner Teil des BGB, 18. Aufl. 2014, S. 467 f., Rn. 58.
96 *Rüthers/Stadler*, Allgemeiner Teil des BGB, 18. Aufl. 2014, S. 468, Rn. 62.
97 BGH, Urt. v. 6.3.1975, (Az. II ZR 80/73), BGHZ 64, 72, 74; BGH, Urt. v. 13.6.1984, (Az. VIII ZR 125/83), BGHZ, 91, 334, 336.
98 BGH, Urt. v. 24.9.1990 (Az. II ZR 167/89), BGHZ, 112, 339, 341; MüKo/*Schubert*, 7. Aufl. 2015, § 181 BGB, Rn. 43; BeckOK/*Schäfer*, 42. Aufl. 2017, § 181 BGB, Rn. 23; *Rüthers/Stadler*, Allgemeiner Teil des BGB, 18. Aufl. 2014, S. 467 f., Rn. 61; *Hübner*, Allgemeiner Teil des Bürgerlichen Gesetzbuchs, 2. Aufl. 1996, S. 549, Rn. 1328; *Brox/Walker*, Allgemeiner Teil des BGB, 40. Aufl. 2016, S. 260, Rn. 593.

Selbstkontrahierens inhaltlich entsprechen. Sie sind jeweils unter dem Titel Interessenkonflikte (Conflict of interest[s]) zu finden (Art. 2.2.7 PICC; Art. 3:205 PECL).

Nach Art. 2.2.7 PICC kann der Vertretene dem vom Vertreter in seinem Namen abgeschlossenen Vertrag die Wirksamkeit nehmen, wenn sich der Vertrag auf einen Interessenkonflikt zwischen dem Vertreter und Vertretenen bezieht und der Geschäftspartner diesen Interessenkonflikt kannte oder kennen musste (Art. 2.2.7 Abs. 1 PICC). Der Vertretene hat ein rechtsvernichtendes Gestaltungsrecht, es sei denn, er hat diesem Interessenkonflikt zugestimmt, kannte ihn oder hätte ihn kennen müssen (Art. 2.2.7 Abs. 2 lit. (a) PICC).[99] Der Vertretene muss das Gestaltungsrecht innerhalb einer angemessenen Frist, nachdem ihm der Vertreter den Interessenkonflikt mitgeteilt hat, ausüben (Art. 2.2.7 Abs. 2 lit. (b) PICC). Das Selbstkontrahieren ist eine der häufigsten Konstellationen für einen derartigen Interessenkonflikt.[100]

Art. 2.2.7 PICC deckt sich im Wesentlichen mit Art. 3:205 PECL. Zentraler Unterschied zwischen beiden Normen ist Art. 3:205 Abs. 2 PECL, der die Mehrvertretung (Art. 3:205 Abs. 2 lit. (a) PECL) und das Selbstkontrahieren (Art. 3:205 Abs. 2 lit. (b) PECL) als Prototypen des Interessenkonflikts benennt.[101]

2. Regelungshistorie

Nach der Erarbeitung der PICC durch das Internationale Institut für die Vereinheitlichung des Privatrechts (UNIDROIT) im Jahre 1994 wurden diese 2004 und 2010 revidiert. Das Stellvertretungsrecht, einschließlich

---

99 MüKo/*Schubert*, 7. Aufl. 2015, § 181 BGB, Rn. 7.

100 Comment 1. zu Art. 2.2.7 Abs. 2 Alt. 2 PICC: The most frequent cases of potential conflict of intrerests are those where the agent concludes the contract with itself.

101 MüKo/*Schubert*, 7. Aufl. 2015, § 181 BGB, Rn. 7.

Art. 2.2.7, wurde erst 2004 in die PICC eingefügt.[102] Die Aufnahme der Regeln über die Interessenkonflikte in Art. 2.2.7 PICC beruhte darauf, „that conflict of interests was too important a topic to be left out of the draft"[103].

Art. 3:205 PECL wurde auf der Grundlage rechtsvergleichender Studien 1996 von der Lando-Kommission erarbeitet und 1998 sowie 2002 revidiert. Daraus ergab sich die Regelung der Interessenkonflikte, insbesondere die Vermutungsregelung in Art. 3:205 Abs. 2 PECL.[104] Die Gründe für diese abweichende Ausgestaltung im Vergleich zu Art. 2.2.7 PICC liegen zunächst darin, dass es an einer einheitlichen Auffassung zum „Interessenkonflikt" und den Konsequenzen einer solchen Vermutungsregelung fehlte.[105] Zudem sollte von Fall zu Fall beurteilt werden, ob in der konkreten Situation ein Interessenkonflikt vorliegt.[106] Daher hat man auf eine Vermutungsregelung in Art. 2.2.7 PICC verzichtet. Im Gegensatz dazu verwies die Lando-Kommission hinsichtlich Art. 3:205 Abs. 2 PECL darauf, dass Selbstkontrahieren und Mehrvertretung als die Hauptfälle des Interessenkonflikts festzuschreiben seien.[107]

3. Normzweck

Bereits aus dem Wortlaut ist ersichtlich, dass Art. 2.2.7 PICC und Art. 3:205 PECL Interessenkonflikte vermeiden sollen. Der Normzweck im Fall des Selbstkontrahierens ist allerdings von anderen Fällen zu unterscheiden. Zunächst beruht der Interessenkonflikt nach Art. 2.2.7 PICC und Art. 3:205 PECL, anders als das Verbot des Selbstkontrahierens nach § 181 Alt. 1 BGB, nicht auf einem abstrakten, sondern auf einem tatsächlichen

---

102 *Wang Jian* (王健), Kursorische Besprechung der PICC, Die revidierte Fassung 2004, Die Rechtsordnung und Gesellschaft («法制与社会») 2007 Heft 8, 90, 90.

103 *Festner*, Interessenkonflikte im deutschen und englischen Vertretungsrecht, 2006, S. 61.

104 *Festner*, Interessenkonflikte im deutschen und englischen Vertretungsrecht, 2006, S. 62 ff.

105 *Festner*, Interessenkonflikte im deutschen und englischen Vertretungsrecht, 2006, S. 62.

106 *Festner*, Interessenkonflikte im deutschen und englischen Vertretungsrecht, 2006, S. 62.

107 *Festner*, Interessenkonflikte im deutschen und englischen Vertretungsrecht, 2006, S. 62.

Interessenkonflikt zwischen Vertreter und Vertretenem.[108] Dies gilt in allen Fällen eines Interessenkonflikts. Außerdem bedarf es für das Vorliegen eines Interessenkonflikts bei beiden Regelungen der Unkenntnis des Geschäftspartners. Somit beziehen sich beide nicht nur auf das Innenverhältnis zwischen Vertreter und Vertretenem, sondern auch auf das Außenverhältnis zum Geschäftspartner.[109] Damit wird – sofern sowohl ein Innenverhältnis als auch Außenverhältnis besteht – weniger der Schutz der Interessen des Vertretenen als der Schutz der Interessen des Geschäftspartners angestrebt.[110] Das Innenverhältnis wird durch andere Vorschriften geregelt.[111] Allerdings spielt die Kenntnis Dritter beim Selbstkontrahieren grundsätzlich keine Rolle, weil der Geschäftspartner und der Vertreter gerade identisch sind. Somit steht der Schutz des Vertretenen im Vordergrund.

Art. 2.2.7 PICC und Art. 3:205 PECL werden auch als Bestimmungen zur Wahrung der Privatautonomie des Vertretenen verstanden.[112] Dem ist zuzustimmen. Nach Art. 2.2.7 Abs. 1 PICC und Art. 3:205 Abs. 1 PECL kann der Vertretene einerseits den Vertrag wegen des Interessenkonflikts anfechten, andererseits verliert er das Gestaltungsrecht nach Art. 2.2.7 Abs. 2 PICC und Art. 3:205 Abs. 3 PECL, wenn er einen solchen Konflikt

108 MüKo/*Schubert*, 7. Aufl. 2015, § 181 BGB, Rn. 7; *Festner*, Interessenkonflikte im deutschen und englischen Vertretungsrecht, 2006, S. 67; *You Hongyan* (尤宏岩), Research on the Agency System of the Principles of International Commercial Contracts 2004, 2007, S. 10.

109 *Zhang Xi* (张曦), The Study on the System of Agency in "UNIDROIT Principles for International Commercial Contracts 2004", Comparative Analysis with Chinese Law, 2007, S. 16; *Wang Jian* (王健), Kursorische Besprechung der PICC, Die revidierte Fassung 2004, Die Rechtsordnung und Gesellschaft («法制与社会») 2007 Heft 8, 190, 191.

110 *Festner*, Interessenkonflikte im deutschen und englischen Vertretungsrecht, 2006, S. 63; *Wang Jian* (王健), Kursorische Besprechung der PICC, Die revidierte Fassung 2004, Die Rechtsordnung und Gesellschaft («法制与社会») 2007 Heft 8, 190, 191.

111 *Zhang Xi* (张曦), The Study on the System of Agency in "UNIDROIT Principles for International Commercial Contracts 2004", Comparative Analysis with Chinese Law, 2007, S. 16; *Wang Jian* (王健), Kursorische Besprechung der PICC, Die revidierte Fassung 2004, Die Rechtsordnung und Gesellschaft («法制与社会») 2007 Heft 8, 190, 191.

112 MüKo/*Schubert*, 7. Aufl. 2015, § 181 BGB, Rn. 7 in Bezug auf das Ziel des Art. 3:205 PECL.

gestattet oder keine Einrede erhoben hat, nachdem ihn der Vertreter hierüber aufgeklärt hat. Insofern hängt das Gestaltungsrecht vom Kennen oder Kennenmüssen des Vertretenen hinsichtlich des Interessenkonflikts ab.[113]

4. Rechtsfolgen des Verstoßes gegen das Verbot des Selbstkontrahierens nach Art. 2.2.7 PICC und Art. 3:205 PECL

Liegt ein Interessenkonflikt nach Art. 2.2.7 PICC und Art. 3:205 PECL vor, kann der Vertretene den Vertrag für unwirksam erklären. Sachlich entspricht das dem Anfechtungsrecht im deutschen[114] sowie im chinesischen Recht, auch wenn im chinesischen Recht eine Gestaltungsklage erhoben werden muss. Der Vertretene muss bei einem solchen Interessenkonflikt aktiv vorgehen. Der Vertrag bleibt ohne entsprechende Erklärung durch den Vertretenen wirksam. Das gewährleistet die Effektivität des Rechtsverkehrs[115] zu Lasten der Rechtssicherheit.[116]

5. Ausnahmen vom Verbot des Selbstkontrahierens nach Art. 2.2.7 PICC und Art. 3:205 PECL

Alle Ausnahmen vom Verbot des Selbstkontrahierens nach Art. 2.2.7 PICC und Art. 3:205 PECL sind von der Kenntnis des Vertretenen vom Interessenkonflikt abhängig. Abgesehen von den unterschiedlichen Kriterien für die fahrlässige Unkenntnis des Vertretenen[117] gilt die Ausnahme übereinstimmend beim Kennenmüssen des Interessenkonflikts (Art. 2.2.7 Abs. 2 lit. (a) Alt. 2 PICC; Art. 3:205 Abs. 3 lit. (a) Alt. 2 PECL) sowie bei der

113 MüKo/*Schubert*, 7. Aufl. 2015, § 181 BGB, Rn. 7.

114 MüKo/*Schubert*, 7. Aufl. 2015, § 181 BGB, Rn. 8; *Festner*, Interessenkonflikte im deutschen und englischen Vertretungsrecht, 2006, S. 270.

115 *Geng Lin/Cui Jianyuan* (耿林/崔建远), Konstruktion des Rechtsinstituts der Stellvertretung in den GRCL des Zivilrechts ("民法总则应当如何设计代理制度"), Die Rechtsanwendung («法律适用») 2016 Heft 5, 51, 58; *Liang Huixing* (梁慧星), Allgemeiner Teil des Zivilrechts («民法总论»), 4. Aufl. 2010, S. 228; *Xie Hongfei* (谢鸿飞), Grundgedanken und wichtige Rechtsinstitute zur Gesetzgebung der Stellvertretung ("代理部分立法的基本理念和重要制度"), Schulzeitung der Ostchinesischen Universität für Politikwissenschaft und Recht («华东政法大学学报») 2016 Heft 5, 64, 70.

116 MüKo/*Schubert*, 7. Aufl. 2015, § 181 BGB, Rn. 7.

117 S. auch *Festner*, Interessenkonflikte im deutschen und englischen Vertretungsrecht, 2006, S. 273 f.

Aufklärung des Vertretenen über den Interessenkonflikt durch den Vertreter (Art. 2.2.7 Abs. 2 lit. (b) PICC; Art. 3:205 Abs. 3 lit. (b) PECL). Zudem besteht eine Ausnahme für den Fall der Gestattung durch den Vertretenen (Art. 2.2.7 Abs. 2 lit. (a) Alt. 1 PICC; Art. 3:205 Abs. 3 lit. (a) Alt. 1 PECL).

Unabhängig von der Schutzbedürftigkeit des Vertretenen ist damit das Verhältnis zwischen den Ausnahmefällen noch nicht geklärt. Insbesondere stellt sich die Frage, ob die Gestattung und die Aufklärung über den Interessenkonflikt überhaupt noch sinnvoll sind, wenn das Kennen oder Kennenmüssen das Anfechtungsrecht des Vertretenen bereits ausschließen. In diesen Fällen ist die Anfechtungsmöglichkeit des Vertretenen also eingeschränkt. Das Bestehen der Willenserklärung im Außenverhältnis hängt nicht allein vom Willen des Vertretenen ab. Der Vertreter hat verschiedene Handlungsalternativen,[118] insbesondere wenn er sich des Bestehens eines Interessenkonflikts nicht sicher ist.

V. Rechtsvergleichende Betrachtung

1. Zur historischen Entwicklung des Verbotes des Selbstkontrahierens

In den vier in diesen Vergleich einbezogenen Regelwerken hat sich das Verbot des Selbstkontrahierens im deutschen Recht etwa ein Jahrhundert früher entwickelt als in den anderen. Zwar kannte das chinesische Recht das Verbot des Selbstkontrahierens bereits vor Erlass des § 168 Abs. 1 GRCL. Die wiederholten Gesetzesänderungen hatten jedoch zur Folge, dass die Auseinandersetzung mit dem Verbot des Selbstkontrahierens in der chinesischen Rechtswissenschaft noch in den Anfängen steckt.

Abzulehnen ist eine einheitliche Herangehensweise für einseitige und vertragliche Rechtsgeschäfte, weil sie erhebliche Unterschiede aufweisen: die Essenz des Vertrages ist die Vertragsfreiheit und die Einigung beider Vertragsparteien,[119] während bei einem einseitigen Rechtsgeschäft die Willenserklärung einer Partei gestaltend wirkt.[120] Aus diesem Grund ist ein

---

118 MüKo/*Schubert*, 7. Aufl. 2015, § 181 BGB, Rn. 8.

119 *Zhu Qingyu* (朱庆育), Allgemeiner Teil des Zivilrechts («民法总论»), 2. Aufl. 2016, S. 137.

120 *Zhu Qingyu* (朱庆育), Allgemeiner Teil des Zivilrechts («民法总论»), 2. Aufl. 2016, S. 136.

Selbstkontrahieren bei einseitigen Rechtsgeschäften, anders als bei einem Vertrag, nicht genehmigungsfähig, sondern unwirksam (§ 180 S. 1 BGB; s. o. Fn. 78). Auch Art. 2.2.7 PICC und Art. 3:205 PECL sind aufgrund des Anwendungsbereiches der PICC[121] und der PECL (Art. 1:101 PECL) auf Verträge beschränkt.

2. Konzeption und Zweck des Verbotes des Selbstkontrahierens

Während sich § 168 Abs. 1 GRCL und § 181 Alt. 1 BGB in ihrer Konzeption ähnlich sind, wählen Art. 2.2.7 PICC und Art. 3:205 PECL einen abweichenden Regelungsansatz. Erstere verbieten das Selbstkontrahieren und erlauben dessen Gestattung, letztere erlauben das Selbstkontrahieren, ermöglichen jedoch die Anfechtung des Vertretergeschäfts. Die Ähnlichkeit des chinesischen zum deutschen Recht beruht darauf, dass bei der Ausarbeitung der GRCL hauptsächlich an die kontinentaleuropäischen Rechtsordnungen angeknüpft wurde.[122]

Art. 2.2.7 PICC und Art. 3:205 PECL sind in ihrer Konzeption darauf ausgerichtet, Interessenkonflikte beim Vertragsschluss durch einen Vertreter umfassend zu regeln, während sich § 181 Alt. 1 BGB und § 168 Abs. 1 GRCL auf das In-sich-Geschäft als Fallgruppe der Interessenkonflikte bei der Stellvertretung beschränken. Das Verbot des Selbstkontrahierens nach § 181 Alt. 1 BGB wirkt durch das Fehlen der Vertretungsmacht präventiv.[123] Ein Selbstkontrahieren liegt bereits vor, wenn aufgrund der Personenidentität allgemein die Gefahr eines Interessenkonflikts besteht, ohne dass es auf eine tatsächliche Interessenverletzung des Vertretenen ankommt (s. o. III. 2.). Das verwirklicht den Schutz der Interessen des Vertretenen und die Rechtssicherheit in besonderem Maße. Einen vergleichbaren Weg hat das chinesische Recht eingeschlagen.

---

121 Der erste Satz der Präambel der PICC: These Principles set forth general rules for international commercial contracts.

122 *Liang Huixing* (梁慧星), Geschichtlicher Rückblick auf die chinesische Zivilrechtswissenschaft und ihre Aussicht ("中国民法学的历史回顾与展望"), Zeitschrift der Wangjianger Rechtswissenschaft («望江法学») 2007, 1, 4.

123 MüKo/*Schubert*, 7. Aufl. 2015, § 181 BGB, Rn. 3; BeckOK/*Schäfer*, 42. Aufl. 2017, § 181 BGB, Rn. 3; *Rüthers/Stadler*, Allgemeiner Teil des BGB, 18. Aufl. 2014, S. 467, Rn. 60; *Flume*, Allgemeiner Teil des Bürgerlichen Rechts, Bd. 2: Das Rechtsgeschäft, 4. Aufl.1992, S. 811; *Hübner*, Allgemeiner Teil des Bürgerlichen Gesetzbuchs, 2. Aufl. 1996, Rn. 1322.

Im Gegensatz dazu erfassen Art. 2.2.7 PICC und Art. 3:205 PECL alle Interessenkonflikte, auch wenn das Selbstkontrahieren gesondert erfasst ist. Anders als bei § 181 Alt. 1 BGB bedarf es eines konkreten Interessenkonflikts bei Vertragsschluss.[124] Der Vertrag ist dann wirksam, aber anfechtbar. Im Interesse des Geschäftspartners an der Aufrechterhaltung des Vertragsverhältnisses ist die Anfechtung nur zulässig, wenn dieser Kenntnis vom Interessenkonflikt hatte (Art. 2.2.7 Abs. 1 PICC; Art. 3:205 Abs. 1 PECL). Das gilt selbstverständlich nicht für die Fälle des Selbstkontrahierens, in denen es allein auf das Bestehen des Interessenkonflikts ankommt (s. o. IV. 3.). Die Anfechtbarkeit hängt allerdings davon ab, dass der Vertretene den Interessenkonflikt nicht kannte oder kennen musste. Ansonsten ist der Vertretene nicht schutzbedürftig. Der Normzweck der Art. 2.2.7 PICC und Art. 3:205 PECL, der Schutz der Privatautonomie, rechtfertigt einen weitergehenden Schutz nicht.[125] Die Begrenzung des Schutzes wird in der deutschen Diskussion zu § 181 Alt. 1 BGB wenig beachtet, zumal die Norm selbst dem Schutz des Vertretenen einen weiterreichenden Vorrang einräumt, den dieser vor allem selbst durch die Gestattung relativieren kann (s. o. III. 2.).

Die chinesischen Autoren gehen überwiegend davon aus, dass sich § 168 Abs. 1 GRCL auch auf den Interessenkonflikt bezieht. Dabei wird nicht deutlich gemacht, ob es dafür auf die abstrakte Gefahr eines Interessenkonflikts wie bei § 181 Alt. 1 BGB ankommt oder auf einen konkreten tatsächlichen Interessenkonflikt wie bei Art. 2.2.7 PICC und Art. 3:205 PECL. Der wichtigste Unterschied zwischen diesen beiden Ansätzen besteht nach dem chinesischen Verständnis bei den Tatbestandsvoraussetzungen und der Beweislast. Es stellt sich die Frage, ob es auf der Seite des Vertretenen für den Interessenkonflikt schon reicht, wenn Personenidentität von Vertreter und Geschäftspartner vorliegt oder ob der Vertretene konkret darlegen und beweisen muss, dass der von ihm behauptete Interessenkonflikt vorliegt. Evident ist, dass eine formale Personenidentität für den Vertretenen leichter zu beweisen ist. Für diese Konzeption spricht außerdem, dass § 168 Abs. 1 GRCL in erster Linie die Interessen des Vertretenen vor der Gefährdung durch ein Selbstkontrahieren des Vertreters schützen will.

---

124 MüKo/*Schubert*, 7. Aufl. 2015, § 181 BGB, Rn. 7; *Festner*, Interessenkonflikte im deutschen und englischen Vertretungsrecht, 2006, S. 67; *You Hongyan* (尤宏岩), Research on the Agency System of the Principles of International Commercial Contracts 2004, 2007, S. 10.

125 MüKo/*Schubert*, 7. Aufl. 2015, § 181 BGB, Rn. 7.

3. Rechtsfolgen des Verstoßes gegen das Verbot des Selbstkontrahierens

Der Schutz der Interessen des Vertretenen nach Art. 2.2.7 PICC und Art. 3:205 PECL auf der einen und nach § 181 BGB auf der anderen Seite unterscheidet sich auch in den Rechtsfolgen. Nach § 181 Alt. 1 BGB ist der Vertrag schwebend unwirksam (s. o. III. 3.), während er nach Art. 2.2.7 PICC und Art. 3:205 PECL wirksam, aber anfechtbar ist (s. o. IV. 4.). Die Abwägung zwischen Rechtssicherheit für den Vertretenen und Effektivität des Rechtsverkehrs ist mit unterschiedlichen Ergebnissen vorgenommen worden.

Gerade diese Frage wird derzeit in der chinesischen Rechtswissenschaft intensiv erörtert (s. o. II. 3.), weil § 168 Abs. 1 GRCL keine Rechtsfolgen bestimmt. Maßgeblich dafür, ob das chinesische Recht die Anfechtbarkeit wie in Art. 2.2.7 PICC und Art. 3:205 PECL oder die schwebende Unwirksamkeit wie in § 181 Alt. 1 BGB für das Selbstkontrahieren bestimmen sollte, sind zum einen die Funktionsunterschiede zwischen der Anfechtung und Stellvertretung und zum andern das Regelungskonzept (s. o. II. 3.). Zu beachten ist weiter, dass die Anfechtbarkeit in Art. 2.2.7 PICC und Art. 3:205 PECL von der fehlenden Kenntnis bzw. vom Nicht-Kennenmüssen des Vertretenen abhängt. Eine solche Vorgabe ergibt sich aus § 168 Abs. 1 GRCL nicht. Somit liegt für das chinesische Recht eine Entscheidung zu Gunsten der schwebenden Unwirksamkeit des Vertrages im Falle des Selbstkontrahierens nahe.

4. Ausnahmen vom Verbot des Selbstkontrahierens

Die Ausnahmen zum Verbot des Selbstkontrahierens vervollständigen die Umsetzung des Regelungszwecks, wo es dem Verbotstatbestand nur unvollkommen gelingt. § 168 Abs. 1 GRCL und § 181 Alt. 1 BGB lassen ein Selbstkontrahieren daher ausnahmsweise vereinzelt zu, so dass das Vertretergeschäft wirksam ist, während Art. 2.2.7 Abs. 2 PICC und Art. 3:205 Abs. 3 PECL teilweise das Anfechtungsrecht des Vertretenen entfallen lassen, so dass der Vertrag endgültig wirksam ist.

§ 168 Abs. 1 GRCL ist aufgrund der dem § 181 Alt. 1 BGB ähnlichen Struktur in vergleichbarer Weise einzuschränken. Die Einschränkungen in Art. 2.2.7 Abs. 2 PICC und Art. 3:205 Abs. 3 PECL passen weder der Konzeption noch dem Inhalt nach. Die Ausnahmen knüpfen an das Kennen oder Kennenmüssen des Vertretenen, § 168 Abs. 1 GRCL hingegen knüpft an die Zustimmung des Vertretenen an. Soweit § 168 Abs. 1 GRCL und § 181

Alt. 1 BGB das Vermeiden der Interessenkonflikte bezwecken, liegt es nahe, sich hinsichtlich der teleologischen Reduktion des § 168 Abs. 1 GRCL an die deutsche Diskussion anzulehnen. Insbesondere ist das Selbstkontrahieren bei lediglich rechtlich vorteilhaften Rechtsgeschäften zuzulassen. Im Gegensatz zum deutschen Recht sieht § 168 Abs. 1 GRCL keine Ausnahme für die Erfüllung einer Verbindlichkeit vor. Da das chinesische Recht kein Abstraktionsprinzip kennt, bedarf es einer solchen Ausnahme aber auch nicht.

Für eine analoge Anwendung des Verbots des Selbstkontrahierens sprechen sich die deutsche und die chinesische Literatur im Fall der Untervertretung übereinstimmend aus. Dem ist zu folgen. Entscheidend für die Analogie ist nicht der Interessenkonflikt, sondern die Rechtsumgehung (s. o. III. 4. b)).

VI. Fazit

Sowohl hinsichtlich der Formulierung als auch des sachlichen Inhalts ist das Verbot des Selbstkontrahierens nach § 168 Abs. 1 GRCL dem § 181 Alt. 1 BGB ähnlich. Daher ist anzunehmen, dass das Selbstkontrahieren im chinesischen Recht die Vermeidung eines Interessenkonflikts zwischen Vertreter und Vertretenem und somit den Schutz der Interessen des Vertretenen bezweckt. Welche Rechtsfolgen beim Verstoß gegen das Verbot des Selbstkontrahierens eintreten, ist in § 168 Abs. 1 GRCL nicht ausdrücklich geregelt. Angesichts der in diesem Beitrag dargestellten Regelungen der § 181 Alt. 1 BGB und Art. 2.2.7 PICC sowie Art. 3:205 PECL, kommen zwei unterschiedliche Rechtsfolgen in Betracht: entweder schwebende Unwirksamkeit des Vertrages wie im Falle der Vertretung ohne Vertretungsmacht (§ 181 Alt. 1 BGB) oder seine schwebende Wirksamkeit, also die Anfechtbarkeit des Vertrages. Vorzugswürdig ist aufgrund der Institutsfunktion der Anfechtung und des Zwecks der Stellvertretung die schwebende Unwirksamkeit. Auch das Argument der Effektivität des Rechtsverkehrs überzeugt nicht, denn die Gefahr des Interessenkonflikts beim Selbstkontrahieren besteht generell. Sofern das Verbot des Selbstkontrahierens auf die Prävention des generellen Interessenkonflikts gerichtet ist, ist das Verbot einzuschränken, wenn eine solche Gefahr nicht ersichtlich ist. Umgekehrt ist § 168 Abs. 1 GRCL analog anzuwenden, wenn das Rechtsgeschäft unter Umgehung der Personenidentität vorgenommen wird.

Einführung in das „neue" Sachenrecht der GRCL: Mit Schwerpunkt auf dem öffentlichen Eigentum am Grundstück (Zusammenfassung)

*Jiayuan Zhuang**

Kapitel 5 der General Rules of Civil Law (GRCL) (民法总则) regelt die Grundlagen des Sachenrechts. Dieses besteht aus fünf Paragraphen (§ 113 bis § 117 GRCL), wobei deren inhaltlicher Ursprung auf frühere Gesetze zurückzuführen ist. § 113 GRCL entstand aus Art. 3 Abs. 3 SachenRG und sieht das bedeutende „Gleichbehandlungsprinzip" vor. Der Begriff Eigentum im SachenRG umfasst drei verschiedene Arten von Eigentum, nämlich Privateigentum, Staatseigentum und Kollektiveigentum. In Übereinstimmung mit der kontinentaleuropäischen Rechtstradition stellt § 114 GRCL klar, dass das chinesische Sachenrecht auch auf den Prinzipien der Unmittelbarkeit und der Absolutheit dinglicher Rechte beruht. Art. 2 Abs. 2 SachenRG diente § 115 GRCL als Vorlage. Dieser normiert, dass ein Unterschied zwischen beweglicher und unbeweglicher Sache besteht. Hinsichtlich der unbeweglichen Sache unterscheiden sich die deutschen und die chinesischen Regelungen deutlich. In China gilt das Gebäude als eigenständige, vom Grundstück losgelöste Sache, während es in Deutschland als wesentlicher Bestandteil des Grundstücks behandelt wird. Art. 5 SachenRG diente § 116 GRCL als Vorlage, welcher das Prinzip des *numerus clausus* normiert. § 117 GRCL ist auf Art. 42 und Art. 44 SachenRG zurückzuführen. Demnach setzen Enteignung und Beschlagnahme von Sachen seitens des Staates das Vorliegen eines Allgemeininteresses voraus. Außerdem ist dem Enteigneten eine gerechte und angemessene Entschädigung zu leisten.

Nach chinesischem Verfassungsrecht stehen Grundstücke in Städten im Staatseigentum (Art. 10 Abs. 1 Verfassung der Volksrepublik China) und Grundstücke auf dem Land und in Vororten sind grundsätzlich Kollektiveigentum (Art. 10 Abs. 2). Um auf einem Grundstück ein Gebäude zu bauen

* *Dr. (Köln)*; Privatdozent (Associate Professor), Jiaotong-Universität Shanghai, Juristische Fakultät. Lehrstuhl für Bürgerliches Recht.

oder um es zu bewirtschaften, muss ein Nutzungsrecht am Grundstück erworben werden. Das Nutzungsrecht am Grundstück spielt in China eine ebenso bedeutende Rolle wie das Eigentum in Deutschland.

Im SachenRG werden drei verschiedene Nutzungsrechte normiert. Das erste ist das Recht zur Nutzung von Bauland, das grundsätzlich nur am Grundstück in der Stadt erworben werden kann. Die beiden anderen Nutzungsrechte, welche sich auf kollektive Grundstücke auf dem Land beschränken, sind das Recht zur Nutzung im Sinne von Bewirtschaftung sowie das Recht zur Errichtung eines Wohnhauses (Holflandrecht oder das Recht zur Nutzung bäuerlicher Hausgrundstücke).

Während das Recht zur Nutzung von Bauland nahezu uneingeschränkt übertragbar ist, ist das Hoflandrecht grundsätzlich nicht übertragbar und das Recht zur Bewirtschaftung nur in relativ begrenztem Umfang übertragbar. Somit monopolisiert der Staat den Grundstücksmarkt.

Nach § 60 SachenRG ist das dörfliche Kollektiv bestehend aus einer Gruppe von Bauern Eigentümer des Kollektiveigentums. Die kollektive Wirtschaftsorganisation oder der Dorfbevölkerungsausschuss üben dieses Eigentumsrecht aus. Allerdings ist der Begriff des dörflichen Kollektives undefiniert, weshalb es eigentlich keinen wirklichen Eigentümer gibt. Zudem werden in der Praxis die Interessen der Bauern durch die verschiedenen autonomen Organisationen oftmals nicht sachgerecht vertreten. Aufgrund der Industrialisierung und Urbanisierung Chinas musste und muss immer mehr „kollektives" Land enteignet werden, um den Bedürfnissen der Stadtentwicklung gerecht zu werden. Obwohl eine solche Enteignung das Vorliegen von Allgemeininteresse voraussetzt, erweist sich eine klare Differenzierung zwischen diesem allgemeinen Interesse und einer bloßen Verfolgung kommerzieller Interessen als schwierig. Bauern werden nicht ausreichend vor Enteignungen geschützt. Auch die neuen Regelungen im Sachenrecht bringen dahingehend keine wesentlichen Verbesserungen mit sich.

Das chinesische Zivilgesetzbuch und die ungerechtfertigte Bereicherung: Bilanz und Perspektive

*Guangyu Fu**

Zusammenfassung: *Das geltende chinesische Recht verfügt nur über wenige Regelungen zur ungerechtfertigten Bereicherung. Schon die Gesetzgebungsgeschichte zeigt, warum dieses Rechtsinstitut sozusagen als Stiefsohn der Zivilrechtsfamilie gilt. Eine reife Rechtsdogmatik und -klarheit auf diesem Gebiet ist noch nicht in Sicht. Das künftige chinesische Zivilgesetzbuch (ZGB) wird wahrscheinlich auf einen Allgemeinen Teil des Schuldrechts verzichten. Die ungerechtfertigte Bereicherung könnte als Quasivertrag im Buch des Vertragsrechts mitgeregelt werden. Die Generalklausel in den GRCL könnte in Verbindung mit den ergänzenden Regelungen im Abschnitt über den Quasivertrag angewendet werden. Dieses Modell birgt jedoch Rechtsunsicherheit, weshalb es empfehlenswert wäre, die Generalklausel von den GRCL in den Abschnitt über den Quasivertrag zu schieben. Was die Typologie angeht, so wäre es zweckmäßig sie der Wissenschaft und der Rechtsprechung zu überlassen. Eine reife Dogmatik entsteht erst mit der intensiven Interaktion zwischen Wissenschaft und Praxis. Schließlich würde es sich wohl lohnen, das Verhältnis zwischen den Kondiktionsansprüchen und den anderen Rückgewähransprüchen gesetzlich klarzustellen, um die Unübersichtlichkeit des Regelungssystems zu vermeiden oder zumindest zu verringern.*

Stichwörter: Kodifizierungshistorie, ungerechtfertigte Bereicherung, Rückgewähransprüche.

---

* *Dr. (Tübingen)*; Privatdozent (Associate Professor), Universität für Außenwirtschaft und Handel, Juristische Fakultät. Lehrstuhl für Bürgerliches Recht, Privatrechtsgeschichte und Rechtsvergleichung.
Dieser Artikel ist das Zwischenergebnis des Forschungsprojekts „Ungerechtfertigte Bereicherung aus Perspektive der Kodifikation des Zivilrechts" (Projektnummer: 13YJC820018), das vom Erziehungsministerium Chinas und dem China Scholarship Council finanziell unterstützt wird. Das Manuskript entstand teilweise während eines Aufenthaltes als Stipendiat am Max-Planck-Institut für ausländisches und internationales Privatrecht in Hamburg von Juni bis August 2016.

I. Einleitung

1. Ungerechtfertigte Bereicherung aus rechtsvergleichender Perspektive

Das Rechtsinstitut der ungerechtfertigten Bereicherung geht auf das römische Recht zurück und gilt seit einigen Jahren als ein wichtiges Thema der Rechtsvergleichung. Gerade die rechtsvergleichende Betrachtung zeigt aber, dass es auf dem Gebiet des Bereicherungsrechts kein einheitliches Modell gibt. Denken wir nur an die zwei wichtigsten kontinentaleuropäischen Länder, Deutschland und Frankreich. Sowohl funktional als auch strukturell bestehen große Unterschiede zwischen diesen beiden Rechtsordnungen in Bezug auf das Bereicherungsrecht. Im BGB erscheint die ungerechtfertigte Bereicherung parallel zum Vertrag und der unerlaubten Handlung als ein selbständiger Entstehungsgrund eines Schuldverhältnisses. Funktional gesehen ist die Leistungskondiktion eng mit dem Abstraktionsprinzip verknüpft. Was das französische Recht angeht, so kennt der *Code Civil* seit Langem keine allgemeine Bereicherungsklage, sondern nur einzelne Bereicherungsfälle, einschließlich der *condictio in debiti* als Quasivertrag.[1] Die umfassende Reform des Schuldrechts in Frankreich im Jahr 2016 hat zwar die von der Rechtsprechung als allgemeine Bereicherungsklage entwickelte *actio de in remverso* als Quasivertrag übernommen, sieht in ihr aber nur einen subsidiären Anspruch.[2] In der Tat kann man schwer sagen, welches Modell besser ist. Beide Regelungen werden unterschiedlich bewertet. Während nicht wenige deutsche Juristen die §§ 812 ff. BGB als ein Unglück ansehen,[3] werden sie von manchen amerikanischen Juristen relativ hoch geschätzt.[4] Im Rahmen der Rechtsvereinheitlichung bietet der *Draft Common Frame of Reference* (DCFR) eine weitere, neue Lösung an, die versucht, einen Mittelweg zwischen den verschiedenen europäischen Rechtsordnungen zu finden.[5]

Es ist von Interesse, mit diesem Wissen Geschichte, Gegenwart und Zukunft des chinesischen Bereicherungsrechts zu betrachten, weil China, wie später noch zu erörtern ist, einerseits die deutsche Rechtsdogmatik rezipiert hat und sich andererseits bei der Kodifizierung des Zivilrechts in gewissem Maße am französischen Quasivertrag-Modell orientieren könnte. Außerdem könnte man in mancher Hinsicht auch vom DCFR lernen.

2. Das geltende chinesische Bereicherungsrecht im Überblick

In der chinesischen Rechtsordnung gab es vor Erlass der *General Rules of Civil Law* (GRCL) im Jahr 2017 nur eine einzige Generalklausel für das Bereicherungsrecht im engeren Sinne, nämlich § 92 der *General Principles of Civil Law* von 1986 (GPCL). Diese genügte den Anforderungen der Praxis aber nicht und führte zu vielen Kontroversen in der Wissenschaft. Die Erläuterungen des Obersten Volksgerichtshofs der Volksrepublik China (OVG) zu den GPCL von 1988 (OVG-Erläuterungen GPCL) ergänzten in

---

1 *Meier*, Bereicherungsrecht, in: Basedow/Hopt/Zimmermann, Handwörterbuch des Europäischen Privatrechts, Bd. 1, 2009, S. 182–187; *Zweigert/Kötz*, Einführung in die Rechtsvergleichung, 3. Aufl. 1996, S. 538 ff.; *Ferid/Sonnenberger*, Das Französische Zivilrecht, Bd. 2, 2. Aufl. 1986, 2 N.

2 *Chiusi*, Die actio de in rem verso im römischen Recht, 2001, S. 193ff.; vgl. *soustitre III* des *titre III* des *livre III* des 2016 reformierten *Code Civil*, abrufbar unter https://www.legifrance.gouv.fr/affichCode.do?cidTexte=LEGITEXT000006070721 (zuletzt abgerufen am 05.06.2017).

3 Staudinger/*Lorenz*, Neubearbeitung 2007, Vorbemerkung zu §§ 812 ff., Rn. 2.

4 So auch *Dawson*, Unjust Enrichment, 1951, S. 91.

5 *Von Bar/Clive* (Hrsg.), Principles, Definitions and Model Rules of European Private Law, Draft Common Frame of Reference (DCFR), Bd. 4, 2009.

ihrem § 131 noch einige Aspekte zu den Rechtsfolgen der ungerechtfertigten Bereicherung. Allerdings ist dieser ergänzende Paragraf einerseits sehr kurz und einfach, andererseits wird er wegen seines öffentlich-rechtlichen Charakters dem Zivilrecht nicht gerecht. Deswegen haben Praxis und Wissenschaft sozusagen die gemeinsame Erwartung, dass durch die Kodifizierung des Zivilrechts die Regelung der ungerechtfertigten Bereicherung verbessert wird.

Genau wie die GPCL verfügen die am 15. März 2017 verabschiedeten GRCL, die als der erste Schritt hin zu einem ZGB gelten, auch nur über einen einzigen Paragrafen zur ungerechtfertigten Bereicherung. Es ist verständlich, dass die GPCL als „kleines ZGB" die ungerechtfertigte Bereicherung nur kurz regeln. Man kann sich indes kaum vorstellen, dass das zukünftige ZGB mit einem einzigen Paragrafen über die ungerechtfertigte Bereicherung in seinem Allgemeinen Teil auskäme. Es sollten weitere Regelungen getroffen werden.

Aus den offiziellen Angaben des Gesetzgebers sowie der Gestalt der GRCL kann man ableiten, dass der Gesetzgeber eine pragmatische Gesetzgebungsstrategie verfolgt hat, die die Kontinuität der vorhandenen Ordnung respektiert.[6] Während die wichtigen Einzelgesetze wie das Vertragsgesetz von 1999 (VG), das Sachenrechtsgesetz von 2007 und das Deliktsrechtsgesetz von 2009 (DG) im künftigen ZGB hinter den GRCL als selbständige Bücher erscheinen werden, ist das Schicksal der ungerechtfertigten Bereicherung nicht ganz klar, obwohl sie logisch gesehen parallel zum Vertrag und der unerlaubten Handlung stehen sollte. Was für eine systematische Stellung wird die ungerechtfertigte Bereicherung im zukünftigen ZGB haben? In welchem Verhältnis sollen die bereicherungsrechtliche Generalklausel und die ergänzenden Regelungen stehen? Wie verhalten sich die bereicherungsrechtlichen Ansprüche zu anderen Rückgewähransprüchen? Um solche Fragen zu beantworten, ist es notwendig und nützlich, sich zunächst die einschlägige Gesetzgebungsgeschichte und deren begleitende wissenschaftliche Diskussion in Erinnerung zu rufen. Nur auf dieser Grundlage kann ein Ausblick gegeben werden.

---

6 So auch *Li Jianguo*, Stellvertretender Vorsitzender des Ständigen Ausschusses des Nationalen Volkskongresses, Offizielle Stellungnahme am 8.3.2017 zum Entwurf der GRCL, in: He Qinhua/Li Xiuqing/Chen Yi (Hrsg.), Sammlung der ZGB-Entwürfe des neuen Chinas, Bd. 3 («新中国民法典草案总览»), 2017, S. 1644–1649.

II. Die unterschiedliche systematische Stellung der ungerechtfertigten Bereicherung von den Anfängen bis zu den GRCL

Wenn wir auf die verschiedenen Versuche der Kodifizierung des Zivilrechts seit der Gründung der Volksrepublik China[7] zurückblicken, dann bemerken wir sofort, dass die ungerechtfertigte Bereicherung immer unterschiedliche systematische Stellungen hatte.

1. Die Entwürfe vor den GPCL

a) Entwürfe der 1950er-Jahre: Anschluss an die kontinentaleuropäische Tradition

Schon im Jahre 1954 begann die neue Volksrepublik China ihr Zivilrecht zu kodifizieren. Nach dem vermutlich 1955 angefertigten Entwurf des Allgemeinen Teils des Schuldrechts[8] können sich Schuldverhältnisse aus „dem ungerechtfertigt Erlangten", „den geplanten Gesetzen und Dekreten", „den Verträgen", „der Geschäftsführung ohne Auftrag" und „den unerlaubten Handlungen" ergeben. Danach ist die ungerechtfertigte Bereicherung ein selbstständiger Entstehungsgrund eines Schuldverhältnisses. Drei Paragrafen (§§ 31–33) widmeten die Macher des Entwurfs der ungerechtfertigten Bereicherung. Ein Paragraf davon ist eine Generalklausel (§ 31). Die zwei folgenden Paragrafen (§§ 32, 33) beziehen sich auf die Rechtsfolgen.

Gemäß dem Plan der Macher des Entwurfs sollte das Zivilgesetzbuch ein Buch des Schuldrechts umfassen, das u. a. einen Allgemeinen Teil enthält. Systematisch gesehen wurden die Vorschriften über die ungerechtfertigte Bereicherung stark durch das sowjetische Zivilgesetzbuch geprägt, das sich seinerseits an die kontinentaleuropäische Tradition anlehnte.[9] In den späte-

---

7 *Reuser/Liang Huixing*, Das chinesische Zivilrecht: Sein gegenwärtiger Zustand und der Erlaß eines Zivilgesetzbuches, AcP 194 (1994), 479 ff.; *Zhang Xinbao/Zhang Hong*, Hundert Jahre Wandlung des chinesischen Zivilrechts ("中国民法百年变迁"), 6 Social Sciences in China, S. 67 ff. (2011).

8 He Qinhua/Li Xiuqing/Chen Yi (Hrsg.), Sammlung der ZGB-Entwürfe des neuen Chinas, Bd. 1 («新中国民法典草案总览»), 2017, S. 136–143.

9 *Wang Liming/Guo Mingrui/Fang Liufang*, Neue Darstellung des Zivilrechts, Bd. 2 («民法新论(下册)»), 1988, S. 421.

ren Entwürfen der 1950er-Jahre wurde dieses Modell, von leicht abweichenden Formulierungen abgesehen, grundsätzlich übernommen: Die ungerechtfertigte Bereicherung als ein selbständiger Entstehungsgrund eines Schuldverhältnisses; eine Generalklausel in Verbindung mitergänzenden Regelungen über die Rechtsfolgen.[10]

Während des Entwurfs des Allgemeinen Teils des Schuldrechts wurden einige Fragen über die Struktur des Schuldrechts und die Gestaltung der ungerechtfertigten Bereicherung zur Diskussion gestellt. Diese Diskussionen hatten kaum ideologischen Charakter. Vielmehr ging es dabei vor allem um technische Probleme. Die diskutierten Fragen waren insbesondere folgende: Sollte die ungerechtfertigte Bereicherung im Allgemeinen Teil oder im Besonderen Teil des Schuldrechts stehen? Wie weit sollte der Anwendungsbereich der bereicherungsrechtlichen Regelungen gefasst werden? Sollten vom Institut der ungerechtfertigten Bereicherung auch die Rückabwicklungsfälle umfasst sein, die sich aus der Nichtigkeit des Rechtsgeschäfts ergeben? Was ist der Unterschied zwischen der ungerechtfertigten Bereicherung und der Geschäftsführung ohne Auftrag und der Verletzung der Vermögensrechte eines anderen? Wie sind die typischen Bereicherungsfälle von anderen besonderen Schuldverhältnissen zu unterscheiden?[11] Solche Fragen sind selbst heute nicht obsolet.

Die neue Volksrepublik China verstand sich zwar als sozialistischer Staat, orientierte sich beim Entwurf des Zivilgesetzbuchs aber an den kontinentaleuropäischen Begriffen und Systemen. Das erinnert an die Ansicht von Franz Wieacker, welcher meinte, dass die modernen Privatrechtsgesetzgebungen vom Typ des französischen *Code Civil* oder des deutschen BGB in Staaten mit ganz unterschiedlichen Weltanschauungen angewendet werden könnten.[12]

---

10 He Qinhua/Li Xiuqing/Chen Yi (Hrsg.), Sammlung der ZGB-Entwürfe des neuen Chinas, Bd. 1 («新中国民法典草案总览»), 2017, passim.

11 He Qinhua/Li Xiuqing/Chen Yi (Hrsg.), Sammlung der ZGB-Entwürfe des neuen Chinas, Bd. 2 («新中国民法典草案总览»), 2017, S. 1000.

12 *Wieacker*, Das Sozialmodell der klassischen Privatrechtsgesetzbücher und die Entwicklung der modernen Gesellschaft, 1952, S. 3.

b) Entwürfe der 1960er-Jahre: Abschied vom bourgeoisen Zivilrecht

Die Orientierung an der kontinentaleuropäischen Tradition wurde in den 1960er-Jahren aber aufgegeben. Nach der damals herrschenden Ansicht bestand das „alte Zivilrechtssystem" aus den abstrakten Rechtsformen wie Rechtssubjekt, Sachenrecht, Forderung, Urheberrecht, Erbrecht usw. Ein solches System müsse aufgegeben werden, weil es dem Inhalt des bourgeoisen Zivilrechts, nicht aber den Anforderungen des sozialistischen Zivilrechts entspreche. Man solle mutig versuchen, ein „neues Zivilrechtssystem", das der Realität der sozialistischen Revolution und dem sozialistischen Aufbau entspreche, zu errichten.[13] Folgerichtig sind das Schuldrecht und mit ihm die ungerechtfertigte Bereicherung als bourgeoise Rechtsformen in den Entwürfen der 1960er-Jahre verschwunden. Für die vorliegende Untersuchung hat diese Epoche daher keine große Bedeutung.

c) Entwürfe der 1980er-Jahre: Ungerechtfertigte Bereicherung als eine besondere Haftungsform

Mit der Reform und Öffnung stand die Zivilgesetzgebung seit Ende der 1970er-Jahre wieder auf der Tagesordnung des Gesetzgebers. Der Gesetzgeber erstrebte zunächst ein umfassendes Zivilgesetzbuch. In den Entwürfen eines Zivilgesetzbuchs der 1980er-Jahre erschien die ungerechtfertigte Bereicherung in anderer Gestalt als in den 1950er-Jahren, nämlich als eine besondere Form der „Haftung". Dabei bezieht sich der Begriff „Haftung" doch vor allem auf die unerlaubte Handlung. Dass die unerlaubte Handlung in einem selbständigen Buch erscheint, ist dem prägenden Einfluss der Zivilgesetzbücher der Tschechoslowakischen Republik und der DDR zuzuschreiben. Hierzu muss man wissen, dass in diesen beiden Staaten die deliktische Haftung deutlich vom vertraglichen Schuldverhältnis abwich: Während das Wesen des vertraglichen Schuldverhältnisses im Vermögensaustausch liegt, zielt die deliktische Haftung vor allem auf den Schutz der Rechte der Bürger ab. Folgerichtig wird die deliktische Haftung vom

13 Zivilrechtliches Institut der Renmin-Universität, Einige Gedanken über den Aufbau eines neuen Systems des Zivilrechts, in: He Qinhua/Li Xiuqing/Chen Yi (Hrsg.), Sammlung der ZGB-Entwürfe des neuen Chinas, Bd. 2 («新中国民法典草案总览»), 2017, S. 1000.

Schuldrecht getrennt und erscheint als ein selbständiges Buch im Zivilgesetzbuch.[14] In den Entwürfen der 1980er-Jahre wird die Materie des traditionellen Schuldrechts nicht mehr als ein Ganzes gesehen, sondern zersetzt sich in verschiedene Teile. Die ungerechtfertigte Bereicherung steht nun neben der unerlaubten Handlung als eine besondere Form der Haftung, sei es als „Schadenshaftung" (Entwurf von 1980), „Deliktshaftung" (Entwurf von 1981) oder „zivile Haftung" (Entwurf von 1982).[15] Insofern kann man die ungerechtfertigte Bereicherung in den 1980er-Jahren als Quasidelikt bezeichnen.

2. Von den GPCL bis zu den GRCL

a) GPCL: Ungerechtfertigte Bereicherung als selbstständiger Entstehungsgrund eines Schuldverhältnisses

Der Versuch, ein umfassendes Zivilgesetzbuch zu entwerfen, wurde Mitte der 1980er-Jahre aufgegeben. Der Gesetzgeber wendete stattdessen eine pragmatische Gesetzgebungsstrategie an. Zuerst sollten die wichtigen zivilrechtlichen Einzelgesetze entworfen werden. Vor diesem Hintergrund wurden die GPCL im Jahr 1986 verabschiedet.

Die GPCL verfügen zwar nur über 156 Paragrafen, regeln aber den wesentlichen Inhalt des Zivilrechts in prägnanter Art und Weise. Insofern kann man sie als „kleines ZGB" bezeichnen. Was die ungerechtfertigte Bereicherung angeht, so widmen sie dieser Problematik nur einen einzigen Paragrafen: § 92 GPCL befindet sich in Kapitel 5 „Zivilrechte" und behandelt die ungerechtfertigte Bereicherung als einen selbstständigen Entstehungsgrund eines Schuldverhältnisses. Als Generalklausel regelt § 92 GPCL sowohl den Tatbestand als auch die Rechtsfolge der ungerechtfertigten Bereicherung in einfacher Weise:

---

14 *Liang Huixing*, Einige Probleme des chinesischen Zivil- und Wirtschaftsrechts («中国民法经济法诸问题»), 1999, S. 112.

15 S. auch He Qinhua/Li Xiuqing/Chen Yi (Hrsg.), Sammlung der ZGB-Entwürfe des neuen Chinas, Bd. 3 («新中国民法典草案总览»), 2017, passim.

> Wer ohne rechtmäßige Grundlage einen unangemessenen Nutzen erlangt und [damit] einen Verlust für eine andere Person herbeiführt, muß den erlangten unangemessenen Nutzen dem zurückgeben, der den Verlust erlitten hat.[16]

Die Grundlage für diese Regelung wurde in der sozialistischen Moral gesehen.[17]

Im Jahr 1988 erließ der OVG eine umfassende Erläuterung zu den GPCL, wobei § 131 zur Rechtsfolge der ungerechtfertigten Bereicherung ergänzend feststellte:

> Die Rückgabe von unangemessenem Nutzen muss die Sache selbst und ihre Früchte einbeziehen. Unter Verwendung unangemessenen Nutzens erlangter anderer Nutzen muss nach Abzug der Aufwendungen für Arbeitsleistungen und Verwaltung eingezogen werden.[18]

Der öffentlich-rechtliche Charakter dieser Regelung wurde von der Wissenschaft kritisiert.[19]

b) Offizieller Entwurf eines Zivilgesetzbuchs von 2002: Ungerechtfertigte Bereicherung im Allgemeinen Teil

Am 23.12.2002 brachte der Gesetzgeber unerwartet einen Entwurf für ein Zivilgesetzbuch ein. Dies war etwas überraschend, weil das VG erst 1999 in Kraft getreten und der Entwurf eines Sachenrechtsgesetzes noch in Bearbeitung war. Der Entwurf von 2002 besteht aus neun Büchern, nämlich

16 In das Deutsche übersetzt durch *Münzel*, der aber das Tatbestandmerkmal „合法根据“ nicht mit „rechtmäßige Grundlage“, sondern „rechtliche Grundlage“ übersetzt, abrufbar unter http://www.chinas-recht.de/index.htm (zuletzt abgerufen am 06.06.2017).

17 *Zhao Zhongfu*, in: Gu Angran/Wang Jiafu/Jiang Ping u. a., Eine Vorlesungsreihe über die GPCL der Volksrepublik China («民法通则讲话»), Lektion 9 „Die Forderung“, 2000, S. 183.

18 In das Deutsche übersetzt durch *Münzel*, abrufbar unter http://www.chinas-recht.de/index.htm (zuletzt abgerufen am 06.06.2017).

19 *Zou Hailin*, Die ungerechtfertigte Bereicherung im chinesischen Zivilrecht (“我国民法上的不当得利”), 5 Civil and Commercial Law Review, S. 1 ff., insb. S. 63 (1995); *Huo Zhengxin*, Construction and Improvement of the Chinese Institution of Unjustified Enrichment (“中国不当得利制度的构建与完善”), 2 Seeking Truth, S. 87 (2006).

dem Allgemeinen Teil und acht weiteren Büchern. Es ist erwähnenswert, dass er nicht die gesamte Materie des traditionellen Schuldrechts regelt. Auch auf einen Allgemeinen Teil des Schuldrechts wurde verzichtet. Dies beeinflusste das Schicksal der ungerechtfertigten Bereicherung entscheidend. Diese erschien nun in Kapitel 6 der GRCL. Nachdem in § 86 des Entwurfs von 2002 die Entstehungsgründe der Schuldverhältnisse einschließlich der ungerechtfertigten Bereicherung aufgezählt werden, übernimmt § 88 wortwörtlich § 92 GPCL. In den anderen Büchern dieses Entwurfs kommt die ungerechtfertigte Bereicherung nicht mehr vor. Dieses Regelungsmodell wurde in der Wissenschaft kritisiert.[20] Laut eines Beamten, der an diesem Entwurf mitgearbeitet hatte, war der Grund für den Verzicht auf einen Allgemeinen Teil des Schuldrechts, dass sich sein Inhalt in großem Umfang mit dem Inhalt des Allgemeinen Teils des VG decken würde.[21] Deshalb stehe die bereicherungsrechtliche Generalklausel im Allgemeinen Teil des Entwurfs von 2002. Es bedürfe aber in Zukunft weiterer Verbesserungen.[22]

c) Die GRCL von 2017: Fortführung des Entwurfs von 2002

Wenn wir dem Entwurf von 2002 nur symbolische Bedeutung zusprechen, weil er nach der Einbringung im Nationalen Volkskongress nicht mehr behandelt wurde, so würden wir seine Bedeutung wohl unterschätzen. Denn in der Tat hat dieser Entwurf die GRCL von 2017 stark geprägt. Dass die GRCL die ungerechtfertigte Bereicherung im Kapitel über die Zivilrechte regeln, setzt offenbar den Gedankengang des Entwurfs von 2002 fort. Anders als der Entwurf von 2002 haben die GRCL in ihrem § 122 den § 92 GPCL nicht wortgetreu, sondern mit leicht abweichender Formulierung übernommen. Erstens orientiert sich § 122 GRCL nicht an der Pflicht des

20 *Huo Zhengxin*, Construction and Improvement of the Chinese Institution of Unjustified Enrichment ("中国不当得利制度的构建与完善"), 2 Seeking Truth, S. 87 (2006); *Yang Daixiong*, The Systematic Constitution of Credit Law in China's Civil Code ("我国民法典中债权法的体系构造"), 6 Law Science Magazine, S. 144 (2007).

21 S. Fn. 22.

22 *Wang Shengming*, The Route that a Country with Legality Must Go: Several Questions in Compiling the Civil Code ("法治国家的必由之路——编纂中华人民共和国民法草案的几个问题"), 1 Tribune of Political Science and Law, S. 26 ff. (2003).

Schuldners, sondern an dem Recht bzw. Anspruch des Gläubigers. Während § 92 GPCL regelt, dass der Bereicherte verpflichtet ist, das Erlangte zurückzugeben, betont § 122 GRCL, dass derjenige, der einen Schaden erleidet, einen Anspruch gegenüber dem Bereicherten hat. Diese Änderung der Formulierung wurde beim zweiten Entwurf der GRCL vorgenommen. M. E. ist eine solche Änderung wohl unnötig. Denken wir nur an § 812 Abs. 1 S. 1 BGB, der den „Anspruch" des Gläubigers auch nicht ausdrücklich betont. Die zweite Änderung bezieht sich auf das Tatbestandmerkmal „ohne rechtmäßige Grundlage" in § 92 GPCL, das nun durch „ohne rechtliche Grundlage" ersetzt wurde. Mit dieser Änderung möchte der Gesetzgeber wohl betonen, dass nicht „Rechtswidrigkeit", sondern „ohne vertragliche oder gesetzliche Grundlage" für das Vorliegen einer ungerechtfertigten Bereicherung entscheidend ist.[23]

3. Fazit

All die Entwürfe eines chinesischen ZGB und auch die GPCL sind von den Rechtstheorien und Gesetzgebungsstrategien ihrer jeweiligen Epoche geprägt. Dabei war die systematische Stellung der ungerechtfertigten Bereicherung immer unterschiedlich. Daher gilt dieses Rechtsinstitut sozusagen als Stiefsohn der Zivilrechtsfamilie. Angesichts der strukturellen Ähnlichkeit zum Entwurf von 2002 könnte das zukünftige chinesische ZGB sehr wahrscheinlich auf einen Allgemeinen Teil des Schuldrechts verzichten. Systematische Stellung und konkrete Gestalt zukünftiger bereicherungsrechtlicher Regelungen sind also von vielen, nicht ganz übersichtlichen Faktoren abhängig.

---

23 Shi Hong (Hrsg.), Die GRCL der Volksrepublik China: Erläuterung der Paragrafen, Gesetzgebungsmotive und einschlägige Bestimmungen («中华人民共和国民法总则：条文说明、立法理由及相关规定»), 2017, S. 286.

III. Ungerechtfertigte Bereicherung aus wissenschaftlicher Sicht

1. Allmähliche Rezeption der deutschen Dogmatik in verschiedenen Varianten

Allein aus dem Wortlaut des § 92 GPCL lässt sich nicht erkennen, dass das chinesische Bereicherungsrecht durch das BGB beeinflusst wird. Doch tatsächlich ist die deutsche Rechtsdogmatik, vor allem die durch Wilburg und von Caemmerer entwickelte „Trennungslehre“, inzwischen von den meisten chinesischen Zivilrechtlern akzeptiert worden. Dies spiegelt sich in zahlreichen Lehrbüchern, Monographien sowie Aufsätzen wider. Auch manche aktuelle Kommentare zu den GRCL bilden hier keine Ausnahme.[24] Es wird in der Wissenschaft weitgehend anerkannt, dass die bereicherungsrechtliche Generalklausel heterogene Fälle erfasst und deshalb eine Typologie zweckmäßig ist. Einige eingehende Darstellungen über die Tatbestandsvoraussetzungen der ungerechtfertigten Bereicherung wie „Leistung“ oder „rechtlicher Grund“ beruhen mit gewissen Einschränkungen auch auf der Trennungslehre.[25] Dass die Trennungslehre in der Rechtsprechung nicht selten ausdrücklich angewendet wird, spiegelt die wissenschaftliche Entwicklung[26] wider. Außerdem vertritt die chinesische Wissenschaft die Ausschlussgründe der Kondiktion weitgehend so wie im deutschen Recht, obwohl das positive chinesische Recht dazu kaum Regelungen enthält.

Es ist erwähnenswert, dass verschiedene Typologien vertreten werden. Denken wir nur an die Typen der Nichtleistungskondiktion. Manche sind der Meinung, dass die Nichtleistungskondition sich aus der Handlung des

---

24 Chen Su u. a. (Hrsg.), Commentary on General Principles of the Civil Code, Bd. 2 («民法总则评注(下册)»), § 122 (Verfasser Chang Peng'ao), 2017, S. 850; *Li Yu*, Grundzüge der GRCL («民法总则要义：规范释论与判解集注»), 2017, S. 382 ff.

25 *Lou Aihua*, The Clarification of the Concept of Unjust Enrichment without Legal Cause ("不当得利没有合法根据之概念澄清"), 6 Science of Law, S. 110 ff. (2012); *Zhao Wenjie*, The Concept of Payment and Return of Unjust Enrichment: ("给付概念与不当得利返还"), 6 Political Science and Law, S. 99 ff. (2012).

26 S. dazu *Li Yu*, Grundzüge der GRCL(«民法总则要义：规范释论与判解集注»), 2017, S. 389 ff.

Bereicherten, der Handlung desjenigen, der einen Schaden erleidet, oder einem Naturereignis ergeben kann.[27] Manche sind demgegenüber der Ansicht, dass die Nichtleistungskondiktion in Eingriffskondiktion, Aufwendungskondiktion und Rückgriffskondiktion zu gliedern ist.[28] All diese Typologien sind eigentlich nicht genuin-chinesisch, sondern gehen auf die kontinentaleuropäische Rechtsdogmatik zurück. Es wird gelegentlich aber auch vertreten, dass die sog. Eingriffskondiktion der Wissenschaft wie der Praxis fremd sei.[29]

2. Ungerechtfertigte Bereicherung in akademischen Vorschlägen für Entwürfe eines ZGB

Von 2003 bis 2004 sind hintereinander drei akademische Vorschläge für ZGB-Entwürfe erarbeitet worden, je einer von Professor Liang Huixing der Chinesischen Akademie der Sozialwissenschaften, von Professor Xu Guodong der Xiamen-Universität und von Professor Wang Liming der Renmin-Universität. Diese drei Vorschläge für ZGB-Entwürfe verkörpern in gewissem Maß auch den wissenschaftlichen Diskurs über die ungerechtfertigte Bereicherung des post-GRCL-Zeitalters.

a) Der Entwurf von Professor Liang Huixing[30]

Dieser Entwurf ist 2003 erschienen und wurde später noch mehrmals überarbeitet und ins Englische[31] übersetzt. Er besteht aus sieben Büchern einschließlich des Allgemeinen Teils des Schuldrechts. Die ungerechtfertigte Bereicherung befindet sich im Allgemeinen Teil des Schuldrechts, genauer

---

27 *Zhang Junhao*, Grundsätze des Zivilrechts («民法学原理»), 2. Aufl. 1997, S. 846 ff.; *Liu Kaixiang*, Allgemeiner Teil des Schuldrechts («债法总论»), 2011, S. 42 ff.

28 *Cui Jianyuan*, Allgemeiner Teil des Schuldrechts («债法总论»), 2013, S. 283 ff.

29 *Li Yongjun*, Vom rechtlichen Schutz der Persönlichkeitsrechte ("从权利属性看人格权的法律保护"), 1 ZUEL Law Journal, S. 13ff., insb. S. 18 (2012).

30 *Liang Huixing* (Hrsg.), A Propositional Version for a Draft Civil Code of China («中国民法典草案建议稿»), 1. Aufl. 2003.

31 *Liang Huixing* (Hrsg.), The Draft Civil Code of the People's Republic of China, in das Englische übersetzt durch die Legislative Research Group der Chinese Academy of Social Sciences, 2010.

im Abschnitt über die „Entstehungsgründe der Schuldverhältnisse“. Wie das deutsche BGB enthält dieser Entwurf eine Generalklausel und einzelne Kondiktionsfälle wie die *condictio in debiti*, die *condictio causa data causa non secuta* und die irrtümliche Geschäftsführung. Die Rechtsfolge der ungerechtfertigten Bereicherung sowie die Ausschlussgründe der Kondiktion sind ebenfalls den einschlägigen Regelungen des BGB ähnlich. Bei der Generalklausel wird aber, anders als im BGB, nicht ausdrücklich danach unterschieden, ob die Bereicherung „durch Leistung“ oder „in sonstiger Weise“ geschehen ist. Allerdings kann man aus den Erläuterungen des Verfassers ableiten, dass seine Generalklausel die Trennungslehre voraussetzt.[32] Was das Verhältnis zwischen den Kondiktionsansprüchen und anderen Ansprüchen angeht, so wird eine Konkurrenz ausdrücklich bejaht.

b) Der grüne Entwurf von Professor Xu Guodong (2004)[33]

Anders als der Entwurf von Professor Liang Huixing enthält der sog. grüne Entwurf von Professor Xu Guodong im Schuldrecht nicht nur einen Allgemeinen Teil, sondern auch einen Besonderen Teil. Die ungerechtfertigte Bereicherung ist im Besonderen Teil des Schuldrechts zu finden und zwar als eines der „anderen aus einseitiger Handlung entstandenen Schuldverhältnisse“. Einige wenige Einzelfälle wie die *condictio in debiti* sind gesondert und nicht in der Generalklausel geregelt. Es ist auffällig, dass dieser Entwurf die Subsidiarität der Kondiktionsansprüche betont. Bei den bereicherungsrechtlichen Regelungen hat sich der Verfasser vor allem an den italienischen und japanischen Zivilgesetzbüchern orientiert.

c) Der Entwurf von Professor Wang Liming (2004)[34]

Dieser im November 2004 erschienene Entwurf betont die Notwendigkeit eines Allgemeinen Teils des Schuldrechts. Die ungerechtfertigte Bereiche-

32 Huixing (Hrsg.), A Propositional Version with Reasons for a Draft Civil Code of China: General Principles of Obligatory Rights («中国民法典草案建议稿附理由：债权总则编»), 3. Aufl. 2013, S. 20.

33 *Xu Guodong* (Hrsg.), Green Draft Civil Code («绿色民法典草案»), 2004.

34 *Wang Liming* (Hrsg.), Vorschlagsentwurf eines chinesischen Zivilgesetzbuchs mit Erläuterungen («中国民法典草案建议稿及说明»), 2004.

rung befindet sich im zweiten Abschnitt des Allgemeinen Teils des Schuldrechts als selbstständiger Entstehungsgrund eines Schuldverhältnisses. Ähnlich wie die beiden anderen akademischen Entwürfe verfügt dieser Entwurf auch über eine Generalklausel. Allerdings findet sich in diesem Entwurf auch die Besonderheit, dass Leistungs- und Nichtleistungskondiktion getrennt voneinander in zwei unterschiedlichen Paragrafen geregelt werden. Anscheinend wurde die deutsche Trennungslehre hier also unmittelbar „in Paragrafen gegossen". Nach den Erläuterungen des Verfassers beruhen diese beiden Paragrafen allerdings auf der „Einheitslehre". Da das chinesische Recht, anders als das BGB, kein Abstraktionsprinzip kennt, sei die Trennungslehre unnötig.[35]

d) Bewertung

Diese drei akademischen Entwürfe sind sich in vielen Aspekten ähnlich: Vorbehalt des „Schuldrechts" als Oberbegriff, Behandlung der ungerechtfertigten Bereicherung als Entstehungsgrund eines Schuldverhältnisses, Verwendung einer Generalklausel in Verbindung mit weiteren gesondert geregelten Einzelfällen der Kondiktion sowie Ablehnung der einschlägigen Erläuterung des OVG wegen ihres öffentlich-rechtlichen Charakters. Außerdem sind nicht wenige Regelungen über den Umfang und die Ausschlussgründe der Kondiktionsansprüche identisch. Es gibt aber auch Unterschiede zwischen diesen drei Entwürfen. Während die Entwürfe von Professor Liang und Professor Wang die Konkurrenz zwischen den Kondiktionsansprüchen einerseits und anderen Ansprüchen andererseits bejahen, sieht der Entwurf von Professor Xu in der Kondiktion eher einen subsidiären Anspruch. Außerdem verhalten sich die drei Entwürfe unterschiedlich zur Trennungslehre. All dies zeigt, dass China im Bereich des Bereicherungsrechts noch keine reife Rechtsdogmatik hat.

---

35 Wang Liming (Hrsg.), Propositional Version for a Draft Civil Code of China with Explanations: General Part of the Law of Obligations, Contract Law («中国民法典草案建议稿及立法理由：债法总则编、合同编»), Xu Xiaofeng, 2005, S. 39–40.

3. Diskussion über die systematische Stellung und die Funktion

Es gab aber nicht nur akademische Vorschläge für den Entwurf eines ZGB. Auch die gesetzgeberischen Entwürfe wurden in der Wissenschaft stets durch intensive Diskussion begleitet. Dabei stehen vor allem zwei Probleme im Vordergrund: Einerseits die systematische Stellung und andererseits die Funktion der ungerechtfertigten Bereicherung.

a) Systematische Stellung der ungerechtfertigten Bereicherung

Die Gestalt des Schuldrechts zählt zu den umstrittensten Fragen im Hinblick auf ein chinesisches ZGB. Dies betrifft auch stets die ungerechtfertigte Bereicherung.

Von den Wissenschaftlern, die sich für einen Allgemeinen Teil des Schuldrechts aussprechen, finden einige, dass sich die ungerechtfertigte Bereicherung im Allgemeinen Teil des Schuldrechtsbefinden sollte.[36] Andere schlagen vor, die ungerechtfertigte Bereicherung im Besonderen Teil des Schuldrechts anzusiedeln.[37]

Auch innerhalb der Gruppe der Wissenschaftler, welche einen Allgemeinen Teil des Schuldrechts ablehnen, gibt es wiederum unterschiedliche Ansichten: Die ungerechtfertigte Bereicherung wird je nach Autor in den

---

36 *Xue Jun*, Über die Struktur des Buchs des Schuldrechts im künftigen chinesischen Zivilgesetzbuch ("论未来中国民法典债法编的结构设计"), 2 ZUEL Law Journal, S. 55 f. (2001); *Cui Jianyuan*, General Rule of Obligation Law and Drafting a Civil Code of the People's Republic of China ("债法总则与中国民法典的制定"), 4 Journal of Tsinghua University (Philosophy and Social Sciences), S. 73 (2003); *Liu Jingwei*, On the Necessity and Feasibility of the General Rule of Obligation Law ("设立债法总则的必要性和可行性"), 2 Xiamen University Law Review, S. 198 ff. (2004); *Yang Lixin*, Whither the Section for "General Principles of Law of Obligations"? ("论民法典中债法总则之存废"), 6 Tsinghua University Law Journal, S. 81 ff. (2014).

37 *Yang Daixiong*, On Systematic Constitution of Credit Law in China's Civil Code ("我国民法典中债权法的体系构"), 2007, S. 144; *Li Shigang*, Coordination of Several Primary Relations in the Construction of China's Law of Obligations ("中国债编体系构建中若干基础关系的协调"), 5 Chinese Journal of Law, S. 22 (2016).

GRCL,[38] als Quasivertrag im Buch des Vertragsrechts[39] bzw. als Quasidelikt im Deliktsrecht gesehen.[40]

Es werden in der Wissenschaft also fast alle Möglichkeiten der systematischen Stellung der ungerechtfertigten Bereicherung vertreten. Und in den genannten offiziellen und akademischen Entwürfen kann man ihre Vorbilder bzw. Entsprechungen finden. Es ist schwer zu sagen, welche Lösung inzwischen die vorherrschende Ansicht darstellt. Angesichts der strukturellen Ähnlichkeit der GRCL zum Entwurf von 2002 wäre das Quasivertrag-Modell wohl die realistischste Wahl, weil der Gesetzgeber sehr wahrscheinlich auf einen Allgemeinen Teil des Schuldrechts verzichten würde.[41]

b) Funktion der ungerechtfertigten Bereicherung

Eng verbunden mit der systematischen Stellung der ungerechtfertigten Bereicherung ist die Frage nach der Funktion dieses Rechtsinstituts. Dabei spielt eine zentrale Rolle, ob in der jeweiligen Rechtsordnung das sog. Abstraktionsprinzip gilt oder nicht. In einem Rechtssystem, das dieses Prinzip im Interesse der Rechtsklarheit anerkennt, spielt die ungerechtfertigte Bereicherung eine besondere Rolle. Nach der wohl h. M. gibt es im chinesischen Recht kein Abstraktionsprinzip. Dies ist der Grund für eine hitzige Debatte über die Funktion des Bereicherungsausgleichs. Manche sind der Meinung, dass bei kausaler Ausgestaltung der Übereignung immer die Vindikation gegeben sei, wenn das schuldrechtliche Geschäft mangelhaft ist. Deshalb sei der Anwendungsbereich der ungerechtfertigten Bereicherung stark eingeschränkt. Die Nichtanerkennung des Abstraktionsprinzips führe

38 *Liu Shiguo*, Über das System des chinesischen Zivilgesetzbuchs ("论中国民法典的体系"), 3 Law and Social Development, S. 132 (2002).

39 *Qin Youtu/Ma Changhua*, The Abolition or not of the General Principles of the Law of Obligations in China's Civil Code ("我国民法典中债法总则的存废"), 5 Legal Science, S. 104 (2003); *Wang Liming*, Legislative Research on the Compilation of Contract of the Civil Code ("民法分则合同编立法研究"), 2 China Legal Science, S. 29 (2017).

40 *Ma Junju/Zhou Ruifang*, The Guiding Ideas in Drawing up the Civil Law Series and the Constructive Thing on Its System ("制定民法典的指导思想及其体系构想"), 5 Jiling University Journal (Social Sciences Edition), S. 60 (2001).

41 *Wang Liming*, Legislative Research on the Compilation of Contract of the Civil Code ("民法分则合同编立法研究"), 2017, S. 28.

zum „Einsturz des Gebäudes der ungerechtfertigten Bereicherung“.[42] Andere finden hingegen, dass die Bedeutung der abstrakten Verfügungsgeschäfte für das Bereicherungsrecht nicht überschätzt werden dürfe. Die Nichtanerkennung des Abstraktionsprinzips schade der Bedeutung des Rechtsinstituts der ungerechtfertigten Bereicherung in keiner Weise. Ganz im Gegenteil könne dies „die Zyste“ dieses Rechtsinstituts entfernen. Eine Bereicherung „durch Leistung“ könne es nicht unbedingt nur bei Anerkennung des Abstraktionsprinzips geben. Außerdem hätten zahlreiche Bereicherungsfälle, wie die Kondiktion wegen unberechtigter Verfügung oder Akzession, mit einer Leistung gar nichts zu tun.[43]

4. Fazit

Auch in der Wissenschaft wird die ungerechtfertigte Bereicherung lebhaft diskutiert, viele Fragen sind aber noch ungeklärt. Dies spiegelt sich nicht nur in zahlreichen Lehrbüchern, Monographien und Aufsätzen, sondern auch in den akademischen Vorschlägen für ZGB-Entwürfe wider. Eine reife Rechtsdogmatik ist in diesem Bereich noch nicht erkennbar. Allerdings ist die Wissenschaft nicht allein an diesem Zustand schuld. Denken wir nur daran, dass erstens die Lösungen der bisherigen Gesetze und offiziellen Gesetzesentwürfe kaum zu befriedigen vermögen und dass zweitens die Haltung der geltenden Rechtsordnung zu manchen Grundlagen wie dem Abstraktionsprinzip nicht ganz eindeutig ist. Außerdem hat der Gesetzgeber noch kein klares Bild davon gegeben, wie er das Schuldrecht im zukünftigen ZGB zu gestalten gedenkt. Nur aufgrund weniger inoffizieller Angaben von Beamten, die in den Gesetzgebungsprozess involviert sind, kann man den Gedankengang des Gesetzgebers nachvollziehen. Vor diesem Hintergrund ist es wohl verständlich, dass die akademischen Meinungen über die ungerechtfertigte Bereicherung stark divergieren.

---

42 *Xu Diyu*, Teleologische Auslegung der Abstraktheit der dinglichen Rechtsgeschäfte (“物权行为无因性的目的论解释”), 2 China Legal Science, S. 89 (2005).

43 *Sun Peng*, Die Lehre des dinglichen Rechtsgeschäfts und die ungerechtfertigte Bereicherung (“物权行为理论与不当得利”), 3 Modern Law Science, S. 117 (2003).

IV. Dogmatische Einordnung anderer Rückgewähransprüche in der geltenden Rechtsordnung

Bisher wurde in diesem Beitrag vor allem das Bereicherungsrecht im engeren Sinne behandelt. In der geltenden Rechtsordnung kommen aber nicht selten auch andere Rückgewähransprüche vor, die bereicherungsrechtliche Funktionen haben. Ob es sich dabei um bereicherungsrechtliche oder selbstständige Ansprüche handelt, ist umstritten. Wie oben erwähnt fanden ähnliche Diskussionen schon in den 1950er-Jahren statt.[44] Im Folgenden sind vier Rückgewähransprüche zu erörtern, die sich aus gescheitertem Rechtsgeschäft, unerlaubter Handlung, Akzession oder geleistetem Brautpreis ergeben.

1. Rückgewähransprüche aus gescheitertem Rechtsgeschäft bzw. Vertrag

Im Bereich des Rechtsgeschäfts, vor allem des Vertrags, kommen eine Reihe von Umständen in Betracht, aus denen sich Rückgewähransprüche ergeben. Als Gründe solcher Rückgewähransprüche sind vor allem folgende zu nennen: (1) Nichtigkeit oder Anfechtung des Rechtsgeschäfts, (2) Rücktritt vom Rechtsgeschäft, (3) Eintritt einer auflösenden Bedingung sowie (4) verbraucherschutzrechtlicher Widerruf. Aus Platzgründen möchte ich mich hier auf (1) und (2) beschränken.

a) Rückgewähr bei Nichtigkeit oder Anfechtung

Nach § 58 VG muss aufgrund eines Vertrags erlangtes Vermögensgut zurückgegeben werden, wenn dieser Vertrag nichtig ist oder angefochten wird. Wenn es nicht zurückgegeben werden kann oder eine Rückgabe unnötig ist, so muss sein Wert ersetzt werden. Ähnliche Regelungen finden sich in § 61 GPCL und § 157 GRCL. Wann eine Rückgabe „unnötig" ist, legt das Gesetz aber nicht ausdrücklich fest. Auch in der Wissenschaft besteht hierüber kein Konsens. Einige vertreten die Ansicht, eine Rückgabe sei unnötig, wenn das Erlangte entweder in einer Dienstleistung oder etwas anderem besteht, das wegen seiner Beschaffenheit nicht zurückgegeben

44 S. o. II. 1. a).

werden kann, oder wenn jemand durch Nutzung des geistigen Eigentums eines anderen etwas erlangt hat.[45] Andere sind demgegenüber der Meinung, dass eine Rückgabe unnötig ist, wenn sie wirtschaftlich unvernünftig ist.[46] Schließlich wird auch vertreten, dass eine Rückgabe unnötig sei, wenn die Parteien bei Bedarf tatsächlich vereinbart haben, dass die Herausgabe des ursprünglich Erlangten nicht notwendig ist.[47]

Manche Autoren äußern sich gar nicht zur Rechtsnatur der Rückgewähransprüche bei nichtigen und angefochtenen Rechtsgeschäften bzw. Verträgen. Sie begnügen sich vielmehr mit der wörtlichen Interpretation der gesetzlichen Regelungen.[48] Die meisten jedoch gehen auf diese Frage ein. Manche von diesen sind der Meinung, dass die Rückgewähransprüche aufgrund von Nichtigkeit oder Anfechtung sowohl Vindikation als auch Kondiktion sein könnten. Ist Gegenstand der Rückgewähr eine Sachleistung, so handle es sich um eine Vindikation, weil dem chinesischen Recht das Abstraktionsprinzip fremd sei, ist Gegenstand eine Geld- oder Dienstleistung, so handle es sich um eine Kondiktion.[49] Es wird manchmal betont, dass die Generalklausel der ungerechtfertigten Bereicherung selbst dann Anwendung findet, wenn die Gesetze in den Abschnitten über das Rechtsgeschäft und den Vertrag die Rückgewähr nicht erwähnen. Die Entscheidung des Gesetzgebers gegen das Abstraktionsprinzip kann allenfalls den Anwendungsbereich der ungerechtfertigten Bereicherung einschränken.[50]

---

45 *Hu Kangsheng* (Hrsg.), Interpretation des Vertragsgesetzes der Volksrepublik China («中华人民共和国合同法释义»), 3. Aufl., § 58, 2013, S. 120.

46 *Wang Liming* (Hrsg.), Bd. 2 («中华人民共和国民法总则详解（下册）»), § 157 (Verfasser Ran Keping), 2017, S. 691.

47 *Jiang Ping* (Hrsg.), Eingehende Interpretation des Vertragsgesetzes der Volksrepublik China («中华人民共和国合同法精解»), 1999, S. 4; *Hu Kangsheng* (Hrsg.), Interpretation des Vertragsgesetzes der Volksrepublik China («中华人民共和国合同法释义»), 3. Aufl. 2013, S. 118 f.

48 *Jiang Ping* (Hrsg.), Eingehende Interpretation des Vertragsgesetzes der Volksrepublik China («中华人民共和国合同法精解»), 1999, S. 48; *Hu Kangsheng* (Hrsg.), Interpretation des Vertragsgesetzes der Volksrepublik China («中华人民共和国合同法释义»), 3. Aufl. 2013, S. 118 f.

49 *Wang Jiafu*, Zivilrechtswissenschaft Chinas: Schuldrecht («中国民法学：民法债权»), 1991, S. 334; *Wang Liming* (Hrsg.), General Principles of the Civil Law of the People's Republic of China, Bd. 2 («中华人民共和国民法总则详解»), § 157 (Verfasser Ran Keping), 2017, S. 690 f.

50 *Zou Hailin*, Ungerechtfertigte Bereicherung im chinesischen Zivilrecht ("中国民法上的不当得利"), 5. Civil and Commercial Law Review, S. 30 f. (1995); *Ma Junju/YuYanman*, The Theory of Civil Law («民法原论»), 2. Aufl. 2005, S.

b) Rückgewähr bei Rücktritt

Über die Rückgewähr nach Rücktritt vom Rechtsgeschäft bzw. Vertrag herrscht ebenfalls Meinungsverschiedenheit. Nach § 97 S. 2 VG kann eine Partei entsprechend den Umständen der Erfüllung und der Natur des Vertrags die Wiederherstellung des ursprünglichen Zustands verlangen und andere Maßnahmen zur Abhilfe ergreifen. Sie ist auch berechtigt Schadenersatz zu verlangen. Diese relativ unklare Formulierung ist Grund für eine heftige Debatte. Nach der wohl herrschenden Lehre von der „direkten Wirkung" vernichtet der Rücktritt den Vertrag rückwirkend. Das bereits Geleistete ist zurückzugeben. Die „Wiederherstellung des ursprünglichen Zustands" in § 97 VG bezieht sich auf die Vindikation. Mit den „anderen Maßnahmen zur Abhilfe" sind Kondiktionsansprüche gemeint. Solche Kondiktionsansprüche gelten vor allem für die Rückgewähr einer Dienst- oder Geldleistung.[51] Nach der Lehre von der indirekten Wirkung vernichtet der Rücktritt einen Vertrag nicht. Vielmehr kann er nur die Wirkung des Vertrags verhindern: Während bei der erfüllten Schuld eine neue Rückabwicklungsschuld entsteht, begründet der Rücktritt bei der noch nicht erfüllten Schuld eine rechtshemmende Einwendung.[52] Nach der vermittelnden Lehre vernichtet der Rücktritt nur die noch nicht erfüllte Schuld. Bei einer schon erfüllten Schuld begründet der Rücktritt hingegen eine neue Rückabwicklungsschuld.[53]

2. Rückgewähransprüche aus sachenrechtlicher Akzession

Die Akzession als Eigentumserwerbsform geht auf das römische Recht zurück und wird von den meisten kontinentaleuropäischen Rechtsordnungen

213 f.; *Wang Liming* (Hrsg.), General Principles of the Civil Law of the People's Republic of China, Bd. 2 («中华人民共和国民法总则详解»), § 157 (Verfasser Ran Keping), 2017, S. 690 f.; *Chen Su u. a.*, Commentary on the General Principles of the Civil Code, Bd. («民法总则评注»), § 157 (Verfasser Ye Jinqiang), 2017, S. 1105 f.

51 *Cui Jianyuan*, Fragen und Antworten zum Rücktrittsrecht, Teil 2 ("解除权问题的疑问与释答(下篇)"), 4 Politics and Law, S. 43 (2005).

52 S. dazu *Wang Hongliang*, Allgemeine Theorie des Schuldrechts («债法总论»), 2016, S. 358.

53 *Han Shiyuan*, Allgemeine Theorie des Vertragsrechts («合同法总论»), 3. Aufl. 2011, S. 526.

anerkannt. Die GPCL und das Sachenrechtsgesetz von 2007 verfügen indessen nicht über entsprechende Regelungen. Da sich in der Praxis aus den Vorschriften über Verbindung, Vermischung und Verarbeitung zahlreiche Streitigkeiten ergeben, hat der OVG diese Problematik in seinen Erläuterungen zu den GPCL berücksichtigt.[54] Außerdem kann z. B. der Vermieter nach den Erläuterungen des OVG über die städtische Wohnungsvermietung von 2009, wenn der Mieter die Wohnung ohne Genehmigung oder sogar gegen den Willen des Vermieters dekoriert hat, entweder Entfernung und Schadensersatz verlangen oder aber dem Mieter seine Aufwendungen ersetzen.

Die h. M. hat beim Eigentumserwerb durch Akzession die Anwendung der bereicherungsrechtlichen Regelungen (früher § 92 GPCL, jetzt § 122 GRCL) bejaht.[55] Die oben genannten Erläuterungen des OVG über die städtische Wohnungsvermietung von 2009 werden mitunter kritisiert, weil sie zu sehr den „Schaden" des Vermieters und das „Verschulden" des Mieters betonen und dadurch die ungerechtfertigte Bereicherung zugunsten der unerlaubten Handlung verdrängen würden.[56] Nach einer Mindermeinung fehlt es beim Eigentumserwerb durch Akzession hingegen nicht an einer „rechtlichen Grundlage". Deshalb kommt eine ungerechtfertigte Bereicherung nicht in Betracht. Vielmehr liege in diesem Fall ein untypisches Schuldverhältnis vor, das in den Allgemeinen Teil des Schuldrechts integriert werden sollte.[57] Diese Ansicht findet aber kaum Anhänger.

---

54 § 86 OVG-Erläuterungen GPCL; §§ 9–13 Erläuterungen des OVG über die städtische Wohnungsvermietung von 2009 (Fashi [2009] No. 11).

55 *Zou Hailin*, Ungerechtfertigte Bereicherung im chinesischen Recht ("中国民法上的不当得利"), 1995, S. 42; *Zhang Junhao*, Grundsätze der Zivilrechtwissenschaft («民法学原理»), 1997, S. 852; *Shi Hong* (Hrsg.), Die GRCL: Erläuterung der Paragrafen, Gesetzgebungsmotive und einschlägige Bestimmungen («中华人民共和国民法总则：条文说明、立法理由及相关规定»), 2017, S. 286; *Wang Liming* (Hrsg.), General Principles of the Civil Law of the People's Republic of China, Bd. 1 («中华人民共和国民法总则详解(上册)»), § 122 (Verfasser Wang Liming), 2017, S. 517.

56 *Cui Jianyuan*, The Ascriptionand Interest Restitution of Leased House Decoration ("租赁房屋装饰装修物的归属及利益返还"), 5 Jurist, S. 135 (2009).

57 *Liu Jingwei*, Von der Begründung des Allgemeinen Teils des Schuldrechts aus der Perspektive der untypischen Schuld ("从非典型之债看债法总则的设立"), 13 Law Review of Xiamen University, S. 48 ff., insb. S. 58 ff. (2007).

3. Rückgewähranspruch im Deliktsrecht: Die sog. Gewinnabschöpfung

Während das Deliktsrecht auf Schadensersatz abzielt, dreht sich das Bereicherungsrecht um die Rückgewähr der Bereicherung. Funktional gesehen ist der Unterschied zwischen diesen beiden Rechtsinstituten erheblich. Die Figur der „Gewinnabschöpfung" bringt aber Abgrenzungsschwierigkeiten mit sich, da sie sowohl deliktische als auch bereicherungsrechtliche Elemente enthält. Eine gesetzliche Regelung der „Gewinnabschöpfung" findet man in China vor allem in § 20 DG:

> Wer Personenrechte anderer verletzt und [damit] Vermögensschäden herbeiführt, leistet Ersatz gemäß dem Schaden, den der Verletzte erleidet; hat der Verletzer damit einen Gewinn erzielt, und lässt sich der Schaden schwer bestimmen, so leistet der Verletzer Ersatz gemäß dem erlangten Gewinn [...].[58]

Zur dogmatischen Einordnung dieses Paragrafen werden verschiedene Meinungen vertreten. Nach einer verbreiteten Meinung handelt es sich bei § 20 DG weder um den Fall einer unerlaubten Handlung noch einer ungerechtfertigten Bereicherung. Vielmehr beziehe er sich auf eine „Übergangszone" und sei die Grundlage eines selbständigen Anspruchs.[59] Nach a. A. ist jener Paragraf zwar Grundlage einer „Eingriffskondiktion", soll aber noch nicht mit anderen Fällen zusammen ein allgemeines Rechtsinstitut der Eingriffskondiktion bilden.[60]

Da offizielle Gesetzgebungsmotive fehlen, könnte die dogmatische Debatte über § 20 DG weitergeführt werden. M. E. ist es wohl schwierig, in diesem Paragrafen eine bereicherungsrechtliche Anspruchsgrundlage zu sehen, weil sich einerseits sein Wortlaut eher an der Schadensberechnung orientiert und andererseits sein Anwendungsbereich streng auf „Personenrechte" beschränkt ist.

---

58 Die deutsche Übersetzung von Frank Münzel, abrufbar unter http://www.chinas-recht.de/inhalt.htm, in 2009.zip (zuletzt abgerufen am 11.07.2017).

59 *Zhu Yan*, Anspruchsgrundlage der Gewinnabschöpfung ("利润剥夺的请求权基础"), 3 ZUEL Law Journal, S. 137 ff. (2011).

60 *Li Yongjun*, Zum rechtlichen Schutz der Persönlichkeitsrechte ("从权利属性看人格权的法律保护"), 1 ZUEL Law Journal, S. 18 (2012).

4. Rückgewähr des Brautpreises im Familienrecht

Im Bereich des Familienrechts spielt der Rückgewähranspruch ebenfalls eine Rolle. Nach § 10 Abs. 1 der zweiten Erläuterung des OVG zum Ehegesetz von 2003 kann eine Partei die Rückgabe des nach der Sitte geleisteten Brautpreises verlangen, wenn die Untersuchung ergibt, dass einer der folgenden Umstände vorliegt: 1. Wenn die Parteien nicht das Eheregistrierungsverfahren durchgeführt haben; 2. wenn die Parteien das Eheregistrierungsverfahren durchgeführt, aber tatsächlich nicht zusammengelebt haben; 3. wenn der Brautpreis vor der Ehe geleistet worden ist und dies den Leistenden in Existenzschwierigkeiten gebracht hat. § 10 Abs. 2 regelt ergänzend, dass Voraussetzung [für die Rückgabe] nach den Nr. 2 und 3 des ersten Absatzes die Scheidung der Parteien ist.[61]

Die Rechtsnatur des Brautpreises wird unterschiedlich gesehen. Eine verbreitete Meinung hält ihn für eine Schenkung mit auflösender Bedingung. Folgerichtig sieht man in der Rückgabe des Brautpreises einen Kondiktionsanspruch und zwar eine *condictio causa finita*. Wegen der Nichtanerkennung des Abstraktionsprinzips sei die Rückgewähr von Sachen Vindikation, die von Geld Kondiktion.[62] M. E. handelt es sich bei § 10 Abs. 1der Erläuterungen eigentlich nur teilweise (Nr. 1) um eine Kondiktion, und zwar um eine *condictio causa data causa non secuta* i. S. v. § 812 Abs. 1 S. 2 Alt. 2 BGB. § 10 Abs. 1 Nr. 2 und Nr. 3 sind eher selbstständige Rückgewähransprüche, die wohl auf Billigkeit beruhen. Außerdem wird von manchen Autoren vertreten, dass die einschlägige gerichtliche Erläuterung die Rückgewähr des Brautpreises noch als eine Strafmaßnahme behandle und damit Interessen der brautpreisempfangenden Partei vernachlässigen könnte. Es empfehle sich daher, in Anschluss an das römische Modell eine Art von „Vorrecht" einzuführen, um solche Nachteile auszugleichen.[63]

61 Vgl. die vollständige deutsche Übersetzung von Frank Münzel abrufbar unter http://www.chinas-recht.de/800910.htm (zuletzt abgerufen am 11.07.2017).

62 *Zou Hailin*, Ungerechtfertigte Bereicherung im chinesischen Zivilrecht («中国民法上的不当得利»), 1995, S. 32; *Zhang Xuejun*, Studie über das Rechtsinstitut der Brautpreisrückgewähr ("彩礼返还制度研究"), 5 Peking University Law Journal, S. 637 f. (2006).

63 *Wu Guozhe/Wen Yu*, Die Bedeutung der römischen actio dotis für China ("罗马嫁资返还制度的中国借鉴"), 6 Gansu Theory Research, S. 151 f. (2014).

5. Fazit

Wie die oben kurz erörterten Rückgewähransprüche dogmatisch einzuordnen sind, ist nicht immer klar. Dies hat teilweise mit den Meinungsverschiedenheiten zu einigen grundlegenden Themen wie dem Abstraktionsprinzip zu tun. Ein technischer Grund dafür liegt aber wohl darin, dass die einschlägigen Regelungen normalerweise die Rechtsfolgen der Rückgewähr selbst regeln und nicht auf andere Anspruchsgrundlagen, seien es Deliktische, seien es Kondiktionale, verweisen, woraus sich viele Interpretationsmöglichkeiten ergeben.

V. Perspektive: Das Bereicherungsrecht im künftigen chinesischen ZGB

Zum Schluss darf ich einen kurzen Ausblick auf das Bereicherungsrecht im künftigen chinesischen ZGB geben.

1. Systematische Stellung: Ungerechtfertigte Bereicherung als Quasivertrag

Obwohl die GRCL das Schuldverhältnis als Oberbegriff bewahrt haben, würde der Gesetzgeber im künftigen Zivilgesetzbuch wahrscheinlich auf einen Allgemeinen Teil des Schuldrechts verzichten. Die GRCL würden gewissermaßen als Allgemeiner Teil des Schuldrechts fungieren. Dabei könnte die ungerechtfertigte Bereicherung als Quasivertrag mitgeregelt werden. Das erinnert an den neu reformierten französischen *Code Civil*, der dem Quasivertrag einen eigenen *sous-titre* widmet, der neben dem *sous-titre* über den Vertrag steht. Allerdings ist das Quasivertrag-Modell logisch insofern etwas mangelhaft, als das moderne Bereicherungsrecht nicht nur Quasivertrag (Leistungskondiktion), sondern auch Quasidelikt (Eingriffskondiktion) umfasst. Man könnte sagen, dass das künftige Zivilgesetzbuch kein rein akademisches Werk, sondern Produkt einer pragmatischen Gesetzgebung ist.

2. Verhältnis zwischen der Generalklausel und den ergänzenden Regelungen

Dass sich die Generalklausel der ungerechtfertigten Bereicherung in den GRCL befindet, ist schon mehrfach kritisiert worden. Wenn die systematische Stellung im künftigen ZGB unberührt bliebe, dann müsste die Generalklausel im Allgemeinen Teil immer in Verbindung mit den ergänzenden Regelungen im Abschnitt über den Quasivertrag angewendet werden. Die ergänzenden Regelungen würden zur Konkretisierung der Tatbestandsmerkmale und der Rechtsfolge der Generalklausel dienen, die ihrerseits nicht allein angewendet werden könnte. Aus der Perspektive der Rechtsanwendung wäre ein solches Modell umständlich. Deshalb empfiehlt es sich, die Generalklausel vom Allgemeinen Teil in den Abschnitt über den Quasivertrag zu schieben.

3. Die Problematik der Typologie

Obwohl die Wissenschaft überwiegend die „Trennungslehre“ und die BGB-Typologie der ungerechtfertigten Bereicherung übernommen hat, werden auch andere Typologien vertreten und daher gibt es dahingehend kein einheitliches Konzept. Die Rechtsprechung hat die Trennungslehre bisher auch nicht einheitlich angewendet. Eine reife Rechtsdogmatik hinsichtlich der ungerechtfertigten Bereicherung ist also noch nicht zu erkennen. Es kommt hinzu, dass die ungerechtfertigte Bereicherung wie oben erwähnt sowohl Leistungskondiktion als auch Nichtleistungskondiktion betrifft. Es wäre merkwürdig, wenn man im Abschnitt über den Quasivertrag die Fälle des Quasidelikts mitregeln würde. Deswegen wäre es zweckmäßig, die Typologie der Wissenschaft und der Rechtsprechung zu überlassen. Eine reife Dogmatik entsteht erst mit der intensiven Interaktion zwischen Wissenschaft und Praxis.

4. Verhältnis zwischen Kondiktionsansprüchen und anderen Rückgewähransprüchen

Über das Verhältnis zwischen den Kondiktionsansprüchen im engeren Sinne und den anderen Rückgewähransprüchen bestehen zurzeit viele Kontroversen. Dies ergibt sich teilweise aus den unterschiedlichen Ansichten zu manchen grundlegenden Fragen, teilweise auch aus der Regelungstechnik, die der Gesetzgeber bei den einschlägigen Bestimmungen verwendet. Um die Unübersichtlichkeit des Systems der ungerechtfertigten Bereicherung zu beseitigen oder zumindest zu verringern, würde es sich wohl lohnen, das Verhältnis von den Kondiktionsansprüchen zu anderen Rückgewähransprüchen gesetzgeberisch klarzustellen, wie es der DCFR schon versucht hat.

Kollidierende AGB im chinesischen Vertragsrecht: Auslegungswege und Gesetzgebungsmöglichkeiten bei der Kodifizierung eines Zivilgesetzbuches

*Jin Jing**

Zusammenfassung: *Die Verwendung von Allgemeinen Geschäftsbedingungen (AGB) im inländischen und internationalen Geschäftsverkehr nimmt heutzutage stetig zu. Das Problem kollidierender AGB wird daher vermehrt auftreten, wenn sich Parteien, die AGB verwenden, bei Vertragsschluss über Vertragsinhalte streiten. Bisher wurde diese Frage in der chinesischen Rechtswissenschaft noch nicht vertieft diskutiert, in der vertragsrechtlichen Literatur wird sie lediglich vereinzelt erwähnt. Die knock-out rule wird unter rechtsvergleichender Perspektive zwar teilweise für sinnvoll erachtet, jedoch wird keine konkrete Möglichkeit für eine Implementierung in das chinesische Recht genannt. Mitunter wird § 31 Vertragsgesetz[1] (VG) als allgemeiner Rechtsgedanke verstanden und bei kollidierenden AGB angewandt, was der last shot rule entspricht. Zu beachten ist jedoch, dass die Auslegung des § 31 VG als last shot rule nicht unproblematisch ist. Eine solche Lösung des Problems kollidierender AGB erscheint im chinesischen Recht kompliziert und birgt Rechtsunsicherheit. Vielmehr ist es möglich und mit der vertragsrechtlichen Wirklichkeit vereinbar, dieses Problem in der künftigen Kodifikation eines chinesischen Zivilgesetzbuches (ZGB) zu behandeln und entsprechende Regelungen einzuführen.*

Stichwörter: Allgemeine Geschäftsbedingungen, Kollision der AGB, Restgültigkeitstheorie, Auslegung des Vertragsgesetzes.

---

* *Dr. (Münster)*; Dozentin, Chinesische Universität für Politikwissenschaft und Recht. Lehrstuhl für Bürgerliches Recht.
Die Erstellung dieses Beitrags wurde unterstützt durch das Programm *The Regional Integration of Contract Law under the Silk Road Economic Belt* des Nationalen Chinesischen Fonds zur Förderung der Sozialwissenschaften unter der Fördernr. 15CFX058 (2015国家社科基金青年项目"丝绸之路经济带合同法区域整合研究"，项目编号15CFX058).

1 Vertragsgesetz der Volksrepublik China (« 中华人民共和国合同法 ») v. 15.3.1999, in Kraft getreten am 1.10.1999, Order No.15 of the President of the People's Republic of China.

Heutzutage nimmt die Verwendung von AGB im inländischen und internationalen Geschäftsverkehr stetig zu. Eine überragende Rolle spielen AGB bei Handelsverträgen. Bei der Verteilung von Transaktionsrisiken werden AGB als Instrument zur Risikobegrenzung in Massengeschäften eingesetzt: Die AGB werden normalerweise von juristischen Experten sorgfältig vorformuliert. Dadurch werden die Interessen des AGB-Verwenders geschützt und seine rechtlichen Risiken vernünftig begrenzt. Allerdings werden durch die Verwendung von AGB wiederum andersartige Transaktionsrisiken erzeugt: Häufig werden durch AGB die Interessen des Vertragspartners verkürzt oder bleiben ganz unberücksichtigt, z. B. bei einer für ihn ungünstigen

Risikoverteilung oder Schiedsklausel. Die Verwendung von AGB ist in diesem Sinne ein „einseitiges Diktat des Verwenders". Während Verkaufsbedingungen normalerweise zugunsten des Verkäufers formuliert sind, wirken Einkaufsbedingungen normalerweise zugunsten des Käufers. Der Verwender von AGB kann diese Vorteile nur verwirklichen und davon profitieren, wenn die von ihm vorgeschlagenen AGB auch tatsächlich wirksam einbezogen werden. Im unternehmerischen Geschäftsverkehr kann es zu einer Kollision von AGB kommen, wenn jede Partei ihre eigenen AGB durchsetzen möchte. So etwa wenn ein Unternehmen bei einer Warenbestellung auf seine Allgemeinen Einkaufsbedingungen verweist und sein Vertragspartner in der Auftragsbestätigung dagegen auf seine Allgemeinen Verkaufsbedingungen Bezug nimmt. Das Problem kollidierender AGB tritt also auf, wenn sich die Parteien über Vertragsinhalte streiten. In Bezug auf das Problem kollidierender AGB stellen sich folgende zwei Fragen: (1) Ist der Vertrag wirksam? (2) Inwieweit werden die kollidierenden Vertragsbedingungen in den Vertrag einbezogen? Diese „Kollision der AGB" zwischen den Parteien wird in der englischen Terminologie als *battle of the forms* bezeichnet.

Dieser Aufsatz konzentriert sich auf drei Fragen, nämlich die Risikoverteilung, existierende Auslegungsparadoxa und künftige Lösungsansätze für kollidierende AGB im chinesischen Vertragsrecht vor dem Hintergrund der Kodifizierung eines Zivilgesetzbuches (ZGB). Der erste Teil beinhaltet einen Überblick über das Problem kollidierender AGB im derzeitigen chinesischen Vertragsrecht und geht dabei auf Rechtsgrundlagen, Rechtsprechung und Auslegung ein. Im Zweiten Teil werden die bestehenden verschiedenen Lösungsmodelle aus rechtsvergleichender Sicht dargestellt und bewertet. Im Schlussteil werden mögliche Lösungsansätze für kollidierende AGB im Hinblick auf ein chinesisches ZGB vorgeschlagen.

I. Ein Überblick über kollidierende AGB im chinesischen Vertragsrecht

1. Die gesetzliche Rechtsgrundlage: *last shot rule* gem. § 30 S. 2 VG

Im chinesischen Recht sind AGB (sogenannte Formularklauseln[2]) in den §§ 39–41 VG und §§ 6–9, 26 Verbraucherschutzgesetz[3] (VSG) verankert. AGB sind gem. § 39 Abs. 2 VG definiert als Vertragsbedingungen, die eine Partei zur wiederholten Verwendung vorformuliert und die bei Vertragsschluss mit der anderen Seite nicht ausgehandelt werden. Nach der gesetzlichen Definition sind „einseitige Vorformulierung" und „ohne individuelles Aushandeln" die zwei wichtigsten Merkmale von AGB[4]: Einerseits werden die Vertragsbedingungen durch eine Partei vor dem Vertragsschluss festgelegt.[5] Andererseits müssen die Vertragsbedingungen für eine Vielzahl von Verträgen vorformuliert sein.[6] Jedoch differenziert das VG nicht zwischen einem Verbraucher und einem Unternehmer als Empfänger der AGB. Das VSG enthält keine weitere Definition des Begriffs der AGB. Daher finden §§ 39 ff. VG sowohl beim Handelsvertrag als auch beim Verbrauchervertrag Anwendung.

Für das Problem kollidierender AGB gibt es im chinesischen Vertragsrecht keine Sonderreglung. Es ist hauptsächlich durch die allgemeinen Reglungen zu Angebot und Annahme im Vertragsgesetz gelöst. § 30 VG[7] und

2 Im chinesischen Vertragsrecht werden AGB als Formularklauseln (格式条款) bezeichnet, in der Praxis werden sie manchmal auch als Standardisierte Klausel (标准条款) bezeichnet.

3 Verbraucherschutzgesetz der Volksrepublik China («中华人民共和国消费者权益保护法») v. 31.10.1993, in Kraft getreten am 1.1.1994, zuletzt geändert am 25.10.2013, Order No.7 of the President of the People's Republic of China.

4 *Weidlich/Shen*, in: Binding/Pißler/Xu, Chinesisches Zivil- und Wirtschaftsrecht, 2015, Rn. 40.

5 Palandt/*Grüneberg*, BGB, 76. Aufl. 2017, § 305 Rn. 8.

6 Palandt/*Grüneberg*, BGB, 76. Aufl. 2017, § 305 Rn. 9.

7 § 30 [Abändernde Annahme]
Der Inhalt der Annahme muss mit dem des Angebots übereinstimmen. Wenn der Empfänger des Angebots gegenüber dem Inhalt des Angebots materielle Änderungen vorgenommen hat, gilt [die Annahme] als neues Angebot. Änderungen in Bezug auf den Vertragsgegenstand, die Menge, die Qualität, den Preis oder das Entgelt, auf Frist, Ort oder Art und Weise der Erfüllung, auf die Haftung für Vertragsverletzungen oder die Art und Weise der Beilegung von Streitigkeiten sind materielle Änderungen gegenüber dem Inhalt des Angebots.

§ 31 VG[8] regeln die abändernde Annahme bzw. die nicht materiellen Änderungen bei der Annahme. § 30 VG besteht aus drei Sätzen. Nach § 30 S. 1 VG muss der Inhalt der Annahme mit dem des Angebots übereinstimmen. Dies entspricht der traditionellen *mirror rule* des Vertragsrechts.[9] § 30 S. 2 VG hingegen enthält eine ausdrückliche Regelung über die materielle Abänderung: Sobald sich die Annahme des Angebotsempfängers materiell vom Angebot unterscheidet, gilt die Annahme als neues Angebot. Dieser Satz entspricht der *last shot rule* und könnte als Lösung für kollidierende AGB herangezogen werden. § 30 S. 1 und S. 2 VG stehen im Regel-Ausnahme-Verhältnis zueinander. Obwohl § 30 S. 2 VG die Ausnahme von der *mirror rule* darstellt, ist es eigentlich die wichtigste Regelung im § 30 VG. Gem. § 30 S. 3 VG sind materielle Änderungen des Angebots solche, die den Vertragsgegenstand, die Menge, die Qualität, den Preis oder das Entgelt, die Frist, den Ort oder die Art und Weise der Erfüllung, die Haftung für Vertragsverletzungen oder die Art und Weise der Beilegung von Streitigkeiten betreffen. Die Beispiele im § 30 S. 3 VG zu materiellen Änderungen stellen eine enumerative Aufzählung dar und sind nicht abschließend. Bei nicht materiellen Änderungen bleibt die Annahme gem. § 31 VG hingegen wirksam und der Inhalt des Vertrages richtet sich nach der Annahme, falls der Anbietende nicht rechtzeitig seine Ablehnung zum Ausdruck bringt oder aus dem Angebot eindeutig hervorging, dass die Annahme den Inhalt des Angebots in keiner Weise ändern darf. Die Beurteilung, ob die Annahme das Angebot materiell oder nicht materiell abändert, erfolgt je nach Einzelfall. Deshalb lassen die Regelungen der §§ 30 f. VG großen Spielraum. Die Regelung des § 30 S. 2 VG, wonach eine materielle Abänderung ein neues Angebot darstellt, gilt als Ausgangspunkt für die Lösung des Problems kollidierender AGB über die *last shot rule*.

---

8 § 31 [Nicht materielle Änderungen in der Annahme]
Wenn in der Annahme gegenüber dem Inhalt des Angebots Änderungen nicht materieller Natur vorgenommen worden sind, ist die Annahme wirksam, und der Inhalt des Vertrages richtet sich nach der Annahme, falls der Anbietende nicht rechtzeitig seine Ablehnung zum Ausdruck bringt, oder das Angebot klargestellt hatte, daß die Annahme den Inhalt des Angebots in keiner Weise ändern darf.

9 *Zhu Guangxin*, Die kollidierenden AGB beim Vertragsabschluss ("论合同订立过程中的格式之战问题"), 7 Law Science, S. 78 ff. (2014).

2. Theoretische Einordnung sowie jüngere Rechtsprechung

In der chinesischen Rechtswissenschaft wurde das Problem kollidierender AGB bisher noch nicht gründlich diskutiert. Vereinzelt wird es in der vertragsrechtlichen Literatur jedoch erwähnt. Hierbei erfolgt die Darstellung entweder im Rahmen einer Rechtsvergleichung von § 30 VG mit § 19 Abs. 3 CISG, allerdings ohne klare Stellungnahme zu den Lösungsansätzen des chinesischen Vertragsgesetzes.[10] Oder es werden unterschiedliche Ansätze aus rechtsvergleichender Perspektive vorgestellt und dabei die *knock-out rule* für das Problem der kollidierenden AGB theoretisch als vernünftige Lösung beurteilt.[11] Jedoch wird für eine konkrete Anwendung der *knock-out rule* in der chinesischen vertragsrechtlichen Literatur kein genauer Lösungsweg vorgeschlagen.[12] Immerhin wurde vereinzelt klargestellt, dass nach der wörtlichen Auslegung der §§ 30 f. VG die *last shot rule* oder zumindest eine „begrenzte" *last shot rule* in Betracht kommen.[13] Insgesamt existiert in der Wissenschaft bisher aber keine h. M. über konkrete Lösungsmodelle für kollidierende AGB. Vereinzelt wird auch § 31 VG als allgemeine Lösung verstanden und ebenfalls auf das Problem kollidierender AGB angewandt, weshalb die Literatur die *last shot rule* bei kollidierenden AGB zu vertreten scheint. Zu beachten ist jedoch, dass die Auslegung des § 31 S. 2 VG als *last shot rule* nicht unproblematisch ist. Der Nachteil dieser Lösung besteht darin, dass sie unerwartete Ergebnisse für den Handelsvertrag mit sich bringen kann. Auch wirkt sich die Anwendung der *last shot rule* negativ auf die Rechtssicherheit und Vorhersehbarkeit von Transaktionen aus.

---

10 *Hu Kangsheng*, Erläuterungen zum Vertragsgesetz der Volksrepublik China («中华人民共和国合同法释义»), 2013, S. 70–71.

11 *Wang Liming*, Studie zum Vertragsrecht, Bd. 1 («合同法研究»（第一卷）), 2011, S. 253 ff.

12 *Wang Liming*, Studie zum Vertragsrecht, Bd. 1 («合同法研究»（第一卷）), 2011, S. 257 ff.

13 *Han Shiyuan*, The Law of Contract («合同法总论»（第三版）), 2011, S. 103–104; *Zhu Guangxin*, Die kollidierenden AGB beim Vertragsabschluss ("论合同订立过程中的格式之战问题"), 7 Law Science, S. 73 (2014); *Wang Jiangyu*, Die allgemeinen Regelungen über Abschluss eines Kaufvertrags und die kollidierenden AGB im internationalen Geschäftsverkehr ("买卖合同成立的一般规则与国际贸易中的格式之战"), 8 Civil and Commercial Law Review, Bd. 8, S. 635 ff. (1997); *Hu Li*, Die kollidierenden AGB beim Vertragsabschluss ("论合同订立中的格式之战"), 6 Modern Law Science, S. 46 (1999).

In der jüngeren Rechtsprechung zu §§ 31 ff. VG spielten kollidierende AGB keine Rolle. Es gibt zahlreiche Entscheidungen über die Wirksamkeit eines Vertrags, jedoch bisher keine explizite Entscheidung über die Wirksamkeit kollidierender AGB. Dies mag überraschen, ist bei einer Reihe von Gerichtsentscheidungen jedoch gerechtfertigt. Erwähnenswert ist hier ein Urteil des Obersten Volksgerichtshofs der Volksrepublik China (OVG) aus dem Jahr 2011 zu einer kaufvertragsrechtlichen Streitigkeit.[14] In diesem Fall hatte der Käufer sieben Bestellungen an den Verkäufer gesendet. Der Verkäufer änderte die Vertragsbedingungen einschließlich Preis und Lieferdatum in fünf von sieben Bestellungen und sandte sie dem Käufer zurück. Nachdem zum Teil erfüllt worden war, stritten die Parteien über den Preis und die Wirksamkeit des Vertrags. Obwohl es in diesem Fall nicht um kollidierende AGB geht, kann er für die Lösung dieses Problems herangezogen werden, denn in der ersten und zweiten Instanz ergingen unterschiedliche Entscheidungen hinsichtlich der Wirksamkeit der Verträge bei den kollidierenden Bestellungen. In der letzten Instanz des OVG wurde festgestellt, dass hinsichtlich der beiden Bestellungen ohne Veränderungen durch den Verkäufer Verträge vorlagen. Bei den fünf kollidierenden Bestellungen wurden die Veränderungen jedoch als neue Angebote gem. § 30 S. 2 VG angesehen. Mangels wirksamer Annahme kam anschließend kein Vertrag zustande. Dies führt zu der Annahme, dass der OVG in der Praxis teilweise die Restgültigkeitstheorie (für das Bestehen der zwei Verträge) und teilweise die *last shot rule* (für das Nicht-Bestehen der fünf Verträge) anwendet. Die Position des OVG ist folglich nicht ganz eindeutig und daher problematisch. Bei der Teilerfüllung erkennt der OVG keine wirksamen Verträge an. Dies ist mit einem Nebeneinander von wirksamen Verträgen und der Förderung von Transaktionen unvereinbar.

Das Problem der kollidierenden AGB ist im chinesischen Vertragsrecht bisher nicht gelöst. Es existieren keine speziellen Regelungen hierfür. Das Problem ist daher nur durch die Anwendung der allgemeinen vertragsrechtlichen Regelungen über die Annahme zu lösen. Allerdings gibt es bei kollidierenden AGB im Handelsverkehr einige Besonderheiten. Das spezifische Problem kollidierender AGB nur mit allgemeinen Regelungen über die Annahme zu lösen, ist daher nicht zufriedenstellend. Die Rechtsprechung bietet ebenfalls keine geeigneten Lösungen hierfür. Es stellen sich deshalb folgende Fragen: Welche Lösungsmodelle für kollidierende AGB stehen

---

14 The ITOCHU Group v. CECT (伊藤忠商事株式会社与中电通信科技有限责任公司买卖合同纠纷再审案), Oberster Volksgerichtshof der Volksrepublik China (OVG) (2011) Min Shen Zi No. 170 ((2011)民申字第170号).

grundsätzlich zur Verfügung? Welcher Lösungsansatz ist für das chinesische Vertragsrecht passend?

II. Rechtsvergleichende Lösungsansätze und Bewertungen

Zusammenfassend unterscheidet man vier Lösungsmodelle für kollidierende AGB: Die Theorie des ersten Wortes, die Theorie des letzten Wortes, die Restgültigkeitstheorie und die Ungültigkeit des gesamten Vertrags. Diese Modelle gehen auf die Gesetzgebung, die Rechtsprechung sowie die Literatur zurück.

1. Das niederländische Burgerlijk Wetboek: Theorie des ersten Wortes

Das erste Modell ist die Theorie des ersten Wortes. Diese wird auch als *first shot rule* bezeichnet. Sie bedeutet, dass die AGB, auf welche zuerst verwiesen wird, angewendet werden. Bei diesem Modell setzt sich der Anbietende durch. Dieses Modell ist beispielsweise im niederländischen Burgerlijk Wetboek[15] (BW) kodifiziert.

2. Das UN-Kaufrecht: Theorie des letzten Wortes

Das zweite Modell ist die Theorie des letzten Wortes. Diese Theorie wird auch *last shot rule* genannt. Das bedeutet, dass die AGB desjenigen angewendet werden, der zuletzt unwidersprochen auf seine eigenen Bedingungen verwiesen hat.[16] In der Regel wird sich danach der Lieferant mit seinen Bedingungen durchsetzen. Diese *last shot rule* wird im *Common Law* von

---

15 Art. 6:225 Abs. 3 BW sieht diesbezüglich vor:
Verweisen Angebot und Annahme auf unterschiedliche allgemeine Geschäftsbedingungen, dann ist die zweite Verweisung unwirksam, wenn durch sie nicht zugleich die Anwendbarkeit der in der ersten Verweisung angegebenen allgemeinen Geschäftsbedingungen ausdrücklich abgelehnt wird.

16 *Schlechtriem/Schroeter*, in: Schlechtriem/Schwenzer, Kommentar zum Einheitlichen UN-Kaufrecht, 5. Aufl. 2008, Art. 19 CISG Rn. 22.

englischen und schottischen Gerichten als herrschende Meinung angewandt.[17]

Im UN-Kaufrecht gibt es keine besondere Regelung für kollidierende AGB, weil entsprechende Vorschläge bei der Gesetzgebung keinen Erfolg hatten.[18] Das Problem der *battle of the forms* wird vielmehr durch Art. 19 CISG[19], welcher sich auf das Gegenangebot bezieht, gelöst. Die Frage des Zustandekommens des Vertrages und des Vertragsinhalts richten sich danach, ob die mit der Annahme zugesandten Allgemeinen Geschäftsbedingungen eine wesentliche oder unwesentliche Abweichung von denjenigen der Gegenpartei beinhalten.

---

17 So der Grundsatz nach section 2-207 Uniform Commercial Code (UCC): *(1) A definite and seasonable expression of acceptance or a written confirmation which is sent within a reasonable time operates as an acceptance even though it states terms additional to or different from those offered or agreed upon, unless acceptance is expressly made conditional on assent to the additional or different terms.*
(2) The additional terms are to be construed as proposals for addition to the contact. Between merchants such terms become part of the contract unless: (a) the offer expressly limits acceptance to the terms of the offer; (b) they materially alter it; or (c) notification of objection to them has already been given or is given within a reasonable time after notice of them is received.
(3) Conduct by both parties which recognizes the existence of a contract is sufficient to establish a contract for sale although the writings of the parties do not otherwise establish a contract. In such case the terms of the particular contract consists of those terms on which the writings of the parties agree, together with any supplementary terms incorporated under any other provisions under this Act.

18 *Schlechtriem/Schroeter*, in: Schlechtriem/Schwenzer, Kommentar zum Einheitlichen UN-Kaufrecht, 5. Aufl. 2008, Art. 19 CISG Rn. 21.

19 Art. 19 CISG:
(1) Eine Antwort auf ein Angebot, die eine Annahme darstellen soll, aber Ergänzungen, Einschränkungen oder sonstige Änderungen enthält, ist eine Ablehnung des Angebots und stellt ein Gegenangebot dar.
(2) Eine Antwort auf ein Angebot, die eine Annahme darstellen soll, aber Ergänzungen oder Abweichungen enthält, welche die Bedingungen des Angebots nicht wesentlich ändern, stellt jedoch eine Annahme dar, wenn der Annehmende das Fehlen der Übereinstimmung nicht unverzüglich mündlich beanstandet oder eine entsprechende Mitteilung absendet. Unterlässt er dies, so bilden die Bedingungen des Angebots mit den in der Annahme enthaltenen Änderungen den Vertragsinhalt.
(3) Ergänzungen oder Abweichungen, die sich insbesondere auf Preis, Bezahlung, Qualität und Menge der Ware, auf Ort und Zeit der Lieferung, auf den Umfang der Haftung der einer Partei gegenüber der anderen oder auf die Beilegung von Streitigkeiten beziehen, werden so angesehen, als änderten sie die Bedingungen des Angebots wesentlich.

a) Wesentliche Abweichungen

Nach Art. 19 Abs. 1 CISG ist eine Antwort auf ein Angebot, die eine Annahme darstellen soll, aber wesentliche Ergänzungen, Einschränkungen oder sonstige Änderungen enthält, eine Ablehnung des Angebots und stellt ein Gegenangebot dar. Im Ergebnis lässt sich demzufolge festhalten, dass das UN-Kaufrecht bei wesentlichen Abweichungen der umstrittenen Theorie des letzten Wortes folgt, was in aller Regel dazu führt, dass die AGB des Lieferanten Anwendung finden.

b) Unwesentliche Abweichungen

Weichen die AGB nur unwesentlich voneinander ab, so gibt Art. 19 Abs. 2 CISG den Lösungsweg vor. Danach stellt die Antwort auf ein Angebot, welche die Bedingungen dieses Angebotes nicht wesentlich modifiziert, eine Annahme dar, sofern der Anbietende das Fehlen der Übereinstimmung nicht unverzüglich mündlich beanstandet oder eine entsprechende Mitteilung absendet. Tut er beides nicht, so bilden die Bedingungen des Angebots mit den in der Annahme enthaltenen Änderungen den Vertragsinhalt. Im Ergebnis wird hier die *mirror rule* des Absatzes 1 bei nicht wesentlichen Abweichungen zugunsten der direkten Anwendung der Theorie des letzten Wortes abgeändert, ohne dass hier – wie bei Art. 19 Abs. 1 CISG – mit der Annahme eines Gegenangebotes gearbeitet werden muss. Der Anbietende kann den Vertragsschluss hier nur verhindern, indem er jede noch so unwesentliche Abweichung vom Angebot unverzüglich ablehnt.

c) Bewertung

In der Regel werden bei unwesentlichen Abweichungen die AGB des Annehmenden gelten, da dieser seine AGB zuletzt übersendet. Verhindern kann der ursprünglich Antragende dies, indem er nochmals eine Auftragsbestätigung mit seinen AGB übermittelt. Allerdings sollte man diesen Schritt nur wohl überlegt vornehmen: Zum einen droht ein „Bedingungs-Ping-Pong", da auch der Vertragsgegner in gleicher Weise reagieren kann. Zum anderen, und dies ist für den Antragenden wohl noch essenzieller, bleibt der Vertrag durch die erneute Übersendung der eigenen Allgemeinen Geschäftsbedingungen weiterhin „in der Schwebe". Er läuft also Gefahr, dass die andere Partei sein neues Angebot weder ausdrücklich noch konkludent annimmt, was letztlich ein möglicherweise unerwünschtes Scheitern des Vertrages zur Folge hat.

3. Das Kaufrecht in Deutschland und der Europäischen Union: Restgültigkeitstheorie

Das dritte Modell geht von der Restgültigkeitstheorie aus. Diese Theorie wird auch als *knock-out rule* bezeichnet. Die Vertreter der Restgültigkeitstheorie sehen den Vertrag trotz kollidierender AGB als zustande gekommen an, die Geschäftsbedingungen hingegen sollen nur insoweit ausfallen, wie sie sich widersprechen; an ihre Stelle sollen die gesetzlichen Regelungen treten. Bestimmungen widersprechen sich, wenn sie sich gegenseitig ausschließen. Die gesetzlichen Regelungen werden als Lückenfüller eingesetzt. Dieser Theorie sind in Übereinstimmung mit einer Grundsatzentscheidung des Bundesgerichtshofs wesentliche Teile der deutschen Rechtsprechung gefolgt. Diese heute wohl herrschende Lösung wird in anderen Rechtsordnungen ebenfalls bevorzugt.

Anders als das UN-Kaufrecht hat auch das Gemeinsame Europäische Kaufrecht (GEK) das Restgültigkeitsprinzip übernommen.[20] Wenn die Parteien den Individualvertrag tatsächlich gewollt haben, ist der Vertrag gültig und von den widerstreitenden AGB unabhängig, soweit diese sich widersprechen. Im B2B-Rechtsverkehr ist die vorgeschlagene Bestimmung als zwingende Vorschrift zu begrüßen, weil sie Rechtssicherheit schafft. Tatsächlich ist es gerade der Normalfall, dass Unternehmen untereinander nur

20 Art. 39 GEK:
Widersprechende Standardvertragsbestimmungen
Haben die Parteien abgesehen davon, dass sich Angebot und Annahme auf einander widersprechende Standardvertragsbestimmungen beziehen, eine Einigung erzielt, so ist der Vertrag dennoch geschlossen. Die Standardvertragsbestimmungen sind insoweit Teil des Vertrags, als sie sich inhaltlich decken.
Unbeschadet des Absatzes 1 ist der Vertrag nicht geschlossen, wenn eine Partei
(a) Im Voraus ausdrücklich und nicht durch Standardvertragsbestimmungen zum Ausdruck gebracht hat, dass sie nicht auf der Grundlage von Absatz 1 durch einen Vertrag gebunden sein will, oder
(b) Die andere Partei unverzüglich davon in Kenntnis setzt, dass sie nicht durch einen solchen Vertrag gebunden sein will.

zu den jeweils eigenen Allgemeinen Vertragsbedingungen kontrahieren wollen.

4. Scheitern des Vertragsschlusses

Vereinzelt wird schließlich auch ein Scheitern des Vertrages insgesamt wegen fehlender Einigung über die Geltung der AGB angenommen.[21]

5. Bewertung der verschiedenen Lösungsmodelle

Wie gezeigt, kommen die vier Lösungsmodelle für kollidierende AGB in verschiedenen Ländern bei der Kodifikation, in der Rechtsprechung sowie in der Literatur zur Anwendung. Zusammenfassend folgt das Niederländische BW der Theorie des ersten Wortes. Die h. M. in England und Schottland sowie Art. 19 CISG folgen der Theorie des letzten Wortes. In Deutschland ging man zunächst von der Theorie des letzten Wortes aus. Mittlerweile vertritt die h.M. und die jüngere Rechtsprechung das Restgültigkeitsprinzip. Letzteres wird auch in Österreich, Dänemark und Polen vertreten. Schließlich folgen auch die UNIDROIT-Prinzipien dem Restgültigkeitsprinzip. Fraglich ist, wie die verschiedenen Lösungsmodelle zu bewerten sind und ob eines davon zu bevorzugen ist.

Die Theorie des ersten Wortes kann zu einem zufälligen Ergebnis zwischen beiden Parteien führen. Zudem muss beachtet werden, dass diese Theorie für die praktische Vertragsverhandlung problematisch ist. Nach diesem Modell ist nämlich die Vertragspartei, die das erste Angebot abgegeben hat, immer in der besseren Lage. Dieses Ergebnis ist unfair und zu unflexibel für die Praxis.

Auch bei der Theorie des letzten Wortes besteht der Nachteil darin, dass dieses Modell in der Praxis häufig zu zufälligen Ergebnissen führt,[22] da die AGB sich durchsetzen, auf die zuletzt unwidersprochen verwiesen wurde. Das Ergebnis können die Vertragsparteien vorher weder sicherstellen noch steuern, was bei lang andauernden Vertragsverhandlungen besonders problematisch ist. Es könnte nämlich zum Beispiel sein, dass nach jahrelangen

---

21 *Schlechtriem/Schroeter*, in: Schlechtriem/Schwenzer, Kommentar zum Einheitlichen UN-Kaufrecht, 5. Aufl. 2008, Art. 19 CISG Rn. 24.

22 *Schlechtriem/Schroeter*, in: Schlechtriem/Schwenzer, Kommentar zum Einheitlichen UN-Kaufrecht, 5. Aufl. 2008, Art. 19 CISG Rn. 22.

Verhandlungen, wie beispielsweise beim Unternehmenskauf, die Parteien selbst nicht mehr wissen, welche Partei das Angebot und welche die Annahme erklärt hat. Außerdem werden die Ergebnisse der Theorie des letzten Wortes als ungerecht angesehen. Um die eigenen Bestimmungen durchzusetzen, müsste man der eigenen Annahme an die andere Partei lediglich eine zusätzliche Klausel hinzufügen und abwarten. Würde der Zusatz nicht bemerkt und würde die andere Partei das Angebot annehmen, hätte man gewonnen. Es geht hierbei um Fälle, in denen wohl absichtlich unbedeutende Änderungen hinzugefügt wurden, um das gewünschte Obsiegen der eigenen Bestimmungen zu erreichen. Solche absichtlichen Verzögerungen sind mit dem Grundsatz der Verlässlichkeit im Handelsverkehr schwer vereinbar und für diesen schädlich.

Die Meinung, die ein generelles Scheitern des Vertragsschlusses annimmt, ist mit Ziel und Absicht der Parteien nicht vereinbar. Obwohl die Parteien bei der Verhandlung die jeweils eigenen AGB eingeführt haben, darf nicht vergessen werden, dass die Vertragsparteien an erster Stelle einen Vertrag abschließen möchten. Wegen der fehlenden Einigung über die Geltung der AGB auf den ganzen Vertrag zu verzichten, widerspricht dem wirklichen Willen beider Parteien. Außerdem ist es mit dem Ziel, den Geschäftsverkehr durch AGB zu vereinfachen und zu fördern, nicht vereinbar. Dieses Modell könnte somit zu einer Schädigung der gesamten wirtschaftlichen Tätigkeit führen.

Folglich erscheint das Restgültigkeitsprinzip als das gerechteste unter den vier Modellen. Eine Einigung auf das „gemeinsame Minimum" und die ausschließliche Geltung der gesetzlichen Vorschriften im Kollisionsbereich können die Interessen sowie den Willen beider Parteien besser berücksichtigen. Zustimmung verdient daher der Lösungsansatz der Restgültigkeitstheorie, der auch im grenzüberschreitenden Warenkauf einen handhabbaren und vor allem sachgerechten Weg zum Umgang mit kollidierenden Standardbedingungen eröffnet. Dieses Lösungsmodell hat auch *Ernst Rabel* in seiner Monographie „Das Recht des Warenkaufs" favorisiert. Seiner Ansicht nach werde im Zweifelsfall das meiste dafür sprechen, dass sich keine der Parteien durchgesetzt hat und dass es demnach bei der dispositiven Regelung des Gesetzes bleibt.

III. Chinesischer Lösungsweg bei kollidierenden AGB

1. Die Auslegung des Vertragsgesetzes

Im chinesischen VG ist keine besondere Regelung über kollidierende AGB vorgesehen. Die Rechtslage nach §§ 30 f. VG für kollidierende AGB ist vergleichbar mit Art. 19 CISG, da die §§ 30 f. VG großteils durch eine gesetzgeberische Rezeption des Art. 19 CISG entstanden sind.[23] Es erscheint daher sinnvoll, das Lösungsmodell des UN-Kaufrechts, die Theorie des letzten Wortes, auch im chinesische Vertragsrecht anzuwenden. Problematisch ist jedoch, dass der Anwendungsbereich des UN-Kaufrechts einerseits auf Verträge zwischen Unternehmern beschränkt ist, die §§ 30 f. VG andererseits für alle Vertragstypen gelten. Daher stellt sich die Frage, ob trotz des großen Unterschieds im Anwendungsbereich zwischen § 19 CISG und §§ 30 f. VG die Theorie des letzten Wortes anzuwenden ist oder ob es möglich ist, mittels Auslegung das Restgültigkeitsprinzip anzuwenden.

Bei kollidierenden AGB stellen sich im chinesischen Vertragsrecht zwei Fragen. Erstens ist zu prüfen, ob ein Vertrag trotz kollidierender AGB zustande gekommen und wirksam ist. Ist dies der Fall, stellt sich die Frage, welche Vertragsbedingungen der Parteien wirksam einbezogen wurden.

a) Zustandekommen eines Vertrags bei kollidierenden AGB

Nach § 25 VG ist der Vertrag mit der Wirksamkeit der Annahme zustande gekommen. Die Annahme wird nach § 26 VG in dem Moment wirksam, in welchem die Mitteilung der Annahme dem Anbieter zugeht. Jedoch ist die Frage des Zustandekommens des Vertrages bei kollidierenden AGB durch §§ 25 f. VG nicht gelöst. Eine solche Problemlösung könnten allerdings die entsprechenden Interpretationen des OVG zum Vertragsgesetz (OVG-Interpretation II VG) bieten.[24] Nach § 1 Abs. 1 OVG-Interpretation II VG ist

---

23 *Wang Liming*, Die Verbesserung des Chinesischen Vertragsrechts und CISG ("«联合国国际货物销售合同公约»与我国合同法的制定与完善"), 5 Global Law Review, S. 119 ff. (2013); *Wang Liming*, Studie zum Vertragsrecht, Bd. 1 («合同法研究»（第一卷）). 2011, S. 255.

24 *Pißler*, Erläuterungen des Obersten Volksgerichtshofs zu einigen Fragen des „Vertragsgesetzes der Volksrepublik China“ (Teil 2) ("最高人民法院关于适用«中华人民共和国合同法»若干问题的解释（二）"), Übersetzung, ZChinR 2009, 288 ff.

für das Zustandekommen eines Vertrags die Bezeichnung des Vertragsgegenstandes und der Bezugsgrößen wie Anzahl oder Menge ausreichend. Daher ist § 1 Abs. 1 OVG-Interpretation II VG die ergänzende Regelung für §§ 25 f. VG. Wenn im Tatbestand der Vertragserklärungen bei kollidierenden AGB zumindest die Voraussetzungen nach § 1 Abs. 1 OVG-Interpretation II VG erfüllt sind, ist der Vertrag zustande gekommen. Kollidieren die AGB aber bereits in Bezug auf die Mindestvoraussetzung gemäß § 1 Abs. 1 OVG-Interpretation II VG, kann auf § 10 Abs. 1 VG i.V.m. § 2 OVG-Interpretation II VG zurückgegriffen werden. Danach kann das Gericht einen Vertragsschluss in „anderer Form" gem. § 10 Abs. 1 VG annehmen, wenn aus den Handlungen der Parteien der Rechtsbindungswille abgeleitet werden kann. Als weiteres Argument für das Zustandekommen eines Vertrags könnte die Verkehrsgewohnheit gem. § 7 OVG-Interpretation II VG herangezogen werden. Wenn der Vertrag schon teilweise erfüllt ist oder die Erfüllung zumindest begonnen hat, ist dies ebenfalls ein Argument für das Zustandekommen des Vertrages. Daher könnte die Frage, ob ein Vertrag trotz kollidierender AGB zustande kommen kann, durch die Auslegung der §§ 25 f. VG i.V.m. § 1 Abs. 1 OVG-Interpretation II VG sowie § 2 OVG-Interpretation II VG unter Heranziehung von § 7 OVG-Interpretation II VG und der Umstände bei Erfüllung des Vertrags gelöst werden.

b) Inhalt des Vertrags bei kollidierenden AGB

(i) Deutscher Auslegungsweg: Auslegung durch Rechtsgedanken des § 306 BGB

Wie oben erwähnt, hat die h. M. bei der Auslegung des deutschen BGB früher die Theorie des letzten Wortes vertreten.[25] Da die Theorie des letzten Wortes der Wirklichkeit des Verkehrs nicht ganz entspricht, hat der BGH in jüngeren Entscheidungen mit dem Restgültigkeitsprinzip die gewandelte h. M. vertreten.[26] Bei gegenseitigem Leistungsaustausch ist der Vertrag trotz des offenen Dissenses gem. § 154 Abs. 1 BGB entsprechend § 306

25 *Schulte-Nölke*, in: Schulze, Handkommentar BGB, 9. Aufl. 2017, § 305 Rn. 20.

26 BGH, Urt. v. 23.1.1991 (Az. VIII ZR 122/90), BGHZ 113, 251 = NJW 1991, 1604; BGH, Urt. v. 26.9.1973 (Az. VIII ZR 106/72), BGHZ 61, 282.

Abs. 1 BGB wirksam.[27] Die einander widersprechenden AGB werden nicht als Vertragsbestandteil anerkannt.[28] Nach dem Rechtsgedanken des § 306 Abs. 2 BGB wird anstelle des sich widersprechenden Teils der AGB grundsätzlich das dispositive Recht angewandt.[29] Lücken werden durch die ergänzende Vertragsauslegung geschlossen.[30]

Der Auslegungsweg des deutschen BGB kann als Vorbild dienen. Die gesetzgeberische Rechtslage gem. § 150 BGB ist fast vergleichbar mit § 30 VG. Dennoch hat man sich bei der Auslegung des BGB für das Restgültigkeitsprinzip entschieden. Nach § 306 Abs. 1 BGB bleibt der Vertrag, sofern AGB ganz oder teilweise nicht Vertragsbestandteil geworden oder unwirksam sind, im Übrigen wirksam. Obwohl § 306 BGB das Problem der kollidierenden AGB nicht direkt löst, konnte dieser Rechtsgedanke durchaus zur Lösung des Problems beitragen, sofern die Parteien schon mit der Durchführung des Vertrags begonnen haben.[31]

(ii) Chinesischer Auslegungsweg: Teleologische Erweiterung des § 39 Abs. 1 VG

Die Auslegung des chinesischen Vertragsgesetzes kann sich für das Problem der kollidierenden AGB an den Erfahrungen des deutschen Rechts orientieren. Der Lösungsweg über die Rechtsvergleichung zwischen dem chinesischen Vertragsrecht und dem BGB hat zur Grundlage, dass beide Rechtsordnungen keine besondere Regelung für kollidierende AGB aufweisen und, was noch wichtiger ist, dass § 30 VG und § 150 BGB überhaupt vergleichbar sind. Jedoch gibt es einen Unterschied zwischen dem deutschen und dem chinesischen AGB-Recht. Die h. M. in Deutschland vertritt das Restgültigkeitsprinzip und löst das Problem der kollidierenden AGB mit Rechtsgedanken aus dem AGB-Recht, durch § 305 BGB bei der Einbeziehung der AGB in den Vertrag, durch § 306 BGB für die Frage der

27 *Dörner*, in: Schulze, Handkommentar BGB, 9. Aufl. 2017, § 150 Rn. 4; BGH, Urt. v. 26.9.1973 (Az. VIII ZR 106/72), BGHZ 61, 282, 288.

28 *Kötz*, Vertragsrecht, 2. Aufl. 2012, S. 56, Rn. 125.

29 *Schulte-Nölke*, in: Schulze, Handkommentar BGB, 9. Aufl. 2017, § 305 Rn. 20.

30 *Kötz*, Vertragsrecht, 2. Aufl. 2012, S. 56, Rn. 125.

31 Palandt/*Grüneberg*, BGB, 76. Aufl. 2017, § 305 Rn. 54; BGH, Urt. v. 26.9.1973 (Az. VIII ZR 106/72), BGHZ 61, 282; BGH, Urt. v. 20.3.1985 (Az. VIII ZR 327/83), NJW 1985, 1838.

Rechtsfolge bei Nichteinbeziehung und Unwirksamkeit. Demgegenüber erscheint das chinesische AGB-Recht nicht so systematisch entwickelt wie das deutsche. Im chinesischen VG behandeln nur drei Artikel AGB, nämlich die §§ 39[32], 40[33], 41[34] VG. Sie definieren den Begriff der AGB, regeln die Unwirksamkeit von AGB und stellen Auslegungsregeln auf. Daher ist es umstritten, ob es im chinesischen VG Regelungen über die Einbeziehung von AGB in den Vertrag gibt. Wenn es keine solche Regelungen gibt, wird es schwierig sein, den deutschen Auslegungsweg in das chinesische Recht zu transformieren.

Sinn und Zweck der §§ 39 ff. VG besteht darin, die schwächere Vertragspartei, normalerweise den Verbraucher, zu schützen. Das bedeutet, dass sich der Anwendungsbereich des chinesischen AGB-Rechts grundsätzlich auf Verträge zwischen Unternehmern und Verbrauchern beschränkt. Jedoch könnte bei der Auslegung der § 39 VG eine teleologische Erweiterung vorgenommen werden, so dass die Regelung in bestimmten Fällen ebenso auf Verträge zwischen Unternehmern angewendet werden kann. Nach der teleologischen Erweiterung des Anwendungsbereichs des chinesischen AGB-Rechts ist Folgendes festzustellen: Nach § 40 VG sind AGB unwirksam, wenn sie eine Haftungsbefreiung enthalten, die die Haftung der anderen

---

32 § 39
Wenn zur Errichtung eines Vertrages allgemeine Geschäftsbedingungen verwandt werden, muss die Partei, welche die allgemeinen Geschäftsbedingungen stellt, wenn sie die Rechte und Pflichten der Parteien gegeneinander festsetzt, sich an den Gerechtigkeitsgrundsatz halten und eine vernünftige Art und Weise wählen, um die andere Seite auf Klauseln aufmerksam zu machen, welche die Haftung dieser [die Geschäftsbedingungen stellenden Partei] ausschließen oder einschränken und auf Wunsch der anderen Seite diese Klauseln erklären. Allgemeine Geschäftsbedingungen sind Klauseln, die von der Partei zur wiederholten Verwendung vorweg entworfen und nicht bei der Errichtung des Vertrages mit der anderen Seite ausgehandelt werden.

33 § 40
Klauseln in allgemeinen Geschäftsbedingungen, bei denen einer der in §§ 52 und 53 bestimmten Umstände vorliegt, oder welche die Seite, welche die Geschäftsbedingungen stellt, von ihrer Haftung befreien, die Haftung der anderen Seite erhöhen und Hauptrechte der anderen Seite ausschließen, sind unwirksam.

34 § 41
Allgemeine Geschäftsbedingungen müssen bei Streitigkeiten über ihre Auslegung im allgemein üblichen Sinne ausgelegt werden. Wenn mehrere Auslegungen möglich sind, müssen sie in dem Sinn ausgelegt werden, der für die Seite, die sie gestellt hat, nicht von Vorteil ist. Wenn allgemeine Geschäftsbedingungen mit Klauseln im Widerspruch stehen, die keine allgemeinen Geschäftsbedingungen sind, gelten die Klauseln, die keine allgemeinen Geschäftsbedingungen sind.

Seite erhöht und die Hauptrechte der anderen Seite ausschließt. Daher sollen widersprechende Bedingungen in kollidierenden AGB entweder von der eigenen Haftung befreien, die Haftung der anderen Seite erhöhen oder die Hauptrechte der anderen Seite ausschließen. Nach dem Rechtsgedanken der § 40 VG scheinen widersprechende AGB daher unwirksam zu sein. Diese Lücke könnte durch die Auslegung des Vertrags nach § 125 VG geschlossen werden. Dies würde zur Anwendung des Restgültigkeitsprinzips im chinesischen Vertragsrecht führen. Im Vergleich zur Theorie des letzten Wortes durch Anwendung von § 30 VG ist das Ergebnis der Anwendung des Restgültigkeitsprinzips mit der vertragsrechtlichen Praxis vereinbar, vorhersehbar und gerecht.

2. Künftige gesetzgeberische Vorschläge

Durch Auslegung das Problem der kollidierende AGB zu lösen, erscheint im chinesischen wie deutschen Recht zunächst kompliziert. Die richtige Konstruktion erscheint unklar. Die Gründe hierfür liegen darin, dass zum Zeitpunkt des Gesetzgebungsprozesses das Problem noch nicht klar ersichtlich war. Außerdem hat die Bedeutung von AGB im Geschäftsverkehr, nicht nur im internationalen Handel, sondern auch innerstaatlich zugenommen. Um ein gesetzgeberisches Beispiel zu nennen: Art. 2.1.22 UNIDROIT PICC sieht eine Sonderregelung für kollidierende AGB vor und stellt eine Ausnahme zur allgemeinen Regelung über die abändernde Annahme in Art. 2.1.11 UNIDROIT PICC dar. Eine solche allgemeine Regelung mit Sonderregelung als Ausnahme kennt auch das GEK.

Daher erscheint es machbar und mit der vertragsrechtlichen Wirklichkeit vereinbar, das Problem der kollidierenden AGB in der künftigen Kodifikation eines chinesischen ZGB zu behandeln und entsprechende Regelungen einzuführen. Diesen Gedanken hat die *Propositional Version with Reasons for Civil Code of China*[35] bereits aufgenommen. Darin wird vorgeschlagen, neben der traditionellen Regelung über die abändernde Annahme (Art. 887) eine Sondervorschrift über den Konflikt von AGB (Art. 894) einzuführen. Nach Art. 894 gilt das Restgültigkeitsprinzip für kollidierende AGB, während die normale materielle Abänderung des Angebots als Gegenangebot betrachtet, also nach der Theorie des letzten Wortes gelöst wird. Es wäre zu begrüßen, wenn das Problem der kollidierenden AGB und die Einführung

35 *Liang Huixing*, A Propositional Version with Reasons for Civil Code of China («中国民法典草案建议稿附理由合同编（上册）»), 2013.

des Restgültigkeitsprinzips im künftigen Gesetzgebungsprozess zur Kodifikation eines Zivilgesetzbuches diskutiert werden könnten und gleichzeitig die traditionelle Regelung für die Abänderung des Angebots im allgemeinen Vertragsrecht erhalten bleibt.

Civil Liability Provisions in the General Rules of Civil Law

*Jieqiong Li**

Abstract: *The General Rules of Civil Law of the People's Republic of China of 2017 (GRCL) contain an independent and separate Chapter 8 entitled "Civil Liability". This chapter covers the assumption of civil liability, several liability, joint and several liability, methods of bearing civil liability, force majeure, self-defense, emergency avoidance of danger, liability concerning brave actions for just causes, Good Samaritan provision, liability for defaming heroes and martyrs, concurrent liability in contract and tort and coincidence of legal liability. In comparison to the General Principles of Civil Law of 1986 (GPCL), the chapter of civil liability of the GRCL focuses more on the protection of private rights. The chapter on civil liability exhibits a strong socialist morality. The core socialist values have been weaved into the clauses and the Chinese culture and traditions are also embodied in the law. The specific rules were designed with necessary adaptations according to the Chinese conditions and realities, which shows a more pragmatic approach in China's civil law codification program. The chapter on civil liability will definitely have a profound impact on the development of the Chinese civil liability system and jurisprudence. However, it should also be admitted that there is still a range of challenges and uncertainties.*

Keywords: Civil Liability, Liability Provisions, Socialist Morality.

---

* *Dr.*; Lecturer, Sun Yat-sen University, Faculty of Law. Chair for Intellectual Property Law and Civil Law.

I. Introduction

On March 15, 2017, the General Rules of Civil Law of the People's Republic of China (GRCL) were adopted at the 5th session of the 12th National People's Congress (NPC) and promulgated the same day.[1] The GRCL consist of 11 chapters and 206 sections, covering, among other subjects, general rules of civil law, civil subjects, civil rights, civil juristic acts, agency and civil liability. The GRCL will come into force on October 1, 2017.[2]

Similarly to Book One of the planned Chinese Civil Code, the GRCL lay down the basic principles for regulating civil activities. Its adoption marks the crucial first step of the civil law codification in China, which is a milestone in the Chinese legislative history of civil law. The GRCL have an

1 The full text of the General Rules of Civil Law of the People's Republic of China (GRCL) is available on the website of the National People's Congress (NPC) npc.gov.cn: http://www.npc.gov.cn/npc/xinwen/2017-03/15/content_2018907.htm (last visited Nov. 24, 2017).

2 Section 206 GRCL:
This Law shall come into force on October 1, 2017.

independent and separate Chapter 8 entitled "Civil Liability". This contains a legislative Chinese tradition established by the General Principles of Civil Law of 1986 (GPCL).[3] Civil liability aims to provide a compensation mechanism in the civil law system, which is very important to guarantee civil rights. Compared to similar provisions of the GPCL and separate statutes of Tort Law or Contract Law, there are some important changes in the chapter of civil liability of the GRCL.

This section aims to provide a detailed analysis of the civil liability provisions of the GRCL. Part I (II.) gives an overview of the chapter on civil liability of the GRCL. The essay also discusses the legislative background and related debates regarding the civil liability chapter. Part II (III.) provides a section-by-section analysis of the civil liability chapter of the GRCL, with emphasis on the new elements in comparison to the former laws. The conclusion part summarizes the main characteristics of the chapter on civil liability of the GRCL and discusses its impact and implications.

II. An Overview of the Chapter on Civil Liability

1. An Independent Chapter on Civil Liability

Through legislation practice and theoretical research in the past 30 years, China has developed a general theory regarding civil liability, including liability composition, imputation rules, rules regarding exemptions from liability, methods of bearing civil liability and others.[4] Regarding the nature of civil liability, there are three different theories in China: (1) *The Punishment Theory* which asserts that civil liability is a punishment to civil subjects when they fail to perform civil obligations, (2) *The Means Theory* which claims that civil liability is a means to realize civil rights, and (3) *The*

3 General Principles of Civil Law of the People's Republic of China (GPCL), adopted and promulgated on Apr. 12, 1986, in force since Jan. 1, 1987, as amended on Aug. 27, 2009.

4 Editing Group from the Legislative Affairs Commission of the NPC Standing Committee, Legislative Background of and Statement on the General Rules of the Civil Law («民法总则立法背景与观点全集»), 628 (2017).

Consequence Theory which states that civil liability is the consequence resulting from a breach of obligations.[5] The Consequence Theory is the current prevailing theory in the academic world of China. As the first comprehensive private law enactment in the People's Republic of China, the GPCL established the civil liability system in China.[6] Traditionally, civil liability belongs to the law of obligations and does not constitute a separate part in the civil codes of civil law countries.[7] However, instead of following the civil law tradition, the GPCL created an independent chapter on liability. Henceforth, a right-obligation-liability triple-layer doctrine has been developed in China. Rights correspond to obligations, and liability is the result of breach of obligations.[8] In other words, liability is separated from obligation. Chapter 6 of the GPCL is entitled "Civil Liability" and it is comprised of 29 sections, covering general rules regarding civil liability, civil liability for breach of contract, civil liability for infringement of rights, and methods of bearing civil liability. This right-obligation-liability triple-layer structure was transmitted into several civil law statutes. For instance, the Contract Law[9] contains a Chapter 7 entitled "Liability for Breach of Contract", and the Tort Law a Chapter 2 entitled "Liability Composition and Liability Methods".[10]

However, a heated debate on whether civil liability should be defined in a separate chapter in the GRCL came up. Some scholars hold that China's new Civil Code should adhere to the traditional civil law structure and that there should not appear an independent chapter on civil liability.[11] Some assert that the liability rules regarding breach of contract and tort are quite

5 Editing Group from the Legislative Affairs Commission of the NPC Standing Committee, Legislative Background of and Statement on the General Rules of the Civil Law («民法总则立法背景与观点全集») , 628 (2017).

6 Wang Liming, Studies on the Tort Law («侵权责任法研究»), 204 (2016).

7 Shen Deyong, Understanding and Application of the General Rules of Civil Law of the People's Republic of China («〈中华人民共和国民法总则〉条文理解与适用»), 1162 (2017).

8 Shen Deyong, Understanding and Application of the General Rules of Civil Law of the People's Republic of China («〈中华人民共和国民法总则〉条文理解与适用»), 1159 (2017).

9 Contract Law of the People's Republic of China, adopted and promulgated on Mar. 15, 1999, in force since Oct. 1, 1999.

10 Tort Law of the People's Republic of China, adopted and promulgated on Dec. 26, 2009, in force since July 1, 2010.

11 Li Shishi, Interpreting the General Rules of Civil Law of the People's Republic of China («中华人民共和国民法总则释义»), 545 (2017).

different, so they should be defined in the book for Contract Law and in the book for Tort Law of the Civil Code respectively.[12] In contrast, the majority of opposing scholars claim that there should be an individual chapter on civil liability that stipulates the general concepts and principles of civil liability in the GRCL.[13] First, the right-obligation-liability triple-layer structure is a Chinese characteristic and innovation in civil law, which has already been accepted in practice and should be carried on in the new GRCL.[14] After stipulating civil subjects and civil rights, a separate civil liability part would make the GRCL a more reasonable, integrated and complete system.[15] It is noted that the concepts of criminal liability and administrative liability exist in criminal law and administrative law respectively. Civil liability should be preserved as a corresponding legal concept in civil law. The scholars are afraid that the legal concept of civil liability might just disappear from the civil law system in China without a general part concerning civil liability.[16] Secondly, civil liability is the consequence of private misconduct. From the point of view of the precautionary function of law, an independent civil liability part can inform a civil subject about the legal consequences of his acts better, and therefore simplifies the fulfilling of his obligations.[17] Thirdly, from the point of view of the relationship between the GRCL and the future individual books of the Civil Code, it is necessary to establish a separate civil liability part, which guides and controls the different types of civil liabilities stipulated in the individual books.[18] The rules regarding civil liability in the GRCL, concluded through abstraction, systemization and logic, could form a basis

12 Li Shishi, Interpreting the General Rules of Civil Law of the People's Republic of China («中华人民共和国民法总则释义»), 545 (2017).

13 Li Shishi, Interpreting the General Rules of Civil Law of the People's Republic of China («中华人民共和国民法总则释义»), 545 (2017).

14 Li Shishi, Interpreting the General Rules of Civil Law of the People's Republic of China («中华人民共和国民法总则释义»), 545 (2017).

15 Li Shishi, Interpreting the General Rules of Civil Law of the People's Republic of China («中华人民共和国民法总则释义»), 545 (2017).

16 Shen Deyong, Understanding and Application of the General Rules of Civil Law of the People's Republic of China («〈中华人民共和国民法总则〉条文理解与适用»), 1162 (2017).

17 Li Shishi, Interpreting the General Rules of Civil Law of the People's Republic of China («中华人民共和国民法总则释义»), 546 (2017).

18 Li Shishi, Interpreting the General Rules of Civil Law of the People's Republic of China («中华人民共和国民法总则释义»), 546 (2017).

for civil liability provisions in the individual books of the Civil Code. It would simplify the Civil Code and provide a chance to represent the spirits and ideas behind the civil liability provisions, such as equal protection and self-responsibility. Finally yet importantly, there will be separate civil law statutes that will neither be codified in the Civil Code, nor promulgated or amended after the enactment of the Civil Code. In view of the *lex generalis* nature of the GRCL, these provisions can apply to these separate civil law statutes. It is considered that a separate general part regarding civil liability can make its application in the individual statutes much more convenient.[19] If necessary, the civil liability provisions in the GRCL can apply to fill in gaps and solve inconsistencies among several applicable laws in the civil law system. Moreover, a separate general part could safeguard the flexibility of civil liability rules, making them more adaptable to changes in society. In conclusion, there would be important positive effects in establishing a separate civil liability chapter.

2. A New Chapter on Civil Liability

Chapter 8 entitled "Civil Liability" in the GRCL consists of 12 sections, which cover the assumption of civil liability, several liability, joint and several liability, methods of bearing civil liability, force majeure, self-defense, emergency avoidance of danger, liability concerning brave actions for just causes, Good Samaritan provision, liability for defaming heroes and martyrs, concurrent liability in contract and tort, and coincidence of legal liability. Although the GRCL are based on the GPCL, they rather constitute an amendment. The civil law codification is neither a process of making new laws, nor a simple compilation of existing laws. It is a process of systemizing existing laws and revising outdated provisions. Therefore, the GRCL include some additional or revised provisions.

The civil liability provisions in the GRCL provide an improved relief mechanism for those whose civil rights have been violated through the actions of others. The chapter on civil liability of the GRCL exhibits the fundamental rules that are abstracted and distilled from civil liability provisions in specific civil law branches, and therefore could apply commonly in the civil law system. Roughly speaking, regarding the general provisions, the

---

19 Shen Deyong, Understanding and Application of the General Rules of Civil Law of the People's Republic of China («<中华人民共和国民法总则>条文理解与适用»), 1162 (2017).

chapter on civil liability in the GRCL followed the legislative style of the GPCL. However, specific rules concerning the civil liabilities arising from breach of contract or torts are no longer contained in the GRCL. According to the legislative schedule, there should be individual and separate books such as a book for Contract and a book for Tort Liability in the forthcoming Civil Code. In these individual books, a wide range of specific rules could be prescribed.

III. Civil Liability Provisions in the General Rules of Civil Law

1. Civil Obligation and Civil Liability

Section 176 GRCL states:

> "Civil subjects fulfil their civil obligations and assume civil liability according to the provisions of the law or the agreement of the parties."

This section is crucial for the realization of civil rights prescribed in Chapter 5 of Civil Rights of the GRCL. It reiterates the corresponding relationship between civil obligation and civil liability. Civil obligation is the premise and foundation on which civil liability arises, and civil liability is the legal consequence resulting from a violation of civil obligations.[20] This section is deemed to have a broader coverage than section 106 Para. 1 GPCL which states that citizens and legal persons who breach a contract or fail to fulfil other obligations shall bear civil liability.

It should be noted that the concept of "civil liability" in section 176 GRCL actually comprises different types of civil liabilities, such as tort liability, liability for breach of contract, unjust enrichment, and *negotiorum gestio*. In practice, besides the provisions in the chapter on civil liability of the GRCL, the judiciary has to take a look at the specific provisions concerning the components, subjects, scope and exemptions, etc. of a specific type of civil liability, which are stipulated in individual civil law statutes such as the Tort Law, the Contract Law, and the Property Law.[21]

---

20 Yang Lixin, Essence of the General Rules of Civil Law of the People's Republic of China and Related Case Study («中华人民共和国民法总则要义与案例解读»), 653 (2017).

21 Shen Deyong, Understanding and Application of the General Rules of Civil Law of the People's Republic of China («<中华人民共和国民法总则>条文理解与适用»), 1165 (2017).

2. Several Liability

Section 177 GRCL prescribes the rule of several liability. When two or more persons assume liabilities according to the law by proportions, if their respective proportion of liability can be determined, they shall bear liability correspondingly. If their respective proportion of liability cannot be determined, they shall bear equal liability. This section is a revised version of section 12 Tort Law.[22] The share of responsibility between the liable persons is determined mainly based on their respective fault and contribution to the damage.

3. Joint and Several Liability

The rules concerning joint and several liability are scattered in the GPCL. In Chapter 5 "Civil Rights", section 87 GRCL sets out rules on joint and several debts. In Chapter 6 "Civil Liability", section 130 GRCL provides that if two or more persons jointly infringe upon another person's rights and cause him damage, they shall bear joint and several liability.

In contrast, section 178, which stipulates joint and several liability in the GRCL, is a general provision that is commonly applicable in civil law. In fact, when considering the clause's structure, section 178 GRCL can be regarded as being constructed based on Secs. 13 and 14 Tort Law which stipulate joint and several liability in the case of joint infringement. The basic rules of joint and several liability in the GRCL are as follows: Initially, if two or more persons are jointly and severally liable, the right holders shall have the right to request all or any one of the persons subject to joint and several liability to bear liability. Secondly, the share of the liability of the persons subject to joint and several liability shall be determined according to the proportion of the respective responsibilities. If it is difficult to determine the proportion of their respective responsibilities, liability shall be borne equally by the persons subject to joint and several liability. Thirdly, if a person subject to joint and several liability has assumed more than his

---

22 Section 12 Tort Law:
If acts of tort by two or more persons severally result in the same damage and their respective liability can be determined, the said persons shall bear liability correspondingly. If their respective liability cannot be determined, the said persons shall bear equal liability for damages.

share of responsibility, he shall be entitled to claim reimbursement from the other person(s) subject to joint and several liability. Finally, the joint and several liability can only occur when provided by law or agreed on by the parties.

The above rules are statutory, which means that the joint and several debtors cannot change the rules by an agreement or anything similar.[23] An agreement between the joint and several debtors regarding the share of responsibility does not have any legal effect on the right holder.[24] Joint and several liability can be incurred from either a breach of contract or a tort. It aims to increase the chance of obtaining adequate compensation for the right holder. The right holder can have more choices when he decides whom he shall request to bear liability. The factors for consideration in determining the share of the responsibility between the joint and several debtors are the same as in the case of several liability. Since joint and several liability is a type of rather strict liability, in order to avoid any extra burden to the debtors, its application can only be allowed when there are related laws or when the parties reached an agreement.[25] Relevant provisions that have prescribed joint and several liability include Secs. 8–11 Tort Law, Secs. 12 and 18 Guarantee Law, some clauses of the Advertisement Law, the Product Quality Law, the Securities Law, etc.

It is notable that some scholars argue that joint and several liability contradicts with the principle of self-responsibility because a person that is jointly and severally liable but has only a minor fault may still be obliged to bear the full liability.[26] However, it needs to be added that the existence of joint and several liability is necessary because it can ensure an adequate protection of the right holder's lawful rights and interests.[27] Sections 177 and 178 have to be adopted in the GRCL, because there is no general provision part in the future Book for Law of Obligations.

---

23 Li Shishi, Interpreting the General Rules of Civil Law of the People's Republic of China («中华人民共和国民法总则释义»), 551 (2017).

24 Li Shishi, Interpreting the General Rules of Civil Law of the People's Republic of China («中华人民共和国民法总则释义»), 551 (2017).

25 Li Shishi, Interpreting the General Rules of Civil Law of the People's Republic of China («中华人民共和国民法总则释义»), 553 (2017).

26 Li Shishi, Interpreting the General Rules of Civil Law of the People's Republic of China («中华人民共和国民法总则释义»), 551 (2017).

27 Li Shishi, Interpreting the General Rules of Civil Law of the People's Republic of China («中华人民共和国民法总则释义»), 551 (2017).

4. Methods of Bearing Civil Liability

Section 179 GRCL provides 11 methods of bearing civil liability: cessation of infringement, removal of obstacles, elimination of danger, return of property, restitution, repair or reconstruction or replacement, payment of damages, continuing to perform, payment of breach of contract damages, elimination of ill effects and rehabilitation of reputation and extension of apology. These civil remedies may be awarded separately or jointly.

In comparison to the corresponding section 134 GPCL there are three important changes. First, "continuing to perform" is a newly added form of civil remedy. However, it seems that the above list is a little confusing because "repair or reconstruction or replacement" is actually a way of "continuing to perform". Secondly, the GRCL contain an additional paragraph concerning punitive compensation. If other laws stipulate punitive compensation, punitive compensation shall be granted. For example, section 47 Tort Law provides that in the event of death or serious damage to health arising from the manufacture or sale of a product known to be defective, the infringed shall be entitled to claim corresponding punitive compensation. Lastly, the GPCL allow the court in a trial of a civil case to serve admonitions, order the offender to sign a pledge of repentance, and confiscate the property used in carrying out illegal activities and the illegal income obtained therefrom. The court may also impose a fine or detain the infringer as stipulated by law. However, the coercive measures that a civil court could take are removed in the GRCL. This illustrates that the private law nature is more emphasized in the Civil Code.

5. Force Majeure

In some circumstances, the infringer may be relieved. Force majeure is one of them. According to section 180 GRCL, civil liability shall not be borne for failure to perform civil obligations if it is caused by force majeure, except as otherwise provided by the law. Force majeure refers to unforeseeable, unavoidable and insurmountable objective conditions. Although different theories exist regarding the definition of force majeure in the academic literature, the concept is defined both by subjective and objective points of view in China's civil law legislation.[28] Section 180 GRCL seems to be a

28 Zhang Xinbao, Interpretation of the General Rules of Civil Law of the People's Republic of China («〈中华人民共和国民法总则〉释义»), 392 (2017).

combination of Sections 107 and 153 GPCL. Except for some changes in wording, the rules are essentially the same. The defense of force majeure is not applicable if the law provides special regulations. For instance, according to Sections 70 and 71 Tort Law, if a nuclear accident at a civilian nuclear facility or a civilian aircraft causes damage to others, the operator cannot be relieved from his civil liability by claiming force majeure.

The defense of force majeure in general belongs to the law of obligations, thus a defendant cannot claim force majeure in a property law dispute. However, since there is no "General Provisions" part in the future Book for Law of Obligations, the force majeure clause has to be regulated in the GRCL.

6. Justifiable Defense

Justifiable defense is another general defense against liability. According to section 181 GRCL, no liability shall be borne for damage arising from justifiable defense. However, if the act of the justifiable defense exceeds its necessary limit and causes undue damage, the person acting in justifiable defense shall bear appropriate liability. This section is deemed to be transferred from section 30 Tort Law. Compared to section 128 GPCL, which fails to specify who should bear the liability arising from disproportionate defensive acts, the GRCL provide regulations about the person(s) liable in case the justifiable defense exceeds the necessary limits and results in undue damage.

Justifiable defense is considered as a statutory lawful excuse in civil law. Since a person acting in justifiable defense causes property damage or personal injury without fault, he should not be held liable. However, there is no explanation as to what kinds of acts constitute justifiable defense in the civil law statutes. Since section 20 Criminal Law defines justifiable defense,[29] the definition could be transferred into the civil law.[30] Justifiable defense refers to a defensive act that is taken to ward off a current unlawful

---

29 Section 20 Para. 1 Criminal Law:
Criminal liability shall not be borne for an act that a person undertakes in justifiable defense to avert an immediate and unlawful infringement of the public interest or of his own or another person's rights of the person or other rights.

30 Li Shishi, Interpreting the General Rules of Civil Law of the People's Republic of China («中华人民共和国民法总则释义»), 564 (2017).

assault directed at oneself or another.[31] In order to be qualified as justifiable defense, (1) the aim of taking a defensive act should be to prevent infringement on personal or property rights of the defender or another person; (2) there must exist an infringing act; (3) the infringing act is happening while the defensive act is taken; (4) there is not enough time to ask for help from governmental authorities; (5) the defensive act is targeted at the infringing person himself; and (6) the defensive act does not exceed the necessary limits.[32] Only if all the above conditions apply, the defender can be relieved from civil liability. It should be noted that although a person shall not be liable for damage inflicted on the assailant during an appropriate act of justifiable defense, the person should still be held liable for damage inflicted on a third party. This means a person defending himself during an attack can be sued for damages by a third party, if the third party's property was destroyed or the defender caused injuries.

With regard to "the necessary limits" of justifiable defense, if a defensive act goes beyond an extent that is necessary to stop the infringement, the act is deemed as exceeding the necessary limits. In practice, the necessary limits are determined on a case-by-case basis by taking into consideration the situation of the infringing act, the infringed rights, the time and means of the defensive act and other factors. Disproportionate defensive acts that cause undue damage may incur "appropriate" liability, which means that even if the defensive act is determined as exceeding the necessary limits, the defender only has to bear an appropriate part of the full liability instead of the whole liability. "Appropriate" liability is determined at the discretion of the court by considering the defender's individual fault.[33]

7. Emergency Avoidance of Danger

Emergency avoidance of danger may also relieve the actor from civil liability. According to section 182 GRCL, for damage arising from emergency avoidance of danger, the person increasing such danger shall bear civil liability. If a person caused the danger, he is obliged to pay damages if the

31 Li Shishi, Interpreting the General Rules of Civil Law of the People's Republic of China («中华人民共和国民法总则释义»), 563 (2017).

32 Li Shishi, Interpreting the General Rules of Civil Law of the People's Republic of China («中华人民共和国民法总则释义»), 565 (2017).

33 Li Shishi, Interpreting the General Rules of Civil Law of the People's Republic of China («中华人民共和国民法总则释义»), 566 (2017).

actor or a third person suffered damage or injury caused by the actor's action to ward off the danger from himself or from another person. If natural reasons caused the danger, the person who undertakes emergency avoidance of danger shall not bear liability but may pay appropriate compensation. However, the person who undertakes emergency avoidance of danger shall bear appropriate liability if undue damage was caused because the measures for emergency avoidance were improper or have exceeded the necessary limits. Section 182 GRCL is basically the same as section 129 GPCL and section 31 Tort Law. However, according to section 129 GPCL, in case of a danger arising from natural factors, the person who takes emergency actions may bear "appropriate liability", while it is "appropriate compensation" that a person who undertakes emergency avoidance of danger may pay under the GRCL. According to section 182 GRCL, as long as the measures for emergency avoidance are not improper and do not exceed the necessary limits, the person who undertakes emergency actions is exempt from civil liability. He may only pay appropriate compensation when necessary.

Just like justifiable defense, there is no definition of emergency avoidance of danger in the civil law statutes. It is considered that the concept should be understood by reference to section 21 Criminal Law[34] which defines emergency avoidance of danger.[35] In order to constitute emergency avoidance of danger, (1) the purpose of taking emergency actions is to avert an immediate danger to the personal or property rights of the actor or another person;[36] (2) the emergency actions should be targeted as the imme-

---

34 Section 21 Criminal Law:
Criminal liability shall not be borne for an act that a person is compelled to commit in an emergency to avert an immediate danger to the country, the public interest or to the personal, property or other rights of his own or another person. Criminal liability shall be borne if an act committed in an emergency to avert danger exceeds the limits of necessity and causes undue harm; however, consideration shall be given to a mitigated punishment or exemption from punishment. The provisions of the first paragraph of this Section with respect to averting danger to oneself shall not apply to a person who is charged with specific responsibility in his post or profession.

35 Li Shishi, Interpreting the General Rules of Civil Law of the People's Republic of China («中华人民共和国民法总则释义»), 568 (2017).

36 There are no provisions as to whether emergency avoidance of danger could be used as a defense when the aim is to protect the public interest. However, the majority opinion is that the rules concerning emergency avoidance of danger can

diate danger; (3) the actor is compelled to commit an act to avert the immediate danger without other choices; (4) the emergency actions do not exceed the necessary limits.[37] Only when all of the above conditions are met can emergency avoidance of danger be recognized and thus the actor be exempt from civil liability. However, the actor shall be held liable if he caused the danger by himself or if undue damage or injury occurred because the emergency actions he took were improper or out of proportion to the danger.

8. Brave Actions for Just Causes

According to section 183 GRCL, the infringer shall be held reliable for the damage a person suffers while taking brave actions to protect the civil rights and interests of others. The intention of the Chinese lawmakers to include such a section in the new General Provisions is to encourage people to act bravely for a just cause[38], and to promote adequate protection.

Section 183 GRCL is established on the basis of section 109 GPCL and section 23 Tort Law, with some changes and revisions. First, if a person suffers damage while preventing other's civil rights from being infringed, the infringer shall bear liability. In such a case, the beneficiary may give appropriate compensation, which is a newly added rule in comparison to section 23 Tort Law. It is worth noting that section 109 GPCL states: "If a person suffers damage from preventing or stopping infringement on state or collective property, or the property or personal rights of a third party, the infringer shall bear responsibility for compensation." In contrast, the GRCL only provide civil liability rules when a person prevents others' civil rights from being infringed. It can be noticed that the lawmakers no longer encourage people to protect state or collective property at the cost of their own

be applied when an emergency action is taken to protect the public interest (Shen Deyong, Understanding and Application of the General Rules of Civil Law of the People's Republic of China («<中华人民共和国民法总则>条文理解与适用»), 1205 (2017)).

37 Li Shishi, Interpreting the General Rules of Civil Law of the People's Republic of China («中华人民共和国民法总则释义»), 569 (2017).

38 The Chinese expression for that is Jian Yi Yong Wei (见义勇为), which means that in order to protect the state interest, the public interest or the rights and interests of others, a person who is not charged with specific legal responsibility or duties performs outstanding acts of bravery and courage, such as stopping criminal acts, saving people in a disaster and so on.

life or health.[39] Secondly, the beneficiary shall give the infringed an appropriate compensation in case no infringer exists, the infringer flees or is in no capacity to assume civil liability. Compared to section 109 GPCL and section 23 Tort Law, the GRCL fill a legal gap by providing an appropriate compensation in the form of a contingent liability of the beneficiary if there is no infringer.

According to the general theory of tort law, since the beneficiary did not commit any infringing acts, and thus has no fault in resulting in the damage suffered by the infringed, he should not be held liable.[40] The infringer should bear full liability for all losses and damages occurred to the infringed, in which case the beneficiary may (not "should") pay appropriate compensation. However, in a case where there is no infringer, the infringer flees or has no capacity to pay damages, the beneficiary, if there is one, should pay appropriate compensation as long as the infringed seeks compensation. In either case, the compensation is an appropriate one, which means that it might not be enough to cover the losses suffered by the infringed. Although there are no specific standards or rules regarding "appropriate compensation", it is generally regarded that the sum of "appropriate compensation" might be determined by considering the financial status of both the infringed and the beneficiary, the benefits received by the beneficiary, whether the beneficiary has any fault in causing the damage. In essence, appropriate compensation paid by the beneficiary is intended for loss sharing between the parties involved from a point of view of fairness.[41]

9. Good Samaritan Provision

By providing in section 184 GRCL that a rescuer that voluntarily carries out emergency aid and as a result causes damage to an imperiled person shall not be held liable, a Good Samaritan provision is introduced into the civil

39 Shen Deyong, Understanding and Application of the General Rules of Civil Law of the People's Republic of China («〈中华人民共和国民法总则〉条文理解与适用»), 1209 (2017).

40 Li Shishi, Interpreting the General Rules of Civil Law of the People's Republic of China («中华人民共和国民法总则释义»), 574 (2017).

41 Shen Deyong, Understanding and Application of the General Rules of Civil Law of the People's Republic of China («〈中华人民共和国民法总则〉条文理解与适用»), 1213 (2017).

law for the first time in China. A Good Samaritan in legal terms refers to a person who voluntarily renders aid in an emergency to an injured or ill person. Good Samaritan laws are designed to afford protection to people who provide assistance on a voluntary basis in an emergency. Usually, if a volunteer comes to the aid of a person in need of emergency help, he has the duty to be reasonably careful while giving aid. In many countries, no liability for emergency aid will arise unless gross negligence is recognized.[42]

According to section 184 GRCL, a Good Samaritan who has caused damage to the person(s) in danger shall not bear civil liability. Although seeming somewhat startling, just as the wording suggests, a Good Samaritan shall never be liable under any circumstances. In fact, this section has its unique legislative background. It comes in the wake of a number of outrageous incidents that seriously distorted peoples' social behavior. Before the GRCL, there was no provision specifying whether a volunteer coming to the aid of an injured or ill person who is a stranger at the site of an emergency should bear civil liability if the volunteer caused damage to the aided. The legislation of this section had started with the famous (or infamous) judicial decision, the Peng Yu Case[43], which has destroyed good social morals greatly. In 2006, Peng Yu was sued by an elderly lady Xu Shoulan for personal injury compensation. Xu claimed that Peng caused her to fall when she disembarked from a city bus and as a result caused her to break her femur. Peng maintained that he only approached Xu in order to provide help after she had fallen. The judge, despite the lack of concrete evidence, held that Peng should be liable and pay 40% of Xu's losses. By "analyzing from the point of view of commonsense"[44], the judge concluded, "The probability that the defendant bumped into the plaintiff is rather high. If the defendant were a Good Samaritan, instead of just offering her help, it would be a more reasonable act that he tried to catch the person who caused Xu to

42 Mitchell McInnes, *Good Samaritan Statutes: A Summary and Analysis*, 26 U. Brit. Colum. L. Rev. 239, 239–240 (1992).

43 Xu Shoulan v. Peng Yu (徐寿兰诉彭宇人身损害赔偿纠纷案), Nanjing Gulou District People's Court, (2007) Gu Min Yi Chu Zi No. 212 ((2007) 鼓民一初字第212号).

44 Xu Shoulan v. Peng Yu (徐寿兰诉彭宇人身损害赔偿纠纷案), Nanjing Gulou District People's Court, (2007) Gu Min Yi Chu Zi No. 212 ((2007) 鼓民一初字第212号).

fall."[45] According to the court's reasoning, because Peng assisted Xu, brought her to the hospital and paid 200 Renminbi (RMB) for her medical treatment, it could be deduced that Peng actually caused Xu to fall. However, the judge held that there was no fault in either of the parties, judging from the circumstances at the scene. Therefore, the court applied the equitable liability principle according to which the defendant was held liable to pay damages (45,876.36 RMB) even though he caused the injury and damage without fault.[46] The decision received widespread media coverage and engendered a loud public outcry about its "reasoning". It has been labeled as a landmark Good Samaritan case, which actually deterred people from attempting to aid others in emergencies. A well-intentioned volunteer lending help to others in emergencies, as a return of his good intention and selfless acts, could find himself facing legal proceedings and paying damages. People hesitate to offer help because they are vulnerable to civil liability. Indifferent bystanders increased and several very egregious incidents happened after the Peng Yu Case.[47] Section 184 GRCL was introduced to cope with this urgent and serious social problem.

In fact, the legislative history also makes it clear that complete immunity is exactly the desired result the lawmakers intended.[48] There was no such provision in the first and second drafts presented to the NPC. Based on the suggestions of some delegates, section 187 was incorporated into the third draft presented to the NPC, which provided that a Good Samaritan shall bear no civil liability unless he has committed gross negligence. However, some delegates worried that "gross negligence" is difficult to define in practice and the provision would just discourage people to offer help to others. What's more, the person who in good faith gives emergency aid on a voluntary basis is not a professional charged with a corresponding duty. In an emergency, it is very difficult for the aider to make the best choice if he is not a professional. Later on, a revised provision stated: "A rescuer that voluntarily carries out emergency aid and thus causes damage to the aided shall

---

45 Xu Shoulan v. Peng Yu (徐寿兰诉彭宇人身损害赔偿纠纷案), Nanjing Gulou District People's Court, (2007) Gu Min Yi Chu Zi No. 212 ((2007) 鼓民一初字第212号).

46 The case was appealed to a higher court and ended with a settlement eventually.

47 Zheng Caixiong, *Law Mulled to Make Aid Compulsory*, China Daily website, Oct. 20, 2011, available at http://www.chinadaily.com.cn/china/2011-10/20/content_13937442.htm (last visited Nov. 27, 2017).

48 Regarding the legislative history of this provision, see Li Shishi, Interpreting the General Rules of Civil Law of the People's Republic of China («中华人民共和国民法总则释义»), 575 (2017).

not be held liable. However, a rescuer shall bear appropriate liability if he caused undue and serious damage to the aided because of his gross negligence." According to this amended version, there are strict conditions for a voluntary helper to bear liability: (1) there must be gross negligence on the part of the volunteer; and (2) the damage should be undue and serious. Even if all of the above conditions are met, the voluntary helper only has to bear "appropriate" liability instead of "corresponding" liability. Many scholars asserted that from the point of view of balancing the parties' rights and obligations, the language specifying liability for the aiders should be maintained. However, some delegates again objected the provision because it fails to eliminate a well-intentioned helper's worries completely. Since it is an urgent business to restore helping behavior and good faith in view of the current social situation, the law should send a clear message to the public that good people and good deeds are encouraged and protected. At a result, the provision was removed. Of course, an aider could not completely be totally exempt from any civil liability. If there are any intentional wrongful acts, the aider should still be held liable.

Scholars are still arguing about whether a person who attempts to aid others in case of emergency should bear civil liability in case of gross negligence. Some fear that this will lead to another extreme situation.[49] It remains unclear how the courts are going to apply this section in future. Some predict that more concretizing rules will be integrated in the future book for Tort Liability or in judicial interpretations.

10. Liability for Defaming Heroes and Martyrs

An important highlight of the GRCL is that it prohibits defaming heroes and martyrs. According to section 185, anyone who harms the name, portrait, reputation, or honor of heroes, martyrs, etc., insofar as the public interest is damaged, shall bear civil liability. Actually, this new section did not appear in the draft and discussions at the NPC resulted in its addition into the GRCL.[50]

---

49 E.g., Cai Lidong, *in* Commentary on General Principles of the Civil Code («民法总则评注»), 1314, 1315 (Chen Su ed., 2017).

50 Li Shishi, Interpreting the General Rules of Civil Law of the People's Republic of China («中华人民共和国民法总则释义»), 579 (2017).

In essence, section 185 is about protecting the personal interests of a deceased person.[51] There were no related provisions regarding the personal interests of dead people in the GPCL. In order to deal with increasing disputes concerning the personal interests of dead people, the Supreme People's Court in 2001 promulgated a judicial interpretation[52] in which the principle of general protection of dead people's personal interests was established. Section 3 of this judicial interpretation provides that anyone who infringes upon the name, portrait, reputation and honor of the deceased by means of insult, slander, derogation, defacement or other methods that go against the social public interest or public morals, shall be liable to pay emotional damages. Close relatives of a deceased person can sue the infringer and claim compensation for mental suffering. However, the new provision in the GRCL cannot be regarded as a mere codification of the above rules set forth in the judicial interpretation of 2001. Section 185 GRCL provides special protection for the personal interests of heroes and martyrs.

In fact, this new provision has a political and social background and purpose. In recent years, there have been some cases in which the reputation and honor of heroes and martyrs was harmed by insult, slander, disparagement or vilification, which damaged the public interest and caused extremely bad social influence. Although the court can adjudicate such cases based on the judicial interpretation of 2001,[53] this is considered to be insufficient. First, according to the judicial interpretation, only the close relatives have the right to bring action for emotional damages. However, many heroes and martyrs do not have any "close relatives", either because they do not have any descendants at all or because their close relatives have already

---

51 Not all of the personal rights of the deceased are protected. E.g., the right of privacy is not included here.

52 Supreme People's Court, Interpretation on Certain Issues Concerning the Determination of Liability for Compensation for Mental Suffering in Civil Torts, Fa Shi [2001] No. 7 (法释(2001)7号).

53 There have already appeared court decisions in which liability was imposed on persons who harmed the reputation and honor of heroes and martyrs in China, e.g. the Five Heroes of Langya Mountain case (Ge Changsheng & Song Fubao v. Hong Zhenkuai (葛长生、宋福保诉洪振快侵害名誉案), Beijing Second Intermediate People's Court, (2016) Jing 02 Min Zhong No. 6272 ((2016)京02民终6272号)) or the Qiu Shaoyun case (Qiu Shaohua v. Sun Jie (邱少华与孙杰等一般人格权纠纷案), Beijing Daxing District People's Court, (2015) Da Min Chu Zi No. 10012 ((2015)大民初字第10012号)).

died, in which case it is impossible to bring such a suit. Secondly, disputes regarding the reputation and honor of heroes and martyrs are not the same as any ordinary defamation-of-the-dead case because the former is strongly related to the public interest. The stories and spirits of heroes and martyrs have already become part of the national spirit and national culture. Section 185 GRCL was introduced with the aim of providing solid protection for personal interests of heroes and martyrs, and therefore promoting the Core Values of Chinese Socialism.[54] It provides an explicit basis for the adjudication of disputes relating to defamation of heroes and martyrs.

However, it should be noted that the personal interests of heroes and martyrs do not receive any extra protection compared to the personal interests of ordinary persons.[55] Even though a special clause exists, the general principles regarding the protection of dead peoples' personal interests are the same.[56] According to section 4 GRCL, all civil subjects have equal status in civil activities. Equal protection is a fundamental principle in civil law. The law provides equal protection for the personal interests of both the heroes and martyrs and the ordinary deceased people.[57] Although seeming contradictory to the literal meaning of section 185 GRCL, as long as the personal interests of heroes and martyrs have been infringed upon, no matter whether there is any damage to the public interest, legal protection is available.[58] In other words, an infringer still has to bear civil liability even though he caused no damage to the public interest. In nature, section 185 is a clause

---

54 The Core Socialist Values refer to the twelve values that should be promoted and followed on national, social, and personal levels in China. The three most important core values are: (1) prosperity, democracy, civility and harmony on the national level; (2) freedom, equality, justice and rule of law on the social level; and (3) patriotism, dedication, integrity and friendship on the personal level.

55 Yang Lixin, Essence of the General Rules of Civil Law of the People's Republic of China and Related Case Study («中华人民共和国民法总则要义与案例解读»), 688 (2017).

56 Therefore, some scholars doubt the necessity of such a special clause in the General Rules of Civil Law (see Yang Lixin, Essence of the General Rules of Civil Law of the People's Republic of China and Related Case Study («中华人民共和国民法总则要义与案例解读»), 691 (2017)).

57 Yang Lixin, Essence of the General Rules of Civil Law of the People's Republic of China and Related Case Study («中华人民共和国民法总则要义与案例解读»), 687 (2017).

58 Zhang Xinbao, Interpretation of the General Rules of Civil Law of the People's Republic of China («〈中华人民共和国民法总则〉释义»), 402 (2017).

dedicated to the protection of private rights instead of public interest.[59] It is essentially a tort law issue and the same legal standards should apply as in an ordinary defamation-of-the-dead case. The wording "public interest" in section 185 means that in case of defamation a public interest litigation is possible.[60] If an infringement upon the name, portrait, reputation or honor of heroes, martyrs, etc. harmed the public interest, even though there are no close relatives to file a suit or the close relatives fail to sue, relevant state authorities such as the People's Procuratorate can file a public interest litigation to hold the infringer liable.

However, some uncertainties regarding this section remain. First, it is unclear how to define "heroes, martyrs, etc." Secondly, it is also a problem how to measure the damages. Section 185 is only a general provision with inevitable vagueness, and detailed rules are expected in the future book for Tort Liability of the Civil Code.[61]

11. Concurrent Liability

Section 186 GRCL provide general principles regarding concurrence of civil liability. It is a revised version of section 122 Contract Law. If a party infringed the personal or property rights and interests of the other party due to a breach of contract, the injured party has the right to choose to claim liability for breach of contract or tort liability. Traditionally, contract and tort claims exist mutually exclusively as different actions. Concurrent liability provides a chance for an injured party to have a choice as to his claims. Concurrent liability does not simply provide two different methods of achieving the same goal. Usually, an injured party chooses between potential claims by considering which would provide the greatest chance of success or the desired damages. However, the injured party can only choose to

---

59 Jiang Bixin & He Dongning, A comparison between the GPCL and the GRCL and the Essentials of Application («民法总则与民法通则条文对照及适用提要»), 99 (2017).

60 Yang Lixin, Essence of the General Rules of Civil Law of the People's Republic of China and Related Case Study («中华人民共和国民法总则要义与案例解读») 688 (2017); Zhang Xinbao, Interpretation of the General Rules of Civil Law of the People's Republic of China («〈中华人民共和国民法总则〉释义»), 403 (2017).

61 Zhang Xinbao, Interpretation of the General Rules of Civil Law of the People's Republic of China («〈中华人民共和国民法总则〉释义»), 403 (2017).

demand the other party to bear one kind of civil liability.[62] Section 186 GRCL established the rules for choosing civil liability when there is concurrent liability in tort and contract, which can also be used as a basis for solving problems when concurrent liability occurs in other areas.[63]

12. Coincidence of Legal Liability

According to section 187 GRCL, when a civil subject bears civil liability, administrative liability and criminal liability for the same act, the assumption of administrative or criminal liability shall not affect the assumption of civil liability. If the properties of the civil subject are insufficient for the payment, civil liability shall take priority. Actually, the above rules were adopted from section 4 Tort Law with some revisions. Compared to section 110 GPCL, the priority of civil liability is a newly added rule, which demonstrates that the idea of priority of private rights is more valued.

IV. Conclusion

In sum, this section presented the major changes and new developments under the GRCL, in particular in comparison to the GPCL. China, despite being a civil law jurisdiction, does not stick to the traditional style and structure of the civil codes of civil law countries. Instead, the GRCL demonstrate some Chinese characteristics and innovations. First, the GRCL adopted the Chinese tradition of a separate chapter on civil liability. Secondly, the chapter on civil liability exhibits a strong socialist morality. The core socialist values have been weaved into the clauses and the Chinese culture and traditions are also embodied in this law. Thirdly, specific rules were designed with necessary adaptation according to the Chinese conditions and realities, which shows a more pragmatic approach in China's civil law codification process.

The chapter on civil liability has reiterated the correspondent relationship between civil obligation and civil liability, established the basic rules

62 Li Shishi, Interpreting the General Rules of Civil Law of the People's Republic of China («中华人民共和国民法总则释义»), 584 (2017).

63 Yang Lixin, Essence of the General Rules of Civil Law of the People's Republic of China and Related Case Study («中华人民共和国民法总则要义与案例解读»), 693 (2017).

concerning several liability and joint and several liability, enriched the list of civil remedies, cleared the rules regarding civil liability immunity, emphasized the protection of the personal interests of heroes and martyrs, and provided the basic principles for concurrent liability and coincidence of legal liability. Additionally, the chapter of civil liability of the GRCL focuses more on the protection of private rights compared to the GPCL. The chapter on civil liability of the GRCL, by furnishing general principles commonly applicable, harmonizing existing rules and filling the legal gaps, has laid a firm foundation for the future books of the Civil Code and for further academic development. It will definitely have a profound impact on the development of the Chinese civil liability system and jurisprudence. However, it should also be admitted that there still exist many challenges, ranging from the uncertainties to some heatedly debated controversies.

Annex

中华人民共和国民法总则	**Allgemeiner Teil des Zivilrechts der Volksrepublik China**[1]	**General Rules of the Civil Law of the Peoples Republic of China**[2]
(2017 年 3 月 15 日第十二届全国人民代表大会第五次会议通过)	(Verabschiedet am 15. März 2017 auf der 5. Sitzung des 12. Nationalen Volkskongresses)	(Adopted at the 5th Session of the 12th National People's Congress of the People's Republic of China on March 15, 2017)
目录	**Inhalt**	**Content**
第一章　基本规定	**1. Kapitel: Grundlegende Bestimmungen**	**Chapter I General Stipulations China**
第二章　自然人	**2. Kapitel: Natürliche Personen**	**Chapter II Natural Persons**
第一节　民事权利能力和民事行为能力	1. Abschnitt: Zivilrechtsfähigkeit und Zivilgeschäftsfähigkeit	Subchapter 1 Legal and Contractual Capacity
第二节　监护	2. Abschnitt: Vormundschaft	Subchapter 2 Guardianship
第三节　宣告失踪和宣告死亡	3. Abschnitt: Verschollenheitserklärung und Todeserklärung	Subchapter 3 Declarations of Missing Persons and Death
第四节　个体工商户和农村承包经营户	4. Abschnitt: Einzelgewerbetreibende und ländliche Übernahmebetreiber	Subchapter 4 Individual Businesses and Operators Taking Over Farm Households
第三章　法人	**3. Kapitel: Juristische Personen**	**Chapter III Legal Entities**
第一节　一般规定	1. Abschnitt: Allgemeine Bestimmungen	Subchapter 1 General Stipulations
第二节　营利法人	2. Abschnitt: Gewinnorientierte juristische Personen	Subchapter 2 For-profit Legal Entities
第三节　非营利法人	3. Abschnitt: Nichtgewinnorientierte juristische Personen	Subchapter 3 Non-profit Legal Entities
第四节　特别法人	4. Abschnitt: Besondere juristische Personen	Subchapter 4 Special Legal Entities

1 Die Herausgeber danken den Herren Peter Leibküchler, Knut Benjamin Pißler und Nils Klages für die Bereitstellung ihrer Übersetzung des Allgemeinen Teils des Zivilrechts der Volksrepublik China.

2 Basierend auf der deutschen Übersetzung ins Englische übersetzt von Sandra Paulson.

第四章　非法人组织	**4. Kapitel: Organisationen ohne Rechtspersönlichkeit**	**Chapter IV Non-incorporated Organisations**
第五章　民事权利	**5. Kapitel: Zivilrechte**	**Chapter V Civil Rights**
第六章　民事法律行为	**6. Kapitel: Zivilrechtsgeschäfte**	**Chapter VI Civil Transactions**
第一节　一般规定	1. Abschnitt: Allgemeine Bestimmungen	Subchapter 1 General Stipulations
第二节　意思表示	2. Abschnitt: Willenserklärungen	Subchapter 2 Declaration of Intent
第三节　民事法律行为的效力	3. Abschnitt: Wirksamkeit von Zivilrechtsgeschäften	Subchapter 3 Validity of Civil Transactions
第四节　民事法律行为的附条件和附期限	4. Abschnitt: Bedingungen und Zeitbestimmung bei Zivilrechtsgeschäften	Subchapter 4 Conditions and Duration of Civil Transactions
第七章　代理	**7. Kapitel: Vertretung**	**Chapter VII Agency**
第一节　一般规定	1. Abschnitt: Allgemeine Bestimmungen	Subchapter 1 General Stipulations
第二节　委托代理	2. Abschnitt: Beauftragte Vertretung	Subchapter 2 Entrusted Agency
第三节　代理终止	3. Abschnitt: Beendigung der Vertretung	Subchapter 3 Termination of Agency
第八章　民事责任	**8. Kapitel: Zivile Haftung**	**Chapter VIII Civil Liability**
第九章　诉讼时效	**9. Kapitel: Klageverjährung**	**Chapter IX Limitation Period**
第十章　期间计算	**10. Kapitel: Berechnung von Zeiträumen**	**Chapter X Calculation of Periods**
第十一章　附则	**11. Kapitel: Ergänzende Regeln**	**Chapter XI Supplementary Stipulations**

第一章　基本规定	1. Kapitel: Grundlegende Bestimmungen	Chapter I General Stipulations
第一条　为了保护民事主体的合法权益，调整民事关系，维护社会和经济秩序，适应中国特色社会主义发展要求，弘扬社会主义核心价值观，根据宪法，制定本法。	**§ 1 [Gesetzgeberisches Ziel, vgl. § 1 AGZR[3]][4]** Um die legalen Rechte und Interessen der Zivilsubjekte zu schützen, die Zivilbeziehungen zu regeln, die gesellschaftliche und wirtschaftliche Ordnung zu wahren, zur Anpassung an die Erfordernisse der Entwicklung des Sozialismus mit chinesischen Besonderheiten [und] zur Förderung der Sozialistischen Grundwerte wird gemäß der Verfassung dieses Gesetz festgesetzt.	**Section 1** These Rules are enacted in accordance with the Constitution to protect the legal rights and interests of civil subjects, regulate civil relations, maintain the social and economic order, adapt to the requirements of the development of socialism with Chinese characteristics, and promote the socialist fundamental values.
第二条　民法调整平等主体的自然人、法人和非法人组织之间的人身关系和财产关系。	**§ 2 [Regelungsgegenstand; vgl. § 2 AGZR]** Das Zivilrecht regelt die Personenbeziehungen und Vermögensbeziehungen zwischen natürlichen Personen, juristischen Personen und Organisationen ohne Rechtspersönlichkeit[5] als gleichberechtigte Subjekte.	**Section 2** Civil law regulates personal relations and property relations between natural persons, legal entities, and non-incorporated organisations as equal subjects.
第三条　民事主体的人身权利、财产权利以及其他合法权益受法律保护，任何组织或者个人不得侵犯。	**§ 3 [Gesetzlicher Schutz legaler Rechte; vgl. § 5 AGZR]** Die persönlichen Rechte, Vermögensrechte und anderen legalen Rechte und Interessen der Zivilsubjekte werden vom Gesetz geschützt; keine Organisation oder Einzelperson darf [diese Rechte] verletzen.	**Section 3** The personal rights, property rights, and other legal rights and interests of civil subjects are protected by the law; no organisation or individual may infringe these rights.

3 Allgemeine Grundsätze des Zivilrechts der VR China (中华人民共和国民法通则) vom 12.4.1986 in der Fassung vom 27.8.2009; deutsche Übersetzung in: *Frank Münzel* (Hrsg.), Chinas Recht, 12.4.86/1.

4 Soweit für eine Vorschrift eine Vorläufervorschrift in den AGZR oder zentralen justiziellen Interpretationen des Obersten Volksgerichts (OVG) auf dem Gebiet des Zivilrechts existiert, wird auf diese in der Paragraphenüberschrift hingewiesen. Auf in anderen (ggf. spezielleren) Gesetzen bereits existierende Vorschriften mit dem gleichen oder einem ähnlichen Regelungsgegenstand wird ohne Anspruch auf Vollständigkeit in Fußnoten hingewiesen.

5 Wörtlich: „Organisationen die keine juristische Personen sind“, vgl. Definition in § 102.

第四条　民事主体在民事活动中的法律地位一律平等。	**§ 4 [Gleichheitsgebot; vgl. § 3 AGZR]** Die rechtliche Stellung von Zivilsubjekten bei Zivilaktivitäten ist ausnahmslos gleichberechtigt.	**Section 4** All civil subjects are legally equal in civil activities.
第五条　民事主体从事民事活动，应当遵循自愿原则，按照自己的意思设立、变更、终止民事法律关系。	**§ 5 [Prinzip der Freiwilligkeit; vgl. § 4 AGZR]** Wenn Zivilsubjekte Zivilaktivitäten unternehmen, müssen sie den Grundsatz der Freiwilligkeit befolgen und gemäß ihrem eigenen Willen Zivilrechtsbeziehungen begründen, ändern [oder] beenden.	**Section 5** Civil subjects engaging in civil activities shall follow the principles of voluntariness and according to their own intentions establish, change, or terminate civil legal relations.
第六条　民事主体从事民事活动，应当遵循公平原则，合理确定各方的权利和义务。	**§ 6 [Prinzip der Gerechtigkeit; vgl. § 4 AGZR]** Wenn Zivilsubjekte Zivilaktivitäten unternehmen, müssen sie den Grundsatz der Gerechtigkeit befolgen [und] die Rechte und Pflichten aller Parteien[6] vernünftig festlegen.	**Section 6** Civil subjects engaging in civil activities shall follow the principles of fairness and reasonably determine the rights and obligations of all parties concerned.
第七条　民事主体从事民事活动，应当遵循诚信原则，秉持诚实，恪守承诺。	**§ 7 [Treu und Glauben; vgl. § 4 AGZR]** Wenn Zivilsubjekte Zivilaktivitäten unternehmen, müssen sie den Grundsatz von Treu und Glauben befolgen, Ehrlichkeit bewahren und Versprechen gewissenhaft einhalten.	**Section 7** Civil subjects engaging in civil activities shall follow the principle of good faith, adhere to honesty, and carefully abide by their commitments.
第八条　民事主体从事民事活动，不得违反法律，不得违背公序良俗。	**§ 8 [Gesetzliches Verbot und gute Sitten; vgl. § 7 AGZR]** Wenn Zivilsubjekte Zivilaktivitäten unternehmen, dürfen sie nicht gegen das Gesetz verstoßen [oder] der öffentlichen Ordnung [und] den guten Sitten[7] zuwiderhandeln.	**Section 8** No civil subject engaging in civil activities may violate law or contravene the public order and morality.

6 Wörtlich „aller Seiten".

7 Bei dem chinesischen Terminus 公序良俗 (hier übersetzt als „öffentliche Ordnung [und] gute Sitten") handelt es sich um einen einheitlichen Begriff, bei dem offenbar die beiden Komponenten jeweils keinen eigenständigen Bedeutungsgehalt haben.

第九条　民事主体从事民事活动，应当有利于节约资源、保护生态环境。

§ 9 [Schutz der Umwelt] Wenn Zivilsubjekte Zivilaktivitäten unternehmen, müssen sie zur Schonung von Ressourcen beitragen [und] die ökologische Umwelt schützen.

Section 9 Civil subjects engaging in civil activities shall contribute to saving resources and protecting the ecological environment.

第十条　处理民事纠纷，应当依照法律；法律没有规定的，可以适用习惯，但是不得违背公序良俗。

§ 10 [Rechtsquellen; vgl. § 6 AGZR] Die Behandlung ziviler Streitigkeiten muss gemäß dem Gesetz [erfolgen]; soweit das Gesetz keine Bestimmungen enthält, können Gebräuche angewendet werden, jedoch darf nicht der öffentlichen Ordnung [und] den guten Sitten[8] zuwidergehandelt werden.

Section 10 Civil disputes shall be resolved in accordance with the law; in the absence of any legal provisions, usual practices may be followed but the public order and morality shall not be contravened.

第十一条　其他法律对民事关系有特别规定的，依照其规定。

§ 11 [Vorrang spezieller Vorschriften] Soweit andere Gesetze besondere Bestimmungen zu Zivilbeziehungen enthalten, gelten diese Bestimmungen.

Section 11 If other laws contain special provisions on civil relations, these provisions are applicable.

第十二条　中华人民共和国领域内的民事活动，适用中华人民共和国法律。法律另有规定的，依照其规定。

§ 12 [Anwendung chinesischen Rechts; vgl. § 8 AGZR] Auf Zivilaktivitäten im Hoheitsgebiet der Volksrepublik China werden die Gesetze der Volksrepublik China angewandt. Gibt es andere gesetzliche Bestimmungen, so gelten diese Bestimmungen.

Section 12 The laws of the People's Republic of China are applicable to civil activities within the territory of the People's Republic of China, unless otherwise provided by the law.

第二章　自然人

2. Kapitel: Natürliche Personen

Chapter II Natural Persons

第一节　民事权利能力和民事行为能力

1. Abschnitt: Zivilrechtsfähigkeit und Zivilgeschäftsfähigkeit

Subchapter 1 Legal and Contractual Capacity

8 S.o. Fn. 7.

第十三条　自然人从出生时起到死亡时止，具有民事权利能力，依法享有民事权利，承担民事义务。	**§ 13 [Rechtsfähigkeit; vgl. § 9 AGZR]** Von der Zeit ihrer Geburt bis zur Zeit ihres Todes besitzen natürliche Personen Zivilrechtsfähigkeit, genießen nach dem Recht zivile Rechte [und] tragen zivile Pflichten.	**Section 13** Commencing at the time of birth and ceasing at the time of death, natural persons possess legal capacity, enjoy civil rights, and assume civil obligations in accordance with the law.
第十四条　自然人的民事权利能力一律平等。	**§ 14 [Unbeschränkbarkeit der Rechtsfähigkeit; vgl. § 10 AGZR]** Die Zivilrechtsfähigkeit natürlicher Personen ist ausnahmslos gleich.	**Section 14** The legal capacity of natural persons is unanimously equal.
第十五条　自然人的出生时间和死亡时间，以出生证明、死亡证明记载的时间为准；没有出生证明、死亡证明的，以户籍登记或者其他有效身份登记记载的时间为准。有其他证据足以推翻以上记载时间的，以该证据证明的时间为准。	**§ 15 [Geburts- und Todeszeitpunkt; vgl. Ziffer 1 AGZR-Ansichten[9]]** Für den Zeitpunkt der Geburt und den Zeitpunkt des Todes einer natürlichen Person ist der in der Geburtsurkunde [bzw.] Todesurkunde aufgezeichnete Zeitpunkt maßgeblich; gibt es keine Geburtsurkunde [bzw.] Todesurkunde, ist der im Haushaltsregistrierungsbuch oder einer anderen gültigen Identitätseintragung aufgezeichnete Zeitpunkt maßgeblich. Gibt es andere Beweise, die ausreichen, um den oben [genannten] aufgezeichneten Zeitpunkt zu widerlegen[10], ist der durch diesen Beweis bewiesene Zeitpunkt maßgeblich.	**Section 15** The time of birth and the time of death of a natural person shall be the time recorded in their birth certificate or death certificate; in the absence of a birth certificate or death certificate, the time recorded in the household registry or any other valid identity registration shall be applicable. If there is any other evidence sufficient to refute the aforementioned time, the time supported by such evidence shall prevail.

---

9 Versuchsweise durchgeführte Ansichten des Obersten Volksgerichts zu einigen Fragen der Anwendung der Allgemeinen Grundsätze des Zivilrechts der VR China [最高人民法院关于贯彻执行«中华人民共和国民法通则»若干问题的意见（试行）] vom 2.4.1988 in der Fassung vom 18.12.2008; deutsche Übersetzung in: *Frank Münzel* (Hrsg.), Chinas Recht, 12.4.86/1.

10 Wörtlich: „umzustürzen“.

第十六条　涉及遗产继承、接受赠与等胎儿利益保护的，胎儿视为具有民事权利能力。但是胎儿娩出时为死体的，其民事权利能力自始不存在。	**§ 16 [Rechtsstellung des nasciturus[11]]** In Bezug auf den Schutz der Interessen eines Fötus wie etwa beim Erben von Nachlass [oder] beim Empfang von Geschenken gilt der Fötus als zivilrechtsfähig. Ist der Fötus jedoch zur Zeit der Entbindung ein Leichnam, so bestand seine Zivilrechtsfähigkeit von Anfang an nicht.	**Section 16** Regarding the protection of the interests of a foetus, as for instance the heir of an estate or receiving gifts, the foetus is considered legally capable. However, if the foetus is stillborn, the legal capacity has never existed.
第十七条　十八周岁以上的自然人为成年人。不满十八周岁的自然人为未成年人。	**§ 17 [Volljährigkeit; vgl. § 11 Abs. 1 AGZR]** Eine natürliche Person von 18 oder mehr Lebensjahren ist ein Volljähriger. Eine natürliche Person von weniger als 18 Lebensjahren ist ein Minderjähriger.	**Section 17** A natural person of 18 or more years is an adult. A natural person under the age of 18 is a minor.
第十八条　成年人为完全民事行为能力人，可以独立实施民事法律行为。	**§ 18 [Geschäftsfähigkeit Volljähriger; vgl. § 11 AGZR]** Ein Volljähriger ist ein voll Zivilgeschäftsfähiger [und] kann eigenständig Zivilrechtsgeschäfte vornehmen.	**Section 18** An adult has full contractual capacity and may perform legal transactions autonomously.
十六周岁以上的未成年人，以自己的劳动收入为主要生活来源的，视为完全民事行为能力人。	Ein Minderjähriger von 16 oder mehr Lebensjahren, dessen hauptsächliche Einkommensquelle[12] Einkommen aus eigener Arbeit ist, gilt als voll Zivilgeschäftsfähiger.	A minor aged of 16 or more years whose main source of income is their own work is considered to be of full contractual capacity.
第十九条　八周岁以上的未成年人为限制民事行为能力人，实施民事法律行为由其法定代理人代理或者经其法定代理人同意、追认，但是可以独立实施纯获利益的民事法律	**§ 19 [Beschränkte Geschäftsfähigkeit Minderjähriger; vgl. § 12 Abs. 1 AGZR]** Ein Minderjähriger von acht oder mehr Lebensjahren ist ein beschränkt Zivilgeschäftsfähiger, die Vornahme von Zivilrechtsgeschäften	**Section 19** A minor aged of eight or more years is of limited contractual capacity, legal transactions shall be performed by their legal agent acting in the capacity or with their consent or approval; however, such minor may

11 Vgl. § 28 Erbgesetz der VR China [中华人民共和国继承法] vom 10.4.1985; deutsche Übersetzung in: *Frank Münzel* (Hrsg.), Chinas Recht, 10.4.85/1 (Erbgesetz).

12 Wörtlich: „Lebensquelle".

行为或者与其年龄、智力相适应的民事法律行为。	[erfolgt] durch seinen gesetzlichen Vertreter in Vertretung oder mit dessen Einverständnis [oder] Genehmigung; er kann jedoch rein vorteilhafte Zivilrechtsgeschäfte, oder Zivilrechtsgeschäfte, die seinem Alter [und seinen] geistigen Fähigkeiten entsprechen, eigenständig vornehmen.	autonomously perform purely beneficial legal transactions or legal transactions corresponding their age and mental capacities.
第二十条　不满八周岁的未成年人为无民事行为能力人，由其法定代理人代理实施民事法律行为。	**§ 20 [Geschäftsunfähigkeit Minderjähriger; vgl. § 12 Abs. 2 AGZR]** Ein Minderjähriger von weniger als acht Lebensjahren ist ein Zivilgeschäftsunfähiger [und] wird von seinem gesetzlichen Vertreter bei der Vornahme von Zivilrechtsgeschäften vertreten.	**Section 20** A minor under the age of eight is not competent for contractual obligations and shall be represented by their legal agent in the performance of legal transactions.
第二十一条　不能辨认自己行为的成年人为无民事行为能力人，由其法定代理人代理实施民事法律行为。	**§ 21 [Geschäftsunfähigkeit Volljähriger; vgl. § 13 Abs. 1 AGZR]** Ein Volljähriger, dem die Einsicht in seine Handlungen fehlt[13], ist ein Zivilgeschäftsunfähiger [und] wird von seinem gesetzlichen Vertreter bei der Vornahme von Zivilrechtsgeschäften vertreten.	**Section 21** An adult lacking the awareness of their activities is a person lacking the contractual capacity and shall be represented by their legal agent in the performance of legal transactions.
八周岁以上的未成年人不能辨认自己行为的，适用前款规定。	Auf einen Minderjährigen von acht oder mehr Lebensjahren, dem die Einsicht in seine Handlungen fehlt[14], wird die Bestimmung des vorherigen Absatzes angewandt.	A minor who has reached the age of eight or more years and lacks the ability to account for their own activities shall be subject to the provision set forth in the preceding paragraph.
第二十二条　不能完全辨认自己行为的成年人为限制民事行为能力人，实施民事法律行为由其法定代理	**§ 22 [Beschränkte Geschäftsfähigkeit Volljähriger; vgl. § 13 Abs. 2 AGZR]** Ein Volljähriger, der keine vollständige Einsicht in seine Handlungen hat[15], ist ein	**Section 22** An adult lacking full awareness to account for their own actions is a person of

13 Wörtlich: „der seine eigenen Handlungen nicht erkennen kann".
14 Siehe Fn. 13.
15 Wörtlich: „der seine eigenen Handlungen nicht vollständig erkennen kann".

人代理或者经其法定代理人同意、追认，但是可以独立实施纯获利益的民事法律行为或者与其智力、精神健康状况相适应的民事法律行为。	beschränkt Zivilgeschäftsfähiger, die Vornahme von Zivilrechtsgeschäften [erfolgt] durch seinen gesetzlichen Vertreter in Vertretung oder mit dessen Einverständnis [oder] Genehmigung; er kann jedoch rein vorteilhafte Zivilrechtsgeschäfte, oder Zivilrechtsgeschäfte, die seinen geistigen Fähigkeiten [und] dem Zustand [seiner] geistigen Gesundheit entsprechen, eigenständig vornehmen.	limited contractual capacity; legal transactions shall be performed by their legal agent or with their consent or approval; however, such adult can autonomously perform purely beneficial legal transactions or legal transactions corresponding their mental capacities and the state of their mental sanity.
第二十三条　无民事行为能力人、限制民事行为能力人的监护人是其法定代理人。	**§ 23 [Gesetzlicher Vertreter; = § 14 AGZR]** Der Vormund eines Zivilgeschäftsunfähigen oder beschränkt Zivilgeschäftsfähigen ist dessen gesetzlicher Vertreter.	**Section 23** The guardian of a person without or with limited contractual capacity is their legal agent.
第二十四条　不能辨认或者不能完全辨认自己行为的成年人，其利害关系人或者有关组织，可以向人民法院申请认定该成年人为无民事行为能力人或者限制民事行为能力人。	**§ 24 [Gerichtliche Bestimmung von Mängeln der Geschäftsfähigkeit; vgl. § 19 AGZR, Abs. 3]** Bei einem Volljährigen, der keine oder keine vollständige Einsicht in seine Handlungen hat[16], kann ein Interessierter[17] oder eine betreffende Organisation beim Volksgericht beantragen, dass dieser Volljährige als Zivilgeschäftsunfähiger oder beschränkt Zivilgeschäftsfähiger festgestellt wird.	**Section 24** An interested person or a concerned organisation may apply to a people's court that an adult lacking full awareness in their actions be determined a person lacking contractual capacity or a person with limited contractual capacity.
被人民法院认定为无民事行为能力人或者限制民事行为能力人的，经本人、利害关系人或者有关组织申请，人民法院可以根据其智力、精神健康恢复的状况，认定该成年人	Wenn [eine Person] vom Volksgericht als Zivilgeschäftsunfähiger oder beschränkt Zivilgeschäftsfähiger festgestellt wurde, kann auf Antrag des Betroffenen, eines Interessierten oder einer betreffenden Organisation das Volksgericht gemäß dem Zustand der Wiederher-	After a person has been determined a person lacking contractual capacity or a person with limited contractual capacity, upon request of the concerned party, an interested person or a concerned organisation the people's court

16 Wörtlich: „der seine eigenen Handlungen nicht erkennen oder nicht vollständig erkennen kann".
17 Wörtlich: „[dazu] in einer [eigenen] Nutzen und Schaden berührenden Beziehung stehende Person".

恢复为限制民事行为能力人或者完全民事行为能力人。	stellung von dessen geistigen Fähigkeiten [und] geistiger Gesundheit feststellen, dass dieser Volljährige als beschränkt Zivilgeschäftsfähiger oder vollständig Zivilgeschäftsfähiger wiederhergestellt ist.	may determine according to their state of recovery of their mental capacities and mental sanity that the adult has recovered to be of limited contractual capacity or to be of full contractual capacity.
本条规定的有关组织包括：居民委员会、村民委员会、学校、医疗机构、妇女联合会、残疾人联合会、依法设立的老年人组织、民政部门等。	Die in diesem Paragraphen bestimmten betreffenden Organisationen umfassen: Einwohnerkomitees, Dorfbewohnerkomitees, Lehranstalten, Gesundheitseinrichtungen, Frauenverbände, Behindertenverbände, nach dem Recht errichtete Seniorenorganisationen und Abteilungen für Zivilangelegenheiten.	The concerned organisations mentioned in this Section include: residents committees, villagers committees, educational institutions, medical institutions, women's federations, federations of persons with disabilities, elderly organisations duly established, and civil affairs authorities.
第二十五条　自然人以户籍登记或者其他有效身份登记记载的居所为住所；经常居所与住所不一致的，经常居所视为住所。	**§ 25 [Wohnsitz natürlicher Personen; vgl. § 15 AGZR]** Der Wohnsitz einer natürlichen Person ist der in der Haushaltsregistrierung oder einer anderen gültigen Identitätseintragung aufgezeichnete Aufenthaltsort; ist der gewöhnliche Aufenthaltsort mit dem Wohnsitz nicht identisch, so gilt der gewöhnliche Aufenthaltsort als Wohnsitz.	**Section 25** The domicile of a natural person shall be their residence recorded in the household register or another valid identity register; if the habitual residence of a natural person is not the same as their domicile, such habitual residence is considered the domicile.
第二节　监护	**2. Abschnitt: Vormundschaft**	**Subchapter 2 Guardianship**
第二十六条　父母对未成年子女负有抚养、教育和保护的义务。	**§ 26 [Pflichten zwischen Eltern und Kindern]** Eltern haben gegenüber ihren minderjährigen Kindern die Pflicht zum Unterhalt, zur Erziehung und zum Schutz.	**Section 26** Parents are obligated to maintain, educate, and protect their minor children.
成年子女对父母负有赡养、扶助和保护的义务。	Volljährige Kinder haben gegenüber den Eltern die Pflicht zum Unterhalt, zum Beistand und zum Schutz.	Adult offspring have the obligation to maintain, support, and protect their parents.

第二十七条　父母是未成年子女的监护人。	**§ 27 [Vormünder Minderjähriger; vgl. § 16 Abs. 1, 2 AGZR]** Die Eltern sind die Vormünder der minderjährigen Kinder.	**Section 27** Parents are guardians of their minor children.
未成年人的父母已经死亡或者没有监护能力的，由下列有监护能力的人按顺序担任监护人：	Sind die Eltern eines Minderjährigen bereits verstorben oder haben keine Vormundschaftsfähigkeit, so fungieren die folgenden Personen, die fähig sind, Vormund zu sein, in der Reihenfolge als Vormund:	If the parents of a minor are deceased or have no guardianship competence, the following persons that have the competence serve as guardians according to this order :
（一）祖父母、外祖父母；	1. Großeltern väterlicherseits, Großeltern mütterlicherseits;	(1) Paternal grandparents or maternal grandparents;
（二）兄、姐；	2. ältere Brüder, ältere Schwestern;	(2) Older brothers, older sisters;
（三）其他愿意担任监护人的个人或者组织，但是须经未成年人住所地的居民委员会、村民委员会或者民政部门同意。	3. andere Personen oder Organisationen, die als Vormund fungieren wollen, allerdings muss das Einwohnerkomitee, das Dorfbewohnerkomitee oder die Abteilung für Zivilangelegenheiten am Ort des Wohnsitzes des Minderjährigen einverstanden sein.	(3) Any other individual or organisation that is willing to act as the guardian, however, the consent of the residents committee, the villagers committee, or the civil affairs authority at the place of the minors' domicile is needed.
第二十八条　无民事行为能力或者限制民事行为能力的成年人，由下列有监护能力的人按顺序担任监护人：	**§ 28 [Vormünder Volljähriger; vgl. § 17 AGZR]** Für einen zivilgeschäftsunfähigen oder beschränkt zivilgeschäftsfähigen Volljährigen fungieren die folgenden Personen, die Vormundschaftsfähigkeit haben, in der Reihenfolge als Vormund:	**Section 28** Any of the following persons with guardianship competence shall act as the guardian of an adult with no or limited legal or contractual capacity according to this order:
（一）配偶；	1. Ehegatten;	(1) Spouses;
（二）父母、子女；	2. Eltern, Kinder;	(2) Parents, children;
（三）其他近亲属；	3. andere nahe Verwandte;	(3) Close relatives;
（四）其他愿意担任监护人的个人或者组织，但是须经被监护人住所地的居民委员会、村民委员会或者民政部门同意。	4. andere Personen oder Organisationen, die als Vormund fungieren wollen, allerdings muss das Einwohnerkomitee, das Dorfbewohnerkomitee oder die Abteilung für Zivilangelegenheiten am Ort des Wohnsitzes des Mündels einverstanden sein.	(4) Any other individual or organisation that is willing to act as the guardian, however, the consent of the residents commit-

		tee, the villagers committee, or the civil affairs authority at the place of the domicile of the adult is needed.
第二十九条　被监护人的父母担任监护人的，可以通过遗嘱指定监护人。	**§ 29 [Testamentarische Bestimmung des Vormunds]** Fungieren die Eltern des Mündels als Vormund, können [sie] durch Testament einen Vormund bestimmen.	**Section 29** If the parents act as the ward's guardian they can designate a guardian by will.
第三十条　依法具有监护资格的人之间可以协议确定监护人。协议确定监护人应当尊重被监护人的真实意愿。	**§ 30 [Vereinbarung des Vormunds]** Zwischen den Personen, die die Befähigung zur Vormundschaft besitzen, kann der Vormund durch Vereinbarung festgelegt werden. Bei der Festlegung des Vormundes durch Vereinbarung muss der wahre Wille des Mündels respektiert werden.	**Section 30** Qualified persons of guardianship may agree to determine a guardian. If a guardian is determined by agreement, the true will of the ward shall be respected.
第三十一条　对监护人的确定有争议的，由被监护人住所地的居民委员会、村民委员会或者民政部门指定监护人，有关当事人对指定不服的，可以向人民法院申请指定监护人；有关当事人也可以直接向人民法院申请指定监护人。	**§ 31 [Bestimmung des Vormunds; vgl. § 16 Abs. 3 und § 17 Abs. 2 AGZR]** Gibt es Streit über die Festlegung des Vormundes, wird der Vormund vom Einwohnerkomitee, Dorfbewohnerkomitee oder der Abteilung für Zivilangelegenheiten am Ort des Wohnsitzes des Mündels bestimmt; unterwerfen sich die betreffenden Parteien nicht der Bestimmung, können [sie] beim Volksgericht die Bestimmung eines Vormunds beantragen; die betreffenden Parteien können auch direkt beim Volksgericht die Bestimmung eines Vormunds beantragen.	**Section 31** If there are disputes about the determination of a guardian, the residents committee, the villagers committee, or the civil affairs authority at the place of the ward's residence may appoint a guardian; if the parties concerned disagree with the appointment, they may apply to a people's court for appointing a guardian; the concerned parties may also directly apply to the people's court for appointing a guardian.
居民委员会、村民委员会、民政部门或者人民法院应当尊重被监护人的真实意愿，按照最有利于被监护人的原则在依法具有监护资格的人中指定监护人。	Das Einwohnerkomitee, das Dorfbewohnerkomitee, die Abteilung für Zivilverwaltung oder das Volksgericht muss den wahren Willen des Mündels respektieren [und] gemäß dem Grundsatz des größten Nutzens für das Mündel unter den Personen, die nach dem Recht die	The residents committee, the villagers committee, the civil affairs authority, or the people's court shall respect the true will of the ward, and shall appoint a guardian within the

	Befähigung für die Vormundschaft besitzen, den Vormund bestimmen.	scope of persons legally qualified for guardianship under the principle of "benefiting the ward to the greatest extent".
依照本条第一款规定指定监护人前，被监护人的人身权利、财产权利以及其他合法权益处于无人保护状态的，由被监护人住所地的居民委员会、村民委员会、法律规定的有关组织或者民政部门担任临时监护人。	Befinden sich vor der Bestimmung eines Vormundes gemäß Absatz 1 dieses Paragraphen die persönlichen Rechte, die Vermögensrechte und die sonstigen legalen Rechte und Interessen des Mündels in einem Zustand, in dem sie von niemandem geschützt werden, so fungiert das Einwohnerkomitee, das Dorfbewohnerkomitee, eine gesetzlich bestimmte betreffende Organisation oder die Abteilung für Zivilangelegenheiten am Ort des Wohnsitzes des Mündels als vorläufiger Vormund.	If the personal rights, property rights and other legal rights and interests of the ward are under no protection prior to the appointment of a guardian in accordance with Clause 1 of this Section, the residents committee or the villagers committee at the place of the ward's residence, the respective organisation that is provided for in law, or the civil affairs authority shall act as the guardian.
监护人被指定后，不得擅自变更；擅自变更的，不免除被指定的监护人的责任。	Nachdem ein Vormund bestimmt wurde, darf [dieser] nicht eigenmächtig ausgewechselt [18] werden; eigenmächtige Auswechslungen[19] entbinden den bestimmten Vormund nicht von [seiner] Haftung.	The guardian, once appointed, shall not be changed without authorisation; unauthorised changes do not exempt the designated guardian from liability.
第三十二条　没有依法具有监护资格的人的，监护人由民政部门担任，也可以由具备履行监护职责条件的被监护人住所地的居民委员会、村民委员会担任。	**§ 32 [Amtsvormundschaft; vgl. § 16 Abs. 4 und § 17 Abs. 3 AGZR]** Gibt es keine Person, die nach dem Recht die Befähigung für die Vormundschaft besitzt, fungiert die Abteilung für Zivilangelegenheiten als Vormund; es kann auch das Einwohnerkomitee [oder] Dorfbewohnerkomitee am Ort des Wohnsitzes des Mündels,	**Section 32** If there is no person legally qualified for guardianship, the civil affairs authority shall act as the guardian; the residents committee, or the villagers committee at the place of the ward's residence that fulfils the requirements of performing the guardianship official duties may act as the guardian.

18 Wörtlich: „geändert“.
19 Wörtlich: „Änderungen“.

bei dem die Voraussetzungen für die Erfüllung der vormundschaftlichen Amtspflichten vorhanden sind, [als Vormund] fungieren.

第三十三条　具有完全民事行为能力的成年人，可以与其近亲属、其他愿意担任监护人的个人或者组织事先协商，以书面形式确定自己的监护人。协商确定的监护人在该成年人丧失或者部分丧失民事行为能力时，履行监护职责。

§ 33 [Gewillkürte Festlegung des Vormunds[20]] Ein Volljähriger, der die vollständige Zivilgeschäftsfähigkeit besitzt, kann seine Verwandten, andere Einzelpersonen oder Organisationen, die als Vormund fungieren wollen, im Voraus konsultieren [und] in schriftlicher Form den eigenen Vormund festlegen. Der durch Konsultation festgelegte Vormund erfüllt die vormundschaftlichen Amtspflichten, wenn der Volljährige seine Zivilgeschäftsfähigkeit verliert oder teilweise verliert.

Section 33 An adult with full contractual capacity may, in prior consultation with their close relatives, or other individuals or organisations who are willing to act as their guardian, determine their own guardian in written form. The agreed guardian shall perform the guardianship official duties when such adult loses or partially loses their contractual capacity.

第三十四条　监护人的职责是代理被监护人实施民事法律行为，保护被监护人的人身权利、财产权利以及其他合法权益等。

§ 34 [Amtspflichten und Haftung des Vormunds; Abs. 1, zu Abs. 2 vgl. § 18 Abs. 2] Die Amtspflichten des Vormunds sind die Vertretung des Mündels bei der Vornahme von Zivilrechtsgeschäften [und] der Schutz der persönlichen Rechte [und] Vermögensrechte sowie anderer legaler Rechte und Interessen des Mündels.

Section 34 The guardian of a ward has the official duties to perform civil transactions and to protect the personal rights and property rights and other legitimate rights and interests of the ward on their behalf.

监护人依法履行监护职责产生的权利，受法律保护。

Die Rechte des Vormunds, die aus der rechtsgemäßen Erfüllung der vormundschaftlichen Amtspflichten entstehen, werden vom Gesetz geschützt.

The guardian's rights arising from lawfully performing the official duties of guardianship are protected by law.

---

20 Vgl. § 26 Gesetz über die Garantie der Rechte und Interessen von Senioren [老年人权益保障法] vom 29.8.1996 in der Fassung vom 24.4.205; chinesisch-englisch abrufbar unter pkulaw.cn [北大法宝], Index-Nr. [法宝引证码] CLI.1.252608(EN).

监护人不履行监护职责或者侵害被监护人合法权益的，应当承担法律责任。	Erfüllt der Vormund seine vormundschaftlichen Amtspflichten nicht oder verletzt er die legalen Rechte und Interessen des Mündels, so muss er die gesetzliche Haftung tragen.	Any guardian who fails to perform the official duties of guardianship or infringes the legal rights and interests of the ward shall be held liable.
第三十五条　监护人应当按照最有利于被监护人的原则履行监护职责。监护人除为维护被监护人利益外，不得处分被监护人的财产。	**§ 35 [Grundsätze der Vormundschaftsausübung; zu Abs. 1 vgl. § 18 Abs. 1 AGZR, Abs. 2, 3]** Der Vormund muss seine vormundschaftlichen Amtspflichten gemäß dem Grundsatz des größten Nutzens für das Mündel erfüllen. Außer zur Wahrung der Interessen des Mündels darf der Vormund über das Vermögen des Mündels nicht verfügen.	**Section 35** A guardian shall perform the official duties of guardianship according to the principle of the greatest benefit for the war. The guardian shall not dispose of the ward's property, unless to protect the ward's interests.
未成年人的监护人履行监护职责，在作出与被监护人利益有关的决定时，应当根据被监护人的年龄和智力状况，尊重被监护人的真实意愿。	Der Vormund eines Minderjährigen muss, wenn er in Erfüllung seiner vormundschaftlichen Amtspflichten eine Entscheidung trifft, die die Interessen des Mündels betrifft, gemäß dem Alter und dem Zustand der geistigen Fähigkeiten des Mündels den wahren Willen des Mündels respektieren.	Performing the official duties of guardianship, the minor's guardian shall, in making the decision relating to the ward's interests, respect the true will of the ward corresponding to the ward's age and mental capacity.
成年人的监护人履行监护职责，应当最大程度地尊重被监护人的真实意愿，保障并协助被监护人实施与其智力、精神健康状况相适应的民事法律行为。对被监护人有能力独立处理的事务，监护人不得干涉。	Der Vormund eines Volljährigen muss bei der Erfüllung seiner vormundschaftlichen Amtspflichten im höchsten Maße den wahren Willen des Mündels respektieren [sowie] gewährleisten und unterstützen, dass das Mündel seinen geistigen Fähigkeiten und dem Zustand seiner geistigen Gesundheit entsprechende Rechtsgeschäfte vornimmt. In Angelegenheiten, die eigenständig zu erledigen das Mündel fähig ist, darf sich der Vormund nicht einmischen.	The guardian of an adult that performs the official duties of guardianship shall respect the true will of the ward to the greatest extent and protect and assist the ward in the performance of legal transactions that are compatible with the ward's mental capacity and health, and shall not interfere with the affairs that the ward is able to perform themselves.
第三十六条　监护人有下列情形之一的，人民法院根据有关个人或者组织的申请，撤销其监护人资格，	**§ 36 [Gerichtliche Aufhebung der Vormundschaft; vgl. § 18 Abs. 3 Satz 2 AGZR]** Wenn bei einem Vormund einer der folgenden Umstände vorliegt, hebt das	**Section 36** Under any of the following circumstances, the people's court may, upon the

安排必要的临时监护措施，并按照最有利于被监护人的原则依法指定监护人：	Volksgericht gemäß dem Antrag einer betreffenden Einzelperson oder Organisation dessen Befähigung zum Vormund auf, arrangiert die notwendigen vorläufigen vormundschaftlichen Maßnahmen und bestimmt gemäß dem Grundsatz des größten Nutzens für das Mündel nach dem Recht einen Vormund:	petition of an individual or organisation concerned, disqualify a guardian, take necessary preliminary measures for guardianship, and appoint another guardian for the ward under the principle of the greatest benefit:
（一）实施严重损害被监护人身心健康行为的；	1. Handlungen, die die körperliche [oder] geistige Gesundheit des Mündels erheblich schädigen, werden vorgenommen;	(1) Actions that substantially damage the physical or mental health of the ward are performed;
（二）怠于履行监护职责，或者无法履行监护职责并且拒绝将监护职责部分或者全部委托给他人，导致被监护人处于危困状态的；	2. die Erfüllung der vormundschaftlichen Amtspflichten wird vernachlässigt oder die Erfüllung der vormundschaftlichen Amtspflichten ist unmöglich und es wird verweigert, vollständig oder teilweise eine andere Person mit den vormundschaftlichen Amtspflichten zu beauftragen, [und dies] führt dazu, dass sich das Mündel in einem gefährlichen Zustand befindet;	(2) The performance of official duties of guardianship is neglected, or the performance of the official duties of guardianship are impossible, and they refuse to delegate part or all of the guardianship official duties to others causing danger for the ward;
（三）实施严重侵害被监护人合法权益的其他行为的。	3. andere Handlungen, die die legalen Rechte und Interessen des Mündels erheblich verletzen, werden vorgenommen.	(3) Perform other acts that seriously infringe the legal rights and interests of the ward.
本条规定的有关个人和组织包括：其他依法具有监护资格的人，居民委员会、村民委员会、学校、医疗机构、妇女联合会、残疾人联合会、未成年人保护组织、依法设立的老年人组织、民政部门等。	Die in diesem Paragraphen bestimmten betreffenden Einzelpersonen und Organisationen umfassen: andere Personen, die nach dem Recht die Befähigung zur Vormundschaft besitzen, Einwohnerkomitees, Dorfbewohnerkomitees, Lehranstalten, Gesundheitseinrichtungen, Frauenverbände, Behindertenverbände, Organisationen für den Schutz Minderjähriger, nach dem Recht errichtete Seniorenorganisationen und Abteilungen für Zivilangelegenheiten.	The concerned individuals or organisations mentioned in this Section include: other persons that are legally qualified for guardianship, residents committees, villagers committees, schools, medical institutions, women's federations, associations of persons with disabilities, minors protection organisations, elderly organisations duly established, and civil affairs authorities.

前款规定的个人和民政部门以外的组织未及时向人民法院申请撤销监护人资格的，民政部门应当向人民法院申请。	Wenn die im vorherigen Absatz bestimmten Einzelpersonen oder Organisationen außer der Abteilung für Zivilangelegenheiten nicht unverzüglich beim Volksgericht die Aufhebung der Befähigung zum Vormund beantragen, muss die Abteilung für Zivilangelegenheiten [dies] beim Volksgericht beantragen.	If individuals and organisations other than civil affairs authorities specified in the preceding clause fail to timely file a petition to a people's court for disqualification of guardianship, the civil affairs authorities shall do so instead.
第三十七条　依法负担被监护人抚养费、赡养费、扶养费的父母、子女、配偶等，被人民法院撤销监护人资格后，应当继续履行负担的义务。	**§ 37 [Fortbestehen von Unterhaltspflichten nach Aufhebung der Vormundschaft]** Eltern, Kinder [oder] Ehegatten, die nach dem Recht Kindesunterhalt, Elternunterhalt [oder] Ehegattenunterhalt für das Mündel tragen, müssen die Erfüllung der zu tragenden Pflicht fortsetzen, nachdem [ihre] Befähigung zum Vormund vom Volksgericht aufgehoben wurde.	**Section 37** Parents, offspring, or spouse providing maintenance for the child, parent, or spouse according to the law for the ward shall continue to perform their obligations after having been disqualified from guardianship.
第三十八条　被监护人的父母或者子女被人民法院撤销监护人资格后，除对被监护人实施故意犯罪的外，确有悔改表现的，经其申请，人民法院可以在尊重被监护人真实意愿的前提下，视情况恢复其监护人资格，人民法院指定的监护人与被监护人的监护关系同时终止。	**§ 38 [Wiederherstellung der Vormundschaft]** Wenn, nachdem die Befähigung zum Vormund der Eltern oder Kinder des Vormunds vom Volksgericht aufgehoben wurde, außer wenn gegenüber dem Mündel eine vorsätzliche Straftat begangen wurde, [der ursprüngliche Vormund] seine Reue tatsächlich zum Ausdruck bringt, kann das Volksgericht auf dessen Antrag, unter der Bedingung, dass es den wahren Willen des Mündels respektiert, unter Beachtung der Situation dessen Befähigung zum Vormund wiederherstellen; das Vormundschaftsverhältnis zwischen dem vom Volksgericht bestimmten Vormund und dem Mündel endet gleichzeitig.	**Section 38** If the parents or offspring of a ward show true repentance after disqualification from guardianship by a people's court, unless a deliberate offence has been committed to the ward, upon their request, the people's court may reinstate the guardianship qualification as appropriate under the condition of respecting the true will of the ward; the guardianship relationship between the guardian appointed by the people's court and the ward is terminated simultaneously.
第三十九条　有下列情形之一的，监护关系终止：	**§ 39 [Beendigung der Vormundschaft]** Wenn einer der folgenden Umstände vorliegt, endet das Vormundschaftsverhältnis:	**Section 39** Under any of the following circumstances, the guardianship relationship terminates:

（一）被监护人取得或者恢复完全民事行为能力； （二）监护人丧失监护能力；	1. das Mündel erlangt seine vollständige Zivilgeschäftsfähigkeit oder diese wird wieder hergestellt; 2. der Vormund verliert die Vormundschaftsfähigkeit;	(1) The ward obtains or reinstates full contractual capacity; (2) The guardian loses the guardianship competence;
（三）被监护人或者监护人死亡； （四）人民法院认定监护关系终止的其他情形。监护关系终止后，被监护人仍然需要监护的，应当依法另行确定监护人。	3. das Mündel oder der Vormund sterben; 4. das Volksgericht stellt andere Umstände der Beendigung des Vormundschaftsverhältnisses fest. Benötigt das Mündel nach Beendigung der Vormundschaftsbeziehung weiterhin eine Vormundschaft, muss nach dem Recht ein anderer Vormund festgelegt werden.	(3) Either the ward or the guardian dies; (4) The people's court identifies other circumstances of the termination of the guardianship relationship. Another guardian shall be determined in accordance with the law after termination of guardianship if the ward still needs guardianship.
第三节　宣告失踪和宣告死亡	**3. Abschnitt: Verschollenheitserklärung und Todeserklärung**	**Subchapter 3 Declarations of Disappearance and Death**
第四十条　自然人下落不明满二年的，利害关系人可以向人民法院申请宣告该自然人为失踪人。	**§ 40 [Verschollenheitserklärung; vgl. § 20 AGZR]** Ist der Verbleib einer natürlichen Person seit vollen zwei Jahren unklar, so kann ein Interessierter beim Volksgericht beantragen, dass diese natürliche Person zum Verschollenen erklärt wird.	**Section 40** If the whereabouts of a natural person have been unknown for two years, an interested person may apply to a people's court fora declaration of disappearance.
第四十一条　自然人下落不明的时间从其失去音讯之日起计算。战争期间下落不明的，下落不明的时间自战争结束之日或者有关机关确定的下落不明之日起计算。	**§ 41 [Zeitpunkt des unklaren Verbleibs; vgl. § 20 Abs. 2 AGZR]** Die Zeit des unklaren Verbleibs einer natürlichen Person wird vom Tag des Abbruchs des Kontakts[21] mit ihr an gerechnet. Wird der Verbleib in Kriegszeiten unklar, so wird die Zeit des unklaren Verbleibs ab dem Tag des Kriegsendes oder dem von den	**Section 41** The time period of the unknown whereabouts of a natural person shall be calculated from the day of loss of contact. If the whereabouts remain unclear in time of war, such time period shall be calculated from the day of the end of war or from the day of the

21 Wörtlich: „Verlust der Nachrichten“.

	betreffenden Behörden festgelegten Tag des unklaren Verbleibs an gerechnet.	natural person's unknown whereabouts as specified by the relevant authorities
第四十二条　失踪人的财产由其配偶、成年子女、父母或者其他愿意担任财产代管人的人代管。	**§ 42 [Vermögensverwaltung; vgl. § 21 Abs. 1 AGZR]** Das Vermögen des Verschollenen wird von seinem Ehepartner, volljährigen Kindern, Eltern oder anderen Personen, die als Vermögensverwalter[22] fungieren wollen, verwaltet[23].	**Section 42** The estate of the missing person shall be administered by their spouse, adult offspring, parents, or other persons willing to serve as custodian of the property.
代管有争议，没有前款规定的人，或者前款规定的人无代管能力的，由人民法院指定的人代管。	Bei Streit über die Verwaltung, wenn es keine der im vorigen Absatz bestimmten Personen gibt, oder wenn die im vorigen Absatz bestimmten Personen nicht die Fähigkeit zur Verwaltung haben, wird [das Vermögen] von einer vom Volksgericht bestimmten Person verwaltet.	If the administration of the assets is disputed, the assets shall be administered by a person determined by the people's court absent any persons as specified in the prior Subchapter, or if the persons specified in the prior paragraph lack the capability of administration.
第四十三条　财产代管人应当妥善管理失踪人的财产，维护其财产权益。	**§ 43 [Grundsätze der Vermögensverwaltung; Haftung; vgl. § 21 Abs. 2 AGZR]** Der Vermögensverwalter muss das Vermögen des Verschollenen zweckmäßig verwalten [und] seine Vermögensrechte und Interessen wahren.	**Section 43** The custodian of the estate of a missing person shall properly manage the assets and preserve the property rights and interests of the missing person.
失踪人所欠税款、债务和应付的其他费用，由财产代管人从失踪人的财产中支付。	Die vom Verschollenen geschuldeten Steuern, Verbindlichkeiten und zu zahlenden sonstigen Ausgaben werden vom Vermögensverwalter aus dem Vermögen des Verschollenen bezahlt.	Any taxes, liabilities, and other expenses owed by the missing person shall be paid by the custodian of the assets of the missing person.

22 Wörtlich: „vertretender Vermögensverwalter".
23 Wörtlich: „vertretend verwaltet".

财产代管人因故意或者重大过失造成失踪人财产损失的，应当承担赔偿责任。	Wenn der Vermögensverwalter vorsätzlich oder grob fahrlässig das Vermögen des Verschollenen schädigt, muss er die Schadensersatzhaftung tragen.	If the custodian of the estate causes damage to the property of the missing person due to intentional or gross negligence, the custodian shall be liable for compensation.
第四十四条　财产代管人不履行代管职责、侵害失踪人财产权益或者丧失代管能力的，失踪人的利害关系人可以向人民法院申请变更财产代管人。	**§ 44 [Auswechslung des Vermögensverwalters]** Wenn der Vermögensverwalter die Amtspflichten der Verwaltung nicht erfüllt, die Vermögensrechte und interessen des Verschollenen verletzt oder die Fähigkeit zur Verwaltung verliert, können Interessierte des Verschollenen beim Volksgericht die Auswechslung[24] des Vermögensverwalters beantragen.	**Section 44** If the custodian of the assets does not perform the custodian duties, infringes the property rights or interests of the missing person, or loses custodian competence, interested persons of the missing person may apply to a people's court for the replacement of the property custodian.
财产代管人有正当理由的，可以向人民法院申请变更财产代管人。	Wenn der Vermögensverwalter einen rechtfertigenden Grund hat, kann er beim Volksgericht die Auswechslung[25] des Vermögensverwalters beantragen.	The property custodian may apply to a people's court with due cause for the replacement of custodian.
人民法院变更财产代管人的，变更后的财产代管人有权要求原财产代管人及时移交有关财产并报告财产代管情况。	Wenn das Volksgericht den Vermögensverwalter austauscht, ist der Vermögensverwalter nach dem Austausch berechtigt, vom ursprünglichen Vermögensverwalter zu verlangen, unverzüglich das betreffende Vermögen zu übergeben und über die Situation der Vermögensverwaltung zu berichten.	If the people's court replaces the property custodian after the replacement, the custodian may require the former custodian to promptly hand over relevant assets and report about the situation of the asset administration.
第四十五条　失踪人重新出现，经本人或者利害关系人申请，人民法院应当撤销失踪宣告。	**§ 45 [Aufhebung der Verschollenheitserklärung; vgl. § 22 AGZR]** Taucht der Verschollene wieder auf, so muss das Volksgericht auf Antrag des Betroffenen oder eines Interessierten die Verschollenheitserklärung aufheben.	**Section 45** If the missing persons reappears, the people's court shall revoke the declaration of disappearance upon the application of the person themselves or an interested person.

---

24 Wörtlich: „Änderung".
25 Wörtlich: „Änderung".

失踪人重新出现，有权要求财产代管人及时移交有关财产并报告财产代管情况。

Wenn der Verschollene wieder auftaucht, ist er berechtigt, vom Vermögensverwalter zu verlangen, unverzüglich das betreffende Vermögen zu übergeben und über die Situation der Vermögensverwaltung zu berichten.

If the missing person reappears, they have the right to require the property custodian to promptly hand over the assets and to report about the asset administration.

第四十六条　自然人有下列情形之一的，利害关系人可以向人民法院申请宣告该自然人死亡：

（一）下落不明满四年；

（二）因意外事件，下落不明满二年。

§ 46 [Todeserklärung; vgl. § 23 AGZR] Wenn bei einer natürlichen Person einer der folgenden Umstände vorliegt, kann ein Interessierter beim Volksgericht beantragen, dass diese natürliche Person für tot erklärt wird:

1. der Verbleib ist seit vollen vier Jahren unklar;
2. aufgrund eines unvorhergesehenen Ereignisses ist der Verbleib seit vollen zwei Jahren unklar.

Section 46 If in relation to a natural person one of the following circumstances applies, an interested person may apply to a people's court to declare the natural person dead:

(1) the whereabouts have remained unclear for four whole years;

(2) due to an unforeseen event the whereabouts have remained unclear for two whole years.

因意外事件下落不明，经有关机关证明该自然人不可能生存的，申请宣告死亡不受二年时间的限制。

Wenn der Verbleib aufgrund eines unvorhergesehenen Ereignisses unklar ist [und] den betreffenden Behörden bewiesen wurde, dass ein Überleben dieser natürlichen Person nicht möglich ist, so gilt für die Beantragung der Todeserklärung nicht die zeitliche Beschränkung von zwei Jahren.

If a natural person's whereabouts are unclear due to an unforeseen event and it has been proved to the relevant authorities that the survival of this natural person is impossible, the temporal restriction of two years is inapplicable to the application for the declaration of death.

第四十七条　对同一自然人，有的利害关系人申请宣告死亡，有的利害关系人申请宣告失踪，符合本法规定的宣告死亡条件的，人民法院应当宣告死亡。

§ 47 [Vorrang der Todeserklärung; vgl. Ziffer 29 AGZR-Ansichten] Wenn hinsichtlich derselben natürlichen Person von einigen Interessierten die Todeserklärung beantragt, und von einigen Interessierten die Verschollenheitserklärung beantragt wird, muss das Volksgericht für tot erklären, wenn die Voraussetzungen für die Todeserklärungen vorliegen.

Section 47 A people's court must declare the death of a natural person if some interested persons apply for the declaration of death of the same natural person while other interested persons apply for the declaration of disappearance, provided that the requirements for the declarations of death are satisfied.

第四十八条　被宣告死亡的人，人民法院宣告死亡的判决作出之日视为其死亡的日期；因意外事件下落不明宣告死亡的，意外事件发生之日视为其死亡的日期。	**§ 48 [Todestag; vgl. Ziffer 36 AGZR-Ansichten]** Bei einer für tot erklärten Person gilt als deren Todestag der Tag, an dem das Volksgericht das Urteil über die Todeserklärung erlassen hat; wurde [eine Person], deren Verbleib aufgrund eines unvorhergesehenen Ereignisses unklar ist, für tot erklärt, so gilt als ihr Todestag der Tag, an dem das unvorhergesehene Ereignis stattgefunden hat.	**Section 48** The date of death of a person declared dead shall be the day the people's court delivered the judgment on the declaration of death; if a person whose whereabouts were unclear due to an unforeseen event was declared dead, the date of death shall be the day the unforeseen event happened.
第四十九条　自然人被宣告死亡但是并未死亡的，不影响该自然人在被宣告死亡期间实施的民事法律行为的效力。	**§ 49 [Wirksamkeit von Rechtsgeschäften nach Todeserklärung; vgl. § 24 Abs. 2 AGZR]** Wurde eine natürliche Person für tot erklärt, aber war sie nicht verstorben, so beeinflusst dies nicht die Wirksamkeit von Rechtsgeschäften, die diese natürliche Person während des Zeitraums der Todeserklärung vorgenommen hat.	**Section 49** If a natural person has been declared dead but has not died, this shall not affect the validity of legal transactions performed by the natural person during the period of the declaration of death.
第五十条　被宣告死亡的人重新出现，经本人或者利害关系人申请，人民法院应当撤销死亡宣告。	**§ 50 [Aufhebung der Todeserklärung; vgl. § 24 Abs. 1 AGZR]** Taucht eine für tot erklärte Person wieder auf, so muss das Volksgericht auf Antrag des Betroffenen oder eines Interessierten die Todeserklärung aufheben.	**Section 50** If a person who has been declared dead reappears the people's court shall revoke the declaration of death upon the application of the person concerned or an interested person.
第五十一条　被宣告死亡的人的婚姻关系，自死亡宣告之日起消灭。死亡宣告被撤销的，婚姻关系自撤销死亡宣告之日起自行恢复，但是其配偶再婚或者向婚姻登记机关书面声明不愿意恢复的除外。	**§ 51 [Ehebeziehungen bei Todeserklärung; vgl. Ziffer 37 AGZR-Ansichten]** Der Ehebund einer für tot erklärten Person erlischt mit dem Tag der Todeserklärung. Wird die Todeserklärung aufgehoben, wird der Ehebund vom Tag der Aufhebung der Todeserklärung an automatisch wiederhergestellt, außer ihr Ehepartner hat erneut geheiratet oder erklärt schriftlich gegenüber der Eheregisterbehörde, dass sie die Wiederherstellung nicht wünscht.	**Section 51** The marriage of the person who has been declared dead shall terminate with effect from the date of the declaration of death. If the declaration of death is revoked, the marriage is automatically restored with effect from the date of the revocation of the declaration of death, except the spouse remarried or by written notice to the marriage

		registration authority, declares the reluctance to restore the marriage.
第五十二条　被宣告死亡的人在被宣告死亡期间，其子女被他人依法收养的，在死亡宣告被撤销后，不得以未经本人同意为由主张收养关系无效。	**§ 52 [Eltern-Kind-Beziehungen bei Aufhebung der Todeserklärung; vgl. Ziffer 38 AGZR-Ansichten]** Wenn das Kind einer für tot erklärten Person während des Zeitraums der Todeserklärung von einem Anderen nach dem Recht adoptiert wurde, darf nach der Aufhebung der Todeserklärung nicht aus dem Grund, dass [die Adoption] ohne das Einverständnis des Betroffenen, [vorgenommen wurde] geltend gemacht werden, die Adoptionsbeziehung sei unwirksam.	**Section 52** If the child of a person declared dead was adopted by another during the time of the declaration of death according to the law, after the revocation of the declaration of death the ineffectiveness of the adoption relationship cannot be claimed due to the lack of consent of the concerned person.
第五十三条　被撤销死亡宣告的人有权请求依照继承法取得其财产的民事主体返还财产。无法返还的，应当给予适当补偿。	**§ 53 [Vermögensbeziehungen bei Aufhebung der Todeserklärung; vgl. § 25 AGZR]** Eine Person, deren Todeserklärung aufgehoben wurde, ist berechtigt zu verlangen, dass ein Zivilrechtssubjekt, das gemäß dem Erbgesetz ihr Vermögen erlangt hat, das Vermögen zurückgibt. Kann es nicht zurückgegeben werden, muss es einen angemessenen Ausgleich leisten.	**Section 53** A person whose declaration of death has been revoked shall be entitled to reclaim assets from a civil legal subject who obtained it according to inheritance law. If it cannot be returned, they must make an appropriate compensation.
利害关系人隐瞒真实情况，致使他人被宣告死亡取得其财产的，除应当返还财产外，还应当对由此造成的损失承担赔偿责任。	Hat ein Interessierter die wahre Situation verheimlicht, so dass ein Anderer für tot erklärt wurde [und der Interessierte] dessen Vermögen erlangt hat, so muss er neben der Rückgabe des Vermögens auch für den hierdurch verursachten Schaden die Schadensersatzhaftung tragen.	If an interested person concealed the truth causing another person to be declared dead to obtain their assets, they shall return the assets and be liable for the damage caused.
第四节　个体工商户和农村承包经营户	**4. Abschnitt: Einzelgewerbetreibende und ländliche Übernahmebetreiber**	**Subchapter 4 Individual Businesses and Lease Holding Farm Households**

第五十四条　自然人从事工商业经营，经依法登记，为个体工商户。个体工商户可以起字号。	**§ 54 [Einzelgewerbetreibende; Firma; vgl. § 26 AGZR]** Eine natürliche Person, die ein Industrie- und Handelsgewerbe betreibt, ist mit Eintragung nach dem Recht ein Einzelgewerbetreibender. Ein Einzelgewerbetreibender kann eine Firma verwenden.	**Section 54** A natural person operating an industrial or commercial business upon registration according to the law is an individual trader. An individual trader may use a trade name.
第五十五条　农村集体经济组织的成员，依法取得农村土地承包经营权，从事家庭承包经营的，为农村承包经营户。	**§ 55 [Ländliche Übernahmebetreiber; vgl. § 27 AGZR]** Mitglieder einer ländlichen kollektiven Wirtschaftsorganisation, die das Recht zur übernommenen Bewirtschaftung von ländlichen Grundstücken nach dem Recht erlangt haben [und] als Familie die übernommene Bewirtschaftung betreiben, sind ländliche Übernahmebetreiber.	**Section 55** Members of a rural collective economic organisation who obtained the right to rural land contract management according to the law and engage in household contract management, are rural contract management households.
第五十六条　个体工商户的债务，个人经营的，以个人财产承担；家庭经营的，以家庭财产承担；无法区分的，以家庭财产承担。	**§ 56 [Haftung Einzelgewerbetreibender und ländlicher Übernahmebetreiber; vgl. § 29 AGZR]** Verbindlichkeiten eines Einzelgewerbetreibenden werden, wenn eine Einzelperson [das Gewerbe] betreibt, mit dem Vermögen der Einzelperson getragen; wenn es von einer Familie betrieben wird, werden sie mit dem Familienvermögen getragen; wenn [dies] nicht unterschieden werden kann, werden sie mit dem Familienvermögen getragen.	**Section 56** If an individual operates the business, liabilities of individual traders shall be borne by the personal assets; if the household operates the business, they shall be borne by the household assets; if the assets cannot be distinguished, they shall be borne by the household assets.
农村承包经营户的债务，以从事农村土地承包经营的农户财产承担；事实上由农户部分成员经营的，以该部分成员的财产承担。	Verbindlichkeiten von ländlichen Übernahmebetreibern werden mit dem Vermögen des bäuerlichen Haushalts getragen, der die übernommene Bewirtschaftung von ländlichen Grundstücken betreibt; wird [das Land] tatsächlich von einem Teil der Mitglieder des bäuerlichen	Liabilities of rural contract management households shall be borne by the assets of the rural household that engages in the rural land contract management; if the business is in fact operated by part of the members of the rural household, the liabilities shall be borne

	Haushalts bewirtschaftet, werden [die Verbindlichkeiten] mit dem Vermögen dieses Teils der Mitglieder getragen.	by the assets of this part of the rural household members.
第三章　法　人	**3. Kapitel: Juristische Personen**	**Chapter III Legal Entities**
第一节　一般规定	**1. Abschnitt: Allgemeine Bestimmungen**	**Subchapter 1 General Stipulations**
第五十七条　法人是具有民事权利能力和民事行为能力，依法独立享有民事权利和承担民事义务的组织。	**§ 57 [Definition „juristische Person"; vgl. § 36 Abs. 1 AGZR]** Eine juristische Person ist eine Organisation, die Zivilrechtsfähigkeit und Zivilgeschäftsfähigkeit besitzt [und] nach dem Recht eigenständig Zivilrechte genießt und zivile Pflichten trägt.	**Section 57** A legal entity is an organisation that has legal capacity and contractual capacity, and independently enjoys civil rights and bears civil obligations according to the law.
第五十八条　法人应当依法成立。	**§ 58 [Zustandekommen juristischer Personen; vgl. § 37 AGZR]** Eine juristische Person muss nach dem Recht zustande gekommen sein.	**Section 58** A legal entity shall be established according to the law.
法人应当有自己的名称、组织机构、住所、财产或者经费。法人成立的具体条件和程序，依照法律、行政法规的规定。	Eine juristische Person muss eine eigene Bezeichnung, Organisationsorgane, einen Sitz[26] [und] Vermögen oder [Mittel für] Regelaufwendungen haben. Für die konkreten Voraussetzungen und Verfahren für das Zustandekommen einer juristischen Person gelten die Bestimmungen in Gesetzen [und] Verwaltungsrechtsnormen.	A legal entity must have its own name, bodies of organisation, headquarters, and assets or resources for regular expenses. The legal provisions and administrative regulations are applicable to the specific requirements and procedures for the establishment of legal entities.
设立法人，法律、行政法规规定须经有关机关批准的，依照其规定。	Bestimmen Gesetze [oder] Verwaltungsrechtsnormen, dass die Errichtung einer juristischen Person von den betreffenden Behörden genehmigt sein muss, gelten diese Bestimmungen.	The establishment of a legal entity shall be subject to approval by the relevant authorities if required by laws and administrative regulations.

26 Wörtlich „Wohnsitz".

第五十九条　法人的民事权利能力和民事行为能力，从法人成立时产生，到法人终止时消灭。	**§ 59 [Rechts- und Geschäftsfähigkeit juristischer Personen; vgl. § 36 Abs. 2 AGZR]** Zivilrechtsfähigkeit und Zivilgeschäftsfähigkeit einer juristischen Person entstehen mit dem Zeitpunkt des Zustandekommens der juristischen Person und erlöschen mit der Beendigung der juristischen Person.	**Section 59** The legal capacity and contractual capacity of a legal entity shall arise with the establishment of the legal entity and terminate on the date of the termination of the legal entity.
第六十条　法人以其全部财产独立承担民事责任。	**§ 60 [Haftbarkeit juristischer Personen; vgl. § 48 AGZR]** Eine juristische Person trägt mit ihrem gesamten Vermögen eigenständig die zivile Haftung.	**Section 60** A legal entity shall independently assume civil liability with all its assets.
第六十一条　依照法律或者法人章程的规定，代表法人从事民事活动的负责人，为法人的法定代表人。	**§ 61 [Organschaftliche Vertretung; vgl. §§ 38, 43 AGZR]** Der Verantwortliche, der gemäß dem Gesetz oder der Satzung der juristischen Person in Repräsentation der juristischen Person Zivilaktivitäten unternimmt, ist der gesetzliche Repräsentant der juristischen Person.	**Section 61** The responsible person undertaking the civil activities as a legal agent of the legal entity according to the law or the Sections of Incorporation of the legal entity is the legal agent of the legal entity.
法定代表人以法人名义从事的民事活动，其法律后果由法人承受。	Unternimmt der gesetzliche Repräsentant im Namen der juristischen Person Zivilaktivitäten, so werden deren Rechtsfolgen von der juristischen Person getragen.	If the legal agent engages in civil activities in the name of the legal entity, the legal consequences shall be borne by the legal entity.
法人章程或者法人权力机构对法定代表人代表权的限制，不得对抗善意相对人。	Eine Beschränkung der Repräsentationsmacht des gesetzlichen Repräsentanten durch die Satzung der juristischen Person oder das Machtorgan der juristischen Person darf einem gutgläubigen Gegenüber nicht entgegengehalten werden.	Bona fide counterparties shall not be reproached with the restriction of the agency powers by the Sections of Incorporation of the legal entity or the governing body of the legal entity.
第六十二条　法定代表人因执行职务造成他人损害的，由法人承担民事责任。	**§ 62 [Haftung für gesetzliche Repräsentanten; vgl. § 43 AGZR]** Wenn der gesetzliche Repräsentant wegen der Ausführung von Amtsaufgaben eine Schädigung eines anderen verursacht, trägt die juristische Person die zivile Haftung.	**Section 62** If the legal agent causes damages due to performance of his duties, the legal entity shall bear the civil liability.

法人承担民事责任后，依照法律或者法人章程的规定，可以向有过错的法定代表人追偿。	Nachdem die juristische Person die zivile Haftung übernommen hat, kann sie gemäß dem Gesetz oder der Satzung der juristischen Person von dem schuldhaft [handelnden] gesetzlichen Repräsentanten Ausgleich verlangen.	After the legal entity has assumed civil liability, compensation may be sought from the legal agent for the culpable conduct according to the provisions of the law or the Sections of Incorporation of the legal entity.
第六十三条　法人以其主要办事机构所在地为住所。依法需要办理法人登记的，应当将主要办事机构所在地登记为住所。	**§ 63 [Sitz juristischer Personen; vgl. § 39 AGZR]** Sitz einer juristischen Person ist der Belegenheitsort ihres Hauptverwaltungsorgans. Ist es nach dem Gesetz notwendig, eine Eintragung der juristischen Person vorzunehmen, so muss als Sitz der Belegenheitsort des Hauptverwaltungsorgans eingetragen werden.	**Section 63** The headquarters of a legal entity is the place of the principal office. If it is necessary according to the law to perform the registration of a legal entity, the principal office shall be registered as the headquarters.
第六十四条　法人存续期间登记事项发生变化的，应当依法向登记机关申请变更登记。	**§ 64 [Eintragung von Änderungen bei juristischen Personen; vgl. § 44 AGZR]** Wenn während des Bestehens einer juristischen Person Änderungen im Hinblick auf Eintragungsgegenstände eintreten, muss nach dem Recht bei der Registerbehörde eine Änderungseintragung beantragt werden.	**Section 64** If the registration items change during the existence of a legal entity, an application to the registration authority for change of registration shall be made according to the law.
第六十五条　法人的实际情况与登记的事项不一致的，不得对抗善意相对人。	**§ 65 [Öffentlicher Glaube des Registers]** Ist die tatsächliche Situation einer juristischen Person nicht identisch mit den eingetragenen Gegenständen, darf [dies] nicht einem gutgläubigen Gegenüber entgegengehalten werden.	**Section 65** If the actual situation of a legal entity is inconsistent with the registered items, a bona fide counterparty shall not be reproached with this.
第六十六条　登记机关应当依法及时公示法人登记的有关信息。	**§ 66 [Registerpublizität]** Die Registerbehörde muss Informationen, welche die Eintragung der juristischen Person betreffen, nach dem Recht unverzüglich bekanntgeben.	**Section 66** The registration authority shall promptly announce information relating to the registration of the legal entity according to the law.

第六十七条　法人合并的，其权利和义务由合并后的法人享有和承担。	**§ 67 [Vereinigung und Spaltung juristischer Personen; vgl. § 44 Abs. 2 AGZR]** Wenn sich juristische Personen vereinigen, genießt die juristische Person nach der Vereinigung deren Rechte und trägt deren Pflichten.	**Section 67** When legal entities merge after the merger, the legal entity enjoys their rights and takes their obligations.
法人分立的，其权利和义务由分立后的法人享有连带债权，承担连带债务，但是债权人和债务人另有约定的除外。	Spaltet sich eine juristische Person, genießen die juristischen Personen nach der Spaltung deren Rechte in Gesamtgläubigerschaft und tragen deren Pflichten als Gesamtschuld, es sei denn Gläubiger und Schuldner haben etwas anderes vereinbart.	If a legal entity splits, after the division the legal entities enjoy their rights and take their obligations jointly and severally, unless otherwise stipulated by the creditor and the debtor.
第六十八条　有下列原因之一并依法完成清算、注销登记的，法人终止：	**§ 68 [Beendigung juristischer Personen; vgl. § 45 AGZR]** Wenn einer der folgenden Umstände vorliegt und nach dem Recht die Abwicklung [und] Löschung der Eintragung der juristischen Person vollendet wurde, endet die juristische Person:	**Section 68** If under any of the following circumstances and according to the law the liquidation and deletion of the registration of the legal entity was completed, the legal entity shall terminate:
（一）法人解散；	1. die juristische Person wurde aufgelöst;	(1) The legal entity has dissolved;
（二）法人被宣告破产；	2. der Konkurs der juristischen Person wurde erklärt;	(2) The legal entity is declared bankrupt;
（三）法律规定的其他原因。	3. andere gesetzlich bestimmte Gründe.	(3) Other reasons prescribed by law.
法人终止，法律、行政法规规定须经有关机关批准的，依照其规定。	Bestimmen Gesetze [oder] Verwaltungsrechtsnormen, dass die Beendigung einer juristischen Person von der betreffenden Behörde genehmigt sein muss, gelten diese Bestimmungen.	If provisions of law or administrative regulations stipulate that the termination of a legal entity must be approved by the relevant authority, these stipulations shall apply.
第六十九条　有下列情形之一的，法人解散：	**§ 69 [Auflösung juristischer Personen; vgl. § 45 AGZR]** Wenn einer der folgenden Umstände vorliegt, wird eine juristische Person aufgelöst:	**Section 69** Under any of the following circumstances a legal entity is dissolved:
（一）法人章程规定的存续期间届满或者法人章程规定的其他解散事由出现；	1. Die in der Satzung der juristischen Person bestimmte Dauer des Bestehens ist abgelaufen oder ein anderer in der Satzung der juristischen Person bestimmter Auflösungsgrund ist eingetreten;	(1) The existence of the legal entity provided by the Sections of Incorporation has expired, or another reason for termination provided by the Sections of Incorporation of the legal entity has occurred;

（二）法人的权力机构决议解散；	2. das Machtorgan beschließt die Auflösung;	(2) The governing body decides on the dissolution;
（三）因法人合并或者分立需要解散；	3. wegen der Vereinigung oder Spaltung der juristischen Person ist die Auflösung notwendig;	(3) Due to the merger or division of the legal entity, the dissolution is necessary;
（四）法人依法被吊销营业执照、登记证书，被责令关闭或者被撤销；	4. der juristischen Person wird nach dem Recht der Gewerbeschein [oder] die Eintragungsurkunde entzogen, [ihre] Schließung wird angeordnet oder [sie] wird aufgehoben;	(4) The business licence or registration certificate has been revoked, or the legal entity has been ordered to be closed down or cancelled;
（五）法律规定的其他情形。	5. andere gesetzlich bestimmte Umstände.	(5) Other circumstances prescribed by law.
第七十条　法人解散的，除合并或者分立的情形外，清算义务人应当及时组成清算组进行清算。	**§ 70 [Abwicklung; vgl. § 47 AGZR]** Wird eine juristische Person aufgrund anderer Umstände als einer Spaltung oder Vereinigung aufgelöst, müssen die zur Abwicklung Verpflichteten unverzüglich eine Abwicklungsgruppe bilden [und] die Abwicklung durchführen.	**Section 70** If a legal entity dissolves due to other circumstances than division or merger, the persons responsible for liquidation shall promptly form a liquidation group and perform liquidation.
法人的董事、理事等执行机构或者决策机构的成员为清算义务人。法律、行政法规另有规定的，依照其规定。	Die Mitglieder des Exekutivorgans oder des Entscheidungsorgans der juristischen Person wie etwa Vorstands [oder] Direktorium sind die zur Abwicklung Verpflichteten. Enthalten Gesetze oder Verwaltungsrechtsnormen [27] anderweitige Bestimmungen, so gelten diese Bestimmungen.	The persons responsible for liquidation are the members of the executive or the decision-making body of the legal entity as, for instance, the executive board or the board of directors, unless otherwise provided by law or administrative regulations.
清算义务人未及时履行清算义务，造成损害的，应当承担民事责任；主管机关或者利害关系人可以申请	Wenn die zur Abwicklung Verpflichteten die Abwicklungspflicht nicht unverzüglich ausführen, tragen sie die zivile Haftung für [hierdurch] herbeigeführte Schäden;	If the persons responsible for liquidation fail to promptly perform the liquidation obligation, they are liable for any damages caused

27 Verwaltungsrechtsnormen bezeichnen gemäß § 65 Gesetzgebungsgesetz der Volksrepublik China [中华人民共和国立法法] vom 15.3.2000 in der Fassung vom 15.3.2015; chinesisch-deutsch in: ZChinR 2015, S. 259 ff., ausschließlich solche Rechtsakte, die der Staatsrat erlässt.

人民法院指定有关人员组成清算组进行清算。	die zuständige Behörde oder Interessierte können beantragen, dass das Volksgericht betreffende Personen als Mitglieder der Abwicklungsgruppe zur Durchführung der Abwicklung bestimmt.	thereby; the competent authority or the interested party may apply to the People's Court for designating the respective persons to form a liquidation group for the performance of the liquidation.
第七十一条　法人的清算程序和清算组职权，依照有关法律的规定；没有规定的，参照适用公司法的有关规定。	**§ 71 [Abwicklungsverfahren]** Das Abwicklungsverfahren und die Amtsbefugnisse der Abwicklungsgruppe bei juristischen Personen, richtet sich nach den betreffenden gesetzlichen Bestimmungen; gibt es keine Bestimmungen, werden die einschlägigen Bestimmungen des Gesellschaftsgesetzes angewandt.	**Section 71** The liquidation procedures and the competence of the liquidation group of legal entities shall be in accordance with the relevant legal provisions; if there is no provision, the relevant provisions of the applicable company law shall be applied.
第七十二条　清算期间法人存续，但是不得从事与清算无关的活动。	**§ 72 [Wirkung der Abwicklung; vgl. § 40, 46 AGZR]** Während der Zeit der Abwicklung besteht die juristische Person fort, [sie] darf jedoch keine Geschäfte tätigen, die nicht die Abwicklung betreffen.	**Section 72** During the period of liquidation the legal entity shall continue to exist, but shall not conduct business that is not related to liquidation.
法人清算后的剩余财产，根据法人章程的规定或者法人权力机构的决议处理。法律另有规定的，依照其规定。	Nach der Abwicklung der juristischen Person wird mit dem Restvermögen gemäß der Satzung der juristischen Person oder dem Beschluss des Machtorgans verfahren. Enthalten Gesetze anderweitige Bestimmungen, so gelten diese Bestimmungen.	The Sections of Incorporation of the legal entity or the order of the governing body regulates how to proceed with the remaining assets after the liquidation of the legal entity, unless otherwise provided by law.
清算结束并完成法人注销登记时，法人终止；依法不需要办理法人登记的，清算结束时，法人终止。	Wenn die Abwicklung beendet und die Registrierung der Löschung der juristischen Person abgeschlossen ist, endet die juristische Person; ist für die juristische Person die Vornahme einer Registrierung nach dem Recht nicht erforderlich, endet die juristische Person mit der Beendigung der Abwicklung.	The legal entity terminates with the completion of the liquidation and the registration of deletion of the legal entity; if the registration is not necessary according to the law, the legal entity shall terminate with the termination of the liquidation.

第七十三条　法人被宣告破产的，依法进行破产清算并完成法人注销登记时，法人终止。	**§ 73 [Auflösung wegen Konkurses; vgl. §§ 46, 47 AGZR]** Wurde der Konkurs einer juristischen Person erklärt, so ist die juristische Person beendet, wenn die Konkursabwicklung dem Recht gemäß durchgeführt wurde und die Registrierung der Löschung der juristischen Person vollendet ist.	**Section 73** If a legal entity is declared bankrupt, the legal entity terminates when the bankruptcy liquidation has been performed according to the law and the registration of deletion of the legal entity is completed.
第七十四条　法人可以依法设立分支机构。法律、行政法规规定分支机构应当登记的，依照其规定。	**§ 74 [Zweigstellen juristischer Personen]** Juristische Personen können nach dem Recht Zweigstellen errichten. Bestimmen Gesetze oder Verwaltungsrechtsnormen, dass für Zweigstellen eine Registrierung vorgenommen werden muss, so gelten diese Bestimmungen.	**Section 74** Legal entities may establish branches in accordance with the law. Such branches shall register if stipulated by laws or administrative regulations.
分支机构以自己的名义从事民事活动，产生的民事责任由法人承担；也可以先以该分支机构管理的财产承担，不足以承担的，由法人承担。	Tätigt eine Zweigstelle im eigenen Namen Zivilaktivitäten, so wird die daraus entstehende zivile Haftung von der juristischen Person getragen; sie kann auch vorrangig mit dem von dieser Zweigstelle verwalteten Vermögen getragen werden; ist dieses zur Tragung [der Haftung] nicht ausreichend, so trägt sie die juristische Person.	If a branch conducts civil activities under their own name, the legal entity is liable for any damage caused thereby; it may also be covered primarily with the assets managed by this branch; if it is not sufficient to bear the liability, it is borne by the legal entity.
第七十五条　设立人为设立法人从事的民事活动，其法律后果由法人承受；法人未成立的，其法律后果由设立人承受，设立人为二人以上的，享有连带债权，承担连带债务。	**§ 75 [Gründerhaftung]** Tätigt ein Gründer Zivilaktivitäten zur Errichtung einer juristischen Person, so werden deren rechtliche Folgen von der juristischen Person getragen; kommt die juristische Person nicht zustande, so trägt der Gründer die rechtlichen Folgen; zwei oder mehr Gründer genießen Rechte als Gesamtgläubiger und haften gesamtschuldnerisch.	**Section 75** If a founder performs civil activities for the establishment of a legal entity, the legal consequences shall be borne by the legal entity; if the legal entity is not established, the founder bears the legal consequences; two or more founders jointly and severally enjoy the rights and are jointly and severally liable.

设立人为设立法人以自己的名义从事民事活动产生的民事责任，第三人有权选择请求法人或者设立人承担。	Ergibt sich aus Zivilaktivitäten, die ein Gründer zur Errichtung einer juristischen Person im eigenen Namen tätigt, eine zivile Haftung, so ist der Dritte[28] befugt, nach seiner Wahl zu verlangen, dass entweder die juristische Person oder der Gründer [die Haftung] trägt.	If a civil liability arises from civil activities that a founder conducts for the establishment of a legal entity under their own name, the third party is authorised to require at his discretion that either the legal entity or the founder is liable.
第二节　营利法人	**2. Abschnitt: Gewinnorientierte juristische Personen**	**Subchapter 2 For-profit Legal Entities**
第七十六条　以取得利润并分配给股东等出资人为目的成立的法人，为营利法人。	**§ 76 [Definition „gewinnorientierte juristische Person"]** Eine gewinnorientierte juristische Person ist eine juristische Person, die zu dem Zwecke gegründet worden ist, Gewinne zu erzielen und an [ihre] Investoren[29] wie etwa Gesellschafter zu verteilen.	**Section 76** A for-profit legal entity is a legal entity that was established for the purpose of drawing profits and distributing them to their investors as, for instance, shareholders.
营利法人包括有限责任公司、股份有限公司和其他企业法人等。	Gewinnorientierte juristische Personen sind die Gesellschaft mit beschränkter Haftung, die Aktiengesellschaft und andere juristische Unternehmenspersonen.	For-profit legal entities are the limited liability company, the stock corporation, and other legal business entities.
第七十七条　营利法人经依法登记成立。	**§ 77 [Zustandekommen der gewinnorientierten juristische Person; vgl. § 41 AGZR]** Eine gewinnorientierte juristische Personen kommt durch Registrierung gemäß dem Recht zustande.	**Section 77** A for-profit legal entity is established by lawful registration.
第七十八条　依法设立的营利法人，由登记机关发给营利法人营业执	**§ 78 [Zeitpunkt des Zustandekommens; vgl. § 41 AGZR]** Einer in rechtmäßiger Weise errichteten ge-	**Section 78** The registration authority issues a business licence to a for-profit legal entity that has been lawfully established. The date

28 Gemeint ist der Haftungsgläubiger.

29 Im Original wird der Begriff 出资人 verwendet, der wie der Begriff 投资人 als „Investor" zu verstehen ist.

照。营业执照签发日期为营利法人的成立日期。	winnorientierten juristischen Person erteilt die Registerbehörde einen Gewerbeschein. Das Ausstellungsdatum des Gewerbescheins gilt als Datum des Zustandekommens der gewinnorientierten juristischen Person.	of issue of the business license is the date of establishment of the for-profit legal entity.
第七十九条　设立营利法人应当依法制定法人章程。	**§ 79 [Zwingende Satzung]** Bei der Errichtung einer gewinnorientierten juristischen Person muss eine Satzung für die juristische Person festgelegt werden.	**Section 79** Establishing a for-profit legal entity the Sections of Incorporation shall lawfully be determined.
第八十条　营利法人应当设权力机构。 权力机构行使修改法人章程，选举或者更换执行机构、监督机构成员，以及法人章程规定的其他职权。	**§ 80 [Machtorgan]** Eine gewinnorientierte juristische Person muss ein Machtorgan errichten. Das Machtorgan übt die Befugnis aus, die Satzung der juristischen Person zu ändern, die Mitglieder des Exekutivorgans oder des Überwachungsorgans auszuwählen oder auszutauschen sowie andere ihm in der Satzung der juristischen Person eingeräumte Befugnisse.	**Section 80** A for-profit legal entity shall set up a governing body. The governing body shall exercise the power to amend the Sections of Incorporation of the legal entity, vote for or change the members of the executive body or supervisory body, and other duties conferred to it by the Sections of Incorporation of the legal entity.
第八十一条　营利法人应当设执行机构。 执行机构行使召集权力机构会议，决定法人的经营计划和投资方案，决定法人内部管理机构的设置，以及法人章程规定的其他职权。	**§ 81 [Exekutivorgan]** Eine gewinnorientierte juristische Person muss ein Exekutivorgan errichten. Das Exekutivorgan übt [die Befugnis] aus, die Versammlung des Machtorgans einzuberufen, über die Geschäftsplanung und das Investitionskonzept zu entscheiden, über die Einrichtung eines internen Verwaltungsorgans der juristischen Person zu entscheiden sowie andere ihm in der Satzung der juristischen Person eingeräumte Amtsbefugnisse.	**Section 81** A for-profit legal entity shall establish an executive body. The executive body exercises the power to convene meetings of the governing body, determine the business plan and investment plan, determine the establishment of the internal administrative body of the legal entity, and other powers prescribed by the Sections of Incorporation of the legal entity.
执行机构为董事会或者执行董事的，董事长、执行董事或者经理按照法人章程的规定担任法定代表人；未设董事会或者执行董事的，法人	Sind der Vorstand oder der geschäftsführende Vorstand das Exekutivorgan, so fungiert gemäß den Bestimmungen der Satzung der juristischen Person der Vorstandsvorsitzende, der geschäftsführende Vorstand oder ein	If the executive body consists of the executive or the managing board of directors, the chairman of the executive board, the ex-

章程规定的主要负责人为其执行机构和法定代表人。	Manager als gesetzlicher Repräsentant; ist noch kein Vorstand oder geschäftsführender Vorstand aufgestellt, so ist der in der Satzung festgelegte Hauptverantwortliche Exekutivorgan und gesetzlicher Repräsentant.	ecutive directors or the managers shall be appointed legal representative; if no board of directors or executive directors have been appointed, the person mainly responsible as determined in the Sections of Incorporation is the executive body and legal representative.
第八十二条　营利法人设监事会或者监事等监督机构的，监督机构依法行使检查法人财务，监督执行机构成员、高级管理人员执行法人职务的行为，以及法人章程规定的其他职权。	**§ 82 [Überwachungsorgane]** Hat die gewinnorientierte juristische Person ein Überwachungsorgan wie Aufsichtsrat oder Aufseher eingerichtet, übt das Überwachungsorgan gemäß dem Recht die Befugnis aus, die Finanzen zu kontrollieren, das Verhalten der Mitglieder des Exekutivorgans und hochrangiges Leitungspersonal bei [Ausübung der] Dienstpflichten zu überwachen sowie andere ihm in der Satzung der juristischen Person eingeräumte Befugnisse.	**Section 82** If a for-profit legal entity has established a supervisory body, such as a supervisory board or supervisors, the supervisory body exercises the power to control the finances, oversee the conduct of the executive body's members and high-ranking managing staff in the performance of their duties, as well as other powers granted to it by the Articles of Incorporation of the legal entity.
第八十三条　营利法人的出资人不得滥用出资人权利损害法人或者其他出资人的利益。滥用出资人权利给法人或者其他出资人造成损失的，应当依法承担民事责任。	**§ 83 [Missbrauch von Investorenrechten]** Investoren einer gewinnorientierten juristischen Person dürfen nicht die juristische Person oder die Interessen anderer Investoren schädigen, indem sie ihre Investorenrechte missbrauchen. Wer durch Missbrauch von Investorenrechte der juristischen Person oder anderen Investoren einen Schaden verursacht, muss dem Recht gemäß die zivilrechtliche Haftung tragen.	**Section 83** The investors of a for-profit legal entity shall not misuse the investors' rights to harm the legal entity or other investors' interests. Misusing the investors' rights that cause losses to the legal entity or other investors shall lead to civil liability according to the law.
营利法人的出资人不得滥用法人独立地位和出资人有限责任损害法人的债权人利益。滥用法人独立地位和出资人有限责任，逃避债务，严	Investoren einer gewinnorientierten juristischen Person dürfen nicht die Gläubiger der juristischen Person schädigen, indem sie die unabhängige Stellung der juristischen Person und die begrenzte Haftung der Investoren missbrauchen. Wer sich Verbindlichkeiten entzieht und die Interessen der Gläubiger der juristischen Person	The investors of a for-profit legal entity shall not abuse the legal entity's independent status and the investors' limited liability to damage the interests of the legal entity's creditors. Abusing the independent status of the legal entity and the limited liability of the investors

重损害法人的债权人利益的，应当对法人债务承担连带责任。

schwerwiegend schädigt, indem er die unabhängige Stellung der juristischen Person und die begrenzte Haftung der Investoren missbraucht, muss gesamtschuldnerisch die Haftung für die Schulden der juristischen Person tragen.

to evade debts which has seriously damaged the interests of the legal entity's creditors shall be held jointly and severally liable for the liabilities of the legal entity.

第八十四条　营利法人的控股出资人、实际控制人、董事、监事、高级管理人员不得利用其关联关系损害法人的利益。利用关联关系给法人造成损失的，应当承担赔偿责任。

§ 84 [Verbot der Schädigung unter Nutzung von Verbindungen] Der beherrschende Investor einer gewinnorientierten juristischen Person, derjenige, der [eine solche] tatsächlich kontrolliert, ein Vorstandsmitglied, Aufsichtsratsmitglied [oder] hochrangiges Leitungspersonal darf nicht unter Nutzung seiner Verbindungen[30] die Interessen der juristischen Person schädigen. Wer unter Nutzung seiner Verbindungen der juristischen Person einen Schaden verursacht, muss die Schadensersatzhaftung tragen.

Section 84 The controlling shareholder of a for-profit legal entity, actual controller, executive board member, supervisory board member, high-ranking managing staff shall not harm the interests of the legal entity by using the affiliated relations. Compensation liability shall be assumed if losses are caused to the legal entity by using the affiliated relations.

第八十五条　营利法人的权力机构、执行机构作出决议的会议召集程序、表决方式违反法律、行政法规、法人章程，或者决议内容违反法人章程的，营利法人的出资人可以请求人民法院撤销该决议，但是营利法人依据该决议与善意相对人形成的民事法律关系不受影响。

§ 85 [Aufhebung von Beschlüssen] Wenn bei einem Beschluss des Machtorgans oder des Exekutivorgans einer gewinnorientierten juristischen Person das Verfahren der Einberufung der Versammlung [oder] die Art und Weise der Abstimmung gegen Gesetze, Verwaltungsrechtsnormen oder die Satzung der juristischen Person verstoßen oder wenn der Inhalt des Beschlusses gegen die Satzung der juristischen Person verstößt, kann ein Investor der gewinnorientierten juristischen Person vom Volksgericht die Aufhebung dieses Beschlusses verlangen; allerdings werden Zivilrechtsbeziehungen,

Section 85 An investor of the for-profit legal entity can petition the people's court to revoke a resolution of the executive body of a for-profit legal entity if this resolution violates the procedure for convocation of the assembly or the manner of voting against laws, administrative regulations, or the Sections of Incorporation of the legal entity; however,

30 Siehe die Definition in § 216 Nr. 4 Gesellschaftsgesetz.

	welche aufgrund dieses Beschlusses zwischen der gewinnorientierten juristischen Person und einem gutgläubigen Gegenüber eingegangen wurden, [hiervon] nicht beeinflusst.	the civil legal relations entered by such resolutions between the legal entity and the counterparties in good faith shall not be affected.
第八十六条　营利法人从事经营活动，应当遵守商业道德，维护交易安全，接受政府和社会的监督，承担社会责任。	**§ 86 [Geschäftsethik; gesellschaftliche Verantwortung]** Bei der Ausübung ihrer Geschäftstätigkeit muss die gewinnorientierte juristische Person die Geschäftsethik befolgen, die Sicherheit des Verkehrs[31] wahren, muss sich der Aufsicht des Staates und der Gesellschaft[32] unterwerfen [und] gesellschaftliche Verantwortung tragen.	**Section 86** A for-profit legal entity who engages in business activities must abide by business ethics, maintain the security of transactions, be subject to state and social oversight, and assume social responsibility.
第三节　非营利法人	**3. Abschnitt: Nichtgewinnorientierte juristische Personen**	**Subchapter 3 Non-profit Legal Entities**
第八十七条　为公益目的或者其他非营利目的成立，不向出资人、设立人或者会员分配所取得利润的法人，为非营利法人。	**§ 87 [Definition „nichtgewinnorientierte juristische Personen"; vgl. § 50 AGZR]** Nichtgewinnorientierte juristische Personen sind juristische Personen, die zu gemeinnützigen Zwecken oder anderen nichtgewinnorientierten Zwecken gegründet worden sind [und] keine erzielten Gewinne an ihre Investoren, Gründer oder Mitglieder verteilen.	**Section 87** Legal entities established for the purpose of public welfare or other non-profit purposes which do not distribute earned profit to the investors, founders, or members are non-profit legal entities.

31 Wörtlich: „Transaktionssicherheit".

32 Gemeint ist die „Öffentlichkeit".

非营利法人包括事业单位、社会团体、基金会、社会服务机构等。	Zu den nichtgewinnorientierten juristische Personen zählen etwa Institutionseinheiten[33], gesellschaftliche Körperschaften[34], Stiftungen und Einrichtungen für soziale Dienste.	Non-profit legal entities include institutions, social bodies, foundations, and social service agencies.
第八十八条　具备法人条件，为适应经济社会发展需要，提供公益服务设立的事业单位，经依法登记成立，取得事业单位法人资格；依法不需要办理法人登记的，从成立之日起，具有事业单位法人资格。	**§ 88 [Institutionseinheit]** Eine Institutionseinheit, welche die Voraussetzungen einer juristischen Person besitzt und errichtet wurde, um den Anforderungen der sozio-ökonomischen Entwicklung zu entsprechen [und] gemeinnützige Dienste zur Verfügung zu stellen, erhält als Institutionseinheit Rechtspersönlichkeit[35], sobald sie dem Recht gemäß durch Registrierung zustande gekommen ist; ist die Registrierung als juristische Person nach dem Recht nicht erforderlich ist, so erlangt sie als Institutionseinheit Rechtspersönlichkeit mit dem Tag [ihres] Zustandekommens.	**Section 88** An institution which satisfies the prerequisites of a legal entity and has been established to satisfy the needs of economic and social development, and to provide public service, shall obtain the legal identity as an institution when the registration is complete according to the law; if the law does not require registration as a legal entity, such institution shall obtain the legal identity with effect from the date of establishment.
第八十九条　事业单位法人设理事会的，除法律另有规定外，理事会为其决策机构。事业单位法人的法	**§ 89 [Organe der Institutionseinheit]** Richtet die juristische Person der Institutionseinheit ein Direktorium ein, so bildet das Direktorium ihr Entscheidungsorgan, es sei	**Section 89** If the legal entity establishes a board of directors for the institution, the board forms a decision-making body, unless

33 „Institutionseinheiten" sind gemäß § 2 „Vorläufig durchgeführte Verordnung zur Verwaltung von Institutionseinheiten" [事业单位登记管理暂行条例] vom 25.10.1998 in der Fassung vom 27.6.2004 „Organisationen sozialer Dienste, die vom Staat für soziale gemeinnützige Zwecke [betraut sind], von staatlichen Organen initiiert werden oder von anderen Organen unter Nutzung staatseigenen Vermögens initiiert werden [und] Aktivitäten [in Bereichen] wie etwa Bildung, Wissenschaft und Technik, Kultur und Gesundheit tätigen" [是指国家为了社会公益目的，由国家机关举办或者其他组织利用国有资产举办的，从事教育、科技、文化、卫生等活动的社会服务组织]. Sie sind daher funktional rechtsvergleichend den Körperschaften oder Anstalten des öffentlichen Rechts ähnlich.

34 Funktional rechtsvergleichend handelt es sich bei dieser Rechtsform um Vereine. Siehe *Josephine Asche*, Vereinsrecht in der Volksrepublik China – Eine Einführung, ZChinR 2008, S. 233 ff.

35 Wörtlich: „Eigenschaft als juristische Person".

定代表人依照法律、行政法规或者法人章程的规定产生。	denn Gesetze enthalten anderweitige Bestimmungen. Der gesetzliche Repräsentant der juristischen Person der Institutionseinheit wird gemäß den Bestimmungen in Gesetzen, Verwaltungsrechtnormen oder der Satzung der juristischen Person gebildet.	otherwise provided by law. The legal representatives of the institution's legal entity shall be formed in accordance with the provisions of laws, administrative regulations, or the Sections of Incorporation of the legal entity.
第九十条　具备法人条件，基于会员共同意愿，为公益目的或者会员共同利益等非营利目的设立的社会团体，经依法登记成立，取得社会团体法人资格；依法不需要办理法人登记的，从成立之日起，具有社会团体法人资格。	**§ 90 [Gesellschaftliche Körperschaft]** Eine gesellschaftliche Körperschaft, die die Voraussetzungen einer juristischen Personen besitzt [und] aufgrund des gemeinsamen Willens der Mitglieder zur Verwirklichung von nichtgewinnorientierten Zwecken wie etwa gemeinnützigen Zwecken oder dem gemeinsamen Interesse der Mitglieder errichtet worden ist, erlangt als gesellschaftliche Körperschaft Rechtspersönlichkeit, sobald sie dem Recht gemäß durch Registrierung zustande gekommen ist; ist die Registrierung als juristische Person nach dem Recht nicht erforderlich ist, so erlangt sie als gesellschaftliche Körperschaft Rechtspersönlichkeit mit dem Tag [ihres] Zustandekommens.	**Section 90** A social corporation that satisfies the prerequisites of a legal entity and which has been established with the collective will of the members for the purpose of realising non-profit purposes as for instance, public welfare, or the common interests of the members, obtains legal identity when registration is complete according to the law; if the law does not require the legal registration of legal entities, such corporation shall obtain the legal identity as a social corporation with effect of the date of establishment.
第九十一条　设立社会团体法人应当依法制定法人章程。	**§ 91 [Satzung und Organe der gesellschaftlichen Körperschaft]** Bei Errichtung einer gesellschaftlichen Körperschaft muss nach dem Recht eine Satzung der juristischen Person bestimmt werden.	**Section 91** The established social corporation shall develop the Sections of Incorporation of the legal entity.
社会团体法人应当设会员大会或者会员代表大会等权力机构。	Eine gesellschaftliche Körperschaft muss ein Machtorgan wie etwa eine Mitgliederversammlung oder eine Mitgliederrepräsentantenversammlung einrichten.	A social corporation must establish an executive body such as a general assembly or a general assembly of representatives.
社会团体法人应当设理事会等执行机构。理事长或者会长等负责人按	Die juristische Person der gesellschaftlichen Körperschaft muss ein Exekutivorgan wie etwa ein Direktorium aufstellen. Der Verantwortliche wie etwa der Leiter des Direktoriums oder der Präsident sind gemäß der	The legal entity of a social corporation shall establish an executive body such as a board of directors. The responsible person, such as

照法人章程的规定担任法定代表人。	Satzung der juristischen Person der gesetzliche Repräsentant.	the head of the board of directors or the president, shall be the legal representative according to the Sections of Incorporation of the legal entity.
第九十二条　具备法人条件，为公益目的以捐助财产设立的基金会、社会服务机构等，经依法登记成立，取得捐助法人资格。	**§ 92 [Spendenfinanzierte juristische Personen; religiöse Einrichtungen]** [Organisationen] wie etwa Stiftungen und Einrichtungen für soziale Dienste, die die Voraussetzungen juristischer Personen besitzen [und] für gemeinnützige Zwecke mit gespendetem Vermögen errichtet worden sind, erlangen als spendenfinanzierte juristische Person Rechtspersönlichkeit, sobald sie gemäß dem Recht durch Registrierung zustande gekommen sind.	**Section 92** Organisations, such as foundations and social service agencies which satisfy the prerequisites of legal entities and have been established by donations for the purpose of public welfare, obtain the legal identity of donors when they have been established by registration according to the law.
依法设立的宗教活动场所，具备法人条件的，可以申请法人登记，取得捐助法人资格。法律、行政法规对宗教活动场所有规定的，依照其规定。	Eine nach dem Recht errichtete religiöse Einrichtung[36], die die Voraussetzungen einer juristischen Person besitzt, kann die Registrierung als juristische Person beantragen [und] als spendenfinanzierte juristische Person Rechtspersönlichkeit erlangen. Enthalten Gesetze oder Verwaltungsrechtsnormen Bestimmungen zu religiösen Einrichtungen, so gelten diese Bestimmungen.	Venues for religious activities established by law which satisfy the prerequisites of a legal entity may apply for registration as a legal entity and obtain the legal identity of a legal entity financed by donations. If the provisions of the laws and administrative regulations have other provisions on the venues of religious activities, such provisions shall apply.
第九十三条　设立捐助法人应当依法制定法人章程。	**§ 93 [Satzung und Organe spendenfinanzierter juristischer Personen]** Bei Errichtung einer spendenfinanzierten juristischen Person muss eine Satzung dem Recht gemäß bestimmt werden.	**Section 93** The established legal entities of legal entities financed by donations shall lawfully develop the Sections of Incorporation of the legal entities.

36 Wörtlich: „Orte für religiöse Aktivitäten“.

捐助法人应当设理事会、民主管理组织等决策机构，并设执行机构。理事长等负责人按照法人章程的规定担任法定代表人。	Eine spendenfinanzierte juristische Person muss ein Entscheidungsorgan wie etwa ein Direktorium [oder] eine demokratische Verwaltungsorganisation sowie ein Exekutivorgan einrichten. Der Verantwortliche wie etwa der Leiter des Direktoriums fungiert gemäß der Satzung der juristischen Person als gesetzlicher Repräsentant.	A legal entity financed by donations shall establish a decision-making body, such as a board of directors or a democratic management organisation, as well as an executive organ. The person responsible, such as the head of the board of directors, acts as the legal representative according to the Sections of Incorporation of the legal entity.
捐助法人应当设监事会等监督机构。	Spendenfinanzierte juristische Personen müssen ein Überwachungsorgan wie etwa einen Aufsichtsrat einrichten.	Legal entities financed by donations must establish a supervising entity, such as a supervisory board.
第九十四条　捐助人有权向捐助法人查询捐助财产的使用、管理情况，并提出意见和建议，捐助法人应当及时、如实答复。	**§ 94 [Rechte von Spendern]** Spender haben gegenüber der spendenfinanzierten juristischen Person das Recht, sich über die Nutzung [und] die Umstände der Verwaltung des gespendeten Vermögens zu erkundigen sowie Ansichten und Vorschläge einzureichen; die spendenfinanzierte juristische Person muss unverzüglich [und] wahrheitsgemäß antworten.	**Section 94** Donors have the right to inquire the legal entity financed by donations about the use and management of the donated property and to submit opinions and suggestions; the legal entities financed by donations shall respond promptly and truthfully.
捐助法人的决策机构、执行机构或者法定代表人作出决定的程序违反法律、行政法规、法人章程，或者决定内容违反法人章程的，捐助人等利害关系人或者主管机关可以请求人民法院撤销该决定，但是捐助法人依据该决定与善意相对人形成的民事法律关系不受影响。	Verstößt das Verfahren bei Erlass einer Entscheidung des Entscheidungsorgans, des Exekutivorgans oder des gesetzlichen Repräsentanten einer spendenfinanzierten juristischen Person gegen Gesetze, Verwaltungsrechtsnormen oder die Satzung der juristischen Person oder verstößt der Inhalt der Entscheidung gegen die Satzung der juristischen Person, so können Interessierte wie etwa die Spender oder die zuständige Behörde beim Volksgericht die Aufhebung dieser Entscheidung verlangen; allerdings werden Zivilrechtsbeziehungen, welche auf-	If the decision-making procedures of resolutions made by the decision-making body, executive organ, or the legal representative of the legal entities financed by donations violates laws, administrative regulations, or the Sections of Incorporation of the legal entity, or if the content of the decision violates the Sections of Incorporation of the legal entity, interested parties, as for example the donor or the concerned authority, may petition the

grund dieser Entscheidung zwischen der spendenfinanzierten juristischen Person und einem gutgläubigen Gegenüber eingegangen wurden, [hiervon] nicht beeinflusst.

people's court for the revocation of this decision; however, the civil relations formed between the legal entities financed by donations and counterparties in good faith shall not be affected.

第九十五条　为公益目的成立的非营利法人终止时，不得向出资人、设立人或者会员分配剩余财产。剩余财产应当按照法人章程的规定或者权力机构的决议用于公益目的；无法按照法人章程的规定或者权力机构的决议处理的，由主管机关主持转给宗旨相同或者相近的法人，并向社会公告。

§ 95 [Restvermögen bei Auflösung] Endet eine nichtgewinnorientierte juristische Person, die zu gemeinnützigen Zwecken gegründet worden war, so darf [diese] das Restvermögen nicht an ihre Investoren, Gründer oder Mitglieder verteilen. Das Restvermögen muss gemäß den Bestimmungen der Satzung der juristischen Person oder dem Beschluss des Machtorgans für einen gemeinnützigen Zweck verwendet werden; wenn nicht gemäß der Satzung der juristischen Person oder dem Beschluss des Machtorgans verfahren werden kann, leitet die zuständige Behörde die Übertragung [des Restvermögens] auf eine juristische Person mit dem gleichen oder einem ähnlichem Zweck an und gibt [dies] gegenüber der Öffentlichkeit bekannt.

Section 95 At the time of termination, a nonprofit legal entity established for the purpose of public benefit shall not distribute the remaining property to the investors, founders, or members. The remaining property shall be used for charitable purposes according to the provisions of the Sections of Incorporation of the legal entity, or the resolutions of the executive body; if proceeding according to the Sections of Incorporation of the legal entity or the resolution of the executive body is not possible, the competent authority shall guide the transfer of such property to a legal entity of the same or a similar purpose, and disclose this to the public.

第四节　特别法人

4. Abschnitt: Besondere juristische Personen

Subchapter 4 Particular Legal Entities

第九十六条　本节规定的机关法人、农村集体经济组织法人、城镇农村的合作经济组织法人、基层群众性自治组织法人，为特别法人。

§ 96 [Besondere juristische Personen] Die in diesem Abschnitt geregelte behördliche juristische Person, die juristische Person der ländlichen kollektiven Wirtschaftsorganisation, die juristische Person der städtischen und ländlichen kooperativen Wirtschaftsorganisa-

Section 96 The governmental legal entities, the legal entities of rural collective economic organisations, the legal entities of urban and rural cooperative economic organisations, and the legal entities of basic-level People's

	tion [sowie] die juristische Person der Selbstverwaltungsorganisation der Volksmassen der Grundstufe sind besondere juristische Personen.	self-governing organisations are the particular legal entities.
第九十七条　有独立经费的机关和承担行政职能的法定机构从成立之日起，具有机关法人资格，可以从事为履行职能所需要的民事活动。	**§ 97 [Behördliche juristische Personen]** Behörden, die über eigenständige [Mittel für] Regelaufwendungen verfügen und gesetzlich bestimmte Einrichtungen, die Verwaltungsfunktionen übernehmen, besitzen vom Tage ihres Zustandekommens an die Rechtspersönlichkeit einer behördlichen juristischen Person [und] können die zur Durchführung ihrer Funktion erforderlichen Zivilaktivitäten ausführen.	**Section 97** The governmental bodies with independent funds and the statutory bodies that bear administrative functions shall have the legal identity of a governmental legal entity from the date of their establishment, and may engage in the civil transactions required for the performance of their functions.
第九十八条　机关法人被撤销的，法人终止，其民事权利和义务由继任的机关法人享有和承担；没有继任的机关法人的，由作出撤销决定的机关法人享有和承担。	**§ 98 [Rechtsnachfolge bei behördlichen juristischen Personen]** Wenn eine behördliche juristische Person aufgehoben wird, endet die juristische Person, ihre zivilen Rechte und Pflichten werden von der ihr nachfolgenden behördlichen juristischen Person genossen bzw. getragen; gibt es keine ihr nachfolgende behördliche juristische Person, so werden diese von der behördlichen juristischen Person, die die Aufhebung entschieden hat, genossen bzw. getragen.	**Section 98** If a governmental legal entity is revoked, the legal entity terminates, the civil rights and obligations shall be enjoyed and borne by its successors. If there is no successive governmental legal entity, the governmental legal entity that decided on the revocation shall enjoy and bear such rights and obligations.
第九十九条　农村集体经济组织依法取得法人资格。	**§ 99 [Ländliche kollektive Wirtschaftsorganisationen]** Ländliche kollektive Wirtschaftsorganisationen erlangen nach dem Recht Rechtspersönlichkeit.	**Section 99** Rural collective economic organisations shall obtain the legal identity according to law.
法律、行政法规对农村集体经济组织有规定的，依照其规定。	Wenn Gesetze oder Verwaltungsrechtsnormen Bestimmungen zu dörflichen kollektiven Wirtschaftsorganisationen enthalten, so gelten diese Bestimmungen.	If laws and administrative regulations contain provisions on rural collective economic organisations, such provisions shall apply.

第一百条　城镇农村的合作经济组织依法取得法人资格。	**§ 100 [Kooperative Wirtschaftsorganisationen]** Städtische und ländliche kooperative Wirtschaftsorganisationen erlangen nach dem Recht Rechtspersönlichkeit.	**Section 100** Urban and rural cooperative economic organisations shall obtain legal identity in accordance with the law.
法律、行政法规对城镇农村的合作经济组织有规定的，依照其规定。	Wenn Gesetze oder Verwaltungsrechtsnormen Bestimmungen zu städtischen und ländlichen kooperativen Wirtschaftsorganisationen enthalten, so gelten diese Bestimmungen.	If laws and administrative regulations contain provisions on urban and rural cooperative economic organisations, such provisions shall apply.
第一百零一条　居民委员会、村民委员会具有基层群众性自治组织法人资格，可以从事为履行职能所需要的民事活动。	**§ 101 [Einwohnerkomitees und Dorfbewohnerkomitees]** Einwohnerkomitees und Dorfbewohnerkomitees besitzen die Rechtspersönlichkeit als Selbstverwaltungsorganisation der Volksmassen der Grundstufe [und] können die zur Durchführung ihrer Funktion erforderlichen Zivilaktivitäten ausführen.	**Section 101** The residents committees and the villagers committees possess the legal identity as the basic-level People's self-governing organisations and may engage in civil transactions needed for performing their duties.
未设立村集体经济组织的，村民委员会可以依法代行村集体经济组织的职能。	Wurde noch keine dörfliche kollektive Wirtschaftsorganisation gegründet, so kann das Dorfbewohnerkomitee dem Recht gemäß die Funktion der dörflichen kollektiven Wirtschaftsorganisation an deren Stelle ausüben.	If rural collective economic organisations have not been established yet, the villagers committee may perform the function of the rural collective economic organisation in its stead according to law.
第四章　非法人组织	**4. Kapitel: Organisationen ohne Rechtspersönlichkeit[37]**	**Chapter IV Non-incorporated organisations**
第一百零二条　非法人组织是不具有法人资格，但是能够依法以自己的名义从事民事活动的组织。	**§ 102 [Definition]** Organisationen ohne Rechtspersönlichkeit sind Organisationen, die [zwar] keine Rechtspersönlichkeit besitzen, die aber nach dem Recht im eigenen Namen Zivilaktivitäten tätigen können.	**Section 102** The non-incorporated organisations are organisations that have no legal

37 Dieser Abschnitt wurde neu eingefügt. Teilweise ist darin der Abschnitt in den AGZR über die „Partnerschaft von Einzelpersonen" [个人合伙] enthalten.

		identity but may lawfully engage in civil activities under their own name according to the law.
非法人组织包括个人独资企业、合伙企业、不具有法人资格的专业服务机构等。	Organisationen ohne Rechtspersönlichkeit umfassen Einzelpersonenunternehmen, Partnerschaftsunternehmen sowie unter anderem Einrichtungen für professionelle Dienstleistungen ohne Rechtspersönlichkeit.	The non-incorporated organisations include individually-owned enterprises, partnerships, and agencies for professional services without legal identity.
第一百零三条　非法人组织应当依照法律的规定登记。	**§ 103 [Registrierung; Genehmigung]** Organisationen ohne Rechtspersönlichkeit müssen sich gemäß der gesetzlichen Bestimmungen registrieren.	**Section 103** The non-incorporated organisations shall register according to the law.
设立非法人组织，法律、行政法规规定须经有关机关批准的，依照其规定。	Wenn Gesetze oder Verwaltungsrechtsnormen bestimmen, dass zur Gründung einer Organisation ohne Rechtspersönlichkeit eine Genehmigung durch die entsprechende Behörde erforderlich ist, so gelten diese Bestimmungen.	If laws and administrative regulations provide that for the establishment of non-incorporated organisations approval from relevant authorities is needed, such provisions shall be followed.
第一百零四条　非法人组织的财产不足以清偿债务的，其出资人或者设立人承担无限责任。法律另有规定的，依照其规定。	**§ 104 [Haftung]** Investoren oder Gründer von Organisationen ohne Rechtspersönlichkeit haften unbeschränkt für Verbindlichkeiten [dieser Organisation], die nicht mit dem Vermögen [dieser Organisation] beglichen werden können. Gibt es andere gesetzliche Bestimmungen, so gelten diese Bestimmungen.	**Section 104** If the property of the non-incorporated organisations is insufficient to pay off the debts, the investors or the founders shall bear unlimited liability, unless otherwise provided by law.
第一百零五条　非法人组织可以确定一人或者数人代表该组织从事民事活动。	**§ 105 [Organschaftliche Vertretung]** Organisationen ohne Rechtspersönlichkeit können eine Person oder mehrere Personen bestimmen, die sie bei der Tätigung von Zivilaktivitäten repräsentiert bzw. repräsentieren.	**Section 105** Non-incorporated organisations may determine one or more persons to represent them in the performance of civil transactions.
第一百零六条　有下列情形之一的，非法人组织解散：	**§ 106 [Auflösung]** Liegt eine der folgende Situationen vor, wird die Organisation ohne Rechtspersönlichkeit aufgelöst:	**Section 106** If one of the following cases is present, non-incorporated organisations are dissolved:

（一）章程规定的存续期间届满或者章程规定的其他解散事由出现；	1. die in der Satzung der Organisation ohne Rechtspersönlichkeit bestimmte Dauer des Fortbestehens ist abgelaufen oder andere in der Satzung bestimmte Auflösungsgründe sind eingetreten.	(1) The existence period provided by the Sections of Incorporation has expired, or other reasons for dissolution have occurred;
（二）出资人或者设立人决定解散；	2. Investoren oder Gründer entscheiden sich zur Auflösung;	(2) The investors or the founders have decided to dissolve;
（三）法律规定的其他情形。	3. andere in Gesetzen bestimmte Situationen.	(3) Other circumstances prescribed by law.
第一百零七条　非法人组织解散的，应当依法进行清算。	**§ 107 [Abwicklung]** Wird eine Organisation ohne Rechtspersönlichkeit aufgelöst, so muss eine Abwicklung gemäß dem Recht durchgeführt werden.	**Section 107** The dissolved non-incorporated organisation shall conduct liquidation according to law.
第一百零八条　非法人组织除适用本章规定外，参照适用本法第三章第一节的有关规定。	**§ 108 [Entsprechende Anwendung allgemeiner Regelungen zu juristischen Personen]** Auf die Organisation ohne Rechtspersönlichkeit sind neben diesem Kapitel auch die Bestimmungen aus Kapitel 3, Abschnitt 1 dieses Gesetzes entsprechend anwendbar.	**Section 108** The provisions of Chapter 3, Subchapter 1 of this law is applicable to non-incorporated organisations.
第五章　民事权利	**5. Kapitel: Zivilrechte**	**Chapter V Civil Rights**
第一百零九条　自然人的人身自由、人格尊严受法律保护。	**§ 109 [Freiheits- und Persönlichkeitsrechte natürlicher Personen]** Die persönliche Freiheit und die Würde der Persönlichkeit natürlicher Personen genießen den Schutz des Gesetzes.	**Section 109** Natural persons' personal freedom and personal dignity is protected by law.
第一百一十条　自然人享有生命权、身体权、健康权、姓名权、肖像权、名誉权、荣誉权、隐私权、婚姻自主权等权利。	**§ 110 [Umfang der Rechte natürlicher und juristischer Personen; vgl. §§ 98 bis 103 AGZR]** Natürliche Personen genießen unter anderem das Recht auf Leben, das Recht auf körperliche Unversehrtheit, das Recht auf Gesundheit, das Recht am eigenen Namen, das Recht am eigenen Bildnis, das Recht [auf Schutz] des guten	**Section 110** Natural persons enjoy the right to life, the right to physical integrity, the right to health, the rights to name, the right of persons to their own likeness, the right to good reputation, the right to the protection of honour, the right to privacy, marriage autonomy, and other rights.

	Rufs, das Recht [auf Schutz] der Ehre, das Recht auf Privatsphäre sowie das eheliche Selbstbestimmungsrecht.	
法人、非法人组织享有名称权、名誉权、荣誉权等权利。	Juristische Personen [und] Organisationen ohne Rechtspersönlichkeit genießen Rechte wie etwa das Recht [an] der [eigenen] Bezeichnung, das Recht [auf Schutz] des guten Rufs [und] das Recht [auf Schutz] der Ehre.	Legal entities and non-incorporated organisations enjoy the rights to name, reputation, honour, and other rights
第一百一十一条　自然人的个人信息受法律保护。任何组织和个人需要获取他人个人信息的，应当依法取得并确保信息安全，不得非法收集、使用、加工、传输他人个人信息，不得非法买卖、提供或者公开他人个人信息。	**§ 111 [Schutz persönlicher Informationen]** Persönliche Informationen[38] natürlicher Personen werden vom Gesetz geschützt. Jedwede Organisation oder Person, für die es erforderlich ist, persönliche Informationen einer anderen Person zu erhalten, muss [diese] nach dem Recht erlangen und die Sicherheit dieser Informationen garantieren, darf persönliche Informationen anderer Personen nicht illegal sammeln, nutzen, verarbeiten, [oder] weitervermitteln, [und] darf nicht persönliche Informationen anderer Personen in unrechtmäßiger Weise kaufen oder verkaufen, [und] zur Verfügung stellen oder veröffentlichen.	**Section 111** Personal information of natural persons is protected by law. Any organisation or individual who needed to obtain personal information of another person shall obtain the information according to law and ensure the security of this information, may not illegally gather, use, process, or share personal information of others and may not purchase or sell personal information of other persons unlawfully. It is not allowed to illegally gather, use, process, or transfer, and make available, or publish the personal information of others.
第一百一十二条　自然人因婚姻、家庭关系等产生的人身权利受法律保护。	**§ 112 [Schutz der Rechte aus Ehe und Familie; vgl. § 104 AGZR]** Die persönlichen Rechte, die natürlichen Personen aus Verhältnissen wie etwa Ehe und Familie erwachsen, genießen den Schutz des Gesetzes.	**Section 112** The personal rights of natural persons arising from marriage or family relations shall be protected by law.
第一百一十三条　民事主体的财产权利受法律平等保护。	**§ 113 [Gleichberechtigter Schutz von Vermögensrechten; vgl. § 75 AGZR]** Die Vermögensrechte von	**Section 113** The property rights of the civil legal subjects are equally protected by law.

38 Wörtlich: „Informationen zu Einzelpersonen".

	Zivilrechtssubjekten genießen gleichberechtigten gesetzlichen Schutz.	
第一百一十四条　民事主体依法享有物权。	**§ 114 [Dingliche Rechte; Definition; vgl. § 71 AGZR]** Zivilrechtssubjekte genießen dem Recht gemäß dingliche Rechte.	**Section 114** The civil legal subjects enjoy property rights according to law.
物权是权利人依法对特定的物享有直接支配和排他的权利，包括所有权、用益物权和担保物权。	Dingliche Rechte sind Rechte des Berechtigten, über bestimmte Sachen gemäß dem Recht unmittelbar zu verfügen und andere von jeder Einwirkung auszuschließen[39], einschließlich Eigentumsrechten, dinglicher Nutzungsrechte und dinglicher Sicherungsrechte.	Property rights are the exclusive rights to legally dispose of a specific object directly and exclude others from any interference including ownership, right of use, and security interests.
第一百一十五条　物包括不动产和动产。法律规定权利作为物权客体的，依照其规定。	**§ 115 [Sachen[40]]** [Der Begriff] Sache umfasst sowohl bewegliche als auch unbewegliche [Sachen]. Soweit Gesetze bestimmen, dass Rechte Gegenstand dinglicher Rechte sind, so gelten diese Bestimmungen.	**Section 115** Property includes movable and immovable property. Where the law provides that the rights are the object of the property rights, such provisions shall apply.
第一百一十六条　物权的种类和内容，由法律规定。	**§ 116 [Sachenrechtlicher Typenzwang[41]]** Die Arten dinglicher Rechte und deren Inhalt wird von Gesetzen bestimmt.	**Section 116** The type and content of the property rights shall be provided by law.
第一百一十七条　为了公共利益的需要，依照法律规定的权限和程序	**§ 117 [Entschädigung bei Entzug und Beschlagnahme von Sachen]** Werden im öffentlichen Interesse[42]	**Section 117** Fair and appropriate compensation shall be granted if in the public interest,

39 Siehe § 2 Abs. 3 Sachenrechtsgesetz der VR China [中华人民共和国物权法] vom 16.3.2007, Amtsblatt des Staatsrates [国务院公报] 2007, Nr. 14, S. 4 ff., deutsche Übersetzung von *ZHOU Mei, QI Xiaokun, Sebastian Lohsse, LIU Qingwen*, in ZChinR 2007, S. 78 ff.

40 Siehe § 2 Sachenrechtsgesetz.

41 Siehe § 5 Sachenrechtsgesetz.

42 Wörtlich: „aufgrund der Erfordernisse des öffentlichen Interesses".

征收、征用不动产或者动产的，应当给予公平、合理的补偿。	gemäß den in Gesetzen bestimmten Befugnissen und Verfahren bewegliche oder unbewegliche Sachen entzogen oder beschlagnahmt, muss eine gerechte [und] angemessene Entschädigung gewährt werden.	movable, or immovable property is withdrawn or seized in accordance with the competence and procedure prescribed by law.
第一百一十八条　民事主体依法享有债权。	**§ 118 [Rechte aus Schuldverhältnissen; vgl. § 84 AGZR]** Zivilrechtssubjekte genießen gemäß dem Recht Rechte aus Schuldverhältnissen[43].	**Section 118** Civil legal subjects enjoy rights arising from creditor/-debtor relations according to law.
债权是因合同、侵权行为、无因管理、不当得利以及法律的其他规定，权利人请求特定义务人为或者不为一定行为的权利。	Ein Recht aus Schuldverhältnis[44] ist das Recht des Berechtigten, aus Vertrag, unerlaubter Handlung, Geschäftsführung ohne Auftrag, unberechtigter Bereicherung und aus anderen gesetzlichen Bestimmungen von einem bestimmten Schuldner ein bestimmtes Handeln oder Unterlassen zu verlangen.	A right arising from creditor/-debtor relation is the right of an entitled person to claim a specific act of omission from a specific debtor arising from a contract, tort, actions performed without due authority, unjustified enrichment, and other provisions of law.
第一百一十九条　依法成立的合同，对当事人具有法律约束力。	**§ 119 [Bindungswirkung von Verträgen; vgl. §§ 85, 88 AGZR]** Nach dem Recht zustande gekommene Verträge haben für die Parteien rechtliche Bindungswirkung.	**Section 119** Contracts established in accordance with the law are legally binding for the parties.
第一百二十条　民事权益受到侵害的，被侵权人有权请求侵权人承担侵权责任。	**§ 120 [Haftung bei unerlaubter Handlung]** Werden zivile Rechte und Interessen verletzt, so ist der Verletzte berechtigt zu verlangen, dass der Verletzer die Haftung wegen der Verletzung von Rechten trägt.	**Section 120** If civil rights and interests are infringed, the injured person has the right to request the infringer to bear tort liability for an infringement of rights.

43 Wörtlich: „Schuldrechte".
44 Wörtlich: „Schuldrecht".

第一百二十一条　没有法定的或者约定的义务，为避免他人利益受损失而进行管理的人，有权请求受益人偿还由此支出的必要费用。	**§ 121 [Geschäftsführung ohne Auftrag; vgl. § 93 AGZR]** Wer ohne rechtlich oder aufgrund Vereinbarung [hierzu] verpflichtet zu sein, Veranlassungen trifft[45], um zu vermeiden, dass Interessen eines anderen Schaden erleiden, ist berechtigt, vom Nutznießer die Erstattung hierbei gezahlter notwendiger Ausgaben zu fordern.	**Section 121** If a person who is not legally or due to agreement obligated to take measures that avoid an infringement of the rights of another person, this person is entitled to claim the compensation of necessary paid expenses from the beneficiary.
第一百二十二条　因他人没有法律根据，取得不当利益，受损失的人有权请求其返还不当利益。	**§ 122 [Ungerechtfertigte Bereicherung; vgl. § 92 AGZR]** Erlangt ein anderer ohne rechtliche Grundlage einen unangemessenen Vorteil, so ist derjenige, der [hierdurch] einen Schaden erleidet, berechtigt, von der anderen Person die Herausgabe des unangemessenen Vorteils zu verlangen.	**Section 122** If another person obtains an unjust enrichment without a legal basis, the person suffering from damages is entitled to claim the surrender of the unjust enrichment from the other person.
第一百二十三条　民事主体依法享有知识产权。	**§ 123 [Rechte an geistigem Eigentum; vgl. §§ 94 bis 97 AGZR]** Zivilrechtssubjekte genießen gemäß dem Recht Rechte an geistigem Eigentum.	**Section 123** Civil legal subjects enjoy intellectual property rights according to law.
知识产权是权利人依法就下列客体享有的专有的权利：	Rechte an geistigem Eigentum sind ausschließliche Rechte, die Berechtigte gemäß dem Recht an folgenden Gegenständen genießen:	Intellectual property rights are exclusive rights of entitled persons to the following objects according to law:
（一）作品；	1. Werke;	(1) Works;
（二）发明、实用新型、外观设计；	2. Erfindungen, Gebrauchsmuster, Design[46]s	(2) Invention, utility models, and designs;
（三）商标；	3. Marken;	(3) Trademarks;
（四）地理标志；	4. geografische Herkunftsangaben;	(4) Geographical indications;
（五）商业秘密；	5. Geschäftsgeheimnisse;	(5) Trade secrets;

45 Wörtlich: „die Verwaltung ausführt“.
46 Wörtlich: „äußere Formgestaltung“.

（六）集成电路布图设计； （七）植物新品种； （八）法律规定的其他客体。	6. Designs integrierter Schaltkreise; 7. neue Pflanzenarten; 8. andere Gegenstände, die in gesetzlichen Bestimmungen genannt sind.	(6) Integrated circuit layout design; (7) New plant species; (8) Other objects as prescribed by law.
第一百二十四条　自然人依法享有继承权。 自然人合法的私有财产，可以依法继承。	**§ 124 [Erbrechte; vgl. § 76 AGZR]** Natürliche Personen genießen gemäß dem Recht Erbrechte. Das rechtmäßige Privatvermögen einer natürlichen Person kann gemäß dem Recht geerbt werden.	**Section 124** Natural persons enjoy inheritance rights as prescribed by law. The lawful personal properties of natural persons may be lawfully inherited.
第一百二十五条　民事主体依法享有股权和其他投资性权利。	**§ 125 [Anteils- und andere Investitionsrechte]** Zivilrechtssubjekte genießen dem Recht gemäß Anteilsrechte und andere Rechte mit Investitionscharakter.	**Section 125** Civil legal subjects enjoy the equity and other investment rights according to law.
第一百二十六条　民事主体享有法律规定的其他民事权利和利益。	**§ 126 [Weitere Rechte]** Zivilrechtssubjekte genießen die in gesetzlichen Bestimmungen vorgesehenen weiteren zivilen Rechte und Interessen.	**Section 126** Civil legal subjects enjoy other civil rights and interests as prescribed by law.
第一百二十七条　法律对数据、网络虚拟财产的保护有规定的，依照其规定。	**§ 127 [Daten- und Vermögensschutz im Internet]** Enthalten Gesetze Bestimmungen zum Schutz von Daten oder virtuellem Vermögen im Internet, so gelten diese Bestimmungen.	**Section 127** The provisions on the protection of data or virtual property on the Internet are applicable.
第一百二十八条　法律对未成年人、老年人、残疾人、妇女、消费者等的民事权利保护有特别规定的，依照其规定。	**§ 128 [Besonderer Schutz bestimmter Personengruppen]** Soweit in Gesetzen besondere Bestimmungen zum Schutz der Zivilrechte etwa von Minderjährigen, Alten, Behinderten, Frauen [oder] Verbrauchern vorhanden sind, gelten diese Bestimmungen.	**Section 128** The special provisions on the protection of civil rights of minors, the elderly, the disabled, women, and consumers are applicable.
第一百二十九条　民事权利可以依据民事法律行为、事实行为、法律规定的事件或者法律规定的其他方式取得。	**§ 129 [Entstehung von Zivilrechten]** Zivilrechte können aufgrund von Zivilrechtsgeschäften, tatsächlichem Verhalten, gesetzlich bestimmten Ereignissen oder anderer gesetzlich bestimmter Weise erlangt werden.	**Section 129** Civil rights may be acquired by civil transactions, de facto acts, acts prescribed by law, or other means provided by law.

第一百三十条　民事主体按照自己的意愿依法行使民事权利，不受干涉。	**§ 130 [Ausübung von Zivilrechten]** Zivilrechtssubjekte üben ihre Zivilrechte nach Maßgabe ihres eigenen Willens nach dem Recht aus und dürfen hierbei nicht gestört werden.	**Section 130** Civil legal subjects exercise their civil rights according to their own will and the law and others shall not be interfered therewith.
第一百三十一条　民事主体行使权利时，应当履行法律规定的和当事人约定的义务。	**§ 131 [Pflichtenerfüllung]** Bei der Ausübung ihrer Zivilrechte müssen Zivilrechtssubjekte ihre gesetzlich bestimmten oder unter den Parteien vereinbarten Pflichten erfüllen.	**Section 131** Exercising their rights civil legal subjects shall fulfil the obligations stipulated by law or agreed on by the parties.
第一百三十二条　民事主体不得滥用民事权利损害国家利益、社会公共利益或者他人合法权益。	**§ 132 [Missbrauchsverbot]** Zivilrechtssubjekte dürfen ihre Zivilrechte nicht zum Schaden staatlicher Interessen, allgemeiner gesellschaftlicher Interessen oder der legalen Rechte und Interessen anderer Personen missbrauchen.	**Section 132** Civil legal subjects shall not abuse their civil rights to damage national interests, general public interests, or the legitimate rights and interests of others.
第六章　民事法律行为	**6. Kapitel: Zivilrechtsgeschäfte**	**Chapter VI Civil Legal Acts**
第一节　一般规定	**1. Abschnitt: Allgemeine Bestimmungen**[47]	**Subchapter 1 General Stipulations**
第一百三十三条　民事法律行为是民事主体通过意思表示设立、变更、终止民事法律关系的行为。	**§ 133 [Definition „Zivilrechtsgeschäfte"; vgl. § 54 AGZR]** Zivilrechtsgeschäfte sind Handlungen, mit denen Zivilrechtssubjekte durch Willenserklärung Zivilrechtrechtsbeziehungen begründen, ändern und beenden.	**Section 133** Civil legal acts are acts of civil legal subjects to establish, alter, or terminate civil transactions by declaration of intent.
第一百三十四条　民事法律行为可以基于双方或者多方的意思表示一	**§ 134 [Zustandekommen von Zivilrechtsgeschäften]** Zivilrechtsgeschäfte können durch übereinstimmende	**Section 134** Civil legal acts can be established by corresponding multi or bilateral

47 Dieser Abschnitt wurde neu eingefügt, wobei einige Bestimmungen aus dem 4. Kapitel der AGZR über „Zivilrechtshandlungen und Vertretung" [民事法律行为和代理] in veränderter Fassung übernommen wurden.

致成立，也可以基于单方的意思表示成立。	zwei- oder mehrseitige Willenserklärungen zustande kommen; sie können auch durch eine einseitige Willenserklärung zustande kommen.	declaration of intent; they can also be established by unilateral declaration of intent.
法人、非法人组织依照法律或者章程规定的议事方式和表决程序作出决议的，该决议行为成立。	Fasst eine juristische Personen [oder] eine Organisation ohne Rechtspersönlichkeit gemäß der gesetzlich oder in der Satzung bestimmten Art und Weise der Beratung und des [dort bestimmten] Abstimmungsverfahrens einen Beschluss, so ist diese Beschlusshandlung zustande gekommen.	The resolutions made by legal entities or non-incorporated organisations in accordance with the law or the manner stipulated in the Sections of Incorporation and the voting procedure shall be valid.
第一百三十五条　民事法律行为可以采用书面形式、口头形式或者其他形式；法律、行政法规规定或者当事人约定采用特定形式的，应当采用特定形式。	**§ 135 [Form von Zivilrechtsgeschäften; vgl. § 56 AGZR]** Für Zivilrechtsgeschäfte können die schriftliche, die mündliche oder eine andere Form verwendet werden; wenn das Gesetz, Verwaltungsrechtsnormen oder eine Parteivereinbarung den Gebrauch einer bestimmte Form bestimmt haben, muss die bestimmte Form verwendet werden.	**Section 135** Civil legal acts may be in written, oral, or other form; special forms may be adopted if provided by laws, administrative regulations, or if the parties agreed on a special form.
第一百三十六条　民事法律行为自成立时生效，但是法律另有规定或者当事人另有约定的除外。	**§ 136 [Bindungswirkung von Zivilrechtsgeschäften; vgl. § 57 AGZR]** Zivilrechtsgeschäfte sind vom Zeitpunkt ihres Zustandekommens an wirksam, es sei denn, dass das Gesetz etwas anderes bestimmt oder die Parteien etwas anderes vereinbaren.	**Section 136** Civil transactions are effective from the time of their conclusion, except as otherwise provided by law or otherwise stipulated by the parties.
行为人非依法律规定或者未经对方同意，不得擅自变更或者解除民事法律行为。	Außer aufgrund gesetzlicher Bestimmung oder mit dem Einverständnis der anderen Seite darf der Handelnde eine Zivilrechtshandlung nicht eigenmächtig ändern oder aufheben.	The acting persons may not alter or cancel a civil transaction without authorisation, unless otherwise provided by law.

第二节　意思表示

第一百三十七条　以对话方式作出的意思表示，相对人知道其内容时生效。

以非对话方式作出的意思表示，到达相对人时生效。以非对话方式作出的采用数据电文形式的意思表示，相对人指定特定系统接收数据电文的，该数据电文进入该特定系统时生效；未指定特定系统的，相对人知道或者应当知道该数据电文进入其系统时生效。当事人对采用数据电文形式的意思表示的生效时间另有约定的，按照其约定。

2. Abschnitt: Willenserklärungen[48]

§ 137 [Wirksamwerden von Willenserklärungen] Wird eine Willenserklärung in einem Gespräch abgegeben, wird sie wirksam, wenn das Gegenüber von ihrem Inhalt Kenntnis erlangt.

Wird die Willenserklärung nicht in einem Gespräch abgegeben, wird sie wirksam, wenn sie dem Gegenüber zugeht. Wenn die Willenserklärung nicht in einem Gespräch abgegeben wird, sondern die Form eines elektronischen Datenschriftstücks verwendet wird, und das Gegenüber ein bestimmtes Computersystem benannt hat, um elektronische Datenschriftstücke zu empfangen, wird die Willenserklärung wirksam, sobald sie in dieses bestimmte System gelangt. Wenn kein bestimmtes Computersystem benannt wurde, wird die Willenserklärung wirksam, wenn das Gegenüber weiß oder wissen musste, dass das elektronische Datenschriftstück in sein Computersystem gelangt ist. Wenn die Parteien für den Zeitpunkt des Wirksamwerdens der von ihnen verwendeten Form eines elektronischen Datenschriftstücks für Willenserklärungen etwas anderes vereinbart haben, gilt diese Vereinbarung.

Subchapter 2 Declaration of Intent

Section 137 The declaration of intent made in a dialogue is effective when the counterparty becomes aware of the content.

The declaration of intent made outside of a dialogue is effective when it reaches the counterparty. If the declaration of intent made outside of a dialogue is used in the form of an electronic document and the counterparty has named a specific computer system for receiving electronic documents, the declaration of intent becomes effective once it enters the system. If no specific computer system was named, the declaration of intent becomes effective if the counterparty knows, or should have known, that the electronic document has entered the system. If the parties have agreed otherwise for the time of the coming into effect of the agreed form of an electronic document, this agreement applies.

48 Dieser Abschnitt wurde neu eingefügt.

第一百三十八条　无相对人的意思表示，表示完成时生效。法律另有规定的，依照其规定。	**§ 138 [Nicht empfangsbedürftige Willenserklärungen]** Nicht empfangsbedürftige Willenserklärungen[49] werden mit Vollendung der Äußerung wirksam. Enthalten Gesetze anderweitige Bestimmungen, so gelten diese Bestimmungen.	**Section 138** Declarations of intent that become effective without receipt by the other party become effective with the conclusion of the declaration, unless otherwise provided by law.
第一百三十九条　以公告方式作出的意思表示，公告发布时生效。	**§ 139 [Willenserklärung durch Bekanntmachung]** Willenserklärungen in Form einer Bekanntmachung werden mit dem Verkünden der Bekanntmachung wirksam.	**Section 139** Declarations of intent by announcement become effective upon announcement.
第一百四十条　行为人可以明示或者默示作出意思表示。	**§ 140 [Ausdrückliche und konkludente Willenserklärung; Schweigen]** Der Handelnde kann Willenserklärungen ausdrücklich oder stillschweigend abgeben.	**Section 140** The acting person can make declarations of intent explicitly or tacitly.
沉默只有在有法律规定、当事人约定或者符合当事人之间的交易习惯时，才可以视为意思表示。	Schweigen kann nur dann als Willenserklärung angesehen werden, wenn es das Gesetz bestimmt, es die Parteien vereinbaren oder wenn dies nach den früheren geschäftlichen Gebräuche zwischen den Parteien üblich war.	Silence can only be considered a declaration of intent if provided by law or agreed by the parties, or if this was common practice between the parties.
第一百四十一条　行为人可以撤回意思表示。撤回意思表示的通知应	**§ 141 [Zurücknahme von Willenserklärungen]** Der Handelnde kann eine Willensklärung zurücknehmen.[50]	**Section 141** The acting person can withdraw a civil transaction. The notice of withdrawal

49 Wörtlich: „Willenserklärungen ohne Gegenüber".

50 Der Begriff 撤回 wird hier in Anlehnung an die Rücknahme von Angeboten vor Zugang beim Erklärungsempfänger nach Art. 15 Abs. 2 Übereinkommen der Vereinten Nationen über Verträge über den internationalen Warenkauf (UN-Kaufrecht, BGBl. 1989 II S. 586, 588) mit „zurücknehmen" übersetzt. Im deutschen Recht würde man von einem Widerruf sprechen. Das chinesische Vertragsgesetz folgt aber insoweit nicht dem deutschen Recht, sondern dem UN-Kaufrecht, indem ein Widerruf von Angeboten nach Art. 16 bis zur Absendung

当在意思表示到达相对人前或者与意思表示同时到达相对人。

Die Mitteilung der Rücknahme der Willenserklärung muss dem Gegenüber vor dem oder zeitgleich mit dem Zugang der Willenserklärung zugehen.

of the declaration of intent shall reach the counterparty before or at the time of the receipt of the declaration of intent.

第一百四十二条　有相对人的意思表示的解释，应当按照所使用的词句，结合相关条款、行为的性质和目的、习惯以及诚信原则，确定意思表示的含义。

§ 142 [Auslegung von Willenserklärungen] Bei der Auslegung einer empfangsbedürftigen Willenserklärung[51] muss anhand des verwendeten Wortlauts unter Einbeziehung relevanter Klauseln, der Natur und des Zwecks der Handlung, der Gebräuche und des Grundsatzes von Treu und Glauben der Inhalt der Willenserklärung bestimmt werden.

Section 142 Interpreting a declaration of intent that becomes effective upon receipt by the other party, the content of the declaration of intent shall be determined by means of the wording taking relevant provisions, the nature of the purpose of the act, practices, and the principle of good faith into account.

无相对人的意思表示的解释，不能完全拘泥于所使用的词句，而应当结合相关条款、行为的性质和目的、习惯以及诚信原则，确定行为人的真实意思。

Bei der Auslegung einer nicht empfangsbedürftigen Willenserklärung kann nicht mit vollständiger Strenge am verwendeten Wortlaut festgehalten werden, sondern es muss unter Einbeziehung relevanter Klauseln, der Natur und des Zwecks der Handlung, der Gebräuche und des Grundsatzes von Treu und Glauben der wahre Wille des Handelnden bestimmt werden.

Interpreting a declaration of intent that becomes effective without receipt by the other party, the wording cannot be fully adhered to, but the true will of the acting party shall be determined by taking relevant provisions, the nature and the purpose of the act, the practices, and the principle of good faith into account.

---

der Annahmeerklärung zulässig ist. In der chinesischen Urschrift des UN-Kaufrechts (siehe dort nach Art. 101) werden die Begriffe 撤回 (in Art. 15) und 撤销 (in Art. 16) verwendet, die in der deutschen Übersetzung mit „zurücknehmen“ bzw. „widerrufen“ wiedergegeben werden.

51 Wörtlich: „Willenserklärung mit Gegenüber“.

第三节　民事法律行为的效力	**3. Abschnitt: Wirksamkeit von Zivilrechtsgeschäften**	**Subchapter 3 Validity of Civil Transactions**
第一百四十三条　具备下列条件的民事法律行为有效：	**§ 143 [Wirksamkeitsvoraussetzungen; vgl. § 55 AGZR]** Ein Zivilrechtsgeschäft, das die folgenden Bedingungen erfüllt, ist wirksam:	**Section 143** A civil transaction fulfilling the following conditions is valid:
（一）行为人具有相应的民事行为能力； （二）意思表示真实； （三）不违反法律、行政法规的强制性规定，不违背公序良俗。	1. Der Handelnde besitzt eine entsprechende Zivilgeschäftsfähigkeit; 2. die Willenserklärung ist wahr[52]; 3. es verstößt nicht gegen zwingende Bestimmungen in Gesetzen [oder] Verwaltungsrechtsnormen [und] läuft nicht der öffentlichen Ordnung und den guten Sitten zuwider.	(1) The acting person has contractual capacity; (2) The declaration of intent is true; (3) It does not violate mandatory provisions of the law or administrative regulations and does not contradict the public order and public decency.
第一百四十四条　无民事行为能力人实施的民事法律行为无效。	**§ 144 [Rechtsgeschäfte Geschäftsunfähiger; vgl. § 58 Abs. 1 Nr. 1 AGZR]** Ein von einem Zivilgeschäftsunfähigen vorgenommenes Zivilrechtsgeschäft ist unwirksam.	**Section 144** Civil transactions entered by a person lacking contractual capacity is invalid.
第一百四十五条　限制民事行为能力人实施的纯获利益的民事法律行为或者与其年龄、智力、精神健康状况相适应的民事法律行为有效；实施的其他民事法律行为经法定代理人同意或者追认后有效。	**§ 145 [Rechtsgeschäfte beschränkt Geschäftsfähiger; vgl. § 58 Abs. 1 Nr. 2 AGZR, Abs. 2]** Ein von einem beschränkt Zivilgeschäftsfähigen vorgenommenes, rein vorteilhaftes Zivilrechtsgeschäft oder ein Zivilrechtsgeschäft, das seinem Alter und seinen geistigen Fähigkei-	**Section 145** A purely beneficial civil transaction entered by a person with limited contractual capacity or a civil transaction that corresponds to their mental capacity and health is valid; other civil transaction entered by them

52 Eine Willenserklärung ist „wahr" [真实] im Sinne dieser Vorschrift, wenn geäußerter und innerer Wille übereinstimmen, *SHEN Deyong* [沈德咏] (Hrsg.), Verständnis und Anwendung der Vorschriften des „Allgemeinen Teils des Zivilrechts der Volksrepublik China" (Band 2) [中华人民共和国民法总则条文理解与适用（下）], Beijing 2017, ebenso zu § 55 Nr. 2 AGZR bereits *Stefanie Tetz*, Abschluss und Wirksamkeit von Verträgen in der Volksrepublik China, Hamburg 1994, S. 89.

	ten und seiner geistigen Gesundheit entspricht, ist wirksam; andere von ihm vorgenommene Zivilrechtsgeschäfte, werden mit dem Einverständnis oder der Genehmigung des gesetzlichen Vertreters wirksam.	become valid upon consent or authorisation of the legal representative.
相对人可以催告法定代理人自收到通知之日起一个月内予以追认。法定代理人未作表示的，视为拒绝追认。民事法律行为被追认前，善意相对人有撤销的权利。撤销应当以通知的方式作出。	Das Gegenüber kann den gesetzlichen Vertreter [durch Mitteilung] auffordern, innerhalb eines Monats beginnend mit dem Tag des Erhalts der Mitteilung, die Genehmigung zu erteilen. Wenn der gesetzliche Vertreter sich nicht äußert, gilt die Genehmigung als verweigert. Solange das Zivilrechtsgeschäft nicht genehmigt ist, hat ein gutgläubiges Gegenüber das Recht zum Widerruf[53]. Der Widerruf muss mittels einer Mitteilung erfolgen.	The counterparty can urge the legal representative upon notice to give authorisation within one month starting on the day of receipt of the notice. If the legal representative does not comment, the authorisation is considered as denied. As long as the civil transaction has not been authorised, a counterparty in good faith has the right to revocation. The revocation shall be made by notice.
第一百四十六条　行为人与相对人以虚假的意思表示实施的民事法律行为无效。	**§ 146 [Scheingeschäft; vgl. § 58 Abs. 1 Nr. 7 AGZR]** Ein Zivilrechtsgeschäft, das der Handelnde mit dem Gegenüber durch falsche Willenserklärung vornimmt, sind unwirksam.	**Section 146** A civil transaction entered by the acting person with the counterparty by fraudulent declaration of intent is invalid.
以虚假的意思表示隐藏的民事法律行为的效力，依照有关法律规定处理。	Auf die Wirksamkeit eines Zivilrechtsgeschäfts, das durch falsche Willenserklärung verdeckt wird, finden die einschlägigen gesetzlichen Bestimmungen Anwendung.	The respective legal provisions are applicable to the validity of civil transaction that are concealed by fraudulent declaration of intent.
第一百四十七条　基于重大误解实施的民事法律行为，行为人有权请	**§ 147 [Anfechtung wegen Irrtums; vgl. § 59 Abs. 1 Nr. 1 AGZR]** Wenn ein Zivilrechtsgeschäft aufgrund	**Section 147** If a civil transaction has been entered due to a grave error, the acting party has

53 An dieser Stelle wird im chinesischen Text ein Begriff verwendet, der ansonsten im Gesetz für die Aufhebung von Rechtsgeschäften verwendet wird („撤销" = „Aufhebung"). Hier wird dieser Begriff jedoch im Zusammenhang mit einem (zumindest nach deutschem Verständnis) schwebend unwirksamen Rechtsgeschäft verwendet. Deswegen wird der Begriff an dieser Stelle abweichend als „Widerruf" übersetzt.

求人民法院或者仲裁机构予以撤销。

eines schwerwiegenden Irrtums vorgenommen wurde, ist der Handelnde berechtigt, beim Volksgericht oder beim Schiedsorgan die Aufhebung zu verlangen.

the right to apply for annulment before the people's court or the arbitration authority.

第一百四十八条　一方以欺诈手段，使对方在违背真实意思的情况下实施的民事法律行为，受欺诈方有权请求人民法院或者仲裁机构予以撤销。

§ 148 [Anfechtung wegen Täuschung; vgl. § 58 Abs. 1 Nr. 3 AGZR] Wenn eine Seite die andere Seite durch Täuschung veranlasst, entgegen [deren] wahren Willen, ein Zivilrechtsgeschäft vorzunehmen, ist die getäuschte Seite berechtigt, vom Volksgericht oder Schiedsorgan Aufhebung zu verlangen.

Section 148 If one party by deception causes the other party to enter a civil transaction against their true will, the deceived party has the right to apply for annulment before the people's court or the arbitration authority.

第一百四十九条　第三人实施欺诈行为，使一方在违背真实意思的情况下实施的民事法律行为，对方知道或者应当知道该欺诈行为的，受欺诈方有权请求人民法院或者仲裁机构予以撤销。

§ 149 [Anfechtung wegen Täuschung durch Dritte] Wenn eine durch einen Dritten vorgenommene Täuschungshandlung eine Seite entgegen dem wahren Willen dazu veranlasst, ein Zivilrechtsgeschäft vorzunehmen [und] die andere Seite die Täuschungshandlung kannte oder kennen musste, ist die getäuschte Seite berechtigt, vom Volksgericht oder Schiedsorgan Aufhebung zu verlangen.

Section 149 If a deceptive act by a third party causes one party against their true will to enter a civil transaction, and the other side knew or should have known of the deceptive act, the deceived party has the right to apply for annulment before the people's court or the arbitration authority.

第一百五十条　一方或者第三人以胁迫手段，使对方在违背真实意思的情况下实施的民事法律行为，受胁迫方有权请求人民法院或者仲裁机构予以撤销。

§ 150 [Anfechtung wegen Drohung; vgl. § 58 Abs. 1 Nr. 3 AGZR] Wenn eine Seite oder ein Dritter die andere Seite durch Drohung entgegen dem wahren Willen dazu veranlassen, ein Zivilrechtsgeschäft vorzunehmen, ist die bedrohte Seite berechtigt, vom Volksgericht oder Schiedsorgan Aufhebung zu verlangen.

Section 150 If one party or a third party causes the other party by threat to enter a civil transaction, the threatened party has the right to apply for annulment before the people's court or the arbitration authority.

第一百五十一条　一方利用对方处于危困状态、缺乏判断能力等情形，致使民事法律行为成立时显失公平的，受损害方有权请求人民法院或者仲裁机构予以撤销。

§ 151 [Anfechtung wegen unangemessener Benachteiligung; vgl. § 58 Abs. 1 Nr. 3 und § 59 Abs. 1 Nr. 2 AGZR] Wenn eine Seite ausnutzt, dass sich die andere Seite in einer gefährlichen [oder] schwierigen Lage befindet, es [ihr]an Entscheidungsfähigkeit mangelt [oder]

Section 151 If one party exploits a dangerous or grave state of the other party that they lack decision-making ability or other circumstances and this causes the civil transaction to

	sonstige Umstände [vorliegen], [und] dies dazu führt, dass das Zivilrechtsgeschäft zur Zeit seines Zustandekommens deutlich ungerecht ist, ist die geschädigte Seite berechtigt, vom Volksgericht oder Schiedsorgan Aufhebung zu verlangen.	be considerably unfair at the time of the conclusion of the civil transaction, the injured party has the right to apply for annulment before the people's court of the arbitration authority.
第一百五十二条　有下列情形之一的，撤销权消灭：	**§ 152 [Anfechtungsfrist]** Das Recht auf Aufhebung erlischt, wenn einer der folgenden Umstände vorliegt:	**Section 152** The right to annulment ceases under one of the following circumstances:
（一）当事人自知道或者应当知道撤销事由之日起一年内、重大误解的当事人自知道或者应当知道撤销事由之日起三个月内没有行使撤销权；	1. das Recht zur Aufhebung wird nicht innerhalb eines Jahres von dem Tag an ausgeübt, an dem die Partei die Gründe für die Aufhebung kannte oder kennen musste; oder es wird nicht innerhalb von drei Monaten von dem Tag an ausgeübt, an dem die Partei mit einem schwerwiegenden Irrtum die Gründe für die Aufhebung kannte oder kennen musste;	(1) The right to annulment is not exercised within a period of one year starting on the day the party knew or should have known the grounds for annulment; it is not exercised within a period of three months starting on the day that the party with the grave error knew or should have known the grounds for annulment;
（二）当事人受胁迫，自胁迫行为终止之日起一年内没有行使撤销权；	2. das Recht zur Aufhebung wird nicht innerhalb eines Jahres von dem Tag an ausgeübt wird, an dem die bedrohende Handlung für die bedrohte Partei endet;	(2) The right to annulment is not exercised within a one year period starting on the day that the threatening act for the threatened party ends;
（三）当事人知道撤销事由后明确表示或者以自己的行为表明放弃撤销权。	3. nachdem die Partei Kenntnis von den Gründen für die Aufhebung erlangt hat, erklärt sie klar oder zeigt durch ihre Handlung deutlich, dass sie auf das Recht zur Aufhebung verzichtet.	(3) After the party gains knowledge of the grounds for annulment they clearly explain or explicitly show that they waive the right to annulment.
当事人自民事法律行为发生之日起五年内没有行使撤销权的，撤销权消灭。	Wenn die Partei das Recht zur Aufhebung nicht innerhalb von fünf Jahren von dem Tag des Zivilrechtsgeschäfts an ausübt, erlischt das Recht zur Aufhebung.	If the parties have not exercised the right to annulment within a period of five years starting on the day of the civil transaction, the right to annulment ceases.
第一百五十三条　违反法律、行政法规的强制性规定的民事法律行为	**§ 153 [Gesetzliches Verbot; Sittenwidrigkeit; vgl. § 58 Abs. 1 Nr. 5 AGZR]** Zivilrechtsgeschäfte, die	**Section 153** Civil transactions violating mandatory provisions of the law are invalid; this

无效，但是该强制性规定不导致该民事法律行为无效的除外。	zwingende Bestimmungen in Gesetzen [oder] Verwaltungsrechtsnormen[54] verletzen, sind unwirksam; dies gilt jedoch nicht, wenn diese zwingenden Bestimmungen nicht dazu führen, dass diese Zivilrechtsgeschäfte unwirksam sind.	does not apply, however, if these mandatory provisions do not cause the invalidity of the civil transactions.
违背公序良俗的民事法律行为无效。	Zivilrechtshandlungen, die der öffentlichen Ordnung [und] den guten Sitten[55] zuwiderlaufen, sind unwirksam.	Civil legal acts are invalid if they contradict the public order and the public decency.
第一百五十四条　行为人与相对人恶意串通，损害他人合法权益的民事法律行为无效。	**§ 154 [Kollusion zum Nachteil anderer; vgl. § 58 Abs. 1 Nr. 4 AGZR]** Zivilrechtsgeschäfte, bei denen der Handelnde und das Gegenüber in böswilliger Kollusion die legalen Rechte und Interessen anderer schädigen, sind unwirksam.	**Section 154** Civil transactions are invalid if the acting party and the counterparty thereby damage the legal rights and interests of others by malevolent collusion.
第一百五十五条　无效的或者被撤销的民事法律行为自始没有法律约束力。	**§ 155 [Ex-tunc-Unwirksamkeit; vgl. § 58 Abs. 2 und § 59 Abs.§ 2 AGZR]** Unwirksame oder aufgehobene Zivilrechtsgeschäfte haben vom Beginn an keine rechtliche Bindungskraft.	**Section 155** Invalid or annulled civil transactions are not legally binding from the beginning.
第一百五十六条　民事法律行为部分无效，不影响其他部分效力的，其他部分仍然有效。	**§ 156 [Teilunwirksamkeit; vgl. § 60 AGZR]** Ist ein Teil des Zivilrechtsgeschäfts unwirksam, ohne dass das die Wirkung der anderen Teile beeinflusst, so bleiben die anderen Teile wirksam.	**Section 156** If part of a civil transaction is invalid while the effect of other parts is unaffected, the other part shall still be valid.
第一百五十七条　民事法律行为无效、被撤销或者确定不发生效力后，行为人因该行为取得的财产，应	**§ 157 [Rechtsfolgen der Unwirksamkeit; vgl. § 61 Abs. 1 AGZR]** Ist ein Zivilrechtsgeschäft unwirksam, aufgehoben worden oder wurde festgestellt, dass es	**Section 157** If a civil transaction is invalid annulled or if it was confirmed to have no effect, the acting persons shall return property

54 S. o. Fn. 25.
55 S. o. Fn. 5.

当予以返还；不能返还或者没有必要返还的，应当折价补偿。有过错的一方应当赔偿对方由此所受到的损失；各方都有过错的，应当各自承担相应的责任。法律另有规定的，依照其规定。

keine Wirkungen entfaltet, so müssen die Handelnden aus dieser Handlung erlangtes Vermögensgut zurückgeben; wenn es nicht zurückgegeben werden kann oder eine Rückgabe unnötig ist, so muss es in seinen Wert umgerechnet ersetzt werden. Die Seite, bei der Verschulden vorliegt, muss der anderen Seite den infolgedessen erlittenen Schaden ersetzen; liegt auf allen Seiten Verschulden vor, so muss jede Seite eine entsprechende Haftung tragen. Wenn gesetzlich etwas anderes bestimmt ist, gelten diese Bestimmungen.

obtained from these acts; if it cannot be returned or the return is unnecessary, it shall be replaced with its converted value. The culpable part shall compensate the other party that suffered the damage; if both parties are culpable, each part shall bear the respective liability. If the law otherwise provides, these provisions shall apply.

第四节　民事法律行为的附条件和附期限

4. Abschnitt: Bedingungen und Zeitbestimmung bei Zivilrechtsgeschäften

Subchapter 4 Conditions and Duration of Civil Transactions

第一百五十八条　民事法律行为可以附条件，但是按照其性质不得附条件的除外。附生效条件的民事法律行为，自条件成就时生效。附解除条件的民事法律行为，自条件成就时失效。

§ 158 [Aufschiebende und auflösende Bedingung; vgl. § 62 AGZR] Ein Zivilrechtsgeschäft kann unter eine Bedingung gestellt werden, außer es darf gemäß seiner Natur nicht unter eine Bedingung gestellt werden. Ein aufschiebend bedingtes Zivilrechtsgeschäft wird mit dem Eintritt der Bedingung wirksam. Ein auflösend bedingtes Zivilrechtsgeschäft wird mit dem Eintritt der Bedingung unwirksam.

Section 158 A civil transaction can be subject to a condition, unless it cannot be subject to a condition due to its nature. A civil transaction under a suspensive condition becomes valid upon the occurrence of the condition. A civil transaction under a resolving condition becomes valid upon the occurrence of the condition.

第一百五十九条　附条件的民事法律行为，当事人为自己的利益不正当地阻止条件成就的，视为条件已成就；不正当地促成条件成就的，视为条件不成就

§ 159 [Fiktion des Bedingungseintritts] Wenn ein Zivilrechtsgeschäft unter Bedingungen gestellt wurde [und] eine Partei zu ihrem eigenen Vorteil den Eintritt einer Bedingung unlauter verhindert, gilt die Bedingung als eingetreten; wenn sie unlauter den Eintritt einer Bedingung herbeiführt, gilt die Bedingung als nicht eingetreten.

Section 159 If a civil transaction is subject to a condition and the party illicitly prevented the occurrence of the condition for their own benefit, the condition is considered to have occurred; if they illicitly cause the occurrence of a condition, it is considered not to have occurred.

第一百六十条　民事法律行为可以附期限，但是按照其性质不得附期限的除外。附生效期限的民事法律行为，自期限届至时生效。附终止期限的民事法律行为，自期限届满时失效。	**§ 160 [Zeitbestimmung]** Ein Zivilrechtsgeschäft kann unter eine Frist gestellt werden, außer es darf gemäß seiner Natur nicht unter eine Frist gestellt werden. Ein Zivilrechtsgeschäft mit einer Frist für den Eintritt der Wirksamkeit wird mit Fristende wirksam. Ein Zivilrechtsgeschäft mit einer Beendigungsfrist wird mit Fristende unwirksam.	**Section 160** A civil transaction can be subject to a grace period, unless it may not be subject to a grace period due to its nature. A civil transaction with a grace period for the occurrence of the validity becomes valid upon the end of the grace period. A civil transaction with a grace period of termination becomes invalid upon the end of the grace period.
第七章　代　理	**7. Kapitel: Vertretung**	**Chapter VII Agency**
第一节　一般规定	**1. Abschnitt: Allgemeine Bestimmungen**	**Subchapter 1 General Stipulations**
第一百六十一条　民事主体可以通过代理人实施民事法律行为。	**§ 161 [Stellvertretung; vgl. § 63 Abs. 1 und 3 AGZR]** Zivilrechtssubjekte können durch Vertreter Zivilrechtsgeschäfte vornehmen.	**Section 161** Civil legal subjects can perform the civil transactions through agents.
依照法律规定、当事人约定或者民事法律行为的性质，应当由本人亲自实施的民事法律行为，不得代理。	Bei Zivilrechtsgeschäften, die nach gesetzlicher Bestimmung, Parteivereinbarung oder der Natur der Zivilrechtshandlung persönlich vorgenommen werden müssen, ist Vertretung unzulässig.	Agency is impermissible for civil transactions that must be performed in person according to a legal provision or agreement by the parties of the nature of the civil transaction.
第一百六十二条　代理人在代理权限内，以被代理人名义实施的民事法律行为，对被代理人发生效力。	**§ 162 [Wirkung von Vertretungshandlungen; vgl. § 63 Abs. 2 AGZR]** Zivilrechtsgeschäfte, die der Vertreter innerhalb der Grenzen der Vertretungsmacht im Namen des Vertretenen vornimmt, entfalten Wirkung gegenüber dem Vertretenen.	**Section 162** Civil transactions that the agent performs within the exercise of their powers in the name of the principal are effective for the principal.
第一百六十三条　代理包括委托代理和法定代理。	**§ 163 [Formen der Stellvertretung; vgl. § 64 AGZR]** Vertretung umfasst die beauftragte Vertretung und die gesetzliche Vertretung.	**Section 163** Agency includes entrusted agency and the statutory agency.

委托代理人按照被代理人的委托行使代理权。法定代理人依照法律的规定行使代理权。	Der beauftragte Vertreter übt die Vertretungsmacht gemäß dem Auftrag des Vertretenen aus, der gesetzliche Vertreter übt die Vertretungsmacht gemäß den gesetzlichen Bestimmungen aus.	The entrusted agent shall exercise the agency powers in accordance with the entrustment of the principal, the legal agent shall exercise the agency powers in accordance with the law.
第一百六十四条　代理人不履行或者不完全履行职责，造成被代理人损害的，应当承担民事责任。	**§ 164 [Schadenersatzhaftung des Stellvertreters; vgl. § 66 Abs. 2 und 3 AGZR]** Wenn der Vertreter, indem er seine Amtspflichten nicht oder nicht vollständig erfüllt, eine Schädigung des Vertretenen herbeiführt, muss er die zivile Haftung tragen.	**Section 164** If the agent fails to perform or fails to fully perform his duties and causes damage to the principal, they shall bear the civil liability.
代理人和相对人恶意串通，损害被代理人合法权益的，代理人和相对人应当承担连带责任。	Wenn der Vertreter und das Gegenüber die legalen Rechte und Interessen des Vertretenen in böswilliger Kollusion schädigen, müssen der Vertreter und das Gegenüber die Haftung als Gesamtschuldner tragen.	If the agent and counterparty cause damages to the legal rights and interests of the principal by malicious collusion, the agent and the counterparty shall bear joint and several liability.
第二节　委托代理	**2. Abschnitt: Beauftragte Vertretung**	**Subchapter 2 Entrusted Agency**
第一百六十五条　委托代理授权采用书面形式的，授权委托书应当载明代理人的姓名或者名称、代理事项、权限和期间，并由被代理人签名或者盖章。	**§ 165 [Vollmachtsurkunde; vgl. § 65 AGZR]** Wird bei der Bevollmächtigung zur beauftragten Vertretung die Schriftform verwendet, muss die Vollmachtsurkunde[56] den Namen oder die Bezeichnung des Vertreters [sowie] den Gegenstand der Vertretung, die Befugnisse und die Frist angeben und vom Vertretenen unterschrieben oder gesiegelt sein.	**Section 165** When written form is used in authorisation for the entrusted agency, the letter of authorisation shall indicate the agent's name, the authorised matters, the powers and time limitation which shall be signed or sealed by the principal.

56 Wörtlich: „Bevollmächtigungs- [und] Beauftragungsurkunde“.

第一百六十六条　数人为同一代理事项的代理人的，应当共同行使代理权，但是当事人另有约定的除外。	**§ 166 [Gemeinsame Vertretung]** Sind mehrere Personen Vertreter hinsichtlich desselben Vertretungsgegenstandes, müssen sie die Vertretungsmacht gemeinsam ausführen, soweit die Parteien nicht etwas anderes vereinbart haben.	**Section 166** If several persons authorised agents for the same matter, they shall jointly exercise the power of agency, unless otherwise agreed by the parties.
第一百六十七条　代理人知道或者应当知道代理事项违法仍然实施代理行为，或者被代理人知道或者应当知道代理人的代理行为违法未作反对表示的，被代理人和代理人应当承担连带责任。	**§ 167 [Haftung für rechtswidrige Vertretungshandlungen; vgl. § 67 AGZR]** Wenn der Vertreter weiß oder wissen musste, dass der Gegenstand der Vertretung gegen das Recht verstößt [und] dennoch die Vertretungshandlung vornimmt, oder wenn der Vertretene weiß oder wissen musste, dass Vertretungshandlungen des Vertreters gegen das Recht verstoßen [und] keinen Widerspruch äußert, müssen der Vertretene und der Vertreter die Haftung als Gesamtschuldner tragen.	**Section 167** If the agent knows or should have known that the matter of the agency violates the law and nonetheless performs agency actions, or if the principal knows, or should have known that actions of the agent violate the law and does not object to it, the principal and the agent must bear joint and several liability.
第一百六十八条　代理人不得以被代理人的名义与自己实施民事法律行为，但是被代理人同意或者追认的除外。 代理人不得以被代理人的名义与自己同时代理的其他人实施民事法律行为，但是被代理的双方同意或者追认的除外。	**§ 168 [Insichgeschäfte]** Vertreter dürfen Zivilrechtsgeschäfte nicht im Namen des Vertretenen mit sich selber vornehmen, außer der Vertretene ist einverstanden oder genehmigt. Vertreter dürfen Zivilrechtsgeschäfte im Namen des Vertretenen nicht mit anderen durch sie selbst zugleich vertretenen Personen vornehmen, außer beide vertretenen Seiten sind einverstanden oder genehmigen.	**Section 168** Agents shall not perform civil transactions in the name of the principal with themselves, unless the principal consents or gives authorisation. Agents shall not perform civil transactions in the name of the principal with other of their principals, unless both parties consent or give authorisation.
第一百六十九条　代理人需要转委托第三人代理的，应当取得被代理人的同意或者追认。	**§ 169 [Untervollmacht; vgl. § 68 AGZR]** Wenn es erforderlich ist, dass der Vertreter einen Dritten unterbeauftragt, muss [er] vorher das Einverständnis oder die Genehmigung des Vertretenen einholen.	**Section 169** If the agent needs to entrust third parties as agents, they shall obtain the consent or authorisation of the principal. The agent shall only be liable for the appointment of third parties and the instruction to third parties.

转委托代理经被代理人同意或者追认的，被代理人可以就代理事务直接指示转委托的第三人，代理人仅就第三人的选任以及对第三人的指示承担责任。	Wenn die Unterbeauftragung zur Vertretung mit Einverständnis oder Genehmigung des Vertretenen erfolgte, kann der Vertretene Anweisungen zur Angelegenheit, in der vertreten wird, direkt dem Dritten geben, an den der Auftrag übertragen wurde; der Vertreter trägt die Haftung nur für die Auswahl des Dritten und die [eigenen] Anweisungen an den Dritten.	If such subcontract for agency was made with the consent or the authorisation of the principal, the principal can directly instruct the third party with whom the subcontract was made on the matter; the agent shall be liable for the selection of the third party and their own instructions to the third party.
转委托代理未经被代理人同意或者追认的，代理人应当对转委托的第三人的行为承担责任，但是在紧急情况下代理人为了维护被代理人的利益需要转委托第三人代理的除外。	Wenn der Auftrag zur Vertretung ohne Einverständnis oder Genehmigung des Vertretenen übertragen wurde, muss der Vertreter für Handlungen des Dritten die Haftung tragen, an den der Auftrag übertragen wurde; außer dann, wenn es unter dringenden Umständen zur Wahrung der Interessen des Vertretenen nötig war, dass der Vertreter den Auftrag zur Vertretung an einen Dritten überträgt.	If the subcontract for agency has been made without the consent or authorisation of the principal, the agent bears the liability for acts of the third party with whom they made the subcontract, unless the transfer of agency to a third person is necessary in urgent cases to preserve the interests of the principal.
第一百七十条　执行法人或者非法人组织工作任务的人员，就其职权范围内的事项，以法人或者非法人组织的名义实施民事法律行为，对法人或者非法人组织发生效力。	**§ 170 [Vertretung durch Personal]** Ein Zivilrechtsgeschäft, das von Personal, das Arbeitsaufgaben für eine juristische Person oder Organisation ohne Rechtspersönlichkeit durchführt, in Bezug auf einen Gegenstand im Bereich seiner Amtsbefugnisse im Namen der juristischen Person oder Organisation ohne Rechtspersönlichkeit vorgenommen wird, entfaltet gegenüber der juristischen Person oder Organisation ohne Rechtspersönlichkeit Wirkung.	**Section 170** A civil legal transaction performed by personnel who completes work assignments for a legal entity or non-incorporated organisation with regard to an item in the scope of their powers in the name of the legal entity or non-incorporated organisation takes effect in relation to the legal entity or non-incorporated organisation.
法人或者非法人组织对执行其工作任务的人员职权范围的限制，不得对抗善意相对人。	Beschränkungen des Bereichs der Amtsbefugnisse von Personal, das Arbeitsaufgaben für juristische Personen oder Organisationen ohne Rechtspersönlichkeit durchführt, dürfen nicht einem gutgläubigen Gegenüber entgegengehalten werden.	Limitations of the powers of personnel performing work assignments for the legal entities or organisations may not be used to object counterparties in good faith.

第一百七十一条　行为人没有代理权、超越代理权或者代理权终止后，仍然实施代理行为，未经被代理人追认的，对被代理人不发生效力。	**§ 171 [Vertretung ohne Vertretungsmacht; vgl. § 66 Abs. 1 und 4 AGZR]** Wenn ein Handelnder keine Vertretungsmacht hat, die Vertretungsmacht überschreitet oder nach Beendigung der Vertretungsmacht dennoch eine Vertretungshandlung vornimmt [und] der Vertretene sie nicht genehmigt, entfaltet [die Vertretungshandlung] gegenüber dem Vertretenen keine Wirkung.	**Section 171** If an agent does not have actual authority, exceeds the powers, or performs an action even though the agency has been terminated and the principal does not authorise it, the agency action does not take effect in relation to the principal.
相对人可以催告被代理人自收到通知之日起一个月内予以追认。被代理人未作表示的，视为拒绝追认。行为人实施的行为被追认前，善意相对人有撤销的权利。撤销应当以通知的方式作出。	Das Gegenüber kann den Vertretenen [durch Mitteilung] auffordern, innerhalb eines Monats ab dem Tag des Erhalts der Mitteilung die Genehmigung zu erteilen. Äußert der Vertretene sich nicht, gilt die Genehmigung als verweigert. Bevor die vom Handelnden vorgenommene Handlung genehmigt wurde, hat ein gutgläubiges Gegenüber das Recht zum Widerruf[57]. Der Widerruf muss in Form einer Mitteilung erfolgen.	The counterparty can request the principal upon notice to give the authorisation within one month from the day of the receipt of the notification. If the principal does not express themselves, the authorisation is considered denied. Before the action performed by the agent was authorised, a counterparty in good faith has the right to revocation. The revocation must be issued by notification.
行为人实施的行为未被追认的，善意相对人有权请求行为人履行债务或者就其受到的损害请求行为人赔偿，但是赔偿的范围不得超过被代理人追认时相对人所能获得的利益。	Wird die vom Handelnden vorgenommene Handlung nicht genehmigt, ist ein gutgläubiges Gegenüber berechtigt, vom Handelnden die Erfüllung der Schuld zu verlangen oder, wenn ein Schaden herbeigeführt wurde, vom Handelnden Schadensersatz zu verlangen; der Umfang des Schadensersatzes darf jedoch nicht den Vorteil überschreiten, den das Gegenüber bei einer Genehmigung durch den Vertretenen erlangt hätte.	If the action performed by the agent is not authorised, a counterparty in good faith has the right to claim the fulfilment of the liability from the agent, or if the damage has been inflicted, to claim damages from the agent; the amount of damages may not exceed the advantage which the counterparty would have obtained in the case of an authorisation by the principal.

57 Vgl. Fn. 51.

相对人知道或者应当知道行为人无权代理的，相对人和行为人按照各自的过错承担责任。	Wenn das Gegenüber weiß oder wissen musste, dass der Handelnde keine Berechtigung zur Vertretung hat, tragen das Gegenüber und der Handelnde gemäß ihrem jeweiligen Verschulden die Haftung.	If the counterparty knows or should have known that the agent does not have the right to agency, the counterparty and the agent assume the liability according to their respective culpability.
第一百七十二条　行为人没有代理权、超越代理权或者代理权终止后，仍然实施代理行为，相对人有理由相信行为人有代理权的，代理行为有效。	**§ 172 [Rechtsscheinvollmacht]** Wenn ein Handelnder keine Vertretungsmacht hat, die Vertretungsmacht überschreitet oder nach Beendigung der Vertretungsmacht dennoch eine Vertretungshandlung vornimmt [und] das Gegenüber Grund zu der Annahme hat, dass der Handelnde Vertretungsmacht hat, ist diese Vertretungshandlung wirksam.	**Section 172** If the counterparty knows or should have known that the agent does not have the right to agency, exceeds their powers, or performs agency actions even though the agency has been terminated, and the counterparty has reason to believe that the agent has authority, this agency action is valid.
第三节　代理终止	**3. Abschnitt: Beendigung der Vertretung**	**Section 3 Termination of Agency**
第一百七十三条　有下列情形之一的，委托代理终止：	**§ 173 [Beendigung der beauftragten Vertretung; vgl. § 69 AGZR]** Wenn einer der folgenden Umstände vorliegt, endet die beauftragte Vertretung:	**Section 173** If one of the following cases applies, the entrusted agency terminates:
（一）代理期间届满或者代理事务完成；	1. Die Vertretungsfrist ist abgelaufen, oder die Angelegenheit, in der vertreten wird, ist abgeschlossen;	(1) The duration of agency has expired or the entrusted matters are completed;
（二）被代理人取消委托或者代理人辞去委托；	2. der Vertretene widerruft den Auftrag, oder der Vertreter kündigt den Auftrag;	(2) The principal revokes the entrustment or the agent cancels the entrustment;
（三）代理人丧失民事行为能力；	3. der Vertreter verliert die Zivilgeschäftsfähigkeit;	(3) The agent loses the contractual capacity;
（四）代理人或者被代理人死亡；	4. der Vertreter oder der Vertretene stirbt;	(4) The agent or the principal dies;
（五）作为代理人或者被代理人的法人、非法人组织终止。	5. die vertretende oder vertretene juristische Person [oder] Organisation ohne Rechtspersönlichkeit endet.	(5) The legal entity, or the non-legal-person acting as agent or principal, terminates.

第一百七十四条　被代理人死亡后，有下列情形之一的，委托代理人实施的代理行为有效：	**§ 174 [Vertretungshandlungen nach dem Tod des Vertretenen]** Vertretungshandlungen, die ein beauftragter Vertreter vornimmt, nachdem der Vertretene gestorben ist, sind wirksam, wenn einer der folgenden Umstände vorliegt:	**Section 174** Agency actions that are performed by an entrusted agent after the principal's death are valid if one of the following circumstances applies:
（一）代理人不知道并且不应当知道被代理人死亡；	1. Der Vertreter wusste nicht und musste nicht wissen, dass der Vertretene gestorben ist;	(1) The agent did not know and could not be expected to know that the principal died;
（二）被代理人的继承人予以承认；	2. der Erbe des Vertretenen gewährt die Anerkennung;	(2) The heir of the principal has authorised the actions;
（三）授权中明确代理权在代理事务完成时终止；	3. in der Bevollmächtigung kommt klar zum Ausdruck, dass die Vertretungsmacht [erst] mit Vollendung der Angelegenheit, in der vertreten wird, endet;	(3) The authorisation clearly provides that the authority shall terminate when the entrusted matters have been completed;
（四）被代理人死亡前已经实施，为了被代理人的继承人的利益继续代理。	4. wenn [Handlungen] vor dem Tod des Vertretenen bereits vorgenommen wurden, [und] die Vertretung im Interesse der Erben des Vertretenen fortgesetzt wird.	(4) If actions have been performed before the principal's death and the agency is being continued in the interest of the principal's heirs.
作为被代理人的法人、非法人组织终止的，参照适用前款规定。	Ist der Vertretene eine beendete juristische Person oder Organisation ohne Rechtspersönlichkeit wird der vorige Absatz entsprechend angewendet.	If the principal is a terminated legal entity or non-incorporated organisation, the previous paragraph applies correspondingly.
第一百七十五条　有下列情形之一的，法定代理终止：	**§ 175 [Beendigung der gesetzlichen Vertretung; vgl. § 70 AGZR]** Wenn einer der folgenden Umstände vorliegt, endet die gesetzliche Vertretung:	**Section 175** In any of the following circumstances, the statutory agency shall terminate:
（一）被代理人取得或者恢复完全民事行为能力；	1. Der Vertretene erlangt die Zivilgeschäftsfähigkeit oder stellt sie vollständig wieder her;	(1) The principal obtains contractual capacity or restores it completely;
（二）代理人丧失民事行为能力；	2. der Vertreter verliert die Zivilgeschäftsfähigkeit;	(2) The agent loses the contractual capacity;
（三）代理人或者被代理人死亡；	3. der Vertreter oder der Vertretene stirbt;	(3) The agent or the principal dies;

（四）法律规定的其他情形。	4. in anderen durch Gesetz bestimmten Umständen.	(4) In other circumstances prescribed by law.
第八章　民事责任	**8. Kapitel: Zivile Haftung**	**Chapter VIII Civil Liability**
第一百七十六条　民事主体依照法律规定和当事人约定，履行民事义务，承担民事责任。	**§ 176 [Pflichten und Haftung; vgl. § 106 AGZR]** Zivilrechtssubjekte erfüllen gemäß den gesetzlichen Bestimmungen oder den Vereinbarungen der Parteien zivile Pflichten und tragen zivile Haftung.	**Section 176** Civil subjects fulfil their civil obligations and assume civil liability according to the provisions of the law or the agreement of the parties.
第一百七十七条　二人以上依法承担按份责任，能够确定责任大小的，各自承担相应的责任；难以确定责任大小的，平均承担责任。	**§ 177 [Teilschuld]** Wenn zwei oder mehr Personen gemäß dem Recht die Haftung nach Bruchteilen tragen, [und] der [jeweilige Beitrag zum] Haftungsumfang festgestellt werden kann, tragen sie jeweils die entsprechende Haftung; ist es schwierig, den [jeweiligen Beitrag zum] Haftungsumfang festzustellen, tragen sie die Haftung gleichmäßig.	**Section 177** If two or more persons according to the law bear the liability for fractional shares and the respective share of the scope of liability can be determined, they bear the liability correspondingly; if it is difficult to determine the respective amount of the scope of liability, they equally bear the liability.
第一百七十八条　二人以上依法承担连带责任的，权利人有权请求部分或者全部连带责任人承担责任。	**§ 178 [Gesamtschuld]** Wenn mehrere gemäß dem Recht die Haftung als Gesamtschuldner tragen, ist der Berechtigte berechtigt, von einem Teil oder von allen Gesamtschuldnern zu verlangen, die Haftung zu tragen.	**Section 178** If two or more persons are jointly and severally liable according to the law, the beneficiary has the right to claim from part of or all the joint and several debtors to bear the liability.
连带责任人的责任份额根据各自责任大小确定；难以确定责任大小的，平均承担责任。实际承担责任超过自己责任份额的连带责任人，有权向其他连带责任人追偿。	Der Anteil der Haftung der Gesamtschuldner wird gemäß dem jeweiligen [Beitrag zum] Haftungsumfang festgestellt; ist der [jeweilige Beitrag zum] Haftungsumfang schwierig festzustellen, tragen sie die Haftung gleichmäßig. Gesamtschuldner, bei denen die tatsächlich zu tragende Haftung den Anteil der eigenen Haftung übersteigt, sind berechtigt, von den anderen Gesamtschuldnern einen Ausgleich zu verlangen.	The share of the liability of the joint and several debtors shall be determined according to the respective share of the scope of liability; if the respective share of the scope of liability is difficult to determine, they equally bear the liability. If the liability they actually bear exceeds the amount of their own liability, joint and several debtors have the right to demand

		compensation from the other joint and several debtors.
连带责任，由法律规定或者当事人约定。	Die gesamtschuldnerische Haftung wird vom Gesetz bestimmt oder von den Parteien vereinbart.	The joint and several liability shall be provided by law or agreed on by the parties.
第一百七十九条　承担民事责任的方式主要有：	**§ 179 [Formen der Haftung; vgl. § 134 AGZR]** Die Formen, zivile Haftung zu tragen, sind hauptsächlich:	**Section 179** The methods of assuming civil liability include:
（一）停止侵害；	1. Einstellung von Verletzungen;	(1) Cease the infringement;
（二）排除妨碍；	2. Beseitigung von Behinderungen;	(2) Eliminate impediments;
（三）消除危险；	3. Beseitigung von Gefahren;	(3) Eliminate dangers;
（四）返还财产；	4. Rückgabe von Vermögensgütern;	(4) Return property;
（五）恢复原状；	5. Wiederherstellung des ursprünglichen Zustandes;	(5) Restitution of the original state;
（六）修理、重作、更换；	6. Reparatur, erneute Herstellung, Austausch;	(6) Repair, remake, or replace;
（七）继续履行；	7. fortgesetzte Erfüllung;	(7) Continue to perform;
（八）赔偿损失；	8. Ersatz des Schadens;	(8) Compensation for losses;
（九）支付违约金；	9. Zahlung von Vertragsstrafe;	(9) Pay contractual penalties;
（十）消除影响、恢复名誉；	10. Beseitigung von Auswirkungen, Wiederherstellung des Rufes;	(10) Elimination of impacts, restoration of the reputation;
（十一）赔礼道歉。	11. Entschuldigung.	(11) Apology.
法律规定惩罚性赔偿的，依照其规定。	Bestimmen Gesetze einen Strafschadensersatz, so gelten deren Bestimmungen.	If laws prescribe punitive damages, these provisions are applicable.
本条规定的承担民事责任的方式，可以单独适用，也可以合并适用。	Die in diesem Paragraphen bestimmten Formen, in denen zivile Haftung getragen wird, können allein oder verbunden angewandt werden.	The methods to assume Civil Liability provided for in this Section may be applied alone or may be combined.
第一百八十条　因不可抗力不能履行民事义务的，不承担民事责任。法律另有规定的，依照其规定。	**§ 180 [Höhere Gewalt; vgl. §§ 107, 153 AGZR]** Kann eine Zivilpflicht wegen höherer Gewalt nicht erfüllt werden, wird dafür keine zivile Haftung getragen. Gibt es andere gesetzliche Bestimmungen, so gelten diese Bestimmungen.	**Section 180** No civil liability is borne if civil duties cannot be performed due to force majeure, unless otherwise provided by law.

不可抗力是指不能预见、不能避免且不能克服的客观情况。	Höhere Gewalt bezeichnet objektive Umstände, die unvorhersehbar, unausweichlich und unüberwindlich sind.	Force majeure means unforeseeable, unavoidable, and insurmountable objective circumstances.
第一百八十一条　因正当防卫造成损害的，不承担民事责任。	**§ 181 [Notwehr; vgl. § 128 AGZR]** Für eine durch Notwehr [58] herbeigeführte Schädigung wird keine zivile Haftung getragen.	**Section 181** There is no civil liability for damages induced by self-defence.
正当防卫超过必要的限度，造成不应有的损害的，正当防卫人应当承担适当的民事责任。	Wenn die Notwehr das Maß des Notwendigen übersteigt [und] zu unnötigen Schädigungen führt, muss der in Notwehr Handelnde eine angemessene zivile Haftung tragen.	If the self-defence exceeds the necessary limits and causes unnecessary damages, the defender shall bear appropriate civil liability.
第一百八十二条　因紧急避险造成损害的，由引起险情发生的人承担民事责任。	**§ 182 [Gefahrenabwehr; vgl. § 129 AGZR]** Wird eine Schädigung durch das dringend notwendige Ausweichen vor einer Gefahr herbeigeführt, trägt die Person, die die Entstehung der gefährlichen Umstände herbeigeführt hat, die zivile Haftung.	**Section 182** If the damages induced by necessarily avoiding a danger, the person who induced the dangerous circumstances bears the civil liability.
危险由自然原因引起的，紧急避险人不承担民事责任，可以给予适当补偿。	Wurde die Gefahr durch natürliche Ursachen herbeigeführt, so trägt die Person, die dringend einer Gefahr ausweichen musste, keine zivile Haftung, kann [jedoch] einen angemessenen Ausgleich gewähren.	If the danger was caused by natural events, the persons who urgently had to avoid a danger does not bear the civil liability, but can grant an appropriate compensation.
紧急避险采取措施不当或者超过必要的限度，造成不应有的损害的，紧急避险人应当承担适当的民事责任。	Waren die Maßnahmen, die ergriffen wurden, um dringend einer Gefahr auszuweichen, unangemessen, oder überschritten sie das Maß des Notwendigen, [und] haben sie zu unnötigen Schädigungen geführt, so muss der, der dringend einer Gefahr ausgewichen ist, eine angemessene zivile Haftung tragen.	If the measures taken to urgently avoid a danger were inappropriate or exceeded what was necessary and caused unnecessary damages, the person that urgently avoided the danger shall bear appropriate civil liability.

58 Wörtlich: „gerechtfertigte Verteidigung".

第一百八十三条　因保护他人民事权益使自己受到损害的，由侵权人承担民事责任，受益人可以给予适当补偿。没有侵权人、侵权人逃逸或者无力承担民事责任，受害人请求补偿的，受益人应当给予适当补偿。	**§ 183 [Hilfe in Gefahrenlagen; vgl. § 109 AGZR]** Wenn [jemand], weil er die zivilen Rechte und Interessen anderer schützt, selbst eine Schädigung erleidet, wird die zivile Haftung vom Verletzer getragen [und] der Nutznießer kann einen entsprechenden Ausgleich leisten. Wenn es keinen Verletzer gibt, der Verletzer flüchtig oder unfähig ist, die zivile Haftung zu tragen, [und] der Geschädigte einen Ausgleich verlangt, muss der Nutznießer einen angemessenen Ausgleich leisten.	**Section 183** If someone suffers damages because they protect the civil rights and interests of others, the infringer bears the civil liability and the beneficiary can grant a corresponding compensation. If there is no infringer, or the infringer is fugitive or unable to bear civil liability and the damaged party claims compensation, the beneficiary shall pay appropriate compensation.
第一百八十四条　因自愿实施紧急救助行为造成受助人损害的，救助人不承担民事责任。	**§ 184 [Nothilfe]** Wenn [jemand], weil er freiwillig eine dringende Hilfehandlung vorgenommen hat, demjenigen, dem er Hilfe leistet, einen Schaden verursacht, trägt der Hilfeleistende keine zivile Haftung.	**Section 184** If the rescuer voluntarily provides urgent assistance and causes a damage to the person they assist, the rescuer shall not bear civil liability.
第一百八十五条　侵害英雄烈士等的姓名、肖像、名誉、荣誉，损害社会公共利益的，应当承担民事责任。	**§ 185 [Schutz von Helden und Märtyrern]** Wer den Namen, das Bildnis, den guten Ruf [oder] die Ehre [von Personen] wie etwa Helden [oder] Märtyrern verletzt [und dadurch] die allgemeinen gesellschaftlichen Interessen schädigt, muss die zivile Haftung tragen.	**Section 185** A person infringing the name, portrait, reputation, and honour of heroes or martyrs and the general public interests are damaged, civil liability shall be assumed.
第一百八十六条　因当事人一方的违约行为，损害对方人身权益、财产权益的，受损害方有权选择请求其承担违约责任或者侵权责任。	**§ 186 [Konkurrierende Ansprüche]** Wenn vertragsverletzende Handlungen einer der Parteien die persönlichen Rechte und Interessen [oder] die Rechte und Interessen an Vermögensgütern der anderen Partei schädigen, ist die geschädigte Seite berechtigt zu wählen, ob	**Section 186** If actions of a party in breach of the contract damage the personal rights and interests or the property rights and interests of another party, the injured party has the right to choose whether to claim the liability for breach of contract or the liability for violation of rights.

sie von diesem verlangt, die Haftung wegen Vertragsverletzung oder die Haftung wegen der Verletzung von Rechten[59] zu tragen.

第一百八十七条　民事主体因同一行为应当承担民事责任、行政责任和刑事责任的，承担行政责任或者刑事责任不影响承担民事责任；民事主体的财产不足以支付的，优先用于承担民事责任。

§ 187 [Verhältnis zur verwaltungs- und strafrechtlichen Haftung] Muss ein Zivilrechtssubjekt wegen derselben Handlung zivile Haftung, verwaltungsrechtliche Haftung und strafrechtliche Haftung tragen, beeinflusst das Tragen der verwaltungsrechtlichen Haftung oder der strafrechtlichen Haftung nicht das Tragen der zivilen Haftung; reicht das Vermögen des Zivilrechtssubjekts zur Zahlung nicht aus, wird es bevorzugt zur Tragung der zivilen Haftung verwendet.

Section 187 If a civil legal subject due to the same action bears civil liability, administrative liability, and criminal liability, bearing the administrative liability or the criminal liability does not influence bearing the civil liability; if the estate of the civil legal subject is insufficient to pay, it will be expended preferentially for bearing the civil liability.

第九章　诉讼时效

9. Kapitel: Klageverjährung

Chapter IX Limitation Period

第一百八十八条　向人民法院请求保护民事权利的诉讼时效期间为三年。法律另有规定的，依照其规定。

诉讼时效期间自权利人知道或者应当知道权利受到损害以及义务人之日起计算。法律另有规定的，依照其规定。但是自权利受到损害之日起超过二十年的，人民法院不予保

§ 188 [Allgemeine Verjährung; vgl. §§ 135, 137 AGZR] Die Klageverjährungsfrist für an das Volksgericht gerichtete Verlangen von Schutz der Zivilrechte beträgt drei Jahre. Gibt es andere gesetzliche Bestimmungen, so gelten diese Bestimmungen.

Die Verjährungsfrist wird von dem Tag an berechnet, an dem der Berechtigte von der Verletzung seines Rechts sowie [der Person] des Verpflichteten erfährt oder erfahren muss. Gibt es andere gesetzliche Bestimmungen, so gelten diese Bestimmungen. Wenn jedoch über 20 Jahre

Section 188 The limitation period of a petition to a people's court for protection of the civil rights is three years, unless otherwise provided by law.

The limitation period is calculated from the date on which the beneficiary knows or should know of the infringement of their right and the person of the obligor, unless otherwise provided by law. If more than 20 years

59 Nach dem – auch die deliktische Haftung regelnden – „Gesetz der Volksrepublik China über die Haftung für die Verletzung von Rechten" [中华人民共和国侵权责任法] vom 26.12.2009; deutsch-chinesisch von LIU Xiaoxiao, *Knut Benjamin Pißler*, in: ZChinR 2010, S. 41 ff.

护；有特殊情况的，人民法院可以根据权利人的申请决定延长。	seit dem Tag der Rechtsverletzung vergangen sind, gewährt das Volksgericht keinen Schutz; wenn besondere Umstände vorliegen, kann das Volksgericht auf Antrag des Berechtigten entscheiden, [die Klageverjährungsfrist] zu verlängern.	have passed since the date of the infringement, however, the people's court does not offer protection; upon request of the beneficiary, the people's court can extend the limitation period in the event of special circumstances.
第一百八十九条　当事人约定同一债务分期履行的，诉讼时效期间自最后一期履行期限届满之日起计算。	**§ 189 [Fristbeginn bei Raten[60]]** Vereinbaren die Parteien die Erfüllung einer Schuld in Raten[61], beginnt die Berechnung der Klageverjährungsfrist mit dem Tag, an dem die Frist für die Erfüllung der letzten Rate abgelaufen ist.	**Section 189** If the parties agree on an instalment plan for the fulfilment of debt, the limitation period shall be calculated from the date of expiry of the last instalment.
第一百九十条　无民事行为能力人或者限制民事行为能力人对其法定代理人的请求权的诉讼时效期间，自该法定代理终止之日起计算。	**§ 190 [Fristbeginn bei Geschäftsunfähigen und beschränkt Geschäftsfähigen]** Die Klageverjährungsfrist für Ansprüche Zivilgeschäftsunfähiger oder beschränkt Zivilgeschäftsfähiger gegen ihre gesetzlichen Vertreter wird vom Tag des Endes dieser gesetzlichen Vertretung an berechnet.	**Section 190** The limitation period of claims by a person lacking contractual capacity or of limited contractual capacity against their legal agent shall be calculated from the date of termination of such statutory agency.
第一百九十一条　未成年人遭受性侵害的损害赔偿请求权的诉讼时效	**§ 191 [Fristbeginn bei Ansprüchen Minderjähriger wegen sexuellen Missbrauchs]** Die Klageverjährungsfrist für Ansprüche auf Schadenersatz Minderjähriger	**Section 191** The limitation period of claims for damages for sexual assault by minors are

60 Vgl. § 5 Bestimmungen des Obersten Volksgerichts zu einigen Fragen der Anwendung des Systems der Klageverjährungsfristen bei der Behandlung von Zivilsachen [最高人民法院关于审理民事案件适用诉讼时效制度若干问题的规定] vom 21.8.2008; chinesisch-deutsch von *Knut Benjamin Pißler*, in ZChinR2009, S. 37 ff. (OVG Verjährungs-Bestimmungen).

61 Wörtlich: „einer einheitlichen Schuld zu getrennten Zeiten".

期间，自受害人年满十八周岁之日起计算。	wegen Erleidens einer sexuellen Verletzung wird vom Tag an berechnet, an dem der Geschädigte das 18. Lebensjahr vollendet.	calculated from the date on which the victim reaches the age of 18 years.
第一百九十二条　诉讼时效期间届满的，义务人可以提出不履行义务的抗辩。	**§ 192 [Einrede der Verjährung; vgl. § 138 AGZR]** Wenn die Klageverjährungsfrist abgelaufen ist, kann der Verpflichtete die Erfüllung seiner Verpflichtung verweigern.[62]	**Section 192** When a limitation period has expired, the obligor may refuse the performance of their duties.
诉讼时效期间届满后，义务人同意履行的，不得以诉讼时效期间届满为由抗辩；义务人已自愿履行的，不得请求返还。	Wenn der Verpflichtete nach Ablauf der Klageverjährungsfrist mit der Erfüllung einverstanden war, darf er nicht auf Grund des Ablaufs der Klageverjährungsfrist einen Einwand erheben; hat der Verpflichtete freiwillig erfüllt, darf er nicht Herausgabe verlangen.	If the obligor agrees to perform their duties after the expiry of the limitation period, they may not raise an objection due to the expiry of the limitation period; if the obligor voluntarily performs the duties, they shall not require return of the payment.
第一百九十三条　人民法院不得主动适用诉讼时效的规定。	**§ 193 [Keine ex-officio-Anwendung]** Das Volksgericht darf die Bestimmungen zur Klageverjährungsfrist nicht von sich aus anwenden.	**Section 193** The people's court shall not volunteer to apply the provisions of the limitation period.
第一百九十四条　在诉讼时效期间的最后六个月内，因下列障碍，不能行使请求权的，诉讼时效中止：	**§ 194 [Verjährungshemmung; vgl. § 139 AGZR]** Wenn während der letzten sechs Monate der Klageverjährungsfrist ein Anspruch auf Grund der folgenden Hindernisse nicht ausgeübt werden kann, ist die Klageverjährung gehemmt:	**Section 194** The limitation period shall be suspended if during the last six months of the limitation period a right cannot be exercised due to one of the following obstacles:
（一）不可抗力；	1. Bei höherer Gewalt;	(1) Force majeure;
（二）无民事行为能力人或者限制民事行为能力人没有法定代理人，	2. wenn ein Zivilgeschäftsunfähiger oder ein beschränkt Zivilgeschäftsfähiger keinen gesetzlichen Vertreter hat oder der gesetzliche Vertreter stirbt, die	(2) If a person that lacks contractual capacity or is of limited contractual capacity does not have a legal agent or the legal

62 Wörtlich: „kann der Verpflichtete den Einwand der Nichterfüllung der Verpflichtung erheben".

或者法定代理人死亡、丧失民事行为能力、丧失代理权；	Zivilgeschäftsfähigkeit verliert oder die Vertretungsmacht verliert;	agent dies, loses the contractual capacity, or the authority for agency.
（三）继承开始后未确定继承人或者遗产管理人；	3. wenn nach Eintritt des Erbfalls die Erben oder der Nachlassverwalter noch nicht bestimmt wurden;	(3) If upon the death of the testator the heirs or the executor have not been determined yet;
（四）权利人被义务人或者其他人控制；	4. wenn die Berechtigten durch die Verpflichteten oder andere Personen kontrolliert werden;	(4) If the beneficiaries are controlled by the obligors or other persons;
（五）其他导致权利人不能行使请求权的障碍。	5. wenn andere Hindernisse dazu führen, dass Berechtigte einen Anspruch nicht ausüben können.	(5) If other obstacles prevent the beneficiary from exercising their rights.
自中止时效的原因消除之日起满六个月，诉讼时效期间届满。	Mit Ablauf von sechs Monaten, beginnend mit dem Tag, an dem der Grund der Hemmung entfällt, läuft die Klageverjährungsfrist ab.	At the end of the six month period, starting on the date that the suspension begins, the limitation period expires.
第一百九十五条　有下列情形之一的，诉讼时效中断，从中断、有关程序终结时起，诉讼时效期间重新计算：	**§ 195 [Verjährungsunterbrechung; vgl. § 140 AGZR[63]]** Wenn einer der folgende Umstände vorliegt, wird die Klageverjährung unterbrochen, vom Zeitpunkt der Beendigung der Unterbrechung [bzw.] des betreffenden Verfahrens an beginnt die Klageverjährungsfrist von neuem:	**Section 195** If one of the following circumstances applies, the limitation period is interrupted, the limitation period starts anew from the time of termination, or interruption of the respective procedure:
（一）权利人向义务人提出履行请求；	1. Der Berechtigte verlangt vom Verpflichteten Erfüllung;	(1) The beneficiary requests performance from the obligor;
（二）义务人同意履行义务；	2. der Verpflichtete ist mit der Erfüllung der Verpflichtung einverstanden;	(2) The obligor agrees to fulfil their obligations;
（三）权利人提起诉讼或者申请仲裁；	3. der Berechtigte erhebt Klage oder beantragt ein Schiedsverfahren;	(3) The beneficiary files a suit or requests arbitration;

63 Vgl. auch § 13 OVG Verjährungs-Bestimmungen.

（四）与提起诉讼或者申请仲裁具有同等效力的其他情形。	4. es liegen andere Umstände vor, die die gleiche Wirkung wie die Klageerhebung oder die Beantragung eines Schiedsverfahrens besitzen.	(4) Other circumstances exist that have the same effect as filing a suit or requesting arbitration.
第一百九十六条　下列请求权不适用诉讼时效的规定：	**§ 196 [Unverjährbare Ansprüche]** Auf die folgenden Ansprüche werden die Bestimmungen über die Klageverjährung nicht angewandt:	**Section 196** The provisions on the limitation period do not apply to the following claims:
（一）请求停止侵害、排除妨碍、消除危险；	1. Forderungen nach Einstellung von Verletzungen, Beseitigung von Behinderungen [und] Beseitigung von Gefahren;	(1) Request to cease infringements, remove obstacle, and eliminate dangers;
（二）不动产物权和登记的动产物权的权利人请求返还财产；	2. wenn Berechtigte dinglicher Rechte an unbeweglichen Sachen und dinglicher Rechte an eingetragenen beweglichen Sachen die Zurückgabe von Vermögensgütern fordern;	(2) If beneficiaries of property rights for real estate and chattel claim the return of property;
（三）请求支付抚养费、赡养费或者扶养费；	3. Forderungen über die Zahlung von Kindesunterhalt[64], Elternunterhalt[65] oder Ehegattenunterhalt[66];	(3) Requests on the payment of alimony, parental maintenance, or matrimonial maintenance;
（四）依法不适用诉讼时效的其他请求权。	4. andere Ansprüche auf welche die Klageverjährung gemäß dem Recht nicht angewandt wird.	(4) Other claims to which the limitation period is not applicable.
第一百九十七条　诉讼时效的期间、计算方法以及中止、中断的事由由法律规定，当事人约定无效。	**§ 197 [Unbeachtlichkeit von Parteivereinbarungen[67]]** Klageverjährungsfristen, Berechnungsmethoden	**Section 197** Limitation periods, calculation methods, and the grounds for suspensions and interruptions are provided by law; agreement of the parties are invalid.

---

64 Siehe § 21 Abs. 2 Ehegesetz der VR China [中华人民共和国婚姻法] vom 10.9.1980 in der Fassung vom 28.4.2001; deutsch in: *Frank Münzel* (Hrsg.), Chinas Recht, 10.9.80/1 (Ehegesetz).

65 Siehe § 21 Abs. 3 Ehegesetz.

66 Siehe § 20 Abs. 2 Ehegesetz.

67 Vgl. auch § 13 OVG Verjährungs-Bestimmungen.

	sowie die Gründe für Hemmungen und Unterbrechungen werden durch Gesetze bestimmt; Vereinbarungen der Parteien sind unwirksam.	
当事人对诉讼时效利益的预先放弃无效。	Der Verzicht der Parteien auf die Vorteile der Klageverjährung im Voraus ist unwirksam.	The parties' waiver of the benefits of the limitation period in advance is invalid.
第一百九十八条　法律对仲裁时效有规定的，依照其规定；没有规定的，适用诉讼时效的规定。	**§ 198 [Verjährungsfristen in Schiedsverfahren]** Bestimmen Gesetze Verjährungsfristen für Schiedsverfahren, so gelten diese Bestimmungen; gibt es keine Bestimmungen, werden die Bestimmungen über die Klageverjährung angewendet.	**Section 198** If provisions provide limitation periods for arbitration, these provisions are applicable; in the absence of such provisions, the provisions on the limitation period are applicable.
第一百九十九条　法律规定或者当事人约定的撤销权、解除权等权利的存续期间，除法律另有规定外，自权利人知道或者应当知道权利产生之日起计算，不适用有关诉讼时效中止、中断和延长的规定。存续期间届满，撤销权、解除权等权利消灭。	**§ 199 [Ausschlussfristen bei Gestaltungsrechten]** Fristen für das Fortbestehen gesetzlich bestimmter oder von den Parteien vereinbarter Rechte wie das Recht zur Aufhebung [oder] das Recht zur Auflösung werden, soweit das Gesetz nichts anderes vorsieht, von dem Tag an berechnet, an dem die Berechtigten erfahren oder erfahren müssen, dass das Recht entstanden ist; die betreffenden Bestimmungen über Hemmung, Unterbrechung und Verlängerung der Klageverjährung werden nicht angewandt. Sind Fristen für das Fortbestehen abgelaufen, erlöschen Rechte wie etwa das Recht zur Aufhebung [oder] das Recht zur Auflösung.	**Section 199** Limitation periods for the continuance of statutory or rights agreed on by the party, such as the right to revoke or dissolve are calculated from the date that the beneficiaries know or should know that the right arose, unless otherwise provided by law; the relevant provisions on suspension, interruption, and expiration of the limitation period are inapplicable. If limitation periods for the continuance have been expired, rights such as revocation or dissolution terminate.
第十章　期间计算	**10. Kapitel: Berechnung von Zeiträumen**	**Chapter X Calculation of Periods**
第二百条　民法所称的期间按照公历年、月、日、小时计算。	**§ 200 [Kalender; vgl. § 154 Abs. 1 AGZR]** Die im Zivilrecht bezeichneten Fristen werden in Jahren, Monaten, Tagen und Stunden des Gregorianischen Kalenders berechnet.	**Section 200** The periods referred to by Civil Law are reckoned in years, months, days, and hours according to Gregorian calendar.

第二百零一条　按照年、月、日计算期间的，开始的当日不计入，自下一日开始计算。	**§ 201 [Fristbeginn; vgl. § 154 Abs. 2 AGZR]** Wird die Frist nach Jahren, Monaten oder Tagen berechnet, so wird der Anfangstag nicht eingerechnet; sie wird vom folgenden Tag an gerechnet.	**Section 201** If the period is calculated in years, months and days, the start date is not included in the calculation; the period shall be calculated from the next day.
按照小时计算期间的，自法律规定或者当事人约定的时间开始计算。	Wird die Frist nach Stunden berechnet, so beginnt sie am gesetzlich bestimmten oder durch die Parteien vereinbarten Zeitpunkt.	When the period is calculated in hours, it starts on the date as determined in the statute or agreed on by the parties.
第二百零二条　按照年、月计算期间的，到期月的对应日为期间的最后一日；没有对应日的，月末日为期间的最后一日。	**§ 202 [Fristende]** Wird die Frist nach Jahren [oder] Monaten berechnet, gilt der entsprechende Tag des Ablaufmonats als letzter Tag; hat der Monat keinen entsprechenden Tag, gilt dessen Endtag als letzter Tag der Frist.	**Section 202** If the period is calculated in years or months, the corresponding date of the month of expiry is the last day of the period; in the absence of a corresponding date, the last day of the month shall be the last day of the limitation period.
第二百零三条　期间的最后一日是法定休假日的，以法定休假日结束的次日为期间的最后一日。	**§ 203 [Feiertage; Ende der Tagesfrist; vgl. § 154 Abs. 3 und 4 AGZR]** Ist der letzte Tag der Frist ein gesetzlicher Feiertag, so gilt der auf das Ende der gesetzlichen Feiertage folgende Tag als letzter Tag der Frist.	**Section 203** If the last day of the limitation period is a public holiday, the following day shall be the last day of the limitation period.
期间的最后一日的截止时间为二十四时；有业务时间的，停止业务活动的时间为截止时间。	Der den letzten Tag einer Frist abschließende Zeitpunkt ist 24 Uhr; gibt es Geschäftszeiten, ist der Zeitpunkt des Geschäftsschlusses[68] der abschließende Zeitpunkt.	The time closing the last day of a limitation period is 24.oo h; during ordinary business hours the closing time is the closing time of the business.
第二百零四条　期间的计算方法依照本法的规定，但是法律另有规定或者当事人另有约定的除外。	**§ 204 [Subsidiarität]** Die Methode für die Berechnung einer Frist [richtet] sich nach den Bestimmungen dieses Gesetzes, soweit das Gesetz oder Parteivereinbarungen nichts anderes vorsehen.	**Section 204** The method of calculation of a limitation period, unless otherwise provided by statutory provision or agreement by the parties.

68 Wörtlich: „Einstellung der Geschäftstätigkeit“.

第十一章　附　则	**11. Kapitel: Ergänzende Regeln**	**Chapter XI Supplementary Provisions**
第二百零五条　民法所称的“以上”“以下”“以内”“届满”，包括本数；所称的“不满”“超过”“以外”，不包括本数。	**§ 205 [Definitionen; vgl. § 155 AGZR]** Wenn das Zivilrecht von „oder mehr“, „höchstens“, "innerhalb" oder "bis zu" spricht, ist die betreffende Zahl eingeschlossen; wenn es von "weniger als"[69], „mehr als“[70] oder "außerhalb" spricht, ist die betreffende Zahl nicht eingeschlossen.	**Section 205** In Civil Law, the terms "or more", "not more than", "within" and "up to" shall include the given figure; the terms "less than", "more than" or "beyond" shall not include the given figure.
第二百零六条　本法自 2017 年 10 月 1 日起施行。	**§ 206 [Inkrafttreten; vgl. § 156 AGZR]** Dies Gesetz wird vom 1. Oktober 2017 an angewandt.	**Section 206** This law shall come into force on October 1, 2017.

69 Wörtlich: „keine vollen“.
70 Wörtlich: „überschreiten“.